Riding With
New York Cavalry

Riding With New York Cavalry
Two Accounts of the American Civil War by a Union Army Officer

Three Years in the Federal Cavalry
and
The Capture, Prison-Pen and Escape

Willard W. Glazier

Riding With New York Cavalry
Two Accounts of the American Civil War by a Union Army Officer
Three Years in the Federal Cavalry
and
The Capture, Prison-Pen and Escape
by Willard W. Glazier

FIRST EDITION

First published under the titles
Three Years in the Federal Cavalry
and
The Capture, Prison-Pen and Escape

Leonaur is an imprint
of Oakpast Ltd

Copyright in this form © 2013 Oakpast Ltd

ISBN: 978-1-78282-188-5 (hardcover)
ISBN: 978-1-78282-189-2 (softcover)

http://www.leonaur.com

Publisher's Notes

The views expressed in this book are not necessarily those of the publisher.

Contents

Three Years in the Federal Cavalry   7

The Capture, Prison-Pen and Escape   233

CAPTAIN WILLARD GLAZIER

Three Years in the Federal Cavalry

Contents

Preface	13
The War for the Union—Contest Begun	15
Camp-Life and its Influences	20
Preparations for Active Service	27
The Advance to the Rappahannock	35
Pope's Campaign in Northern Virginia	50
Rebel Invasion of Maryland	65
McClellan Succeeded by Burnside	72
Organisation of a Cavalry Corps	83
Rebel Chiefs and their Raids	96
Chancellorsville and Stoneman's Raid	108
From Yorktown to Falmouth	135
Second Invasion of Maryland—Gettysburg	149
Retreat of the Rebels from Gettysburg	177
Kilpatrick's Gunboat Expedition	198
Capture of the Author	221

To the gallant and unassuming soldier,
Major-General Henry E. Davies, Jr.
whose star always shone brightest
on the front line of battle,
this volume is respectfully dedicated
by the author.

Preface

The cavalry arm of the service during the late Rebellion has never been fully appreciated, and that is my reason for writing this book; for I feel that such a work will not only be found interesting to the public, but will be doing justice to the brave men with whom it was my fortune to be associated during the dark hours of the Rebellion. To serve them, is and ever will be my greatest pleasure.

The remarkable features and events of our late cavalry movements in Virginia and elsewhere, visible to me during the campaigns of the Army of the Potomac, were noted daily in my journal, sometimes in camp, sometimes during the halt of the march, again at the bivouac fire, and often jotted down with pencil during the lull of battle. From that diary this story of our raids, expeditions, and fights is prepared.

My descriptions of battles and skirmishes, in some cases, may seem too brief and unsatisfactory; to which I can only reply, that scores of engagements, which to the participants appear to be of vast importance, have very little general interest. On the other hand, however, it is to be regretted that, where our cavalry-men have done the most brilliant things, it has been impossible for me, in many instances, to secure reliable and detailed accounts with which to do them full justice; still, my work contains many truths not cognizant to the public, and is creditable to our gallant horsemen, who have too often been entirely overlooked.

Willard Glazier.

New York, October 8th, 1870

Our Cavalry

CHAPTER 1

The War for the Union— Contest Begun

The eleventh of April, 1861, revealed the real intention of the Southern people in their dastardly assault upon Fort Sumter. The thunder of Rebel cannon shook the air not only around Charleston, but sent its thrilling vibrations to the remotest sections of the country, and was the precursor of a storm whose wrath no one anticipated. This shock of arms was like a fire-alarm in our great cities, and the North arose in its might with a grand unanimity which the South did not expect. The spirit and principle of Rebellion were so uncaused and unprovoked, that scarcely could anyone be found at home or abroad to justify them.

President Lincoln thereupon issued a call for seventy-five thousand men to uphold and vindicate the authority of the government, and to prove, if possible, that secession was not only a heresy in doctrine, but an impracticability in the American Republic. The response to this call was much more general than the most sanguine had any reason to look for. The enthusiasm of the people was quite unbounded. Individuals encouraged individuals; families aroused families; communities vied with communities, and States strove with States.

Who could be the first and do the most, was the noble contention which everywhere prevailed. All political party lines seemed to be obliterated. Under this renovating and inspiring spirit the work of raising the nucleus of the grandest army that ever swept a continent went bravely on. Regiments were rapidly organised and as rapidly as possible sent forward to the seat of government; and so vast was the number that presented themselves for their country's defence, that the original call was soon more than filled, and the authorities found themselves unable to accept many organisations which were eager to press into the fray.

Meanwhile the great leaders of the Rebellion were marshalling the hordes of treason, and assembling them on the plains of Manassas, with the undoubted intention of moving upon the national capital. This point determined the principal theatre of the opening contest, and around it on every side, and particularly southward, was to be the Aceldama of America,—the dreadful "field of blood."

The first great impulse of the authorities was in the direction of self-defence (and what could be more natural and proper?), and Washington was fortified and garrisoned. This done, it was believed that the accumulating forces of the Union, which had become thoroughly equipped and somewhat disciplined, ought to advance into the revolted territory, scatter the defiant hosts of the enemy, and put a speedy end to the slaveholders' Rebellion. But the hesitation and indecision which prevailed in our military circles were becoming oppressive and unendurable, and hence the cry of "On to Richmond!" was heard from the Border States to the St. Lawrence, precipitating the first general engagement of the war.

Our defeat at Bull Run was a totally unexpected disaster, which, for a time, it was feared, would chill the enthusiasm and greatly weaken the energy of the North. But though the South was much strengthened and emboldened by their victory, our defeat had its own curative elements: it taught us that the enemy was determined and powerful, and that to overcome him the ranks of the Union army must be filled with something besides three months' men, or men on any very limited term of enlistment.

Other lessons were also gained: our men had formed some acquaintance with the citizens and the country; they had learned the importance of a more thorough discipline and organisation; and those who had gone forth as to a picnic or a holiday, sat down "to count the cost" of "enduring privations as good soldiers." The nation discovered that this struggle for life was desperate and even dubious, and it was thoroughly aroused.

Under the military *régime* of General Winfield Scott, the cavalry-arm of the service had been almost entirely overlooked. His previous campaigns in Mexico, which consisted mainly of the investments of walled cities, and of assaults on fortresses, had not been favourable to extensive cavalry operations, and he was not disposed at so advanced an age in life materially to change his tactics of war. What few regiments of cavalry we had in the regular army were mostly broken up into small detachments for the purpose of ranging our Western frontiers, while a few squads were patrolling between the outposts of our new army, carrying messages from camp to camp, and pompously escorting the commanding generals in their grand reviews and parades.

But the Black Horse Cavalry of Virginia, at Bull Run, unmatched by any similar force on our side, had demonstrated the efficiency and importance of this branch of the service, and our authorities began to change their views. The sentiment of the people at large seemed to turn in the same channel, and a peculiar enthusiasm in this direction was perceptible everywhere. It was as though the spirit of the old knight-errantry had suddenly fallen upon us.

I was in Troy, New York, when the sad intelligence of the reverse to our arms at Bull Run, was received. This was followed quickly by another call for volunteers, and I decided without hesitation to enter the army. In accordance with my resolve I enlisted as a private soldier at Troy, on the sixth day of August, 1801, in a company raised by Captain Clarence Buel, for the cavalry service. To encounter the chivalrous Black Horse Cavalry, of Bull Run fame, it was proposed to raise a force in the North, and as Senator Ira Harris, of New York, was giving this organisation his patronage and influence, a brigade was formed, whose banners should bear his name.

Originally the regiment to which my company was assigned was intended for the regular army, and was for some time known as the Seventh United States Cavalry; but the government having decided to have but six regiments of regular cavalry, and as New York had contributed the majority of the men to the organisation, we were denominated the Second Regiment of New York Cavalry, "Harris Light." This regiment was organised by J. Mansfield Davies, of New York, as colonel, assisted by Judson Kilpatrick, of New Jersey, as lieutenant-colonel. The men were mostly from the States of New York, New Jersey, Connecticut, Vermont, Pennsylvania, and Indiana.

On the thirteenth of August, Captain Buel's Trojan Company was summoned together for the purpose of leaving for the South. Under a severe drenching rain we were drawn up in line fronting the residence of General John E. Wool, when the old veteran delivered a most heroic address, which led us quite to forget the pelting rain, and prepared us for our departure. The boys then found a very pleasant shelter on board the *Vanderbilt*, bound for New York City. The day following all the New York State men rendezvoused at G48 Broadway, and were mustered into the service of the United States by Lieutenant-Colonel D. B. Sackett, of the regular army.

At four o'clock p. m. we were ordered aboard a train of cars, and told that our destination was Camp Howe, near Scarsdale, twenty-four miles north of the city, between the Harlem and East rivers. We reached the place just in time to pitch our tents for the night—an operation which was not only new and strange, but performed in anything but a workman-like manner. We had everything to learn, and this was our first lesson in soldiering.

Captain A. N. Duffié, a French officer and graduate of the military school of St. Cyr, is in command of the camp, and is to be the superintendent of our discipline and drill. He is somewhat eccentric, but is undoubtedly well qualified for the duties of his position.

August 16.—This morning we commenced the inevitable drill on foot, as we are still without horses. We find this exercise very severe, and yet, in view of its great importance, we accept it with a good degree of relish. Our drill-master is thorough and rigidly strict, after the fashion of the French schools. We cannot avoid learning under his tuition. In the afternoon we were set to policing camp. This comprises the cleaning of one of the roughest farms in the country of stone. And as a remuneration to the owners for the use of this most unsightly of God's forsaken ground, we are compelled to build stone fences—a very unpleasant introduction to military life, and an occupation which by no means accords with our ideas of a soldier's duties. But our hands toil with a protest in our hearts, and with a certain resolve that this kind of fencing must not long continue.

After a week spent in drill and the stone-wall enterprise, we were all surprised one morning with an order to fall into line to receive a Napoleonic harangue from Captain Duffié. So many and even loud had been our protests, and so glaringly manifest our rebellious spirit on the subject of fortifying a farm in the State of New York, that the captain undoubtedly feared that he might not be very zealously supported by us in his future movements, and so, like Napoleon, on assuming command of the army of Italy, he sought to test the devotion of his men.

After amusing us awhile in his broken English, and arousing us by his touching appeals to our patriotism and honour, at length he shouted, "Now as many of you as are ready to follow me to the cannon's mouth, take one step to the front." This *dernier resort* to pride was perfectly successful, and the whole lino took the desired step. We were then ordered to be ready to leave camp at eleven o'clock that morning, which was on the twentieth of August, assured that Washington, D. C, was our destination.

Our ranks were quickly broken, and all due preparation made for our departure. After marching to Scarsdale we took cars and were soon landed in the metropolis, through the principal streets of which our command passed to the Jersey City ferry. Without much delay we reached Philadelphia in the evening, where we were bountifully supplied with rations by her proverbially generous and patriotic people. True to the instinct of "Brotherly Love," the citizens are making arrangements such as would indicate that millions of Union soldiers might be fed at their tables. Here we spent the night. The next morning at 6.30 we were on our way southward. A brief halt was made in Baltimore, whose streets still seem to be speaking of the blood of the brave Massachusetts men. And as we march along, we can but recall the poet's prophesy:

> *And the Eagle, never dying, still is trying, still is trying,*
> *With its wings upon the map to hide a city with its gore;*
> *But the name is there forever, and it shall be hidden never,*
> *While the awful brand of murder points the Avenger to its shore;*
> *While the blood of peaceful brothers God's dread vengeance*
> *doth implore,*
> *Thou art doomed, Baltimore!*

At four o'clock in the afternoon we beheld the dome of the nation's Capitol, and, after landing, marched a few hundred yards beyond the eastern boundary of the city, where we pitched tents near Camp Oregon—named thus in honour of Colonel Edward D. Baker, who represented that Territory in the United States Senate previous to his acceptance of a military commission, and who is now in command of the famous California regiment—a noble body of men, who will ever follow with devotion the lead of their gallant colonel.

CHAPTER 2

Camp-Life and its Influences

Drill! drill! and camp-police are the order of the day. Indeed we have nothing else to do, and to do nothing at all is the hardest kind of work. We expect soon to have some accoutrements to enable us to drill something besides our feet. Our preparations for war have commenced at the extremities; for thus far nothing but our heads and feet have been instructed. However, as we become better acquainted with this part of our duty, we relish it better than at first, and flatter ourselves that we are making no very mean progress.

For some time after our arrival here, the government was unable to supply us with uniforms, or weapons of war, and our appearance was far from being *à la militaire*, as Captain Duffié would have it. Coming as we did from colleges and schools, from offices and counting-rooms, from shops and farms, and some from no occupation at all, each with the peculiar dress he wore when he enlisted, and already pretty well worn out by our labours at Camp Howe and extensive travelling, we were a most unsightly, heterogeneous mass of humanity, and were a subject of no little sport to our better-clad fellow-soldiers.

Especially was this the case when on a certain day General B. F. Butler reviewed the troops of this department, and we were made to appear before him and the multitude with our hats and caps, our coats and jackets, in nearly all colours, and many of them in rags and shags. We certainly had nothing to recommend us to the consideration of military men, except the courageous spirit that throbbed in our generally robust frames. But we were hopeful of better days, when we might have the appearance and equipage as well as the internal qualities of soldiers.

But the government was so wholly unprepared for war, that our supplies were received very slowly. First came our uniforms, which every man donned gladly, and yet with a feeling that the last link to civil life, for the present, was severed, and that henceforth in a very peculiar sense we belonged to our common country.

A few days after our arrival at Camp Oregon, we were joined by the men who belonged to our regiment from other States. This added fresh enthusiasm, as well as new strength, to our ranks. However, there is as yet nothing in our *tout ensemble* to distinguish us from infantry or artillery, except the yellow trimming of our blue uniforms, whereas the infantry has the light blue trimming, and the artillery bright red,

August 23.—Today I am happy to make the following entry in my diary, namely: the regiment was furnished with sabres, Colt's revolvers and all the necessary appendages, consisting of belts and ammunition-boxes. Every man has now a new care and pride—to keep his sabre bright, and his entire outfit clean, that he may wear them with pleasure to himself and honour to his comrades. The morning of the twenty-fourth was spent in sabre exercise, with which we were all delighted. This is the first development in us of the cavalry element as such, and we begin to feel our individuality.

We desire to have this growth continue uninterruptedly, and in aid of it, in the early part of September, came quite a large instalment of horses and equipments. This occurred while the regiment occupied a camp about three miles from Washington, on the Bladensburg road, which we named Sussex, in honour of Sussex county, New York, our colonel's native county. As the number of horses furnished us at this time was not sufficient to mount the whole command, the number received by each company was proportioned to the maximum roll of its men. After the non-commissioned officers of each company, including all the sergeants and corporals, had drawn their horses according to rank, the privates were made to draw lots for the remainder—a performance which produced no little amount of excitement.

Several of our comrades were of course unfortunately compelled for several days to march on foot, though much against their wishes; for nothing could be more humiliating to a dragoon than to be trudging through the mud and dust, while his companions are gliding past him with their neighing steeds, on their way to the drill-ground, or to any other post of duty.

It was my good fortune to be the recipient of a beautiful black mare, only five years old, full of life and fiery metal, fourteen hands high, and weighing not less than ten hundred pounds. She was a gem for the cavalry service, or anything else, and a friendship was destined to grow up between us worthy of future mention.

We are now fairly out upon the ocean of our new life, and are beginning to feel its influence. It does not take the careful observer long to notice the effects which outward changes and circumstances have upon the characters of most men. Indeed, no man remains unaffected by them; he either advances or retrogrades, and it is very apparent already among us that while soldiering does make some men, it *un*makes many. The very lowest stratum of life among us, such as represents the loungers in the streets and lanes of our cities,—those who have neither occupation nor culture, is amazingly influenced for the better by military discipline. These men now find themselves with something to do, and with somebody to make them do it. The progress is very slow, it is true, and in some cases exceptional, but this is evidently the general tendency.

On the other hand, however, our regiment is made up principally of young men from highly respectable families, reared under the influences of a pure morality, who find that the highest standard of morality presented here is much lower than they were wont to have at home, and they soon begin to waver. Thus, having, lost their first moorings of character, they start downward, and in many instances are precipitated to horrible depths.

When once a shaking monarchy declines,
Each thing grows bold and to its fall combines.

Only a very few have sufficient force in themselves to effectually resist these evils. It must be remembered that the wholesome and normal restraints of virtuous female society are wholly removed from us. And from what we daily see around us we are convinced that a colony of men only, however virtuous or moral, would in a short time run into utter barbarism. No candid observer can doubt the teaching of the old scripture, that *it is not good for man to be alone.*

Moreover, the friends and associates of our childhood's innocence, whose presence always calls forth the purest memories, are not with us; nor do we feel the almost omnipotent influences of the old school-house gatherings, of the church-going bell, and of the home-fireside. When you sever all these ties and helps to a moral life, and throw a man in the immediate association of the vicious, he must be only a little less than an angel not to fall. Here we are all dressed alike, live alike, and are all subject to like laws and discipline.

The very man who shares our blanket and tent-cover, who drawls rations from the same kettle, who drinks from the same canteen, and with whom we are compelled to come in contact daily, may be the veriest poltroon, whose diploma shows graduation at the Five Points, and whose presence alone is morally miasmatic. Consequently our camp is infested more or less with gambling, drunkenness, and profanity, and all their train of attendant evils, and at times we long for campaigning in the field, whore it seems to us we may rid ourselves of this demoralisation. Hannibal's toilsome marches across the Alps and through Upper Italy only gave hardihood and courage to his legions, who came thundering at the very gates of Rome, and threatening its immediate overthrow; but a winter's camp-life at Capua left them shorn of their strength.

But then we have remedial influences even in camp, and we hail them with no little delight. Daily the news-boys make their appearance, calling out: "*Washington Chronicle* and New York papers!" They enjoy an extensive patronage. With these sheets many moments are pleasantly spent, as their columns are eagerly perused. Then, following hard on the track of the news-boys, comes our adjutant's orderly or courier with a mail-bag full of letters, precious mementos from the loved ones at home. These messages are the best reminders we have of our homelife, especially when they are brimfull, as is usually the case, with patriotic sparkling, and with affection's purest libations.

These letters have a double influence; while they keep the memories of home more or less bright within us, and at times so bright that as we read we can almost see our mothers, wives, and sisters in their tender Christian solicitude for us, they also stimulate us to greater improvements in the epistolary art. Men who never wrote a letter in their lives before, are at it now; those who cannot write at all, are either learning, or engage their comrades to write for them, and the command is doing more writing in one day than, I should judge, we used to do in a month, and, perhaps, a year.

No sooner are the contents of the mail-bag distributed, and devoured by the eager newsmongers, than active preparations are made for responding. Some men carry pocket-inkstands and write with pens, but the majority use pencils. Here you see one seated on a stump or fence, addressing his "sweet-heart," wife, or mother; another writes standing up against a tree, while a third is lying flat on the ground. Thus either in the tents or in the open air, scribbling is going on, and the return mail will carry many sweet words to those who cannot be wholly forgotten. I suppose in this way we are not only making, but writing history. Camp-life then is not entirely monotonous.

The Bugle-Corps

Sights and sounds of interest may be seen and heard at almost every hour of the day. The morning is ushered in with the shrill reveille, which means awake and arise. This is well executed by our bugle-corps, which Colonel Davies has organised, and is drilling thoroughly. All our movements are now ordered by the bugle. By its blast we are called to our breakfast, dinner and supper. Roll-call is sounded twice a day, and the companies fall into line, when the first sergeants easily ascertain whether every man is at his post of duty. The bugle calls the sick, and sometimes those who feign to be, to the surgeon's quarters, and their wants and woes are attended to.

By the bugle we are summoned to inspections, to camp-guard, to the feeding and watering of our horses and to drill. A peculiarly shrill call is that which brings all the first or orderly sergeants to the adjutant's quarters to receive any special order he may have to communicate. Thus call after call is sounded at intervals throughout the day, ending with "taps," which is the signal for blowing out the lights and seeking the rest which night demands. Any neglect of the latter call usually brings the offender to the guard-house, or sends him to extra duty.

Our principal duties now are camp guard and drill, which we perform by turns. Every morning quite a large force is detailed, with a commissioned officer in command, for guard duty. These form a line of dismounted pickets, or *vedettes*, around the entire camp. They are stationed within sight and hailing distance of each other, enabling them to prevent anyone from leaving or entering camp without a written pass in the daytime, or the countersign at night. The rule is to have each man stand post for two hours, when he is relieved. This is the maximum time, and is sometimes made less at the discretion of the commandant.

We are told, as we perform this duty, that it is not very unlike the picketing that will be required of us if we are ever permitted to take the field which confronts the enemy. Indeed, this is picketing on a small, scale. And our enthusiasm in this branch of our work increases, as we are almost daily in receipt of accounts of attacks on our pickets along the line of the Baltimore and Ohio Railroad and the Cumberland Canal.

It appears that a certain Colonel Turner Ashby, with a force of cavaliers (?) acting as guerrillas, singly and in squads, is nightly endeavouring to sever our telegraph-wires, to burn our railroad-bridges, and to destroy the canal, or fire at our men on the passing boats; and not unfrequently we read of skirmishes in which several of our pickets have been either captured, wounded, or killed. We, of course, expect before long to face Colonel Ashby and his confederates, and are preparing ourselves for the issue.

Mounted Drill

The regiment was supplied with its full complement of horses a few days since, and mounted drill is now the general order of the day; nearly all our time not otherwise occupied is now devoted to this exercise. At first we had some exciting times with our young and untrained horses. One of our men received a kick from his horse which proved fatal to his life. Several of our wildest and seemingly incorrigible ones we have been compelled to run up the steepest hills in the vicinity, under the wholesome discipline of sharp spurs, until the evil has been sweated out of them.

We find, however, that the trouble is not only with the horses, but frequently with the men, many of whom have never bridled a horse nor touched a saddle. And then, too, these curbed bits in the mouths of animals that had been trained with the common bridle, produced a most rebellious temper, causing many of them to pitch up into the air as though they had suddenly been transformed into monstrous kangaroos, while the riders showed signs of having taken lessons in somersaults. Some of the scenes are more than ludicrous. Horses and men are acting very awkwardly, also, with the guiding of the animal by the rein against the neck, and not by the bit, as we were accustomed to do at home.

We do not wonder much that the chivalrous Black Horse gentry have expressed their contempt of Northern "mudsills and greasy mechanics," and have made their brags that we could never match them. But then it is said that these Southrons were born in a saddle, and were always trained in horsemanship. They generally perform their pleasure excursions, go on their business journeys, and even to church, on horseback. They were therefore prepared for the cavalry service, before we had so much as thought of it. But let them beware of what they think or say, for we can learn, and it does frequently occur that somewhere in the experience of contending parties, "the first is last, and the last first."

We are improving rapidly. There is so much exhilaration in the shrill bugle-notes which order the movements of the drill, and so much life in its swift evolutions, that the men and horses seem to dance rather than walk on their way to the drill grounds, and both are readily learning the certain sounds of the trumpet, and becoming masters of motions and dispositions required of them. Like all other apprentices, of course, we occasionally indulge in the reveries of imagination, and think we are laying the foundation of a career which is destined to be important and glorious. Be this as it may, we do not mean to be outstripped by the most efficient in our knowledge and practice of cavalry tactics, and of the general manoeuvrings of war.

CHAPTER 3

Preparations for Active Service

October 15, 1861.—The Harris Light broke camp at eight o'clock, a. m., and marched proudly through Washington, crossed the famous Long Bridge over the Potomac, and moved forward to Munson's Hill, in full view of our infantry outposts, where we established a new camp, calling it "Advance." For the first time our horses remained saddled through the night, and the men slept on their arms. To us this was a new and exciting phase of life.

Since our retreat from Bull Run, the Rebel army has made itself formidable on this line, and though no active movements have been attempted on Washington, we are, nevertheless, apprehensive of such a measure on their part. Hence our picket lines are doubly strong and vigilant, while every means is resorted to to ascertain the position, strength, and intention of our wily foe.

Frequently "contrabands" feel their way through the enemy's pickets under cover of the night, and through the tangled brushwood which abounds, and reach our lines safely. From them we gain much valuable information of the state of things in "Dixie." Some of them, we learn, were employed by Rebel leaders in constructing forts and earthworks, and in various ways were made to contribute muscle to the Southern Confederacy. They have strange and exciting stories to tell us, and yet it seems as though they might be of great service to us, if we saw fit to employ them, as guides in our movements.

Their hearts are with us in this conflict. They hail us as friends, and entertain wild notions about a jubilee of liberty, for which they are ever praying and singing, and look upon us as their deliverers. How they have formed such opinions is somewhat difficult to conjecture, especially when we consider the anomalous treatment they have received from our hands. The authorities have seemed to be puzzled with regard to them; and there are cases where they have even been returned to their former owners.

And yet there seems to be an instinctive prophecy in their natures, which leads them to look to Northmen for freedom. Their presence in our camps becomes a sort of inspiration to most of us, and we earnestly hope that their prayers may be answered, and that every chain of servitude may be broken. This sentiment at times breaks out in such as the following poetic strain:

> *In the beauty of the lily Christ was born across the sea,*
> *With a glory in His bosom that transfigures you and me*
> *As He died to make men holy, let us die to make them free,*

And as slavery was the cause, and not, as some say, the pretext, of the war, if the Union arms succeed, this "irrepressible conflict" and villainous wrong must come to an end.

Our confidence in the ultimate success of our arms is daily increasing. Since the first of August our ranks have been wonderfully swelled; and now regiment after regiment, battery after battery, is pouring in from the North, filling the camps of instruction, and manning the fortifications around Washington.

Meanwhile, earthworks are being constructed on all the high hills and commanding positions; strong abatis are made of the forest-trees, and everything done that can give the city an air of security, and the country round about the appearance of a bristling porcupine. Should this influx of troops continue, we shall be compelled to advance our lines for very room on which to station them. We have some intimations that our advance to this point today is preparatory to such a movement.

The day following our advance to Munson's Hill I was promoted to the rank of corporal, on recommendation of Captain Buel, my appointment to date from the fifteenth.

On the sixteenth our lines were advanced to Vienna, a station on the Leesburgh Railroad, and on the seventeenth as far as Fairfax Court House, the Confederate force falling back towards Centreville and Manassas Junction without offering us the slightest opportunity to bring them into an engagement.

We are spending our time mostly in foraging, scouting, and patrolling. In consequence of imperfect transportation, the cavalry especially is compelled to seek its own forage, with which, however, the country abounds. Corn is found in "right smart heaps," as the natives say, either

CAVALRY COLUMN ON THE MARCH

in the fields or barns, and hayricks dot the country on every side. But there is a certain degree of scrupulousness on the part of some of our commanders with regard to appropriating the produce of the "sacred soil" to our own use, which greatly embarrasses our foraging expeditions, and exasperates not a little those of us who are needy of the things we are at times ordered not to take.

It is no uncommon thing to find one of our men stationed as safeguard over the property of a most bitter Rebel—property which, in our judgment, ought to be confiscated to the use of the Union, or utterly destroyed. We do not believe in handling Rebels with kid gloves, and especially when we know that the very men whom we protect are constantly giving information to the enemy of all our movements, and using their property whenever they can to aid and comfort the cause of treason. We are too forcibly reminded of the fable we used to read in our schoolboy days, of the Farmer and the Viper. We are only warming into new life and strength this virus of Rebellion, to have it recoil upon ourselves. We hope our authorities will soon discover their error, and change their tactics.

Our scouting is on a limited scale, though it affords considerable exercise and excitement. Thereby we are learning the topography of the country, and making small maps of the same. We are traversing the forests, through the wood-roads and by-paths which run in every direction; strolling by the streams and ravines, and gaining all the information which can be of use to us in future manoeuvrings. We scout in small squads over the entire area occupied by our forces, and often beyond; and, now and then, more frequently in the night, we patrol between our picket posts, to ascertain that all is well at the points most exposed to danger. The principal object of scouting is to learn the strength and position of the enemy, while the object of patrolling is to learn our own.

October 20.—Today the regiment was honoured by a visit from its patron, Senator Ira Harris. After witnessing a mounted drill and parade, which pleased him much, he presented us a beautiful stand of colours, accompanied by an appropriate and eloquent address. He made especial reference to the object of the organisation, the hopes of its friends, and their earnest prayers for its future usefulness and success. He dwelt enthusiastically upon the work before us. At the close of the speech the command responded with a rousing round of cheers, expressive of their thankfulness for the banner and of their determination to keep it, to stand by it, and to defend it. even with their lives. The occasion was one to be remembered.

BALL'S BLUFF

Another great pall of sadness has fallen upon our soldiers. The papers bring intelligence of our terrible disaster at Ball's Bluff, and the promising Colonel E. D. Baker has fallen, while gallantly leading his noble Californians. Discussions as to the cause or causes of that fatal advance and retreat are now in vogue throughout our camps. It does seem to many as through gross incompetency or treachery must have influenced the authorities having immediate oversight of the affair, and that our fallen braves have been needlessly immolated upon their country's altar.

Big Bethel, Bull Run, and Ball's Bluff,
Oh, alliteration of blunders!
Of blunders more than enough.
In a time full of blunders and wonders.

But the boys are enthusiastic over the bravery of our nineteen hundred, who fought against a force more than twice their number, with all the advantage of position and knowledge of the country. All our battles have proven that our men can fight, and, though Providence seems to have been against us thus far, for reasons most inscrutable, we will not waver in our determination to dare or die in the contest. Our chief difficulties are not in the rank and file of the army, but in the general management of the forces, and we trust that ere long right men will be found to take the places of incompetent ones.

RECRUITING SERVICE

Being detailed by Colonel Davies for recruiting service, I left camp on the twenty-eighth of October, and proceeded, in company with Lieutenant Charles E. Morton, to New York. We went on to Newburgh, near the lieutenant's native home, where we remained a few days together; but on the first of November I was ordered to Troy, to act independently. I spent several weeks in this peculiar work and with good success.

Though recruiting offices could be found on all the principal streets of our cities and villages, yet a good business was done by them all, such was the enthusiasm which prevailed among the people. War-meetings were frequently held, and addressed by our best orators. The press, with few exceptions, poured forth its eloquent appeals to the strong-bodied men of the country to range themselves on the side of right against wrong. Violence would be done to truth did we not mention, also, that the pulpits of the land were potent helpers in this work, by their religious patriotism and persistent efforts to keep the great issue distinctly before the people.

Thus the mind and heart of the North were kept alive to the great problem of the nation's existence, and men were rallying to our standard. It was no uncommon thing to receive applications to enter our lists from young men or boys too young and slender to be admitted, who left our offices in tears of disappointment, unless we could find for them a position as drummers and buglers.

A single instance of enlistment under my observation might be mentioned, as it gives a specimen of the manner in which our work went on. Having taken passage on the cars one day from one point of my labours to another, I fell in with a young man who was on his way to college, where he expected to be matriculated the following day. His valise was full of books and other students' requisites, and his heart full of literary ambition. Attracted to me by my uniform, he soon learned my business, and, after a few moments of pensiveness, to my surprise, he told me to inscribe his name among my recruits. Then, turning to a friend on board the car, he said, "Take this trunk to my home, and tell mother I have enlisted in a cavalry regiment."

On the fourth of December I returned from recruiting service, bringing with me all recruits who had not been previously sent to the regiment. I found the Harris Light occupying Camp Palmer, on Arlington Heights, the confiscated property of the Rebel General Robert E. Lee. On arriving in camp I found that the papers from Washington contained a letter of Secretary Seward, directing General McClellan not to return to their former owners contrabands in our lines.

This order, when fully understood by our coloured friends, will undoubtedly increase their exit "from Egypt," as many of them style their escape from bondage. The government will probably adopt measures to give these fugitives systematic assistance and labour, that they may be of use to us. Already I find that a large number of our officers have adopted them for cooks and hostlers, in which positions they certainly excel; and there is no good reason why we may not employ them as teamsters on our trains and helpers in our trenches. They are generally very powerful, and show signs of great endurance.

Nor do we find them unwilling to labour, as we have been so

often told they were. However, we do not wonder much that they have acquired the "reputation" of being lazy, for what but a thing or an animal could take pleasure in unrequited toil? Now they have a personal interest, and take a peculiar delight in what they do for us. Their great willingness and ability to work for Uncle Sam or any of his boys, would indicate that they will become eminently useful in the service of their country.

From Camp Palmer the regiment had gone out to drill for some time; and here we continued through the month, generally occupying the large plain which lies between the Arlington House and the Potomac, and in full view of Washington. On this field Kilpatrick, Davies, Duffié, and others, began to develop their soldierly qualities, infusing them into their commands, and imparting that knowledge of cavalry tactics which would prepare us for the duties of war.

We have recently been greatly encouraged by the movements of Colonel George Dashiel Bayard, of the First Pennsylvania Cavalry, who, on the twenty-seventh of November, while on a scout on the road to Leesburg, Loudon County, met a band of the Chivalry near Drainesville, with whom he had a spirited skirmish. The whole affair would indicate that Colonel Bayard is destined to be no mean cavalry leader.

Cavalry regiments from most of the loyal States have been organised, and are now in camps of instruction. Occasionally they go out scouting, picketing, etc., and are thus preparing for the coming campaigns.

December 20.—Today a brigade of Pennsylvanians, including two squadrons of Colonel Bayard's cavalry regiment, the whole force under command of General E. O. C. Ord, while foraging in the vicinity of Drainesville, were attacked by a Rebel force nearly equal in numbers, with General J. E. B. Stuart commanding in person. A lively contest followed, in which the Rebels were thoroughly beaten and driven from the field, losing, according to their own accounts, about two hundred and fifty in killed, wounded, and captured. They left twenty-five dead horses on the field, with the debris of two caissons, disabled and exploded by the well-directed fire of Easton's battery, which accompanied the expedition.

The Rebels, who had undoubtedly come out for the purpose of forage as well as ourselves, having a long wagon train, retreated toward Fairfax Court House, with their wagons laden with their wounded.

Our loss includes only nine killed and sixty wounded. Unimportant as this victory might seem, it caused an immense rejoicing in the Union ranks. It was a fitting answer to the calumny heaped upon us from both North and South, that our soldiers could not fight, and were no match for their boastful enemy.

Chapter 4

The Advance to the Rappahannock

The winter was one of preparation, not of operation. Why we were kept "all quiet along the Potomac," until the announcement, reiterated through the press, elicited only disdainful merriment among our friends, was never satisfactorily explained. The month of December had been beautiful, the roads in excellent condition, the army well supplied and disciplined, so that nothing but hesitancy in our leaders stood in the way of army movements.

The North and West, which had supplied myriads of men and millions of money, were becoming very impatient with such a state of things. This feeling was intensified by the fact that it was known that the enemy was tireless in his efforts to increase his army and to fortify his strongholds, while he was also gaining the sympathy of foreign powers, and, by means of blockade-running, was adding not a little to his munitions of war. The army shared largely this general discontent. "Why do we not advance?" was everywhere the interrogation of eager officers and men.

However, we were not wholly unemployed; for while we waited for reinforcements and cannon, as demanded by the general in command, and for the leaves to fall from the trees to facilitate movements in a country so thickly wooded as is Virginia, we were kept busy with the camp curriculum, namely, the drill, the guard, the inspection, and parade. General Lee's plantation, on Arlington Heights, and the surrounding country, was thoroughly trodden by loyal feet, as men and horses were acquiring the form and power of military life.

Incidents of the March

But our quiet was to be broken by our grand advance, which commenced on the 3rd of March. The Harris Light broke camp at three o'clock in the morning, and, with several regiments of cavalry, under the command of Colonel W. W. Averill, led the advance, the Harris Light having the position of honour as van-guard. We were ordered to move slowly and cautiously, which we did, on the main thoroughfare known as the Little River Turnpike, and, at four o'clock, p. m,, we arrived at Fairfax Court House, having marched only about fourteen miles.

What was our surprise to find the place entirely deserted by the enemy, who had left the day previous with the design of retiring beyond the Rappahannock. This change of affairs seemed so sudden as to be full of mystery, and was wholly unknown even to our secret corps. We could not doubt but that this movement was performed in anticipation of some of our contemplated manoeuvrings, of which the Rebel leaders are generally informed by their spies in Washington and all through our lines, even before they are known to our army.

Our march was resumed the following day at ten o'clock a.m., and early in the afternoon we captured the "Quaker Guns" at Centreville. The enemy had actually placed in the earthworks or forts which commanded the road, large trunks of trees, resembling cannon of heavy calibre, which frowned down upon us from the heights. Had it not been for the information we had received from contrabands on the march, that the enemy had evacuated, a report confirmed by the curling smoke which rose from various parts of the field, this formidable array of threatening cannon would have greatly retarded our progress.

Indeed, it was not until after the suspicious works had been thoroughly scanned with field-glasses that we were ordered to advance, when the strong position was carried without the snapping of a cap, or a sabre-stroke. Chagrin was written upon every face. Not a sign of the enemy was visible, save the deserted remains of their winter-quarters, which fell into our hands.

A very brief halt was here made, and, hurrying our steps, we soon crossed the memorable Bull Run, and came up with the rear-guard of the retiring arm at Manassas Junction. Here we pitched into them, and kicked up a little dust on the road to Bristoe. This expedition, or wild-goose chase, was continued to Warrenton Junction, where General George D. Stoneman found the enemy in force, but returned without attacking them.

Having loitered about these historic fields a few days, our whole force began to fall back towards its old position on the Potomac, establishing our advanced picket-lines, however, as far forward as Centreville, with Fairfax Court House as headquarters. Our line of pickets intercepts the Leesburg turnpike at Drainesville and extends to the Potomac, a distance of about twenty miles.

GUERRILLAS AND BUSHWHACKERS

As guerrillas and their brethren, the bushwhackers, infest the country more or less, picketing is dangerous as well as difficult. Between the Rappahannock and the Potomac lies a vast territory which abounds in creeks, marshes, deep, dark forests, with only here and there a village or settlement. A little to the west of this plain extend the Bull Run Mountains, with their ravines and caverns. This is a very fit hiding-place for mischief-makers. The guerrillas consist mostly of farmers and mechanics, residents of this region, who, by some means, are exempt from the Rebel conscription. Most of them follow their usual avocations during the day, and have their rendezvous at night, where they congregate to lay their plans of attack on the pickets.

They resort to every stratagem which a vile and savage spirit could inspire. Sometimes a picket is approached by the stealthiest creeping through the dark thickets, when the unfortunate sentinel is seized and quickly despatched by a bowie-knife, or other like weapon, which a Southron can always use most dexterously. When mere stealth cannot accomplish the task, other methods are used. For instance, on a dark night, a *vedette*, stationed by a thick underbrush, heard a cow-bell approaching him, and supposing that the accompanying rustle of leaves and crackling of dry limbs was occasioned by a bovine friend, unwittingly suffered himself to be captured by a bushwhacker.

But the boys soon learned to be suspicious of every noise they heard; so much so, that one night a picket, hearing footsteps approaching him, cried out, "Halt! Who comes there?" His carbine was instantly brought to a ready, and as no halt occurred nor answer was made, a second challenge was given; but failing to effect anything, he fired in the direction of the noise, when he distinctly heard a heavy fall, and then groans, as of somebody dying. The sergeant of the post, running up to ascertain the cause of the alarm, found that an unfortunate ox, that had been grazing his way through the forest, lay dying, with his forehead perforated by the faithful sentry's bullet. The incident caused considerable merriment, and the pickets were supplied with poor Confederate beef during the remainder of their term of duty.

But the attacks are frequently of a more disastrous character, resulting in the killing of men and horses, in wounds and in captures. The utmost care and strictest vigilance cannot secure us perfectly from depredations. Our general plan is as follows: The major part of the regiment or picket detail establishes what we denominate the "main reserve" within a mile or two in rear of the centre of the line of *vedettes*, or at a point where their assistance, in case of an attack, can be secured at any place in the line, at the shortest possible notice. About midway between the main reserve and the picket line are stationed two, three, or four picket reliefs, so situated as to form, with the line of *vedettes* for a base, a pyramid, with its apex at the main reserve.

Picket Duty

The boys will not soon forget the long, dreary, dangerous hours they spent along this line. Here we find ourselves shivering around a miserable fire among the sighing pines (though in times of special danger we are not permitted to have even this slight comfort, for fear of detection), often compelled to sit or lie down in snow or mud, or to walk about smartly to prevent freezing to death. Sometimes, when much exhausted, we have laid ourselves down on the damp and muddy ground, which was frozen stiffly and held us as a vice when we awoke. Frozen fingers and toes were no uncommon occurrence.

In this wretched plight we hear the summons to get ready to stand post. We go out upon our shivering horses, to sit in the saddle for two hours or more, facing the biting wind, and peering through the storm of sleet, snow, or rain, which unmercifully pelts us in its fury. But it were well for us if this was our worst enemy, and we consider ourselves happy if the guerrilla does not creep through bushes impenetrable to the sight, to inflict his mortal blows. The two hours expire, relief comes, and the *vedette* returns to spend his four, six, or eight hours off post, as best he may.

Once, at least, during the night, we are visited by the grand guard, which consists of the officer of the day, accompanied by others, whose duty it is to make a thorough, though usually swift, inspection of the picket line. Most of our time is spent in this duty.

March 29.—Considerable excitement prevailed among us today, as Colonel Bayard was dispatched with a detachment of his regiment to repulse a dastardly raid made by some of General J. E. B. Stuart's men, on the house of a Mrs. Tenant, a Union lady, residing near Difficult Run, about six miles from Chain Bridge. Colonel Bayard reached the place a few moments too late, and the raiders succeeded in taking Mrs.

Tenant as a prisoner, and making off with their prey.

For several weeks the main portion of our grand army has been sent by transports to the Peninsula, with the evident intention of moving upon Richmond by shorter land routes than by way of Manassas. This change in our plan of attack was probably known by the Rebels before they were matured at Washington, and we now understand why they so quietly evacuated their positions on our front.

General McDowell remains in command of the defences of Washington, with a force sufficient, it is believed, to give safety to the Capital, and to harass the Rebels who continue before us. With the departure of General McClellan to the Peninsula, our picket lines were immediately withdrawn to Annandale and Falls Church, within a few miles of the fortifications surrounding Washington.

April 4.—The Harris Light and the First Pennsylvania Cavalry were recalled from the picket lines and sent out on a reconnaissance in force, with a division in command of General McDowell. Our march led us through Fairfax Court House and Centreville, near which we bivouacked for the night.

The Atmosphere and the People.

Already, at this early spring time, a luxurious vegetable growth of green is beautifully carpeting the fields through which we pass and in which we halt. Flowers of great beauty and variety of hues and sweetness of perfume greet us on every hand. It would seem as though Nature were struggling to hide the desolations which war has made, and were weaving her chaplets of honour around the graves of our fallen brothers. And it really seems as though Destruction himself had contributed to this lavish growth. Thus,

> *Life evermore is fed by death,*
> *In earth, or sea, or sky;*
> *And, that a rose may breathe its breath,*
> *Something must die.*

On the fifth we continued on our march to Bristoe Station, on the Orange and Alexandria Railroad, where we encountered one of the most furious snow storms ever known in this region of country. The wind which bore the snow was cold and cutting. It was a season never to be forgotten by those who were quartered in mere shelter tents, or had no tents at all.

So sudden are the changes of the atmosphere here that *no man knoweth what a moment may bring forth.* Yesterday we sought shelter from the sun's heat under the budding trees, while grass and flowers and singing birds indicated settled weather. Today the storm howls music through the bending pines, and snow several inches deep covers the earth.

We are thoroughly convinced that the character of the people here greatly partakes of the nature of these surroundings. Is not this the case everywhere? But we see it here more plainly than we ever did before. The people are fitful, and their spasms are terrible; and yet we find them at times to be as kind and hospitable as any we have ever found elsewhere.

After one has witnessed their beautiful days, cooled with a gentle sea-breeze, which generally blows from about nine o'clock in the morning till six at night, and then their cool, calm evenings, he can see why there are so many lovely traits in the nature of the people.

But if he experience some of their sudden and terrific snow storms and showers, when the thunder and the lightning are such that a Northerner feels that all the storms he has ever witnessed are only infantile attempts, he is inclined to extenuate, on mere climactic principles, the outbursts of wrath, and "fire-eating" propensities of the people. He who is gendered of fire and brimstone must have some vim in his composition. We believe this study is not unworthy the Christian philosopher and philanthropist.

The day following the storm, the sun came out warmly, and the snow suddenly disappeared, but left us in a bed of mud. The soil, naturally rich and tender, consisting of a reddish loam, trodden by many feet, and cut by the wheels of heavy vehicles, became almost impassable. But it has this advantage, that it soon dries. So the soil, as well as the atmosphere and the people, is suddenly changeable.

April 7.—Today our expedition continued its march to Catlett's Station, a few miles south of Bristoe. General Augur commands the advance, which consists of a brigade of infantry and two regiments of cavalry.

On the eighth of the month a detachment of the Harris Light was ordered out on picket at six o'clock p.m., and we enjoyed a quiet, pleasant trip on this usually unpleasant duty. Here we spent a few days picketing, scouting and patrolling, and on the seventeenth we advanced from Catlett's in the direction of Falmouth, on the Rappahannock.

Death of Lieutenant Decker

Our march was rapid and lay through a country altogether new to us, which, however, presented no very interesting features. The Harris Light had the advance, and was followed by the Fourteenth Brooklyn. As our infantry comrades became foot-sore and weary, we exchanged positions with them, for mutual relief, until at last one half of the two regiments were bearing each other's burdens. This incident paved the way for a strong friendship to grow up between us.

Seventeen miles were travelled quietly, when a sudden fire on our advance-guard brought every cavalry man to his horse and infantry man to his musket. Everything assumed the signs of a fight. Kilpatrick, who was in command of the regiment, ordered his band to the rear. This precaution of the commander was no sooner taken than the vanguard, in command of Lieutenant George Decker, was making a furious charge upon Field's Cavalry, which was doing outpost duty ten miles from Falmouth.

On the very first assault Lieutenant Decker fell from his horse, pierced through the heart with a fatal bullet. He was a daring young man, well formed, light complexion, blue eyes, and about twenty-three years of age. He was much lamented by his many friends. His fall, shocking as it was to the command, being our first fatal casualty, only seemed to nerve the men for bold revenge. And we had it. Like chaff before the whirlwind the outpost was quickly scattered, and the whole regiment entered upon its first charge with a will, a charge which continued for several miles with wild excitement. Picket reliefs and reserves were swept away like forest trees before the avalanche, and we fell upon their encampment before time had been afforded them for escape.

Here we captured several men and horses, with large quantities of stores, and then rested our tired steeds and fed them with confederate forage. The men enjoyed the captured rations. It was nearly night, and as the sun disappeared the infantry force came up to our newly-possessed territory.

The cavalry was ordered to "stand to horse," and a strong picket, was thrown out to prevent any surprise attack or flanking movement of the enemy. In the early part of the evening one of our pickets was surprised by the friendly approach of a citizen of Falmouth, who had come, as he said, "to hail once more the 'old star-spangled banner,' and to greet his loyal brethren of the North."

Such a patriotic and fearless individual among the white population of that section of country was a great rarity, and his protestations of friendship were at first received with some suspicion. He was, however, brought to General Augur's headquarters, where he gave satisfactory proof of his kind intentions, and then gave the general a full description of the position and strength of the enemy.

Night Attack on Falmouth Heights

A plan for a night attack was thereupon laid and committed to Bayard and Kilpatrick. Our instructions were conveyed to us in a whisper. A beautiful moonlight fell upon the scene, which was as still as death; and with a proud determination the two young cavalry chieftains moved forward to the night's fray. Bayard was to attack on the main road in front, but not until Kilpatrick had commenced operations on their right flank by a detour through a neglected and narrow wood-path. As the Heights were considered well nigh impregnable, it was necessary to resort to some stratagem, for which Kilpatrick showed a becoming aptness.

Having approached to within hearing distance of the Rebel pickets, but before we were challenged, Kilpatrick shouted with his clear voice which sounded like a trumpet on the still night air,

"Bring up your artillery in the centre, and infantry on the left."

"Well, but, Colonel," replied an honest, though rather obtuse captain, "we haven't got any inf——"

"Silence in the ranks!" commanded the leader. "Artillery in the centre, infantry on the left."

The pickets caught and spread the alarm, and thus greatly facilitated our hazardous enterprise.

"Charge!" was the order which then thrilled the ranks and echoed through the dark, dismal woods, and the column swept up the rugged Heights in the midst of blazing cannon and rattling musketry. So steep was the ascent that not a few saddles slipped off the horses, precipitating their riders into a creek which flowed lazily at the base of the hill; while others fell dead and dying, struck by the missiles of destruction which at times filled the air. But the red field was won; and the enemy, driven at the point of the sabre fled unceremoniously down the Heights, through Falmouth, and over the bridge which spanned the Rappahannock, burning the beautiful structure behind them to prevent pursuit. Quite a number of prisoners and various materials of war full into our hands. Kilpatrick and Bayard were both highly complimented for their personal bravery on this occasion.

April 18.—This morning, at eight o'clock, General Augur took peaceful possession of Falmouth; and here, with military honours, the remains of Lieutenant Decker and about fifteen others, who fell in the late struggle, were interred. Later in the day, and after considerable hesitation, the mayor of Fredericksburg formally surrendered the city to the Yankee general, whose guns on Falmouth Heights commanded obedience.

A bridge of canal boats, similar to a pontoon, was constructed across the river, and we took possession of this beautiful, proud city. This was the first appearance of Yankees in this Rebel locality, and we were the subject of no little curiosity. Many of the people, who, by the misrepresentations of their licentious press and flaming orators, had been led to believe that Yankees were a species of one-eyed Cyclops, or long-clawed harpies, or horned and hoofed devils; who had been deceived into the notion that President Lincoln was a deformed *mulatto*, degenerated into a hideous monkey, and that all his followers were of that sort, on seeing us, expressed great surprise and wished to know "if we were specimens of the Lincoln army."

They had forgotten that our fathers fought side by side in our common country's early struggles, and that now we, their children, as brothers, ought all to sit unitedly under the tree of liberty which they had planted and nourished with their hearts' blood.

But it is painful to observe how the spirit of secession has blotted out the memories of the past, and filled their hearts with bitterness toward the friends of the Union. A few Union families in these parts, whose acquaintance we have made, assure us that their neighbours, who were formerly most hospitable and humane, have become, through this Rebel virus, incarnate fiends. To secede from the Union was evidently to secede from the God of virtue and charity.

April 25.—After spending a few days of tolerable quietness on the banks of the Rappahannock, with our camp near the Phillips House, Falmouth, a most lovely spot, we were today ordered out as escort or guard to a train destined for the Shenandoah Valley. Such a job is generally anything but pleasant to a cavalry force, for the movement is altogether too slow, especially when bad roads are encountered. And in case a team becomes balky or gives out, or a wagon breaks down (incidents which occur frequently), the whole column is in *statu quo* until the difficulty or disability is removed.

And so we are halting, advancing, halting and advancing again, with this monotonous variety repeated *ad libitum*, while the halts are often longer than the advances. But our slow motion gives us some opportunity to scout the country through which we pass, and to obtain, large quantities of rations and forage for man and beast. By this means we are not compelled to consume much, if any, of the contents of our train.

On the twenty-eighth we reached Thoroughfare Gap, through which the Manassas Gap railroad finds its way over the Bull Run mountains. Here we met a force from General Nathaniel P. Banks' army, to whose care we delivered the train. We remained a few days to scout through the country.

On the first of May we started back toward Falmouth, but stopped several days at Bristersburg, a small town, where we spent our time very pleasantly, scouting through the country and living upon its rich products. Here we are very much isolated from the rest of our army. We seldom get a mail or receive any papers, except from rebel sources, and these are so meagre of literary taste and especially of reliable army news, that we dare not put much trust in their representations.

However, we are satisfied from what we read, that our grand Peninsular army is making some telling demonstrations toward Richmond, and that the Rebel General Thomas J. Jackson, surnamed "Stonewall," since his famous defeat by General James Shields at Kernstown, near Winchester, is still in the valley.

We reached Falmouth on the twenty-fifth of May, and took possession of our old camping-ground in front of the Phillips House. We have but little to do except to graze our horses in the surrounding fields, and to recruit our strength. We also have the usual camp work, namely, policing, drilling, etc. This department is very quiet at present, though we hear of active movements elsewhere.

On the thirtieth we had a severe rain storm, with thunder and lightning, *à la Virginie*. The streams were greatly swollen, and mud was abundant, so as to retard movements before Richmond.

June 6.—The Harris Light crossed the Rappahannock and advanced six miles beyond Fredericksburg, where we got only a glimpse of some of Field's cavalry, who had not forgotten us. They kept themselves at a very respectful distance from us, and made themselves "scarce" whenever we made signs of an attack. For several days we bivouacked on that side of the river, and on the twelfth we returned to our old camp at Falmouth Heights. On the sixteenth we were again thrown across the river, and made a reconnaissance several miles south, without finding any force of the enemy.

Nothing of importance occurred until the Fourth of July, when the Troy company of the Harris Light, commanded by Lieutenant Robert Loudon, was sent out to celebrate this national holiday by a reconnaissance on the Telegraph Road, south of Fredericksburg. We left camp at eight o'clock in the morning, and soon came in sight of a detachment of Bath Cavalry, doing patrol duty. After following them for some time, though not rapidly, we halted a few moments, and they lost sight of us, concluding doubtless that we had retired. This was just what we wanted.

Attack at Flipper's Orchard

On the south bank of the Po River, about twenty miles from Fredericksburg, was a beautiful orchard, owned by a Dr. Flipper. This lovely spot had been chosen by our Bath friends for their outpost, their main reserve being a few miles farther south. On arriving at the orchard, with its luscious fruit and inviting shade, the squad we were still pursuing unsuspectingly unsaddled their horses, began to arrange preparations for their dinner, and to make themselves generally comfortable. Of this state of things we were informed by a contraband we chanced to meet.

We then resolved either to share or spoil their coffee; so, moving forward at a trot until in sight of them, we swooped down upon the orchard like eagles. The surprised and frightened cavaliers fired but a few shots, and we captured twelve men and nine horses, and escaped with our lawful prey without having received a scratch. It was my good fortune to take prisoner Lieutenant Powell, the officer in command, and to receive as my own a silver-mounted revolver, which he reluctantly placed in my hand. It will be a fine souvenir of the war, and of this Fourth of July victory to the Troy Company.

Shenandoah Valley

Sometime in May Colonel Bayard with his regiment and a large portion of General McDowell's division were sent to the Shenandoah Valley to share in the shifting military panorama which was there displayed. With the removal of the Army of the Potomac to the Peninsula the Confederate authorities despatched General Jackson to the Valley, to threaten the upper Potomac and Maryland, thus making it necessary for a large Federal force to remain in this quarter. General Banks was in command of that department.

After the Battle of Kernstown, in which Jackson received the sobriquet of "Stonewall" and a sound thrashing, General Banks, who had set out for Warrenton, returned to the Valley, and pursued Jackson, but was unable to bring him to bay. The enemy's cavalry under Colonel Turner Ashby was frequently attacked by the Union Cavalry under General John P. Hatch. On the sixth of May, the Fifth New York Cavalry, First Ira Harris Guard, had a hand to hand encounter with Ashby's men near Harrisonburg, where Yankee sabres and pluck had established a reputation.

A portion of the same regiment under Colonel John R. Kenly, at Front Royal, added new lustre to their fame, on the twenty-third of the same month, during "Stonewall's" flank movement on General Banks at Strasburg, and fought bravely during that memorable retreat to Maryland.

At this juncture of affairs, a division of General McDowell's forces, under General Shields, was dispatched to the valley to intercept Jackson, while General John C. Fremont was ordered by telegraph to the same scene from the Mountain Department. But unavoidably detained by almost impassable mountain roads and streams enormously swollen by recent rains, Fremont reached Strasburg just in time to see Jackson's last stragglers retreating through the town. His pursuit was very rapid, though no engagement was brought about until the fifth of June, at Harrisonburg.

Here Colonel Percy Wyndham, on our side, and Turner Ashby, now a general, on the Rebel side, distinguished themselves in the cavalry. Ashby was killed. His loss was greatly lamented by his comrades. He always fought at the head of his men, with the most reckless self-exposure, and for outpost duty and the skirmish line he left scarcely an equal behind him in either army. His humaneness to our men who had fallen into his hands caused many of them to shed tears at the intelligence of his death. Men of valour and kindness are always worthy of a better cause than that in which the Rebels are engaged; but their merit is always appreciated.

Upon the heel of this fight followed the battles of Cross Keys, and Port Republic, where Jackson eluded the combined Union forces which had been directed against him.

During this memorable campaign, a curious military *modus operandi* had been resorted to in the Luray Valley, in which the cavalry had made itself doubly useful. A small force of our infantry and cavalry were surrounded by the enemy on the south bank of the Shenandoah

Night attack on Falmouth Heights

River, which was so high as to be unfordable. As a last resort the cavalrymen plunged into the stream, swimming their horses, and towing across the infantrymen, who clung to the animals' tails!

A striking case of personal daring in this Valley campaign, is worthy of record here. During Banks' retreat from Winchester, on the twenty-fourth of May, four companies of the Fifth New York Cavalry, under command of Captain Wheeler, were moving on the left flank of our retreating columns, to protect them from any attacks by the Rebel cavalry, which infested the wooded hills that lay along our route. Emerging from a thick wood, Captain John Hammond, who had the advance with eight or ten men, suddenly came upon a squad of mounted Rebels, and immediately called on them to surrender.

However, they fled, firing as they went, but were closely pursued. Captain Hammond was riding a powerful horse, which he had taken from his home, and as his blood was up, he determined to capture one of the party at least, at all hazards. He soon came up to the hindmost, a strong man, with whom he exchanged several shots at close quarters, but without effect on either side, owing to their fearful gait through the timber and down a hill. Hammond's pistol became fouled by a cap, and the cylinder would not revolve.

The Rebel had two charges left. Quick work was now necessary. Another spurring of his horse brought him within arm's length of the flying Rebel, whereupon he seized his coat collar with both his hands, and dragged him backward from his saddle. Holding firmly his grasp, both horses went from under them, and they fell pell-mell to the ground.

Luckily Hammond was uppermost, with one hand at the enemy's throat and the other holding the band of the pistol with which the Rebel was trying to shoot him. As the two men were powerful, a fearful struggle ensued for the mastery of the pistol. Meantime up rode one of Hammond's boys, who, by his order, fired at the upturned face of the obstinate foe, the ball grazing his scalp and causing him to relinquish his hold of the revolver, when he was forced to surrender. Thus ended one of the roughest yet amusing contests of the war.

The prisoner proved to be one of Ashby's scouts, and the remainder of the party were all captured. But notwithstanding the personal bravery of our men, disaster and defeat had attended our operations in the Valley. Nor was this the only field of disastrous changes. On the Peninsula sieges had been laid and raised, terrible battles fought, won, and lost, and thousands of our brave comrades had succumbed to the impure water and miasmatic condition of the country.

The Rebel General J. E. B. Stuart had astounded everybody by a raid around our entire army, cutting off communications, destroying stores, and capturing not a few prisoners. On the second of July this jaded army found a resting place at Harrison's Landing on the James River.

CHAPTER 5

Pope's Campaign in Northern Virginia

Our prospects as a nation were anything but promising about the fourth of July, 1862. Our operations in the Shenandoah Valley had been very expensive and fruitless. The Peninsular campaign, which promised so much at its beginning, which had proceeded at so fearful a cost of treasure and blood, was pronounced a failure at last, and the great armies, depleted and worn, were well nigh discouraged. The celebration of the anniversary of our national birthday was observed throughout the loyal North in the midst of gloomy forebodings, and only the pure patriotism of governors of States, and of the President of the United States, gave the people any ground of hope for success. In the army changes of leaders were occurring, which produced no little amount of jealousy among the "stars," and upon which the opinion of the rank and file was divided.

On the fourteenth of July, General John Pope, having been called from a glorious career in the West, took command of the Army of Virginia, which was a consolidation of the commands of Fremont, Banks, and McDowell.

Before General Pope left Washington, he ordered General Rufus King, who was in command at Fredericksburg, to make a raid on the Virginia Central Railroad, for the purpose of destroying it at as many points as possible, and thus impede communications between Richmond and the Valley. This work was committed to our regiment.

At six o'clock in the evening of July nineteenth the Harris Light was set in rapid motion almost directly south. By means of a forced march of forty miles through the night, at the gray dawn of morning we descended upon Beaver Dam depot, on the Virginia Central, like so many ravenous wolves upon a broken fold. Here we had some lively work. The command was divided in several squads, and each party was assigned its peculiar and definite duty. So while some were destroying culverts and bridges, others were playing mischief with the telegraph wires; others still were burning the depot, which was nearly full of stores, and a fourth party was on the lookout.

During our affray we captured a young Confederate officer, who gave his name as Captain John S. Mosby. By his sprightly appearance and conversation he attracted considerable attention. He is slight, yet well formed; has a keen blue eye, and florid complexion; and displays no small amount of Southern bravado in his dress and manners. His gray plush hat is surmounted by a waving plume, which he tosses as he speaks in real Prussian style. He had a letter in his possession from General Stuart, recommending him to the kind regards of General Lee.

After making general havoc of railroad stock and Rebel stores, we started in the direction of Gordonsville, but having ascertained that a force of Rebels much larger than our own occupied the place, we turned northward, and reached our old camp at midnight, having marched upward of eighty miles in thirty hours. Some of us will not soon forget the ludicrous scenes which were enacted, especially during the latter portion of the raid. In consequence of the jaded condition of our horses it was necessary to make frequent halts. To relieve themselves and animals, when a halt was ordered, some men would dismount, and, sinking to the ground through exhaustion, would quickly fall asleep. With the utmost difficulty they were aroused by their comrades when the column advanced.

Calling them by their names, though we did it with mouth to ear, and with all our might, made no impression upon them. In many instances we were compelled to take hold of them, roll them over, tumble them about, and pound them, before we could make them realise that the proper time for rest and sleep had not yet come.

Others slept in their saddles, either leaning forward on the pommel of the saddle, or on the roll of coat and blanket, or sitting quite erect, with an occasional bow forward or to the right or left, like the swaying of a flag on a signal station, or like the careerings of a drunken man. The horse of such a sleeping man will seldom leave his place in the column, though this will sometimes occur, and the man awakes at last to find himself alone with his horse which is grazing along some unknown field or woods. Some men, having lost the column in this way, have fallen into the enemy's hands.

Sometimes a fast-walking horse in one of the rear companies will bear his sleeping lord quickly along, forcing his way through the ranks ahead of him, until the poor fellow is awakened, and finds himself just passing by the colonel and his staff at the head of the column! Of course, he falls back to his old place somewhat confused and ashamed, and the occurrence lends him just excitement enough to keep him awake for a few moments.

It is seldom that men under these somnambulic circumstances fall from their horses, yet sometimes it does happen, and headlong goes the cavalier upon the hard ground, or into a splashing mud-puddle, while general merriment is produced among the lookers-on. But, as no one is seriously injured, the "fallen brave" retakes his position in the ranks and the column proceeds as though nothing had happened. We had all these experiences in one form or another in our raid, and on reaching camp found that several men had lost their caps by the way.

The day following our arrival at camp the general in command issued his complimentary message, namely:

>Headquarters Army of Virginia,
>Washington, July 21.
>
>To Hon. E. M. Stanton, Secretary of War:
>Sir: The cavalry expedition I directed General King to send out on the nineteenth instant has returned.
>They left Fredericksburg at seven p. m., on the nineteenth, and after a forced march during the night made a descent at daylight in the morning upon the Virginia Central Railroad at Beaver Dam Creek, twenty-five miles north of Hanover Junction and thirty-five miles from Richmond. They destroyed the railroad and telegraph line for several miles, burned the depot, which contained forty thousand rounds of musket ammunition, one hundred barrels of flour, and much other valuable property, and brought in the captain in charge as a prisoner.
>The whole country round was thrown into a great state of alarm. One private was wounded on our side. The cavalry marched eighty miles in thirty hours. The affair was most successful, and reflects high credit upon the commanding officer and his troops.
>As soon as full particulars are received I will transmit to you the

name of the commanding officer of the troops engaged.
I am, Sir, very respectfully,
Your obedient servant,
John Pope,
Major-General Commanding,

The above order was received with great gladness by the boys of the Harris Light, and Kilpatrick had just reasons to feel proud of his brave boys and their noble deeds. As we had done so well in this branch of business, it was natural for the commanding general to be looking out for more similar jobs for us, and, indeed, they came.

July 24.—Kilpatrick was again launched out with his men on another raid upon the Virginia Central Railroad, which, this time, we struck at Anderson Turnout. However, we did not reach the railroad before we had surprised a camp of Rebel cavalry, with which we had a sharp skirmish on the south bank of the North Anna River. But having the advantage of the enemy, we defeated them, captured their camp, with several prisoners and horses.

A huge quantity of camp and garrison equipage fell into our hands, which we burned. Unfortunately for us we did not come just in time to take the cars, but we created an alarm quite as extensive as that which prevailed at Beaver Dam, on our former visit. The *Richmond Examiner*, commenting upon the affair, gave the following truthful rendering:

Another Scare on the Central Road

When the train from the west on the Central Railroad reached Frederick's Hall, a station fifty miles from this, it was met by a rumour that the Yankee cavalry had made another raid from Fredericksburg, and had possession of the track at Anderson Turnout, ten miles below Beaver Dam, and thirty miles from Richmond. The telegraph wire not being in working order, there was no means at hand of ascertaining the truth of this report.

Under the circumstances the conductor, not choosing to risk the passengers and train, took an extra locomotive and ran down to Anderson's on a reconnaissance. When he reached this place he found the report of the Yankees at that point correct, but they had left several hours previous to his arrival. He learned the following particulars:

At a quarter past nine a. m., just a quarter of an hour after the passage of train from Richmond, the Yankee cavalry, several hundred in number, made their appearance at the Turnout. Having missed the train, they seemed to have no particular object in view, but loitered about the neighbourhood for a couple of hours.

They, however, before taking leave, searched the house of Mr. John S. Anderson, which is near the railroad, and took prisoner his son, who is in the Confederate service, but at home on sick furlough. They also took possession of four of Mr. Anderson's horses. They made no attempt to tear up the railroad, having no doubt had enough of that business at Beaver Dam last Sunday.

They did not interfere with the telegraph wire through prudential motives, shrewdly guessing that any meddling with that would give notice of their presence.

Of the movements of our troops occasioned by this second impudent foray it is unnecessary to say anything. The Central train reached this city at eight o'clock, three hours behind its usual time.

It is evident that we are greatly embarrassing the Rebel travelling public by our raids, destroying public property, capturing prisoners and horses, and gaining some valuable information. We have learned from contrabands and other sources that Rebel forces in considerable numbers are being transported westward over this route. Some grand movements are undoubtedly on foot.

We have received word that on the fourteenth General John P. Hatch, with all his cavalry, was ordered by General Banks to proceed at once upon Gordonsville, capture the place and destroy all the railroads that centre there, but especially to make havoc of the Central road, as far east as possible, and west to Charlottesville.

For some reason General Hatch was too slow in his movements, and General Ewell, with a division of Lee's army, reached the place on the sixteenth, one day ahead of Hatch. Thereupon Hatch was ordered to take from fifteen hundred to two thousand picked men, well mounted, and to hasten from Madison Court House, over the Blue Ridge, and destroy the railroad westward to Staunton.

He commenced the movement; but after passing through the narrow defiles of the mountains at Swift Run Gap, he felt that there was no hope of accomplishing anything, and returned. General Pope immediately relieved him from command, and appointed General John Buford, General Banks' chief of artillery, in his place.

After some months had elapsed, the following correspondence between General Hatch and his former command will partly vindicate, if it does not fully justify, his course:

SECOND CAVALRY BRIGADE, THIRD ARMY CORPS,

Near Fort Scott, Va., —— 1862.

To Brigadier-General John P. Hatch:

General: The accompanying sabre is presented to you by the officers of the First Vermont and Fifth New York Cavalry.

We have served under you while you commanded the cavalry in Virginia—a period of active operations and military enterprise—during which your courage and judgment inspired us with confidence, while your zeal and integrity have left us an example easier to be admired than imitated.

We, who have passed with you beyond the Rapidan and through Swift Run Gap, are best able to recognise your qualities as a commander.

Accept, therefore, General, this testimonial of esteem offered long after we were removed from your command,—when the external glitter of an ordinary man ceases to affect the mind, but when real worth begins to be appreciated. On behalf of the officers of the Fifth New York,

Robert Johnstone,
Lieutenant-Colonel, Fifth New York Cavalry.

To the Officers of the Fifth New York and First Vermont Regiments of Cavalry:

Oswego, N.Y., —— 1862.

Gentlemen: A very beautiful sabre, your present to myself, has been received. I shall wear it with pride, and will never draw it but in an honourable cause.

The very kind letter accompanying the sabre has caused emotions of the deepest nature. The assurance it gives of the confidence you feel in myself, and your approval of my course when in command of Banks' Cavalry, is particularly gratifying. You, actors with myself in those stirring scenes, are competent judges as to the propriety of my course, when it unfortunately did not meet with the approval of my superior; and your testimony, so handsomely expressed, after time has allowed opportunity for reflection, more than compensates for the mortification of that moment.

I have watched with pride the movements of your regiments since my separation from you. When a telegram has announced that "in a cavalry fight the edge of the sabre was successfully used, and the enemy routed," the further announcement that the First Vermont and Fifth New York were engaged, was unnecessary.

Accept my kindest wishes for your future success. Sharp sabres and a trust in Providence will enable you to secure it in the field.

Your obedient servant,
John P. Hatch,
Brigadier-General,

On the fifth of August we were again sent out on a reconnaissance to the Central Railroad, which we struck on the sixth, about ten o'clock a. m., at Frederick's Hall. The depot, which contained large supplies of commissary and quartermaster stores, was burned. The telegraph office was also destroyed, with considerable length of wire, while the railroad track was torn and otherwise injured, principally by the fires we built upon it. In a factory near the station were found huge quantities of tobacco. The men took as much as the jaded condition of their horses would permit, and the remainder was wrapped in flames.

All this was accomplished without loss on our side. These daring and successful raids made Kilpatrick very conspicuous before the army and country. He was complimented by the general commanding both in orders and by telegraph, and his name became a synonym of courage and success. This gave wonderful enthusiasm to his men, and their devotion to him was unbounded.

Wherever he led us we gladly went, feeling that however formidable the force or dangerous the position we assailed, either by main force we could overcome, or by stratagem or celerity we could escape. This gave our young hero a double power.

August 8.—Today Kilpatrick was ordered with his regiments to reconnoitre in the direction of Orange Court House. We advanced by way of Chancellorsville and old Wilderness Tavern; but on approaching the Court House we found it occupied by a heavy force of the enemy. It is evident that the Rebel army is advancing with a show of fight towards the upper fords of the Rapidan, where, we understand, Generals Buford and Bayard are picketing. After ascertaining all we could about present and prospective movements, we returned to our old camp, having made a swift and tedious march.

BATTLE OF CEDAR MOUNTAIN

On the ninth was fought the memorable Battle of Cedar or Slaughter's Mountain, in which both sides claimed the victory. The Confederates certainly had the advantage of position, having taken possession of the wooded crest before the arrival of our advance; and they also greatly outnumbered the Union force. But their loss was nearly double our own, and nearly the same ground was occupied by the combatants at night, which each held in the beginning of the fight. The cavalry was not conspicuously engaged in this bloody fray, except such portions of it as were escort or bodyguard to officers in command, and among these some were killed. The main cavalry force watched the flanks, doing good service there.

August 10.—At an early hour of the day the Harris Light was ordered to report at Culpepper Court House, and we were soon on the march. On arriving at our destination we found the place well nigh filled with our wounded from the battle of yesterday. It is estimated that not less than fifteen hundred of our men were killed and wounded, about a thousand of the latter having found a refuge here. The seventh part of the casualties of a battle, on an average, will number the killed and mortally wounded; the others claim the especial attention of their comrades.

It is heart-sickening to witness their bloody, mangled forms. All the public buildings and many private residences of this village are occupied as hospitals, and the surgeons with their corps of hospital stewards and nurses are doing their work, assisted by as many others as have been detailed for this purpose, or volunteer their services. The Rebel wounded who have fallen into our hands receive the same attention that is bestowed upon our own men, many of them acknowledging that they are far better off in our care than they would be among their confederates.

These hospitals are all much more quiet than one would naturally suppose. How calmly the brave boys endure the wounds they have received in defence of their beloved country! Only now and then can be heard a subdued sob, or a dying groan; while those who are fully conscious, though suffering excruciating pain, are either engaged in silent prayer or meditation, or reading a Testament or a last letter from loved ones, and patiently awaiting their turn with the surgeon or nurse.

In the most available places tables have been spread for the purpose of amputations. We cannot approach them, with their heaps of mangled hands and feet, of shattered bones and yet quivering flesh, without a shudder. A man must need the highest style of heroism willingly to drag himself or be borne by others to one of these tables, to undergo the processes of the amputating blade. But thanks be to modern skill in surgery, and to the discoverer of chloroform; for by these aids operations are performed quickly and without the least sensation, until the poor brave awakes with the painful consciousness of the loss of limbs, which no artificer can fully replace.

Thus the skill displayed and the care taken greatly mitigate the horrors of battle. Men here are wounded in every conceivable manner, from the crowns of their heads to the soles of their feet, while some are most fearfully torn by shells. It had been thought that men shot through the lungs or entrails were past cure, yet several of the former have been saved, and not a few of the latter. Indeed, it would seem as though modern science was measuring nearly up to the age of miracles.

Important Cavalry Movements

We found that a large force of cavalry was concentrating at Culpepper, awaiting new developments. Reconnaissances are of frequent occurrence, and all of them reveal that the enemy is in motion, concentrating on our front. Our picket lines are made doubly strong, and the utmost vigilance is enjoined. Scouts and spies are on the rampage, and more or less excitement prevails everywhere.

August 10.—Today a small detachment of cavalry under Colonel Broadhead, of the First Michigan Cavalry, was despatched on a scout in the direction of Louisa Court House. Having penetrated to within the enemy's lines, and not far from the Court House, they made a swift descent upon a suspicious looking horse, which proved to be General Stuart's headquarters. The general barely escaped through a back door, as it were "by the skin of his teeth," leaving a part of his wardrobe behind him. His belt fell into our hands, and several very important despatches from General Lee. Stuart's adjutant-general was found concealed in the house and captured. General Pope, in his official reports, speaks of this affair as follows:

The cavalry expedition sent out on the sixteenth in the direction of Louisa Court House, captured the adjutant-general of General Stuart, and was very near capturing that officer himself. Among the papers taken was an autograph letter of General Robert E. Lee to General Stuart, dated Gordonsville, August fifteenth, which made manifest to me the disposition and force of the enemy and their determination to overwhelm the army under my command before it could be re-enforced by any portion of the Army of the Potomac.

Had it not been for the timely discovery of this Rebel order. General Pope's army, only a handful to the multitudes which were gathering against him from the defences of Richmond, would have been flanked and probably annihilated. Assured, however, that re-enforcements from McClellan's army could certainly reach him before long, General Pope held his advanced position to the last, our pickets guarding the fords of the Rapidan.

On the eighteenth, the entire force of cavalry relieved the infantry pickets, and evident preparations were being made for a retreat. On the day following a sharp skirmish took place with Rebel cavalry which appeared across the narrow, rapid river. In this engagement Captain Charles Walters, of the Harris Light, was killed, and his remains were interred at midnight just as orders were received to retreat on the road to Culpepper.

The cavalry under General Bayard is acting as rear guard to our retreating columns. Stuart's cavalry, with whom we are engaged at almost every step, is vanguard of the Rebel army, which is advancing as rapidly as possible. The prospect before us is exceedingly dark. Nothing is more discouraging to a soldier than to be compelled to retreat, especially under a general whose first order on assuming command contained the following utterances:

> Meantime, I desire you to dismiss from your minds certain phrases which I am sorry to find much in vogue among you.
>
> I hear constantly of taking strong positions and holding them—of lines of retreat and of bases of supplies. Let us discard such ideas.
>
> The strongest position a soldier should desire to occupy is one from which he can most easily advance against the enemy.
>
> Let us study the probable lines of retreat of our opponents, and

leave our own to take care of themselves. Let us look before, and not behind. Success and glory are in the advance. Disaster and shame lurk in the rear.

We all felt that the moment we begin to turn our backs to the enemy, that moment we acknowledge ourselves either outgeneralled or whipped, a thing most disheartening, and to which pride never easily condescends. Our only hope was based on early re-enforcements. Should these fail us we saw nothing but defeat and disaster in our path.

August 20.—While our cavalry forces were feeding their horses on the large plains near Brandy Station, about six o'clock this morning, a heavy column of Stuart's cavalry was discovered, approaching from the direction of Culpepper. Kilpatrick was ordered to attack and check this advance, which he did in a spirited manner. The Harris Light added fresh laurels to its already famous record, and made Brandy Station memorable in the annals of cavalry conflicts. Stuart's advance was not only retarded, but diverted; and it was made our business to watch closely his future movements.

On the twenty-first we reached Freeman's Ford, on the Rappahannock, which we picketed, preventing the enemy from effecting a crossing. As the fords of the river were generally heavily guarded up to this point, the enemy kept moving up the stream toward our right, evidently designing to make a flank movement upon us.

On the twenty-second a notable cavalry engagement, with light artillery, took place at Waterloo Bridge. During this fight a Rebel shell took effect in our ranks, killing instantly three horses ridden by three officers of the same company, dismounting the gallants very unceremoniously, but injuring no one seriously. Through the darkness of the night following, Stuart, with about fifteen hundred picked cavalrymen, effected a crossing of the river, and after making quite a detour *via* Warrenton, came down unperceived through the intense darkness and the falling rain upon General Pope's headquarters near Catlett's Station.

He captured the general's field quartermaster and many important documents, made great havoc among the guards, horses, and wagons, and finally escaped, without injury to himself, with about three hundred prisoners, and considerable private baggage taken from the train. His victory was indeed a cheap one, but we all felt its disgrace, which the darkness to some extent explained, but did not fully excuse.

August 23.—A severe contest occurred today at Sulphur Springs. The enemy is pressing us hard at every crossing of the river, and continues to move towards our right. Skirmishing occurs at nearly every hour of the day and night, occasioning more or less loss of life. Yesterday in a skirmish led by General Sigel, who had crossed the river, General Bohlen was killed, and our forces driven back to the north side of the river. While this manoeuvring was in progress along the Rappahannock, General Lee had despatched Stonewall Jackson, to pass around our right, which he did by crossing about four miles above Waterloo, and, on the twenty-fifth, he struck our forces at Bristoe Station, where a severe contest took place, the losses in killed and wounded being heavy on both sides.

But the enemy was successful in taking possession of the railroad; and in the evening a portion of Stuart's cavalry, strengthened by two regiments of infantry, advanced to Manassas Junction, where they surprised and charged our guards, capturing many prisoners, also ten locomotives, seven trains loaded with immense quantities of stores, horses, tents, and eight cannon. They destroyed what they could not take away. The Rebel General Ewell, having followed closely in the track of Jackson, also came upon the railroad in rear of General Pope's army.

Our commander, greatly astonished at this embarrassing juncture of affairs, began to make the best disposition of his forces, to extricate himself from the toils that had been carefully laid for him; still hoping that new forces would come to his aid from McClellan's army *via* Alexandria. But hope in this instance availed him nothing, and he was compelled to encounter the immense Rebel hosts, not only massed on his front, but also lapping on his flanks, and penetrating, as we have seen, even to his rear. The situation was critical in the extreme; and had not the available forces behaved themselves with undaunted courage and, at times, with mad desperation, the disaster would have been unprecedented.

Several unimportant and yet hotly contested battles were fought at Sulphur Springs, Thoroughfare Gap, Bristoe Station, etc., and early on the morning of the twenty-ninth commenced the Battle of Groveton, by some called the second Bull Run. The Rebels were in overwhelming numbers, though driven badly during the earlier hours of the day; and had Fitz-John Porter brought his forces into the action, the victory must have been ours. The cavalry, though quiet most of the day, made an important charge in the evening. The carnage had been terrible, and the fields were strewn with the dead and dying. It is estimated that the casualties would include not less than seven thousand men on our side alone; and it is fair to suppose that the enemy has lost not less than that number.

August 30.—Our lines having fallen back during the night, the battle was renewed today on the field of the first Bull Run. But the fates were again against us, and, though not panic-stricken, our men retired from the field at night, until they rested themselves on the heights of Centreville. The enemy pursued us with great caution, not attempting even to cross Bull Run.

On the thirty-first General Pope expected to be attacked in his strong position at Centreville, but the enemy was too cautious to expose himself in a position so advantageous to ourselves, where the repulse of Malvern Hill might have been repeated. Quiet reigned along our entire line during the day.

Kearny's Death at Chantilly

September 1.—Becoming aware that a flank movement was in operation. General Pope started his entire army in the direction of Washington, But his army had not proceeded far, before one of his columns, which had been sent to intercept the Little River Turnpike, near Chantilly, encountered Stonewall Jackson, who had led his weary, yet intrepid legions entirely around our right wing, and now contested our farther retreat. General Isaac J. Stevens, commanding General Reno's Second division, who led our advance, at once ordered a charge and moved with terrible impetuosity upon the foe; but he was shot dead, on the very start, by a bullet through his head. His command was thereupon thrown into utter disorder, uncovering General Reno's First division, which was also demoralised and broken.

Just at this critical moment, General Philip Kearny, who was leading one of General Heintzelman's divisions, advanced with intrepid heart and unfaltering step upon the exultant foe. This was during a most fearful thunder-storm, so furious that with difficulty could ammunition be kept at all serviceable, and the roar of cannon could scarcely be heard a half dozen miles away.

The Rebel ranks recoiled and broke before this terrible bolt of war. Just before dark, while riding too carelessly over the field and very near the rebel lines, Kearny was shot dead by one of the enemy's sharpshooters. His command devolved upon General Birney, who ordered another charge, which was executed with great gallantry, driving the enemy from the field, and defeating the great flanker in his attempts farther to harass our retreating columns. But our success had been dearly bought. Two generals had been sacrificed, and Kearny especially was lamented all over the land. Of him the poet sings:

> Our country bleeds
> With blows her own hands strike. He starts, he heeds
> Her cries for succour. In a foreign land
> He dwells; his bowers with luxury's pinions fanned,
> His cup with roses crowned. He dashes down
> The cup, he leaves the bowers; he flies to aid
> His native land. Out leaps his patriot blade!
> Quick to the van he darts. Again the frown
> Of strife bends blackening; once again his ear
> War's furious trump with stern delight drinks in;
> Again the Battle-Bolt in red career!
> Again the flood, the frenzy, and the din!
> At tottering Williamsburg his granite front
> Bears without shock the battle's fiercest brunt.
> So have we seen the crag beat back the blast,
> So has the shore the surges backward cast.
> Behind his rock the shattered ranks reform;
> Forward, still forward, until dark defeat
> Burns to bright victory!
>   Fame commands
> The song; we yield it gladly; but the glow
> Fades as we sing. The dire, the fatal blow
> Fell, fell at last. Full, full in deadliest front
> Leading his legions, leading as his wont,
> The bullet wafts him to his mortal goal!
> And not alone War's thunders saw him die;
> Amid the glare, the rushing, and the roll.
> Glared, crashed, the grand dread battle of the sky!
> There on two pinions,—War's and Storm's,—he soared
> Flight how majestic! Up! His dirge was roared
> Not warbled, and his pall was smoke and cloud;
> Flowers of red shot, red lightnings strewed his bier,
> And night, black night, the mourner.
>   Now farewell,
> O hero! In our Glory's Pantheon

*Thy name will shine, a name immortal won
By deeds immortal; In our heart's deep heart
Thy statued fame, that never shall depart,
Shall tower, the loftier as Time fleets, and show
How Heaven can sometimes plant its Titans here below.*

CHAPTER 6

Rebel Invasion of Maryland

By the almost continual fighting of General Pope's campaign, our ranks had been greatly depleted. Of the cavalry in general one correspondent makes the following remark:

> They picket our outposts, scout the whole country for information, open our fights, cover our retreats, or clear up and finish our victories, as the case may be. In short, they are never idle, and rarely find rest for either men or horses.

We had felt the influence of this wear and tear so sadly, that our once full and noble regiment was now reduced to about three hundred and fifty men, scarcely one third of our original number. Nearly every regiment of cavalry which had participated in the misfortunes of the campaign, had suffered a like decimation. To replenish our weakened ranks and to infuse new vigour and discipline into the various commands, became a question of no little moment. Consequently a large number of regiments, under the direct supervision of General Bayard, were ordered to Hall's Hill, about ten miles from Washington, where we established camps of instruction and drill.

During the disasters of the Peninsular campaign, and the subsequent defeats and retreats from the Rapidan to the Potomac, the country had awakened to the importance of increasing the army by new organisations, and of filling up the broken ranks by fresh levies of recruits. This feeling was greatly intensified by the exposure of Washington to the victorious and advancing enemy, and by the invasions of Northern soil, which the triumphs of the Rebellion made imminent.

Hence multitudes of recruits were pouring into Washington principally, and into other places, gladly donning the uniform, and eager to learn the duties, of the soldier. Camps of instruction were, of course, necessary. And as the attention of young men was turning very favourably to the cavalry service, our camps at Hall's Hill were the scenes of daily arrivals of line specimens of patriots, whose hands were warmly grasped by us; and gladly we initiated them into the mysteries of this new science. We were not a little elated at the epithet of "Veteran," which these recruits lavished upon us.

The experiences and labours of our old camps "Oregon" and "Sussex" were repeated with somewhat of new combinations and interests, as we sought to prepare ourselves and others more thoroughly than before to meet the foe in coming campaigns.

We had scarcely reached our new camps and entered upon our new labours, when we learned that General Lee was marching his confident hosts into Maryland. This movement at first was regarded as a feint only, with the intention of uncovering Washington; but as column after column was known to have crossed the Potomac, and to be advancing through the State with more or less rapidity, the tocsin of alarm was sounded everywhere, and a general movement was made to repel the invaders. Pennsylvania was thoroughly aroused, and her loyal and true governor issued a proclamation calling upon all the ablebodied men of the Commonwealth to organise for defence. The militia promptly responded to the call, and military preparations were going on, not only in the old Keystone State, but throughout the land.

Up to this time the attitude of the Rebels had been defensive, but their recent great victories had led them to change their tactics, and thinking that ultimate success was almost within their grasp, they now assumed the offensive policy. Aside from this consideration they doubtless hoped to awaken in the Border States a sympathy and an enthusiasm on their behalf, which thus far they had failed to create; and that their brilliant march northward would not only carry a strong political influence, but that their ranks would be greatly swollen by accessions of recruits from those States. This indication of Rebel thought is evidently found, in the address which General Lee issued to the people of Maryland on the eighth day of September. In it are found the following sentences:

> The people of the Confederate States have long watched with the deepest sympathy the wrongs and outrages that have been inflicted upon the citizens of a Commonwealth allied to the States of the South by the strongest social, political, and commercial ties, and reduced to the condition of a conquered prov-

Burial of Captain Walters at midnight, during Pope's retreat

ince.

Believing that the people of Maryland possess a spirit too lofty to submit to such a government, the people of the South have long wished to aid you in throwing off this foreign yoke, to enable you again to enjoy the inalienable rights of freemen, and restore the independence and sovereignty of your State.

In obedience to this wish, our army has come among you, and is prepared to assist you with the power of its arms in regaining the rights of which you have been so unjustly despoiled.

But the fond hopes which prompted this address were destined to be blasted. Lee's advancing columns met no resistance, and marched directly upon Frederick City, where recruiting offices were opened under the superintendence of General Bradley T. Johnson, who had left this city, at the beginning of the war, to serve in the Rebel army. But the Confederate chiefs were disappointed. The number who were marshalled under their stars and bars did not exceed the number of those who, tired of training in Rebel gray, deserted their banner.

The enemy's peaceful march through the State and its quiet possession were not of long duration; and the invaders soon found other work to do, than to make political orders and harangues, and to increase their ranks by recruits. From Washington the Union army began to advance with considerable strength and determination, compelling General Lee to relinquish his design of penetrating into Pennsylvania.

Initiatory steps were now being taken for a great battle, the first encounter of which took place, under General Pleasanton, who commanded our cavalry during this campaign, at the Catoctin Creek, in Middletown, Maryland. The enemy's rear-guard, consisting of cavalry, was struck with some force, the prelude of the Battle of South Mountain, at Turner's Gap. The enemy having taken possession of this mountain pass, was driven from it only after the most obstinate resistance and severe loss, and forced to leave only before superior numbers. This occurred on the fourteenth; and the victory, though somewhat dearly bought, inspired our troops with new courage, and gave them a foretaste of better days.

Harper's Ferry and Antietam

But during the day we have received sad tidings from Harper's Ferry, a point of no little importance to the invaders. Unfortunately for us the place was under the command of Colonel Miles, who, for his drunkenness and general incompetency, had made himself conspicuous during the first Battle of Bull Run. Why such a man was left in command of at least ten thousand men, and at a place of so much interest, cannot well be accounted for.

Aware as he must have been several days ago, that this position was a coveted prize and would undoubtedly be assailed, he neither retreated, nor fortified himself as he easily could have done to hold out for a long time against a superior force. Nothing but imbecility or treachery could have controlled his conduct. On the eleventh his command was increased largely by a force under General Julius White, who had evacuated Martinsburg on the approach of Stonewall Jackson,

But today he was attacked from various positions, and his forces driven; and on the fifteenth, being attacked from at least seven commanding positions, early in the day the white flag was raised, which the enemy failing to see, continued to fire for several minutes, during which time Colonel Miles was killed, some say by a Rebel shell, others assert by some of his own men.

By this shameful surrender there fell into the hands of the enemy nearly twelve thousand men, half of them New Yorkers, who had just entered the service; also seventy-three guns good and bad; thirteen thousand small arms; two hundred wagons, and a large supply of tents and camp equipage.

Stonewall Jackson, who had commanded the expedition from Frederick to Harper's Ferry, now moved forward to join Lee's main army, which he did on the sixteenth. From South Mountain General McClellan began to collect his forces well in hand and to move towards Boonsborough. Here General Pleasanton again struck the Rebel cavalry rear-guard, capturing two hundred and fifty prisoners and two field-pieces. Infantry supports were following our cavalry very closely, and, after marching about twelve miles, they discovered the Rebels in force posted on the south bank of Antietam Creek, just in front of the little village of Sharpsburg.

Our troops entered into bivouacs for the night, expecting to attack the enemy early next morning. But the morning and most of the day passed in idleness, while the Rebels were fortifying their positions, and gathering their forces which had been more or less scattered. Had McClellan ordered an advance that morning early, the sixteenth of September, 1862, would have witnessed a comparatively easy and complete victory.

At four o'clock p. m. General Joseph Hooker was sent out on the right. Moving at a sufficient distance to keep out of sight of the Rebel batteries, he forded the Antietam, and, soon afterward turning sharply to the left, came down upon the enemy near the road to Hagerstown. But darkness soon coming on put a speedy end to the conflict.

September 17.—This day has witnessed the grand and glorious Battle of Antietam, the particulars of which I need not record. It is enough to say, that the daring of our men and their heroic deeds upon this field, wiped out forever, in Rebel blood, the disgrace and foul stain cast upon our arms in the momentous military blunders and defeats which have followed us since the beginning of this great American conflict.

The losses were heavy on both sides, but the enemy was fairly beaten, and driven from his chosen positions; and night closed the most sanguinary day ever known to the American continent. McClellan ought to have followed up his victory early next morning, but hesitating, the enemy made good his escape across the Potomac, leaving only his dead and desperately wounded, the latter numbering about two thousand, in our hands.

October 4.—We are still in our camps at Hall's Hill, teaching and learning the tactics of war. Today Kilpatrick detailed me to act as drillmaster, and gave me the command of a detachment of recruits. This gives me a new phase of army experience, and though it has its difficulties, as one will always find when he endeavours to control "men of many minds," yet I find a good exercise of my little knowledge of human nature, and realise that the influence of my new labour upon myself is very salutary.

I had thought that I was master of all the preliminary steps of the science and art of a soldier's discipline, but in endeavouring to teach the same to others, I have learned so much myself, that it now seems to me that what I knew before was the merest rudiment. This I learn is the experience of others who are engaged in similar work. Helping others has a wonderful reflex influence upon ourselves. I often wonder if this may not explain in part the philosophy of that passage of Holy Writ, which says, *It is more blessed to give than to receive.* In this exercise of drilling, and in the comparative monotony of camp life, we spent the month of October.

All was quiet along the entire lines of the great armies. Our ranks had been greatly swollen by new accessions; yet General McClellan was constantly calling for re-enforcements, and all kinds of supplies, alleging that the army was in no condition to move. At length about the twenty-sixth of October a feeble advance was made across the Potomac. Several days were spent in putting the Federal army on the sacred soil and under marching orders. No opposition was encountered in the march. Our forces moved along the east side of the Blue Ridge, the enemy still occupying the Shenandoah Valley, and moving southward on a line parallel with our own.

November 2.—The Harris Light broke camp at Hall's Hill and advanced to the Chantilly Mansion, bivouacking on its beautiful grounds. This property is said to be owned by one of the Stuarts, who is reported to be a quartermaster-general in the Rebel service. Pleasant as was the place, with its fine walks, bordered with flowers and evergreen shrubbery; its fruitful gardens and groves, the cold of the night made our stay not the most agreeable.

The next morning we pursued our line of march to Sudley Church, near Bull Run, where we encountered a strong force of Stuart's cavalry. After a sharp conflict, in which Yankee ingenuity and grit were fairly tested, the chivalry retired southwestwardly, acknowledging themselves badly defeated.

November 4.—Today the regiment was ordered to move to Leesburg, near which we pitched our shelters. This is an old, aristocratic village, the shire-town of Loudon County. It is situated in a lovely valley, at the terminus of the Loudon and Hampshire Railroad, and is only about two miles from the Potomac, and an equal distance from Goose Creek, which is a considerable stream. Though this county sent many brave men into the Union ranks, probably more than any other county of the same population in Virginia, yet Leesburg is almost a *fac-simile* of Charlestown, the capital of Jefferson County, the scene of John Brown's execution, where all the people, including women and children, are "secession to a man."

All this while the Grand Army of the Potomac was moving southward at a snail's pace; and on the seventh of November, just after reaching Warrenton, General McClellan was relieved from command, and directed to report to the authorities by letter from Trenton, New Jersey. Thus ended another indecisive campaign, which though it had witnessed a greater victory than ever won before, yet had failed to reap the fruits thereof.

CHAPTER 7

McClellan Succeeded by Burnside

Upon General Ambrose Burnside fell the choice of the Executive for commander of the great Union army. He assumed it with great reluctance and unfeigned self-distrust, and only as a matter of obedience to orders. this change in the commanding officer, deleterious and dangerous as it might be upon the morale of the army, was nevertheless considered necessary and expedient.

Having secured, by somewhat formidable forces, the principal gaps or passages of the Blue Ridge, which had been occupied by the enemy since their advance into the Valley, General Burnside began to make preparations to move his army to Fredericksburg, as being the most feasible and direct line from Washington to Richmond. To mask as long as possible his real design, he threatened an attack upon Gordonsville; but General Lee, by the aid of his emissaries and raiders, soon ascertained his plans, and moving his army across the Blue Ridge, through the western passes, he took his position on the south bank of the Rappahannock, to prevent Burnside's crossing.

November 8.—The Harris Light broke camp at Leesburg early in the morning, and advanced to White Plains, where we encountered and defeated a detachment of Rebel cavalry, driving them towards the mountains. Continuing our journey through this pleasant valley between the Blue Ridge and the Bull Run mountains, we soon joined our main army, whose headquarters were at Warrenton.

This is the most beautiful village in this region of country, situated on the crest of fruitful hills, and elegantly laid out. It is the shire-town of Fauquier County. Here a few days were consumed in effecting the alterations incident upon a change of commander, and on the fourteenth the Army of the Potomac was constituted into three grand divisions, to be commanded respectively by Generals Sumner, Franklin, and Hooker.

The following day Warrenton was abandoned, and the army swept down towards the Rappahannock. The sight was a grand one. On our march, orders were received from President Lincoln enjoining a stricter observance of the Sabbath in the army and navy, than had been done before. As a general thing the Sabbath had not been regarded as any more than any other day. Indeed, very few men in the rank and file kept any calendar of time, and seldom knew the date or day.

This was occasionally the case even with officers. The only possible way of keeping pace with flying time in the army, is by writing a diary. But even when it was known that the Sabbath had been reached, no regard was taken of its sacred character. One of the causes of our disaster at the first Battle of Bull Run was supposed by many to be, that we had desecrated the holy Sabbath by our attack. However true or false such a view may have been, the order we received today from Washington was universally felt to be opportune.

Two days' march brought our advance to Falmouth, and on the twenty-first General Patrick, our provost-marshal general, was directed to repair to Fredericksburg under a flag of truce, and request the surrender of the city. The authorities replied, that while its buildings and streets would no longer be used by Rebel sharpshooters to annoy our forces across the river, its occupation by Yankee troops would be resisted to the last. Had the means of crossing the river been at hand, General Burnside would have made hostile demonstrations at once; but through some misunderstanding between himself and General Halleck, at Washington, the pontoons were not in readiness.

November 28.—A strong force of Rebel cavalry, under General Wade Hampton, dashed across the river at some of the upper fords, raided up around Dumfries and the Occoquan, captured several prisoners and wagons, and returned to their side of the river without loss. As a sort of offset to this, on the twenty-ninth. General Julius Stahel, who commanded a brigade of cavalry at Fairfax Court House, commenced an expedition of great daring and success, to the Shenandoah Valley.

Having advanced to Snicker's Gap in the Blue Ridge, a strong Rebel picket-post was captured by our vanguard. Pressing forward on the main thoroughfare, they soon reached the Shenandoah River, and were not a little annoyed by Rebel carbineers, hidden behind old buildings across the stream. Captain Abram H. Krom, commanding a detachment of the Fifth New York Cavalry, and leading the advance, dashed across the river, though deep and the current swift, closely followed by his men. On reaching the opposite bank, a charge was ordered, and executed in so gallant a manner that several Rebels wore made prisoners, and the remainder of the squad was driven away at a breakneck speed.

Our men pursued them in a scrambling race for nearly three miles, when they came upon a Rebel camp, which was attacked in a furious manner. Our boys made music enough for a brigade, though only a squadron was at hand. The enemy attempted a defence, but utterly failed. Re-enforcements coming to our aid, the Rebels were thoroughly beaten and driven away, leaving in our hands one captain, two lieutenants, thirty two privates, one stand of colours, and several wagons and ambulances. Most of these were laden with booty taken by White's guerrillas in a recent raid into Poolesville, Maryland. Sixty horses and fifty heads of cattle were also captured in this gallant charge. With all their spoils the expedition returned, *via* Leesburg, arriving at their camp in safety.

But all eyes were turned expectantly towards Fredericksburg, with its two vast armies preparing for a grand encounter. Nearly all the citizens of the city had left their homes and fled southward. While General Burnside waited for his pontoons, General Lee was fortifying the Heights in rear of the city, and concentrating his forces for the anticipated onset. This state of things was greatly regretted.

December 11.—The laying of the pontoons commenced in the night, but the task was only partially performed when daylight made the sappers and miners at work a fair mark for the sharpshooters, who were hidden among the buildings which lined the opposite shore, and whose numbers had largely increased within a few days. Battery after battery was opened on Falmouth Heights, until not less than one hundred and fifty guns, at good range, were belching fire and destruction upon the nearly tenantless city, and still the sharpshooters prevented the completion of the pontoons, and disputed our crossing.

At this critical moment the Seventh Michigan regiment of Infantry immortalised their names. Failing, after some entreaty, to secure the assistance of the engineer corps to row them across, they undertook the perilous labour themselves, and amid the rattling of bullets and the cheers and shouts of our own men, they reached the opposite shore, with five of their number killed, and sixteen wounded, including Lieutenant-Colonel Baxter.

They immediately dashed through the streets of the city, and being quickly re-enforced by other regiments, they soon cleared the rifle-pits and buildings adjacent to the stream of all annoyance. Foremost among the noble men who performed this heroic work was the Rev. Arthur B. Fuller, chaplain of the Sixteenth Massachusetts Infantry, who was killed by a rifle-shot.

Our pontoons were now laid in quietness to the city; and about three miles below General Franklin laid his pontoons without opposition. Several bridges were thus constructed, and before night the main body of infantry and cavalry filed across the river, preparatory to a grand engagement. On the twelfth General Bayard moved his cavalry down the river six miles, and was posted on picket. Several shots wore exchanged with the Rebel pickets during the day, and the demon of fight seemed to exist everywhere.

December 13.—The night had been cold, and the morning was dimmed by a heavy fog which covered friend and foe. But orders for an attack upon the formidable works of the enemy had been given, and even before the mist arose. General Gibbon opened fire with his heavy artillery, which was responded to, but without much effect, owing to the fog, which, however, disappeared about eleven o'clock. The engagement now became general, and the fighting was of a character more desperate and determined than ever known before.

The line of Rebel fortifications was so far back from the river, that our artillery, posted on the Falmouth Heights, was out of range, and made more havoc in our advancing ranks than in the ranks of the enemy, until the fire was silenced by order of General Burnside. About one o'clock, one of the most brilliant movements of the day was performed by General George G. Meade's division, which by a terrific charge, gained the crest of the hill, which was near the key of the position. But not being sufficiently supported, they were compelled to retire, bringing away several hundred prisoners with them.

Another masterpiece of gallantry was presented nearer the town, at Marye's Heights, where General Meagher's Irish Brigade repeatedly charged the Rebel works, until at least two-thirds of his stalwart men strewed the ground, killed and wounded. Brigade after brigade was ordered to take these heights, and though their ranks were mown down like grass before the scythe, in the very mouth of Rebel guns the effort was again and again made.

Midway up the Heights was a heavy stone wall, behind which lay the hosts of the enemy, who delivered their fire with scarcely any exposure, sweeping down our columns as they approached. This hillside was completely strewn with our dead and disabled, and at length our assailing ranks retired, compelled to abandon their futile and murderous attempts. But in the language of General Sumner, "they did all that men could do." This could be applied to all the troops engaged.

Night at length threw her sable mantle over the bloody field, covering in her sombre folds the stiffened corpses and mangled forms of not less than fifteen thousand dead and wounded, including the casualties of both armies.

Not one of all our dead fell more lamented than Major-General George D. Bayard, who was struck by a shrieking shell, dying early in the evening. He was only twenty-eight years of age, of prepossessing appearance and manners, with as brave a heart as ever bled for a weeping country, and a capacity of mind for military usefulness equal to any man in the service.

Gradually he had arisen from one position of honour and responsibility to another, proving himself tried and true in each promotion, while his cavalry comrades especially were watching the developments of his growing power, with unabating enthusiasm. But *death loves a shining mark*, and our hero, with his own blood, baptized the day which had been appointed for his nuptials. The recital of his early death brought tears to many eyes, and caused many a loving heart to bleed.

Death lies on him like an untimely frost—
Upon the sweetest flower of all the field.

The night following this bloody conflict was horrible in the extreme. Every available spot or building in the city was sought for a hospital, to which the wounded were brought on stretchers by their companions. Now and then there came a poor fellow who was able to walk, supporting with one hand its bloody, mangled mate. At times two men might be seen approaching through the darkness, supporting between them their less fortunate comrade, whose bloody garments told that he had faced the foe.

But many of our hospitals proved to be very unsafe refuges, into which Minié balls and broken shells would come rattling, and in some instances destroying the precious lives that had escaped—though not without suffering—the terrible and deadly shock of battle. Many of the wounded were taken across the river, and made perfectly safe and as comfortable as circumstances would permit. The Sanitary and Christian Commissions rendered very effective service, enshrining themselves in the memory of a grateful people.

Their deeds of charity and mercy can never be forgotten. By their timely supplies and personal labours many lives were saved, and thousands of the wounded were comforted.

December 14.—The light of this holy Sabbath was hailed with gladness by many a poor soldier, who had suffered from the chill of the night alone upon the bloody field. The weather, however, is unusually clement for this season of the year. A little firing occurred this morning, but no general engagement resulted. This was greatly feared, for had General Lee advanced upon us, it is difficult to see how our men, though somewhat covered by the fire of our batteries from Falmouth Heights, could have recrossed the stream without fearful loss.

But both armies spent most of the holy day in the sacred task of caring for the wounded and burying their dead. Monday was also spent mostly in the same employment, and in the night, so skilfully as to be unknown even to the Rebel pickets, our whole army was withdrawn to the north side of the river in perfect order and without loss. Our pontoons were then taken up.

General Burnside was not willing to remain totally idle, and, after some time had elapsed, he planned another grand movement, which, with more or less opposition from his subordinates, who did not confide in his judgment, he endeavoured to execute. But he had just taken the first step in the programme when he was signalled to desist by a telegram from the president, who had been informed that the temper of the army was not favourable to a general move under its present commander.

With the Battle of Fredericksburg terminated the campaign of 1862, and the two great armies established their winter quarters facing each other along the line of the Rappahannock. Our camps extend for several miles along the northern shore above and below Falmouth, and the enemy occupy the south bank above and below the Heights of Fredericksburg.

Indeed, nearly the whole territory between the Rappahannock and the Defences of Washington, a dark, forsaken, wilderness region, with only here and there a plantation or a village, was soon converted into a vast camping ground, and became the most populous section of Virginia.

To avoid the distant transportation of forage, the greater portion of the cavalry is encamped near Belle Plain, where government transports land with supplies from Washington. The Harris Light has established its camp on the Belle Plain and Falmouth Turnpike, about four miles from the former place, and has named it "Bayard," in honour of our lamented commander, whose fall at Fredericksburg is still a subject of universal sorrow.

It is wonderful to witness how the forests are disappearing in and around our camps. From morning till night the woodman's axe resounds from camp to camp, echoing dolefully along the river-shore and far back into the dense, dark woods. Soon after the Battle of Fredericksburg, as we had no quarters, and nothing but worn and torn shelter-tents, our only way to prevent freezing at night was to cut and heap together a large number of logs, which, through green, when fully ignited made a rousing fire.

These fires, numerously built in rows throughout; the streets of our camps, presented, especially at night, a most beautiful and lively scene. The few trees which still remained as shelters were generally lighted up by our fires into grand chandeliers, reflecting upon our white tents a weird light of gold and green, which might have furnished the pen of the romancer, and the pencil of the artist, their most interesting plots and designs. Around these fires gathered the comrades of many a march and battle, to discuss the experiences of the past, to applaud or censure certain men and measures, and to lay plans, and to entertain rumours with regard to future operations.

The gallantry and merits of companions fallen in strife were presented by those most intimate with them; and otherwise dreary hours were pleasantly whiled away with narratives of personal encounters, of terrible sufferings of prisoners while in the hands of the enemy, and of hair-breadth escapes. These accounts were generally enlivened with extra colouring drawn from the enchanting and fairy-like scenes which surrounded the speaker, and an entire group was thrilled and electrified until frequently the night was made to ring with uproarious applause.

Occasionally the friends and home scenes we have left behind us became the subjects of conversation, and it is astonishing how that word "home," with its hallowed associations, touches the tender feelings of our hearts. These colloquies often ended with the good old hymn, "Home, sweet home," and with the sound of the last bugle-call we hastened to our rest, to spend, it may be, a miserable night of cold and storm.

No soldier can ever forget these camp and bivouac scenes, for they are deeply photographed upon his memory. He will often recall their ludicrous as well as romantic side, when the mud was knee-deep and over, up to within a few feet of the fire, compelling him often to stand so near the burning pile as to set his clothes on fire. In very cold weather he would freeze one side while the other burned, unless he frequently performed that military feat, changing "his base of operations." If the wind blew, making his fantastic gyrations among the tents, so that you never knew whence he would come nor whither he would go, you were sure to get your face smoked horribly.

With thousands of camps thus circumstanced, it may be conjectured that no little amount of fuel would suffice us. At first the trees were cut down without much regard to the height of the stumps, but as the forest receded from the camps, making transportation difficult, the stumps were dug up by the roots, leaving the ground perfectly smooth, and made ready for the ploughman, whenever our swords are beaten into ploughshares and our battle spears into pruning hooks.

And besides the consumption of wood for fires, no little amount is used for the construction of our houses or huts. Nearly every man has suddenly become a mason or a carpenter, and the hammer, the axe, and the trowel are being plied with the utmost vigour, if not with the highest skill. Many of us, however, are astonished at the ingenuity that is displayed in this department.

Large logs, notched at the ends so as to dovetail together, and sometimes hewn on the inside, compose the body of the hut. By the careful application of mud—that Virginia mortar or plaster with which every soldier is so familiar—to the crevices between the logs, a very comfortable structure is made ready for its covering and occupancy. Shelter-tents, buttoned or sewed together, form the roof, which, by the aid of *talmas* or *ponchos*, is generally made water-proof.

Three or four men usually unite in the construction of a hut, and share one another's skill and stores. If they can afford it, they purchase of the sutlers small sheet-iron stoves, which will keep them very comfortably warm, and afford them an opportunity to do their own cooking on extra occasions, such as come with the issues of supplies from the Christian or Sanitary Commissions, or the reception of boxes from friends at home.

The ordinary cooking of a company is done by men detailed for that purpose. Often good fireplaces and chimneys are erected in the tents. These are sometimes made of sticks of wood laid in thick mud, or of stones or bricks taken from the foundations and remains of buildings that have been destroyed in the neighbourhood of our camps. Every means is resorted to which Yankee ingenuity can devise to make our soldier-homes as comfortable and convenient as possible.

Punch says, *that a Yankee baby will creep out of his cradle, take a survey of it, invent an improved style and apply for a patent, before he is six months old,* and this he said some time ago; what he would say now, we cannot tell. If a house has been abandoned by its inmates anywhere within our lines, it is taken as *prima facie* evidence that the owners must be Rebels—and it matters but little whether they are or not, so long as the house stands alone; and in nearly as short a period of time as it takes to tell the story, the building is torn in pieces, and the materials are used in the construction of officers' quarters, huts for the enlisted men, and stables for our horses. The dying year left us engaged thus in the work of policing and adding comfort to Camp Bayard.

January 1, 1863.—The Harris Light was ordered to the Rappahannock, where we were posted on picket near Port Conway. The Federal and Rebel pickets have mutually arranged that there shall be no firing on either side, unless an advance is undertaken. This agreement is of course among ourselves, neither approved nor disapproved at headquarters.

For several days the most perfect harmony has prevailed between the blue and the gray. Yankees and Johnnies wash together in the same stream, procure water to drink and for culinary purposes from the same spring, and, curious to relate, often read the news from the same papers. Squads of soldiers from both armies may be observed seated together on either side of the Rappahannock, earnestly discussing the great questions of the day, each obstinately maintaining his views of the matters at issue.

On one occasion a soldier from our ranks took from his pocket a copy of the *New York Herald,* and read the Union account of one of the great battles to an attentive crowd of Rebel soldiers. When he had concluded, up sprang one of the chivalry, who brought to view a dingy copy of the *Richmond Examiner,* and proceeded to read his side of the story. No one was offended, and all relished the comparison of views, and then began to discuss the merits of the two accounts.

During all these interviews trading was the order of the day, and a heavy business was carried on in the tobacco, coffee, and hardtack line. There was also a special demand on the part of the Rebels for pocket-knives and canteens, these articles evidently being very scarce in Dixie.

January 12.—The weather has been very uneven since the year began. Wind, rain, sleet, and snow, singly and combined, have been our portion, and as a natural consequence, oceans of mud have thus far given Camp Bayard a most unwelcome appearance. Our only remedy is to corduroy our streets, which we do by bridging them with the straightest timber we can find. Usually this is pine, with which thousands of acres are covered in Virginia. As it is mostly of a recent growth, averaging about six inches in diameter, and shooting up to an immense height before you can reach the branches, it is well suited to our purpose.

Rough as these corduroyed streets are, they are very passable, and prevent us from sinking with our horses into a bottomless limbo. On the fourteenth of the month our picket details returned to camp, after being several days on duty. The weather is becoming delightful. The sun is often so brilliant and warm that we are compelled to seek shelter in our tents or in the fragrant shades of the woods. We are reminded of pleasant April weather in Northern New York. Under this *régime* of old Sol, the roads are rapidly improving, and should no adverse change occur, we may soon look for some important army movement.

January 21.—Today we received two months' pay, and, as is usually the case on pay-day, the boys are in excellent spirits. Whatever trouble or difficulty the soldier may have, pay-day is a wonderful panacea, at least if his pay-roll and accounts are all satisfactory and right. But the men do not all make the same use of their money. Many on receiving the "greenbacks" hasten to Adams' Express, or despatch an agent, and send home all the money that can be spared.

Some repair to their tents and enter upon gambling schemes, with cards generally, or other games; and it is no uncommon thing to hear that someone has lost all he had, and has gone so far even as to borrow more, in less than twelve hours of the time he was paid. A small portion of the men visit the sutlers, those army vampires, whose quarters are converted into scenes of dissipation, drunkenness, and folly. Men whose families at home are waiting for means to live, thus waste all their wages, disgrace themselves, and cast their dependents upon the charities of the cold world.

January 22.—For about two days the army has been prepared for an advance across the Rappahannock. Today the grand movement was commenced. Several regiments, supposing that they would never again need their winter huts, have burned or otherwise demolished them. But the weather, which was fine at the outset, has suddenly changed, and about ten o'clock at night there poured upon us, untented and unprotected, a furious storm of rain, sleet, and snow, making our condition almost unendurable.

We are now left in a bed of almost fathomless mire. None of the men who flounder through these oozy roads, under the inclement sky, will ever forget the "Muddy March." We had scarcely reached the river-shore before we were compelled to return. In one instance a piece of artillery with its horses had to be abandoned, submerged so deeply in the mud that it was considered impracticable to extricate them. Men are frequently compelled to assist one another, unable to proceed alone.

The ground is covered with snow, and yet the mud is so deep that it is almost an impossibility to move artillery or supplies. All our forage and rations are brought from Belle Plain on horses and pack-mules, all wheeled vehicles being entirely shipwrecked.

The Rebels appear to understand what had been our designs, and know fully the cause of our failure in the expedition. Consequently, to tantalize us, they have erected an enormous sign-board on their side of the river, but in full view of our pickets, bearing the inscription: "Stuck in the mud!"

General Burnside, beset on every hand with misfortunes and disasters, tendered his resignation, but was simply relieved, as at his own request, from the command of the Army of the Potomac.

CHAPTER 8

Organisation of a Cavalry Corps

On the twenty-sixth of January, General Joseph Hooker assumed command of the Army of the Potomac, whose vicissitudes and defeats have well-nigh broken its spirit and wiped out its efficiency. The patriotic fire is burning dimly in shrines where it has blazed brightly before. The tide of military life has possibly readied its lowest ebb, and the signs of the times are ominous of ill. Desertions are reported to be fearfully large. For this many of our friends at the North are responsible.

Not only do their letters speak discouraging words to the soldier, but many of them sent by express citizens' clothes, with which many of the boys quickly invest themselves, throwing away the blue, and thus disguised find their way to their false friends at home. I esteem him false to me who would thus rob me of my honour. I would rather say, "despoil me of my life, but my integrity never." Discouraging as all this depression of mind and dispersion of comrades may be, many still remain steadfast at their trust and unflinchingly go ahead in the discharge of their duty.

General Hooker's first work seems to be in the direction of checking this loosening of discipline, and in reorganising and strengthening the bands of military order. As the infantry needed but little further solidification, the commander-in-chief turned his attention to the cavalry. In the possible efficiency of this arm of the service the general seems to have full faith. But it is currently reported that the general has said "that he has yet failed to see or hear of a dead cavalryman."

Of course this cannot be strictly true, for we could cite him multitudes, including our noble Bayard, whose bravery and sacrifice of themselves upon their country's altar, are worthy of recognition at the hand of their commander. But it is quite evident that the cavalry has not yet come up to the *beau*-ideal of the general. And, indeed, it has been a source of speculation to us, that while the efficiency of the infantry is known to depend largely upon its organisation into brigades, divisions, and corps, with their general commander, the same may not be true of the cavalry.

General Bayard, the great cavalry chief of the Army of the Potomac during General Burnside's administration, made several efforts at consolidation, resulting, however, in no very permanent changes. It was reserved for General Hooker to bring about the desired result; and, at last, the Cavalry Corps of the Army of the Potomac is organised, with General George D. Stoneman for its commanding officer. By this change regiments which have been scattered here and there on detached service are brought together, and made to feel the enthusiasm which numbers generally inspire, especially when those numbers are united into a system, with a living head, whose intelligence and authority control the whole.

Under this new regime some very beneficial changes have been wrought. Schools or camps of instruction have been established, with a more rigid discipline than before, and boards of examination, with all the experience of the past before their eyes, have been organised. Old and incompetent officers have been dismissed, or have slunk away before this incisive catechism, giving way generally to intelligent, young, and efficient men, who, placed at the heads of regiments and brigades, give promise of success in the struggles that await us.

The Rebel cavalry under Stuart has long been organised into an efficient body, which, at times, has sneered at our attempts to match them; and yet they have been made to feel, on some occasions, that we are a growing power, which time and experience may develop into something formidable. But the general successes of the Rebel army have made them all very insolent, in the hope that final victory is already in their grasp.

February 11.—My old friend and comrade. Sergeant Theodore May, of Pittstown, New York, died this afternoon at two o'clock, after a brief illness, of typhoid fever, which is a great scourge throughout the army. The death of this valiant fellow-soldier casts a deep gloom over the entire command, in which he has so faithfully served. When we entered the army together at the organisation of the regiment, he came a perfect stranger, but his gentle manners and soldierly deportment soon made for him hosts of warm friends. By his gallantry on the field of battle, as well as by the gentleness of his manners and his unblemished conduct in camp, he has won the respect, and even admiration, of all who knew him.

The patriotic motives which induced Sergeant May to quit his pleasant home in the beautiful valley of the Tomhannock, for the privations, hardships, and dangers of military life, have always proved him to be a true and warm sympathizer in his country's cause. It was evidently not the mere love of adventure, or the mere pageantry or glory of war, that led him to make the great sacrifice. He has been with us in every conflict, and shared with us the varied fortunes of the Harris Light.

His death, which he would rather have met on the field of strife, battling manfully against traitors, was reserved for the calm and quiet of the camp, where he spent his last moments urging his comrades to "cheer up and fight on," offering as his dying reason, that "our cause is just, and must triumph." Such a death is a rich legacy to a command. "*He being dead, yet speaketh.*" We would emulate his virtues.

February 12.—On recommendation of Lieutenant Frederick C. Lord, I was today appointed by Colonel Kilpatrick First Sergeant of Company E, *vice* Henry Temple, promoted to Sergeant Major. My appointment is to date from the first of January, making me a very desirable New Year's gift, which I shall strive to honour.

February 22.—Snow has been falling uninterruptedly the livelong day, and yet the boys have been unusually merry, as they were wont to be on this anniversary before the war. Our celebration has been on a scanty scale, and yet we have felt the patriotic stimulus which comes from the great men and days of the past. And truly, the birth of the great Washington gives birth to many interesting thoughts, especially at this period of our history. A national salute has been fired from our fortifications on the Potomac, and the whole country round about us has been made to reverberate with the sound that welcomes in the day.

But all these patriotic manifestations have not prevented the snowstorm and the cold. When we left our home in the North for what was termed "the sunny South," we little expected to find such storms as this here. While the summers are much cooler than we expected to find them, the days being generally fanned by a beautiful sea-breeze, the winters exceed for cold our highest expectation. The cold is not continuous, but very severe.

We have seen the soft ground and water-puddles freeze sufficiently in one night to bear a horse; and in several days and nights the frost has penetrated the earth several inches deep. The snowstorm of today is as severe as most storms experienced in the North. The wind has howled from the north-west, burdened with its cold, feathery, flakes, which tonight lie at least twelve inches deep in places undisturbed. It is such a storm as our suffering pickets, and indeed our entire army, cannot soon forget.

It may be that the vast forests of Virginia have much to do with its peculiar temperature. As we travel from place to place we are strongly impressed with the vastness of the wilderness, which covers thousands of acres of as fine arable soil as can be found on the continent. How different is this from the notions we had formed of the Old Dominion, while reading of its early settlements, and of its great agricultural advantages.

But when we look into its system of land-owning, and find that one individual monopolizes a territory sufficient for a dozen farms, and consequently neglects eleven twelfths of his acres; and then look into its even worse system of labour, we need search no farther for the causes of this backwardness in agricultural pursuits. The implements made use of here on the plantations are such as were rejected by New England farmers over half a century ago; and the methods of cultivation are a century behind the times. Slavery and land-monopoly are the incubus.

Who does not sincerely hope that the time is not far distant, when the rich acres of this great State shall be properly shared by its inhabitants, and when, freed from a burden and curse which have long paralyzed their energies, instinct with new life and enterprise, the people will realise the dignity of labour? Then will the almost interminable forests disappear, and in their stead the industrious yeoman will behold his rich fields of waving grain. Then, too, along the now comparatively useless streams and swift water-courses, will spring up the factory and the mill, whose rolling wheels and buzzing spindles will bring wealth and prosperity to the nation.

We are convinced, from what we have seen, that Virginia has water-power enough to turn the machinery of the world. With these changes the schoolhouse will be found by the side of every church, and intelligence and virtue will bless the home of the Presidents.

We have also many times been led to think, while lying in these chilly woods, that a greater warmth would be imparted to the atmosphere if the forest-trees were felled and the land put under cultivation,—a change sufficiently great to be appreciable throughout the State.

"Unchronicled Heroes."

Sunday, March 1.—The usual Sunday morning inspection was omitted on account of rain. Rain, rain had fallen for many days almost incessantly. The regiment has been earnestly at work throughout the day in building stables for the horses, which have suffered greatly from being kept standing too long in the mud.

Under these circumstances our horses are afflicted with the scratches, many of them so badly as to render them unserviceable, and occasionally they lose their lives.

By this cause and through hard work my little black mare, which I drew by lot at Camp Sussex in the autumn of 1861, has at last succumbed, and, with a grief akin to that which is felt at the loss of a dear human friend, I have performed the last rite of honour to the dead. The Indian may love his faithful dog, but his attachments cannot surpass the cavalryman's for his horse. They have learned to love one another in the most trying vicissitudes of life, and the animal manifests affection and confidence quite as evidently as a human being could.

The cavalier, it is true, is often compelled to ride at a most fearful rate, as when bearing hurried despatches or making a charge, frequently causing almost immediate blindness to the animal. Or, perhaps, he continues on a march for many days and nights in succession, as on a raid, averaging at least sixty-five miles in twenty-four hours, with little water and less forage; unable to remove the saddle, which has to be tightly bound, until the animal is so badly galled that the hair comes off with the blanket at its first removal.

Sufferings like these often cause the death of a large proportion of a command; and to a careless looker-on these things would appear to be mere neglects. But these cruel military necessities only develop more perfectly the rider's sympathy for his suffering beast, and bind them in closer and more endearing bonds.

Some men had rather injure themselves than have their horses harmed, and the utmost pains are taken to heal them in case they are wounded. Each regiment has its veterinary surgeon, whose skill is taxed to the utmost in his branch of the healing art.

Among the most touching scenes we have witnessed, are those in which the mortally wounded horse has to be abandoned on the field of carnage. With tearful eyes the rider and perhaps owner turns to take a last look of the "unchronicled hero," his fellow-sufferer, that now lies weltering in his blood, and yet makes every possible effort to follow the advancing column. the parting is deeply affecting. Often the cavalryman finds no object to which he may hitch his horse for the night save his own hand; and thus with the halter fast bound to his grasp he lies down with a stone, or perhaps his saddle, for a pillow, his faithful horse standing as a watchful guardian by his side.

At times the animal will walk around him, eating the grass as far as he can reach, and frequently arousing him by trying to gain the grass on which he lies; yet it is worthy of note, that an instance can scarcely be found where the horse has been known to step upon or in anywise injure his sleeping lord. Such a scene the poet undoubtedly had in his mind when he sang:

> *The murmuring wind, the moving leaves*
> *Lull'd him at length to sleep,*
> *With mingled lullabies of sight and sound.*

Such experiences as these had taught me to love my faithful and true friend. But I found I was not the only man in the command who was bereaved of his first love. Only a few horses of the original number which we drew still remain, and several of them are either partially or totally blind, though yet serviceable. the hardships of the camp and the campaign are more destructive of animal than human flesh.

Men are often sheltered from the storm when the horses are exposed, and the men are sometimes fed when the horses have to go hungry.

In battle the horse is a larger mark than the man, and hence is more frequently victimized than his rider, so that there is always a much larger proportion of casualties among the horses than men of a cavalry command in every engagement. The horse's head and shoulders will often receive the bullet which was intended for the rider's body. This is true also of the elevated portions of the saddle, with the rolls of blankets and coats and bag of forage.

A difference has also been noticed between the casualties in cavalry and infantry regiments under equal exposure. This difference is wholly explained when we consider the jolting and swift motion of the man as his horse leaps forward in the fray, making him a very uncertain mark for the enemy.

Bright Days

March 3.—This is the first bright day we have seen in more than three weeks. The mud around our camps, especially in the neighbourhood where we water our horses, is terrible, and the roads are almost bottomless. However, long trains of forage and commissary-wagons may be seen passing to and fro, with horses and mules in mud from "stem to stern." Cavalcades of mudded horses and riders traverse the camps and adjoining fields in various directions.

Large flocks of crows—the most soldier-like bird in the world—with their high-perched *vedettes* when alighted, and their military line of march when on the wing, afford some lessons of diversion and instruction. It would seem as if all the ravens of the United States had congregated here, having been attracted by the carrion of battlefields and the refuse of camps. Turkey buzzards, birds which are always on the wing, and that none of us ever yet saw alighted wheel through the air like eagles, gazing down Upon us with seeming defiance. These sights are of daily occurrence.

Kilpatrick

Today several details were made from the regiment for brigade headquarters, where Kilpatrick, the senior colonel in the brigade, now commands. In the afternoon we raised the "stars and stripes" in front of his tent, after which three cheers were given for the flag and three for the Union. Kilpatrick was then called upon for a speech, and responded in his usually felicitous style. He is certainly an orator as well as a warrior. He speaks, too, as he fights, with dash and daring.

What he has to say he says with such perspicuity that no one doubts his meaning. Frequently there are flashes of eloquence worthy of a Demosthenes. His voice and diction seem to be well-nigh faultless. His speech today elicited frequent outbursts of applause, and the men cheered him enthusiastically at the close, and left his quarters with a deeper affection for him than before. Strict as he is to enforce discipline, and thorough, yet he is not severe; and the men love him for his personal attention to their wants, and for his appreciation of their labours. If he gives us hard work to do in march or battle, he endures or shares with us the hardship.

If by the losses of men he has sustained he is truly entitled to the nickname of "Kill Cavalry," which has been quite generally accorded to him, his men know that these casualties have fallen out in the line of duty, in bold enterprises that cost the enemy dearly, the wisdom of which will ever exculpate our loved commander from the imputation of rashness with which, by uninformed parties, he is sometimes charged.

In preparation for, and during, a battle, none can excel him. His plans are quickly made and executed, while all possible contingencies seem to have been foreseen. His selection of positions and disposition of forces always exhibits great sagacity and military genius. He generally holds his men under perfect control. His clarion voice rings like magic through the ranks, while his busy form, always in the thickest of the tight, elicits the warmest enthusiasm. His equanimity of mind seems never to be overcome by his celerity of motion, but are equally balanced. Rarely is so great prudence found blended with so undaunted courage. He has an indomitable will that cannot brook defeat. The word impossible he never knows, whatever difficulties intervene between him and duty. He feels like Napoleon, "*that impossible is the adjective of fools.*"

Added to all these mental qualifications, is that perfect physique, which makes Kilpatrick the model soldier. As an equestran we have never seen his superior. He rides as though he had been made for a saddle. Rocks, stumps, fallen trees, brooks, and fences are nothing before him. His well-trained steeds understand him perfectly, and are never at a loss to know what is meant by the sharp spurs on their sides, whatever obstacles stand in their path.

We have seen him leap over barriers where only few could follow him. To accomplish such feats the horse must have confidence in the rider as well as the rider in the horse. While in a charge, Kilpatrick has more the appearance of an eagle pouncing upon his prey, than that of a man pouncing upon a man. Then, too, he has a wonderful power of endurance. Though somewhat slender in form and delicate in mould, with complexion and eyes as light as a maiden's, yet it would seem as though his bones were iron and his sinews steel, while the whole is overlaid with gold. He is certainly compactly built. He has undoubtedly his faults, but his men fail to see them, so that to them he is as good as perfect.

What so young a champion of the right may yet achieve for his country, is a matter of much hopeful conjecture among us. He is now only twenty-five years of age, having had his birth in the beautiful valley of the Clove, in Northern New Jersey, in 1838. He entered the Military Academy at West Point on the twentieth of June, 1856, and graduated with honours in 1860, just in time to be ready for the great

Federal and Rebel cavalry pickets meeting in the Rappahannock

conflict then impending.

He was present at Baltimore when the mob endeavoured to stop the trains for Washington, and the blood of Massachusetts men was spilt upon the streets. He there exhibited that bold intrepidity which has ever characterized his actions. He was wounded at the Battle of Big Bethel, one of the first engagements of the war, where as a lieutenant he commanded Duryea's *Zouaves*, June eleventh, 1861, He had just recovered from his wound when he entered upon the organisation of the Harris Light, and became its lieutenant-colonel.

March 5.—We had regimental drill at the usual time this morning. I rode my black pony recently drawn in place of my little black mare, deceased. This was his first experience in cavalry discipline; and I infer that the men in the front rank of the platoon, which I commanded, hoped it might be his last entry; for it must have been most emphatically evident to those who followed him that he was determined to introduce a new system of tactics, in which heels were to go up in no gentle manner at every change of movement.

He is certainly the most ungovernable horse on drill I ever mounted; and nothing but long marches and raids can effectually subdue his kicking propensities. I am encouraged, however, with the consideration that such fiery metal, when properly controlled and moulded, is usually very valuable.

The rain fell so fast on the sixth, that we were prevented from drill, and recall was sounded immediately after drill-call.

Sunday, March 8.—Details from the regiment were ordered out on picket. The night had been stormy, but the day has been lovely. At such times, were it not for the mud, we would feel that we are very comfortably circumstanced.

On the eleventh, in the morning, the ground was covered with snow which had fallen in the night. A brilliant sun soon dissolved the pure mantle and left us in much mire. But our attention was diverted from the going by a novel scene which we were called to witness in camp. The regiment was instructed in the best method of packing a mule, by one who has had experience in the business.

The most mulish mule in the whole braying family was selected for the operation, and if we did not have some tall fun I will admit that I am no judge. A hog on ice or a bristling porcupine are bad enough, but an ugly mule outstrips them all. It seems as if the irascible animal tried to do his prettiest, flouncing around in a most laughable manner, pawing and kicking at times furiously. But the desperate Yankee teacher was not to be outwitted, and conquered him at last, when the pack was satisfactorily poised, and the ornamented mule was promenaded about camp as in triumph.

We are informed that it is the intention of the authorities to have pack-mules used in the cavalry corps henceforward in place of army wagons. The reason of this change seems to be to facilitate rapid movements or forced marches. It is the prevailing opinion, however, that the experiment will prove a failure. Too many mules would be required for this purpose, and our forage and rations would be very insecure, especially from the storms. But we will see how the thing works. At times it may be expedient.

March 12.—I had the misfortune to have my quarters burned this morning while getting out a detail for picket. All my extra clothing, equipments, and some little mementoes or valuables were speedily converted into ashes. But I immediately went to work, and with some kind assistance, which every brother-soldier is so ready to bestow, I put up a new establishment which in every respect is superior to the old one.

Details from the regiment, with pack-mules, were sent out to the Rappahannock on the thirteenth, to carry rations and forage to our pickets. The mule-train looks oddly enough, and yet through these muddy roads it seems to be a necessity.

March 14.—Having been detailed to act as officer of the guard, I am today engaged in the performance of that duty. We were not a little amused this morning by the arrest of Kilpatrick's coloured servants. It was their misfortune to be discovered by Captain Southard, the officer of the day, while engaged in a fierce contest, in which their heads were used as the chief weapons of attack and defence. The blows they dealt upon each other were most terrible, reminding one of the battering-rams of old, used for demolishing the walls of forts or cities.

Such ancient modes of warfare, of course, could not be tolerated here, especially as no order for battle had been promulgated from headquarters, and the captain arrested the offenders and brought them to the guard-house, where they were placed in my charge. I immediately ordered them out under guard to police camp as a punishment for their bad conduct.

While thus engaged, Kilpatrick happened to see them, and, not wishing to have his faithful servants subjected to such humiliating labour, issued an order for their immediate release from durance vile, asserting that he would be responsible for their fighting in the future, if at least they did not put their heads together more than half a dozen times a day.

The day following this laughable farce, in the afternoon, we experienced one of the most terrific storms ever known in this part of the country. The day had been quite pleasant until about two o'clock, when dark clouds began to obscure the sky, and the wind shifted from the south to the north-west.

At four o'clock the elements were ready for battle, and a fierce engagement commenced. Gleaming and forked lightnings cleft the canopy, while booming thunder shook the trembling earth. The artillery of Heaven had not long been opened before the musketry commenced, and down poured a shower of hail, which came near demolishing our tents, and brought suffering and sorrow upon all unsheltered heads.

Mules brayed horribly, vying with the hoarse, muttering thunder, making the camp most hideous and lonely. The wind and cold increased with every passing hour, the hail fell faster and more heavily, and night came suddenly down to hide, though not to prevent, the storm. The night was one of great suffering, especially on the lines of picket—it was bad enough anywhere.

March 23.—A beautiful sabre was presented to Major E. F. Cooke this afternoon, by the members of his old company, for his gallantry and soldierly character, which have earned his promotion. Captain O. J. Downing, of company B, made the presentation speech, in which he beautifully alluded to the happy relation which always exists between a faithful commander and his men. As a token that such relation existed between the major and those whom he had often led through perilous scenes and conflicts, their gift was presented.

An appropriate response was made by the major, in which he very humbly attributed his military success thus far to the bravery of the noble men who had always stood by him, and whose gift he accepted not only as a mark of their appreciation of himself as a man, but of their devotion to the cause which he hoped, by the edge of the sabre and trust in Providence, we may yet win,

March 24.—Kilpatrick's brigade was reviewed this morning by General Gregg, who commands the Second division of the cavalry corps. Kilpatrick commands the First brigade, which is composed of the First Maine, the Tenth New York, and Harris Light. On the twenty-fifth General Gregg again reviewed us. We were ordered to turn out in "heavy marching orders," that is, with all our clothing, rations, forage or grain, and fully equipped. For some reason inspections and reviews are frequent of late. The Harris Light maintains its established reputation, as being second to none in the corps, for its efficiency in drill and discipline, and in its general appearance. The men take pride in keeping up the morale of the regiment.

March 28.—Colonel Clarence Buel is paying us a visit today. This gallant and noble officer, who organised and formerly commanded the Troy company of the Harris Light, has recently been promoted to the colonelcy of the Hundred and Sixty-ninth New York Infantry. The colonel has taken a temporary leave of absence from his new command for the purpose of making us a friendly call; and he is again surrounded by his old tried friends and comrades.

Company E hails with pleasure its former loved captain, and though sad at his loss, still rejoices in his well-earned and merited promotion. All the men of the company showed their respect and admiration for him by falling into line upon the announcement of his arrival in camp, and thus greeted the Christian soldier. It was a very delightful and enjoyable occasion.

As a soldier, Colonel Buel stands among the bravest and the best. Always attentive to the wants of his command, his men are always the last to be out of supplies of rations or clothing. He generally exercised that fatherly care over us which called forth in return a filial love. He is dignified, and yet perfectly affable. As a commander, he is intrepid and cool, and manages his troops with admirable skill. He possesses a naturally well-balanced mind, thoroughly cultivated, and a heart always full of Christian hopefulness and benevolence. We wish him great success in his new field of labour and responsibility.

CHAPTER 9

Rebel Chiefs and their Raids

The Rebel cavalry has been very active all winter, as may be seen by the many raids which they have made, beginning as far back as December twenty-fifth, when their chief, J. E. B. Stuart, anxious to obtain something suitable with which to celebrate the holidays, crossed the Rappahannock, advanced on Dumfries, where it would seem that our boys, freezing dumb (Dumfries), suffered the raider to capture not less than twenty-five wagons, and at least two hundred prisoners. Moving boldly northward, he struck the Orange and Alexandria Railroad, burning the bridge across the Accotink Run, and from Burke's Station he swung around Fairfax Court House, and returned, by long, circuitous route, into their lines with their hard-earned spoils.

A lull of operations followed this bold holiday enterprise, until the sixteenth of February, when a party of General John D. Imboden's rangers, in the Shenandoah Valley, made a rapid raid to Romney, farther west, where they captured several men, horses, and wagons, having taken our forces entirely by surprise. The success which characterized these forays was not only disgraceful to ourselves, and very disheartening, but it gave the Rebels an audacious effrontery and malignant boldness, which led them into more frequent and reckless movements. But our men were a little more on the alert, and thus averted, to a great extent, the injury which was intended.

February 25.—Today Fitz-Hugh Lee, almost in the very face of our pickets, crossed the Rappahannock near Falmouth, attacked by surprise a camp, where he captured one hundred and fifty prisoners, but was not able to return without some loss. The next day General W. E. Jones marched with a brigade into the Valley, attacked and routed two regiments of General Milroy's cavalry, and, with slight loss from his command, escaped with about two hundred prisoners. The most daring, however, of all these raids was made by Major White, with his band of Loudon County rangers, which differs not much from guerrillas, into Maryland, where they captured a few prisoners, but spent most of their time and strength in plunder. Poolesville was the scene of their depredations.

It did seem as though nearly every Rebel cavalry officer had been touched with a magic wand which filled him with the most weird and romantic views of warfare, and led him into enterprises almost wild as any of Dick Turpin's. Fauquier County was the theatre of several of these movements by Captain Randolph, of the Black Horse Cavalry. And in these days appeared another partisan, whose name for the first time flashes out in big capitals in the official as well as other bulletins, amid most startling manoeuvrings: it is John S. Mosby.

To the Harris Light this gentleman was not wholly unknown, and we distinctly remember the time when he was a prisoner in our hands. It appears that he was then sent to Old Capitol Prison at Washington. Not long thereafter he was released; and, being bent on revenge, and naturally fitted for guerrilla operations, he soon received permission from his chief, to operate on an independent plan.

This Mosby, as we have been informed by an acquaintance of his, a Rebel soldier who has known him from early life, has always been a sort of guerrilla—deserting from his father's house in mere boyhood—fighting duels as a pastime—roving the country far and wide in search of pleasure or profit—a thorough student of human nature and of the country in which he operates—bold and daring to a fault and romantic in his make—and finding now his chief delight in the adventures of guerrilla life.

His commission is a roving one, and his command seems to be limited neither to kind or number. Many of his men are citizens, who spend a portion of their time in their ordinary business pursuits, and who hold themselves in readiness for any movements indicated by their commander.

Occasionally he is accompanied and assisted in his forays by daring men from various commands, who are at home on leaves of absence or furloughs, while a few seem to be directly and continually under his control. the principal stimulus of the entire party (except the bad whiskey which they are said to use), is the plunder which they share. It is their custom at times to parole their prisoners and send them back to our lines, though often, when large numbers are taken, they are sent to Richmond; but all horses and equipments, which now command enormous prices in Dixie, are the property of the captors.

The region of the country they have chosen for their operations is certainly well adapted to facilitate their designs. Deep ravines traverse the country, skirted with dense, dark foliage, which affords them shelter, and through which they pass like so many wild turkeys or wild boars, knowing, as they do, all the roads and by-paths. Indeed, some of their parties are dwellers in these regions, and are acquainted with every nook and corner, where they can hide securely with their prey and elude their pursuers. When the immediate neighbourhoods of their depredations do not offer a sufficient asylum, they fly to the fastnesses and caverns of the Bull Run Mountains.

Then, too, there is a certain degree of carelessness on the part of our own men, which merits censure and causes trouble. For instance, calls are frequently made at the homes of bitter Rebels, for the purpose of securing articles of food, which are usually purchased or taken, and while at these places they are too often unguarded in their conversations about the condition of our army, the position of picket lines, etc.—information which is grasped with wonderful avidity and as readily transmitted to Mosby and his men.

Scarcely does any important event transpire among us, that is not fully understood immediately by the Rebel families within our lines, and is very easily borne to those outside the lines between two days. Thus movements even in contemplation have been heralded before the incipient steps had been taken, and consequently thwarted. Our only safety from this source of trouble would be to drive out of our lines all Rebel families, thus preventing the means of communicating the news to the outer world.

Another simple statement will explain the chances of the enemy and the causes of many of our casualties. Our picket-lines are too much extended, covering too wide a territory to make them as strong as they should be. Only a brigade is doing the work of a division, and consequently the picket-posts are not sufficiently near each other. Thus, in the night, it requires no very great dexterity to creep through the bushes between the pickets unobserved, and, once within our lines, any amount of mischief may be done by the miscreants. The method indicated here is usually the one employed by these active guerrillas, and it forms the chief stratagem of all their movements upon us.

Their first important attack upon our pickets took place on or about the tenth of January. A small Federal picket was doing duty at

Herndon Station, on the Loudon and Hampshire Railroad. Mosby determined to effect their capture. Led by a skilful guide, he dismounted his command some distance from the picket-lines. Then they all crept cautiously between the *vedettes*, until they reached the rear of the post, and from that direction advanced upon the unsuspecting boys, whose forms could be distinctly seen by the flaring light of their bivouac fire.

While the pickets were thus a fine shot and mark for the enemy, the attacking force was concealed perfectly by the darkness of night and the shades of the thick pines. A pistol-shot from the guerrillas was followed by a charge, when our boys were suddenly surrounded and captured.

This attack and capture was followed by another similar enterprise a few nights afterwards at Cub Run, near the Little River Turnpike. The picket relief was captured by a charge made in their rear, and only the two *vedettes* made their escape. Later in the same night a similar assault was made upon our post at Frying-Pan Church. Not far from this church resides a Miss Laura Ratcliffe, a very active and cunning Rebel, who is known to our men, and is at least suspected of assisting Mosby not a little in his movements. The cavalry brigade doing picket duty at this point is composed of the First Virginia (many of whose men were raised in these parts), the First Vermont, the Fifth New York, and the Eighteenth Pennsylvania.

The latter of these regiments has but recently been mustered into the service, is poorly drilled and worse equipped, and is by no means fitted to picket against so wily a foe as Mosby. Though great caution is exercised by Colonel Percy Wyndham, who is in command of the brigade, to arrange and change the alternation of the pickets, so that the regiments to picket at a given point may not be known beforehand; yet by means of Miss Ratcliffe and her rebellious sisterhood, Mosby is generally informed of the regiment doing duty, and his attacks are usually directed against the unskilled and unsuspecting.

Having approached, under cover of the night above alluded to, within a few hundred yards of the pickets, whose position and strength he knew very well from information received by the neighbours, the horses were left in charge of one man, while the party skulked along through the thick underbrush, until they could approach the post from the direction of the Union camp. The picket relief was mostly quartered in an old house nearby, with a single sentinel stationed at the door.

Seeing the Mosby party approaching, he supposed that they were a patrol, and consequently allowed them to come within a few paces of the house before he challenged them. But it was now too late; and springing forward like panthers, the guerrillas presented their pistols at his head, ordering a surrender. The house was immediately surrounded and the assailants began to fire through the thin weather-boarding upon the men shut up within. This fire, however, was vigorously returned for a time, but yielding at last to superior numbers, who had greatly the advantage, the whole party was compelled to surrender.

The success with which Mosby carried on his operations made him a sort of terror to our pickets, while it attracted to him from all quarters of Rebeldom a larger and more enthusiastic command. They became wonderfully skilled and bold, as may be seen by the following daring exploit. On the night of the eighth of March, during rain and intense darkness, Mosby led a squadron of his conglomerate command through the pines between the pickets near the Turnpike from Centreville to Fairfax Court House. Striking through the country, so as to avoid some infantry camps, he soon reached the road leading from Fairfax Station to the Court House. Moving now with perfect confidence, as no pickets along this route would suspect the character of such a cavalcade several miles inside our lines, about two o'clock in the morning he entered the village and began operations.

The first thing was to capture the pickets stationed along the streets in a quiet manner, so as to arouse no one from their slumbers, and this was easily accomplished. The way was now fully open to the Confederate band. Divided into parties, each with its work assigned, they quickly accomplished the mischief they desired.

Mosby, with a small band, proceeded to General Stoughton's headquarters, in the house of a Dr. Gunnel. Dismounting, he soon stood knocking at the door. A voice from an open window above demanded their business at such an unseasonable hour.

"Despatches for General Stoughton," responded Mosby. The door was quickly unlocked, and the guerrilla chief stood by the bedside of the sleeping general, who had but a few moments before retired from a dancing and convivial party. Fancy now the re-enactment of the scene in old Ticonderoga Fort, when Ethan Allen, by stratagem, stood in the presence of His Majesty's sleeping commander.

Stoughton was soon apprised of the character of his nightly visitors, and quickly making his toilet, he was hurried away with a portion of his escort, and several other prisoners, including Captain Augustus

Barker, of the Fifth New York Cavalry. Fifty-eight of the finest horses from the officers' stables were also captured; and Mosby retraced his sinuous route through our lines of pickets so rapidly, that he escaped all his pursuers.

The morning light of the ninth of March revealed the boldness and success of the raiders, and no little excitement prevailed. Several parties of cavalry were ordered out in pursuit of the flying partisans, but all returned at night unsuccessful. This was an occasion for great humiliation on the part of our troops, stationed about the Court House, while in Washington and throughout the nation not a little humour was drawn from the remark made by the president when someone told him of the loss we had sustained; "Yes," he characteristically replied, "that of the horses is bad; but I can make another general in five minutes."

Suspicious that Rebel citizens within our lines were more or less implicated in this and other raids, quite a number of arrests were made among them, which cleared the country of the most flagitious cases. However, it is very probable that some innocent ones were made to suffer, while the most guilty were allowed to escape.

March 23.—The pickets near Chantilly had been quiet for several days, but toward night a company of cavaliers, mostly dressed in blue uniforms, emerged from a piece of wood within a mile of the Chantilly mansion, and moved directly toward the picket post stationed near a small run on the Little River Turnpike. The picket, supposing them to be Union troops, watched their approach without suspicion; and when they had come within a few feet of him they introduced themselves by shooting him through the head.

The alarm being thus given, the nearest reserve made a sudden descent upon the attacking party, which proved to be Mosby's, and the guerrillas retreated for some distance up the turnpike, closely pursued. Having followed them about three miles, they came to a barricade of trees which had been fallen across the road. Back of this obstruction Mosby had formed a large part of his command, and our column was stopped by a heavy fire from carbines and pistols in their front and also by a flank-fire from the woods.

At this inopportune moment Mosby made a charge which broke our column. The boys were driven back at a furious rate, and had not strength to rally. Some horses giving out, the hapless riders were captured.

But as Rebels and Yankees were uniformed much alike, it gave some of our boys an opportunity for stratagem. For instance, one of our fellows finding himself overtaken by the enemy, began to fire his pistol in the direction of his flying comrades (with care not to harm them), but with sufficient aim to be taken by the enemy, in their haste, as one of their number. In this way they passed him by, and he effected his escape.

This scrambling race continued for about three miles, back to the ground where the affair commenced, when our men were re-enforced by the reserve from Frying-Pan Church. The Mosbyites were now compelled to halt, and a charge made upon them drove them back up the pike. They were pursued several miles, but night came on and our men were compelled to return. Three of our men were killed, and about thirty-five were taken prisoners, including one lieutenant. Several horses were also taken away. The enemy suffered no appreciable loss.

Mosby's plans were certainly made with great wisdom and forethought, and executed with a dash and will which were at times very astonishing. His men must have been warmly attached to him as their leader, while the gain they made by their plunder greatly increased their zeal. The command was truly unique in its leader, its composition, and its *modus operandi*, while its results, assisted as they were by the topography of the country, and the Rebel sympathizers within and just without our lines, attracted no little attention.

The orders of General Stuart and even those of General Lee associated the name of Mosby with consummate daring and continual success, stimulating the band to greater deeds. We append one specimen of those orders, furnished us by one of their own number:

Headquarters, Cavalry Division,
Army of Northern Virginia, March 27, 1863.

Captain—Your telegram, announcing your brilliant achievements near Chantilly, was duly received and forwarded to General Lee. He exclaimed upon reading it, "Hurrah for Mosby! I wish I had a hundred like him!"

Heartily wishing you continued success, I remain your obedient servant,

J. E. B. Stuart,
Major-General Commanding.

Captain J. S. Mosby, commanding, etc., etc.

But it is not often permitted one man always to prosper in his enterprises, and even the wonderful Mosby was destined to meet equals, and to be worsted in engagements. Later in the season, while General Stahel's cavalry division was picketing the line of the Orange and Alexandria Railroad, Mosby made a sudden descent one morning upon the First Virginia Cavalry at Warrenton Junction.

Unfortunately, these Union Virginians, who were one of the best regiments in our service, were just then unprepared for any such manoeuvring. They had just been relieved from duty, and were taking their rest. Many of the men were lounging about under the shade of trees, or quartered for the time in a few block buildings situated in an angle formed by the two railroads. Their horses were mostly "unsaddled and unbridled, and hence not fit for a fight," while many of them were grazing loosely and quietly in the adjoining fields.

Mosby advanced upon them from the direction of Warrenton—was at first mistaken for a squadron of our own cavalry, which had been sent out on a scouting expedition. The error was soon corrected by a fierce charge made by the guerrillas. Such of the men as were roaming about the premises, mostly unarmed, of course immediately surrendered; but about one hundred of them fled for refuge in one of the largest buildings, resolved to sell themselves (if it came to that) at the dearest price. And now commenced a fearful struggle.

The Confederates would ride up near the windows and discharge their pieces at the men within, while the brave fellows inside, commanded and inspired by Major Steele, one of the bravest of the brave, defended themselves with a noble determination. All efforts of Mosby to make them surrender were in vain. Finding at last that he could not intimidate them with bullets, he ordered the torch to be applied to a pile of hay nearby, and the house was set on fire. Just at this juncture of affairs a strong party of Mosby's gang, having dismounted from their horses, rushed against the door of the building with such force as to burst it open. Surrounded now by the flames, which were spreading rapidly, and attacked with desperation by the foe, the whole party was compelled to surrender.

Flushed with success, the guerrillas were making preparations to retire from the field with their booty, when the Fifth New York Cavalry, which had been bivouacked in a grove not far from Cedar Run Bridge, arrived at the Junction, whither they had been attracted by the firing, and immediately fell upon the foe like an avalanche. Major Hammond commanded in person. Mosby was heard to exclaim, "My

God! it is the Fifth New York!"

A hand-to-hand encounter now took place, in which bravery was fired with desperation, and Yankee sabres were used with fearful effect. The Rebels soon broke and fled in every direction, demoralised and panic-stricken, leaving behind not only the captures they had made, but many of their own number. Some Rebel heads were fearfully gashed and mangled, one of them exhibiting his lower jaw-bone not only dislocated, but almost entirely severed with one determined blow from the strong hand of a cavalryman.

General Stahel, in his despatch to General Heintzelman, says:

> The Rebels, who fled in the direction of Warrenton, were pursued by Major Hammond, Fifth New York Cavalry, who has returned, and reports our charge at Warrenton Junction as being so terrific as to have thoroughly routed and scattered them in every direction. I have sent in twenty-three prisoners of Mosby's command, all of whom are wounded—the greater part of them badly. Dick Moran (a notorious bushwhacker) is among the number. There are also three officers of Mosby's. The loss of the enemy was very heavy in killed, besides many wounded, who scattered and prevented capture. I have no hopes of the recovery of Major Steele, of the First Virginia. Our loss is one killed and fourteen wounded.

Templeman, one of Stonewall Jackson's best spies, was killed; and the partisans confessed themselves thoroughly whipped. They were wont to call this their first retreat, in which they did some tall running. The following complimentary order was issued:

> Headquarters Stahel's Cavalry Division,
> Fairfax Court House, Va. ——, 1863
> Special Orders No. 30.
>
> When soldiers perform brave deeds, a proper acknowledgment of their services is justly their due. The commanding general, therefore, desires to express his gratification at the conduct of the officers and men of Colonel De Forest's command, who were engaged in the fight at Warrenton Junction, on Sunday, ———, 1863. By your promptness and gallantry the, gang of guerrillas who have so long infested the vicinity has been badly beaten and broken up. The heavy loss of the enemy in killed, wounded, and prisoners, proves the determination of your resistance and the vigour of your attack. Deeds like this are

worthy of emulation, and give strength and confidence to the command.

By command of

Major-General Stahel.

Thoroughly as Mosby had been whipped on this occasion, and diminished as was his command, it was not long before he was again heard from. It must be confessed that he possessed remarkable recuperative powers. His qualities of heart and mind seemed to attach his men to him peculiarly, while his mode of warfare was calling many young and daring Virginians to his standard. By this means his numbers were soon recruited, and he was again on the rampage.

At this time the government was sending supplies to the army on the Rappahannock *via* the Orange and Alexandria Railroad. Each train was in charge of a guard, and all the principal bridges and exposed places on the route were under pickets. Besides this, frequent patrols were sent from one picket post to the other, so that the entire road was under a close surveillance. One morning, between seven and eight o'clock, the cavalry pickets and reserves about Catlett's Station were startled by artillery firing just below them on the railroad.

A train laden with rations and forage had just passed on its way to the Rappahannock. It was soon ascertained that during the night the guerrillas had carefully unfastened one of the rails in the woods, and by means of a wire attached to it and extended to some distance from the road, in a manner to be unobserved by the patrols, a man concealed behind a tree had drawn the rail out of place just as the engine was approaching it, throwing it off the track.

A mountain howitzer, which had been placed in position, immediately plunged a shell through the engine, and at the same time a charge was made upon the guard.

This consisted mostly of men whose term of service expired that very day, and their resistance amounted to nothing. They soon fled in shameful confusion, leaving the ground to the Rebels, who, after taking such plunder as they could carry, fired the train, and then started on the road to Haymarket. But the cavalry had been aroused, and detachments of the First Vermont and Fifth New York, each in separate routes, commenced a vigorous pursuit. Mosby, who commanded in person, evidently had not reckoned on so sudden and sharp an encounter. He had not proceeded two miles before he espied the boys in blue eagerly flying after him. His howitzer was quickly brought into position, and a shell was accurately thrown among his pursuers, suddenly dismounting one of the officers, whose horse was killed.

But the detention of the column was only temporary, the boys being determined once more to cross sabres with the chivalry. The nature of the ground was unfavourable for a cavalry charge, and the enemy showed no disposition to fight, but fled as rapidly as possible, firing an occasional shell, but without inflicting any injury. Eagerly the boys spurred on their chargers, and were soon joined by the Vermonters, who added fresh excitement to the chase.

Mosby, finding himself too closely followed for his comfort, and knowing; that something desperate must be done, determined to sell his howitzer as dearly as possible. Having reached the head of a narrow lane, near the house of a Mr. Warren Fitzhugh, he wheeled the piece into position and commenced a rapid fire. There was no way for our boys to reach the howitzer except through the lane, the whole length of which was raked by every discharge. "That gun must be captured," exclaimed Lieutenant Elmer J. Barker, of the Fifth New York, "and who will volunteer to charge it with me?"

About thirty brave fellows responded promptly, and suiting the action to the words, "charge, boys!" he rushed furiously forward at their head, while the fields rang with their maddening yell. But the brave lieutenant fell severely wounded before a murderous discharge of grape and canister, which killed three of his men and wounded several. The lieutenant's faithful horse was also mortally wounded. But before the piece could be reloaded with its only one remaining shell, the surviving comrades were crossing sabres with the gunners over the gun.

The conflict here was desperate, but of short duration. Mosby's lieutenant, Chapman, fought with the rammer of the gun, but fell wounded and was captured. At length those who could not escape surrendered, and the howitzer was ours. It bore an inscription which showed that it had been captured by the Rebels from the lamented Colonel Baker, at Ball's Bluff.

Among the enemy's wounded and captured was a Captain Hoskins, formerly of the British Army, who had run the blockade and espoused the Rebel cause.

He received his death-wound as follows: having wounded a private soldier in a hand-to-hand encounter, he roughly cried out, "Surrender, you d——d Yankee!!

"I'll see you d——d first," was the characteristic reply, while the

Yankee boy lodged a pistol ball in the captain's neck, from which he did not long survive. An interesting diary was found in Captain Hoskins' possession, describing mainly his private life since entering Mosby's command.

Mosby himself barely escaped being captured on this occasion, and he carried the mark of a sabre-cut on his arm. The fight had been desperate on both sides, but the guerrillas were badly worsted, and driven away as far as the jaded condition of our horses would permit us to pursue them. In their flight the spoils, which had been taken from the captured train, were left behind, strewn in every direction. This fight occurred near the little village of Greenwich, and gave Mosby a blow quite as severe as any he had ever received.

CHAPTER 10

Chancellorsville and Stoneman's Raid

April 1.—April-fool day always brings its trains of fun and broods of annoyances, the boys being determined to make the most of it. The usual plan is to induce a comrade to believe that either the colonel, his captain, or lieutenant, wants to see him. This scheme is generally successful; for the victim dare not refuse to report whenever called for, and as he is unable to learn whether he is really wanted or otherwise, he finds it necessary to call upon his superior to ask his pleasure.

Receiving the assurance that nothing is wanted of him, he sees that he has been "sold," and returns to his comrades in the midst of their hilarity at his expense. But he is generally determined to have revenge, and to get the "laugh" on them before the day is spent. Sometimes these jokes are carried rather too far for sport, and recoil upon their perpetrators with unpleasant force.

But, then, this soldier-life of ours is so grave and solemn that our buoyant natures seek relief in all such in means as the above. The bow, always bent to its utmost tension, would soon break or become useless; it must be straightened to send the arrow. So our natures would break were they not elastic, and were there no opportunities for reaction as well as action. Then, too, there is a kind of monotony to our life in winter quarters, to which it is difficult to accustom ourselves.

And he who can suggest anything laughable is a great benefactor to his comrades; for then the monotony is broken, and we enjoy a little sprinkling of variety, which is truly said to be *"the spice of life."* A good joke, that runs through the command like a bubbling brook along the flowering meadows, is worth more to us than a corps of nurses with cart-loads of medicine.

On the second of April, from nine to eleven o'clock in the morning, we had a mounted brigade-drill. Colonel Kilpatrick was in command. He appeared well pleased, at the close, with the proficiency of his men, and they are all enthusiastic over him, There seems to be a wonderful unanimity of feeling in the brigade, all regarding Kilpatrick as the right man in the right place.

April 6.—Today the Cavalry Corps, consisting of twenty-five regiments, well filled and drilled, was reviewed by President Lincoln and Generals Hooker and Stoneman. A salute of twenty-one guns was fired upon the arrival of the presidential party. The review took place on Falmouth Heights, in full view of the Rebel encampment in rear of Fredericksburg. The scene we presented to our enemies must have been grand, for we appeared in our best uniforms and with flying colours.

It was an occasion not to be forgotten, the sight being one of the most magnificent many of us ever saw. The column was between three and four hours passing in review. It seemed to do us all good to get a glimpse of the solemn, earnest face of the president, who reviewed us with apparent satisfaction.

April 7.—Picket details returned from the river today. In the afternoon several horse-races came off near our camp, between the First Pennsylvania, the First New Jersey, and Harris Light. One of Kilpatrick's favourite horses was badly beaten, much to his mortification, owing, as was alleged, to the stupidity of the rider, who was sent off the ground in disgrace. We are frequently training our horses for swift motions, and teaching them to jump ditches and fences.

These are occasions of excitement and amusement. Men are frequently thrown from their horses while endeavouring to jump them beyond their ability, though seldom is anyone hurt. Much practice is necessary to make perfect in this exercise.

The papers bring us good news of a "Great Union Victory in Connecticut." Such victories, though bloodless, have a powerful influence upon the rank and file of the army. Every ballot cast to sustain the administration is equal to a well-directed bullet against the foe.

April 8.—The brigade was called out this morning on the old drill-ground to witness a somewhat sad and novel scene, namely, the branding and drumming out of service of two deserters from Company K. The command was formed into a hollow square, facing inward. Upon the arrival of the blacksmith's forge, the deserters were partially stripped of their clothing, irons were heated, and the letter "D" was burnt upon their left hip. Their heads were then shaved, after which they were marched about the square under guard, accompanied by a corps of buglers playing "the rogue's march."

It was a humiliating and painful sight, and undoubtedly it left its salutary impression, as it was designed, upon all who witnessed it. A deserter should be regarded as only next to a traitor, and when the military law against such offenders is enforced with becoming rigor, we will probably have fewer infractions. This part of our army discipline has thus far been evidently too loosely administered, giving occasion for demoralisation.

In the afternoon we enjoyed a very pleasing change of programme, when true merit was rewarded. A beautiful sabre was presented by the officers of the brigade to Kilpatrick. Affairs of this kind are much enjoyed by the major part of the command; and when night came on we all felt that today, at least, we have learned that "the way of the transgressor is hard," and also that:

Good actions crown themselves with lasting days;
Who deserves well needs not another's praise.

April 9.—To increase the variety of our experience, and to give it a pleasing tone, Kilpatrick's brigade-band made its first appearance in front of headquarters this evening. They discoursed national airs in a manner that thrilled and elated us, making the welkin ring with their excellent music. As the last echoes of a plaintive air died over the distant woods, and I crept into my lowly quarters for my rest, the poet's verse seemed full of hallowed potency:

Music exalts each joy, allays each grief,
Expels diseases, softens every pain.
Subdues the rage of poison and of plague.

An exciting game of "baseball" was played on the eleventh, near our camp, between boys of the "Fourteenth Brooklyn" and the Harris Light. The contest resulted in a drawn game, so that neither could claim the victory. Our time, of late, is slipping rapidly along. The weather is warm and beautiful, the mud is disappearing, and flowers and birds remind us that winter is over and gone.

For several weeks preparations have been evidently made for the opening of the Spring campaign. Each branch of the service has been thoroughly recruited and drilled, and the entire force is computed to be at least one hundred and twenty-five thousand strong. All seem to be anxious for a good opportunity to advance upon the enemy.

April 13.—On the evening of the twelfth, at regimental inspection, orders were received to be ready for march at daylight the next day. Consequently, early this morning our winter-quarters were abandoned, and General Stoneman, at the head of about thirteen thousand cavalry, took up a line of march in the direction of the upper fords of the Rappahannock, in the neighbourhood of the Orange and Alexandria Railroad.

General Hooker's order to his cavalry-chief had the ring of bright metal in it, and contained the following terse sentences:

> Let your watchword be fight, and let all your orders be *fight!* fight! FIGHT! bearing in mind that time is as valuable to the Federal as the Rebel authorities.
> It devolves upon you, General, to take the initiative in the forward movement of this grand army; and on you and your noble command must depend, in a great measure, the extent and brilliancy of our success. Bear in mind that celerity, audacity, and resolution are everything in war; and especially is it the case with the command you have, and the enterprise on which you are about to embark.

We moved at a sufficient distance from the Rappahannock to screen our columns from the enemy's posts of observation. We marched to the vicinity of Elkton, where we bivouacked for the night. The next morning we resumed our march, and soon struck the railroad at Bealeton, where we met and drove a detachment of Rebel cavalry.

After a sharp skirmish they fell back to Beverly Ford, where their crossing was covered by artillery and sharpshooters. A neat little fight enabled us to advance carbineers down to the ford, which we held, though subjected to the fire of rifled cannon on the opposite bank.

At another of the numerous fords of the river (Sulphur Springs), which was not guarded, an entire division was forded across before night. But during the night a heavy rain-storm set in *à la Virginie,* which so suddenly raised the stream, that the order for crossing more troops was not only countermanded, but the forces already across were ordered to return. This was not very easily done. Meanwhile the separated division, by rapid movement and some fighting through the rain, had swung down the river to Beverly Ford, where they commenced recrossing, without pontoons, and with the ford unfordable.

The enemy, taking advantage of this unhappy predicament, attacked the rearguard with furious determination, killing and capturing quite a number. As our artillery could not be brought into position, the only help we could afford to our unfortunate comrades was to play on the Rebels with our carbines, which kept them somewhat at bay. In the haste and difficulty of crossing, where horses were compelled to swim a considerable distance through the strong current, several animals and men were drowned and borne down the stream. It was certainly a very sad experience—a disheartening commencement of operations.

April 16.—The Harris Light was relieved from picket, and moved to Bealeton, leaving Beverly Ford at four o'clock a. m. The roads are almost impassable. The rain has continued almost uninterruptedly for forty-eight hours, making our sojourn in these parts very disagreeable. But, notwithstanding the mud, on the seventeenth a squadron of the Harris Light, composed of Companies E and F, in command of Captain Charles Hasty, left our bivouac at Bealeton, early in the morning, with instructions to proceed to Warrenton, and, if possible, to occupy the place until four o'clock p. m. When we had approached to within three miles of the place the captain learned that the famous Black Horse Cavalry, under Captain Randolph, was in possession of the village, and would undoubtedly give us a splendid entertainment.

The boys were unanimously pleased at the prospect of an opportunity to cross sabres with those heroes of Bull Run, and, concluding from their worldwide reputation that nothing short of a desperate fight would ensue, we made preparations accordingly. The squadron was formed in column of platoons, and two detachments, consisting each of a sergeant and eight men, were instructed to advance upon the town from two parallel streets, thus giving our small force the appearance of being only the vanguard of a very large army.

It was my privilege to command one of these detachments; and, on entering the village, we found the foe formed into line of battle on Main street, with the apparent intention of giving us a warm reception. They had been notified of our approach by a sentinel posted in a prominent church-steeple, and were, therefore, ready for us. We immediately drew sabres and bore down upon them with the usual yell; and, strange as it may seem to those who laud the daring of the Southern Black Horse, they advanced to receive us, fired a few shots, unsheathed their bloodless sabres, but wheeled about suddenly and dashed away to the rear at a break-neck pace, without even halting to pay us the compliment of an affectionate farewell.

Actually it seemed as though they did not so much as look behind them until fairly out of the range of our best carbines. It was quite evident to us that they agreed perfectly with that most ungallant poet, who sings:

He who fights and runs away,
Will live to fight another day.

The beautiful and aristocratic village was now in our possession. Being informed that the proprietor of the Warrenton House was a conspicuous Rebel, Captain Hasty decided to try his hospitality and sound his commissary department. Accordingly he accosted the chivalrous gentleman, and ordered a dinner for the entire squadron.

When all had partaken freely of the good things provided, our Rebel landlord showed signs of uneasiness in his desire to ascertain who would foot the bill. After a while the captain politely directed him to charge it to Uncle Sam. This ended all controversy on the subject. We left Warrenton in accordance with instructions, at four o'clock, and, well satisfied with our excursion, rejoined the regiment during the following night.

April 18.—The enemy "opened the ball" this morning by shelling the cavalry pickets in the woods near Rappahannock Station. Under this fire we advanced some distance toward the river, and then retired slowly with a view of drawing the Rebels across to our side. But they were too wily to be caught in such a trap, and our attempt failed. A stream is a great barrier between two contending forces, and no careful leader will place his men with a stream behind them, unless he is quite certain of victory. We had a sad lesson of this in the Battle of Ball's Bluff.

On the day following this useless cannonade, each regiment of the corps had dress-parade at six o'clock p. m. Orders from General Stoneman were read by the adjutants of their respective regiments, informing them that the entire cavalry force would move at an early hour next day. A portion of the evening was spent in preparation. However, when in the bivouac, as we have been for some time, it takes but a few moments to prepare for a move.

All surplus baggage, which naturally accumulates during winterquarters, has been disposed of, either by sending it home, or to some quartermaster depot, established for the purpose, as at Alexandria, or by destruction; and each man carries only what little articles he can stow away in his saddle-bags and roll up in his blanket. His inventory might run as follows: A shirt, a pair of socks (and often he has only those he wears), a housewife or needle-book, paper and envelopes, a tin cup, and bag which contains his coffee and sugar mixed together. Some men carry a towel and soap. The great effort is to learn to get along with the very least possible.

At first the soldier thinks he must have this article of luxury and the other, until he finds that they are positive burdens to himself and horse, and gradually he throws off this weight and that incumbrance, until his entire outfit is reduced to nearly "the little end of nothing, whittled to a point!" Possessed of a coffee-bag and cup and a hard tack or biscuit, the most essential things, he seldom now borrows much trouble about his surroundings.

We commenced march at four o'clock on the morning of April twentieth, and advanced toward Sulphur Springs. Scarcely had we gone out of our bivouacs before a drenching rain-storm set in, and continued incessantly until we were forced to halt, the mud being really oceanic. The day being quite warm, we experienced but little discomfort from the wet until night.

The weather then became cold, and everything being so wet, it was difficult to make fires; consequently we had a very tedious night. A fellow considered himself fortunate, if, after toiling long through the cold and dark, he could succeed to cook a little coffee. But the soldier will have his coffee, if it be possible, and then he is quite contented with his lot.

On the twenty-first, all we could do was to change our position, to get out of the very deep mud, which one night's treading of the horses' feet produced. On the following day in the afternoon the Cavalry Corps moved from Waterloo Bridge to Warrenton Junction. The day was pleasant, though the roads are still in a fearful condition. Our infantry is engaged in repairing the railroad to Rappahannock Station. We are evidently on the eve of some important movements.

Before night, many of the boys were made glad by the reception of a large mail from the North, which is the first we have received since we left our winter-quarters on the thirteenth instant. Nearly every man had a letter, and there was general contentment all around. The mail-bag is always a welcome visitor, especially in times like this, and it is not the least of the instrumentalities which mould our character and give tone to our morale.

April 23.—Another drenching rain set in this morning and continued without cessation throughout the day. We were all drowned out of our little shelter-tents, and many preferred to take the chastisement face to face with the merciless elements. We were a sorry looking company of men, drenched with the rain, bespattered with mud, and chilled with the cold. Our fires, well-nigh quenched by the falling floods, were of very little use to us. Men and horses all suffered together. Thus far the month has been very wet, and this April is certainly entitled to be classed among the Weeping Sisters.

We spent the dreary night hoping for a better morrow. But the twenty-fourth followed the example of its predecessor, and rain poured upon us in torrents.

The yielding clay of this region of country is soon trodden into a soft mud, under so many hoofs, until it seems quite impossible to find a dry spot large enough to lie down upon at night. This makes our bivouacs very dreary and uncomfortable. And yet under these melancholy circumstances we are not totally bereft of pleasant entertainment. The woods and fields in this vicinity abound with quails and rabbits, whose presence has been the cause of some excitement and not a little fun.

Ever and *anon* a sportive cavalier starts up a nimble rabbit and chases the frightened little creature through the camp, crying at the top of his voice, "stop him! stop him! catch that rabbit," etc. Poor pussy comes flying down the road, pursued by a throng of men, while the shouts are caught up and repeated along the entire line of escape, men jumping up at every bound of the animal, and joining in the sport.

Occasionally the rabbit is so perfectly surrounded as to be compelled at last to surrender, when the trembling prisoner is caught, but carefully treated. At this time of the year they are so very small and lean as to be scarcely eatable, and yet now and then they are shot, as well as quails, to increase our commissary supplies, and the cooks display considerable skill in dressing and preparing them *à la Delmonico*.

April 27.—Colonel Davies, after quite a lengthy absence from us, rejoined the regiment at ten o'clock a.m. He reported having a narrow escape from guerrillas near Elkton, where he was fired at and pursued for some distance, while on his way from Falmouth. Details were ordered out immediately to those infested regions, with instructions to capture everything in the shape of a bushwhacker. Captain Coon, of the Connecticut squadron, was put in command of the reconnoitring party. We had a rich and delightful ride, but did not succeed in overhauling the offenders.

On the twenty-eighth the first battalion of the Harris Light, commanded by Captain Samuel McIrvin, was ordered to reconnoitre as far as Brentsville. We went *via* Elkton and Bristerburg, at which places we captured several guerrillas, who were not looking for us. The first part of the day was very pleasant, but from eleven o'clock till night we had a continually drizzling rain, which made our march exceedingly disagreeable.

We had but just halted for the night, when an order was received from a messenger, to rejoin the regiment without delay. Through the rain, mud, and darkness we hastened back to Catlett's Station where we found everything in motion, preparing for some grand movement.

With the gray light of the morning of the twenty-ninth, after marching most of the night, we reached the banks of the Rappahannock at Kelly's Ford. In addition to the Cavalry Corps we found here the Fifth, Sixth, Seventh, and Twelfth Corps of the Army of the Potomac, making preparation to cross the river. The Engineer Corps soon laid the pontoons, and the grand columns effected a passage without material resistance or difficulty.

STONEMAN'S RAID.

We are credibly informed that other columns of our army are crossing the river at other points, and that a great battle is imminent. There has been occasional skirmishing, on the front, during the day. The Rebels, however, seem to have been taken wholly by surprise and are not making the demonstrations we had good reason to anticipate; but we shall be greatly disappointed if they do not soon awake, and come to their work.

The going is far from pleasant, though today the weather is favourable. The streams are dreadfully swollen and nearly all bridgeless, compelling us to ford them. This process, through the cold, high water, is attended with more or less difficulty and suffering.

Soon after crossing the river the Cavalry Corps broke away from the infantry, in the direction of Stevensburg; and it is rumoured among us that a grand raid upon the enemy's communications is contemplated, while the two armies engage in deadly combat, it is thought not far from the river.

April 30.—This afternoon our column reached the Rapidan at

Raccoon Ford, and began to cross over. The water being much above the fording mark and very rapid, we had an exciting time. Several horses and men were swept down the stream by the swift current and were drowned; and none of us escaped the unpleasant operation of getting wet.

After reaching the high plateau on the south bank of the river, the entire corps were formed in line of battle, in which hostile position we were ordered to spend the night. For more thorough protection, pickets had been sent out in every direction, and posted with much care. It was a season of considerable anxiety to all, and of great fatigue especially to those of us who had been in the saddle several consecutive days and nights. Standing to horse as we were compelled to do, very little rest could be obtained, though many were so exhausted, that, dropping to the earth, with bridle and halter in hand, they fell asleep, while their comrades wished for the morning, which came at last.

After our frugal breakfast, which consisted mostly of hard-tack and coffee, a thorough inspection of the command was made, and all men reported to have unserviceable or unsafe horses, were sent to the rear. The weather is perfectly charming today, although quite too warm, in the mid-day heat, to be comfortable marching.

Early in the morning of May second our column reached the railroad in the rear of General Lee's army, and, with slight opposition from scattered pickets, the work of destruction began. Culverts and bridges, telegraph lines and posts, disappeared like the smoke of their burning.

While this work was going on, Kilpatrick was ordered to lead the Harris Light into Louisa Court House, which he did in a gallant manner. The inhabitants, taken by surprise, were greatly terrified at our approach and entry into the place; but finding themselves in the hands of men, and not fiends, as they had been wont to regard us, and receiving from us neither disrespect nor insult, soon dispelled their needless fears. We remained in town until two o'clock in the afternoon, collecting supplies of rations and forage for men and horses, tearing up railroad track and destroying railroad property, as well as commissary and quartermaster stores found in public buildings.

At the hour above named we were ordered out to support the First Maine Cavalry in a spirited skirmish with Rebel cavalry. In this engagement our Troy company had one sergeant wounded, and one corporal and four men taken prisoners.

By eleven o'clock at night General Stoneman's forces had reached the neighbourhood of Thompson's Cross Roads, where the command was broken up into several independent expeditions to scour the country in every direction, and to destroy as completely as possible all the enemy's means of supply. Colonel Percy Wyndham, with the First New Jersey and First Maine, was sent south to Columbia on the James River, to destroy the great canal which feeds Richmond from the west.

Lieutenant Colonel Davis, with the Twelfth Illinois, was despatched to the South Anna River, in the neighbourhood of Ashland Station, on the Fredericksburg and Richmond Railroad, to destroy the important bridges in that vicinity. General Buford was to march westward and do all the mischief he could. But it was reserved for Kilpatrick to advance upon Richmond, enter the Rebel capital, if possible, and lay waste the public property and communications there.

Sunday, May 3.—We marched steadily after leaving General Stoneman, long into the night, halting only long enough for a little refreshment and rest. At two o'clock this afternoon the command, which consists of only about three hundred men, well mounted, was marched into a pine thicket, where we were ordered to destroy or throw away all our extra clothing and blankets, with everything which we could possibly spare, to lighten the burdens of our horses. This halt in the shade of the pines was very refreshing both to men and beasts. The sun is very warm and shelter is very agreeable.

Leaving the fragrant shade, we moved on until night. We are now within fifteen miles of Richmond, where vigilance is the price, not only of liberty, but of life. Sergeant Northrup, while on a scout to the front, was fired upon by a guerrilla undoubtedly, and wounded. Kilpatrick and Lieutenant-Colonel Henry E. Davies, Jr., slept on their arms in the road with the men. Very little sleep was had through the night, but what we did get was precious.

At two o'clock on the morning of the fourth we resumed our hazardous journey toward the rebellious city. Had it not been for the intrepidity of our leader, and the utmost confidence of the men in his ability to accomplish whatever he undertook, it would have been impossible to proceed. Fearing as we did the desolation and sorrows of "Libby Prison," ignorant of the forces we might soon encounter, and the ambuscades that might be laid for us, we nevertheless pushed bravely on, because we were bound to follow our chief, be the consequences what they might.

Soon after daybreak we came down upon Hungary Station, on the Fredericksburg and Richmond Railroad. Here we destroyed the telegraph lines, tore up the track, and burned the depot. Near the station we ran into the enemy's pickets, the first we have encountered since leaving our main column. Only two of them were discovered, and they fled so rapidly that it was useless for us to try to overtake them with our jaded horses. They kept generally about three hundred yards ahead of us, and as we had orders to fire on no one unless positively necessary, they proceeded unmolested, in the direction of Richmond.

Having arrived within five miles of the city, we advanced more cautiously. There was good reason for this, for our condition was critical. There we were, only a remnant of a regiment, many miles away from any support, with no way to retreat, as we had burned all the bridges and ferries in our rear, nearer to the Confederate capital than ever any Union troops were before, and ignorant of the forces that garrisoned it. Still on we moved, looking only to our leader, who seemed especially inspired for the work assigned him.

We soon arrived in sight of the outer line of fortifications, and moved steadily upon them. To our surprise, we found them unmanned, and we safely passed in towards the second line of defence. We had scarcely entered these consecrated grounds, when General Winder's assistant adjutant-general pompously rode up to the head of our column, and inquired, "What regiment?"

Astonishment and blight accompanied the answer of Kilpatrick, who said, "The Second New York Cavalry," adding, "and you, sir, are my prisoner."

Ceremonies were short, and Kilpatrick very quickly appropriated Winder's favourite charger, upon which the captured adjutant was mounted when he made his fatal challenge.

We continued still to advance, until the smoke from workshops, and the church steeples were plainly visible, and we began to think that we were about to enter Richmond without opposition. We were now within two miles of the city, and yet we halted not until we had reached the top of a hillock just before us. Here was an interesting scene. There stood a handful of cavalrymen, far within the fortifications of a hostile city, almost knocking at the door of her rebellious heart. On every hand were frowning earthworks, and just ahead of us the coveted prize.

But just at the foot of the hill on which we stood, we discovered a battery of artillery, drawn up in the road, supported by infantry, ready to receive us. It became evident that we had advanced as far as prudence would permit us. We had also reached and secured the road to the Meadow Bridge across the Chickahominy, over which we were expected to escape, and which it was very desirable to destroy. These facts or circumstances decided the direction of our march. We moved leisurely on our way, the cavalry refusing to give us even the semblance of a pursuit.

Having crossed Meadow Bridge, it was set on fire. Following the railroad a little distance, a train of cars was met and captured, much to the astonishment of the bewildered conductor, who was in charge of government stores *en route* for Richmond. After firing the cars, the engine was set in motion under a full head of steam, and the blazing and crackling freight went rushing on until it reached the burning bridge, when the whole thing well-nigh disappeared in the deep mud and water of the sluggish stream.

No particular line of escape seemed to have been agreed upon. Our main object was to do all the mischief in our power to the Rebel cause. The men were much exhausted for want of rations and rest, but you could not hear a word of complaint from one of them. They were all inspired with the greatness of the deeds which they were required to perform, feeling much as Napoleon's legions must have felt, when he said to them: "The eyes of all Europe are upon you." Sustained by such considerations, and cheered by the voice and still more potent example of their leader, they pressed onward, resolved to do all within their power, and then, if the worst came, they could go to "Libby" or "Belle Isle," with the pleasing consciousness that they had done their duty.

All night we marched with only an occasional and brief rest. On the morning of the fifth we arrived at the Pamunkey River. Here we captured a Rebel train laden with commissary stores, just the prize we coveted. After appropriating a generous supply for the day, the remnant was reduced to ashes. All the serviceable animals captured were added to our cavalcade, and the prisoners paroled and sent on their way rejoicing. The river was crossed on a one-horse platform ferry-boat, whose capacity was only twenty horses and their riders. Considerable precious time was consumed in this tedious operation. When the last man had reached the desired shore, the ferry-boat was destroyed, and the column resumed its line of march.

About four o'clock in the afternoon a cold rain-storm set in, borne on the flapping wings of a chilly wind. Cold, hungry, and fatigued, we still pressed onward, suffering not a little. Fearful of encountering heavy forces of the enemy on the main thoroughfares, we filed along the byways and neglected paths, where we were frequently immersed in almost impenetrable bushes dripping with rain.

May 6.—Today we crossed the Mattapony, at Aylett's, burning the ferry behind us. We then took the road to Tappahannock, a small village on the Rappahannock. We had not proceeded far in this direction before we met and captured another wagon-train, laden with ham and eggs and other luxuries, which had been smuggled across the Rappahannock.

This, of course, was thoroughly confiscated, appropriated, and destroyed. A consultation of officers was here instituted, and it was decided to try to reach Gloucester Point, opposite Yorktown, which we knew was in possession of Union forces.

Not far from King and Queen Court House we captured and burned a depot of ordnance and several wagons. We have been much annoyed by bushwhackers on the way today. Their plan is to hide in the thick bushes, and tire upon the rear of our column as we pass, in places where it is not possible to pursue them without much loss of time, which is too precious to be wasted thus. Several men and horses have been wounded by these skulkers during the day.

As night was settling down upon us, we discovered a body of cavalry in our front, and quickly made preparations to meet them. Kilpatrick deployed skirmishers and advanced in column of squadrons. Our supposed enemies were also prepared for fight, and a spirited conflict was anticipated. Several shots were exchanged, when the contending parties discovered their mutual mistake. Our opponents proved to be the Twelfth Illinois, which, after leaving the main column at Thompson's Cross Roads, had swept down through the enemy's communications about Ashland Station, destroyed several important bridges and some stores, and was now, like ourselves, endeavouring to reach Gloucester Point.

This rencontre was very pleasing. Our column was greatly increased and encouraged. We needed this stimulus exceedingly, for we had been marching all day through a cold drizzling rain, which had dampened our ardour somewhat, and chilled our blood. Many of our horses had given out by the way, and were killed to prevent their falling into the enemy's hands.

A few days of rest and care will so recruit such horses that they become again serviceable. their places were filled by those horses and mules which were brought to us by the contrabands, which all along our journey flocked to our standards, and by such other animals as were captured by our flankers and advance guards. Exhausted as most of us were, no bivouac fires were kindled until we reached our lines of pickets from Gloucester Point, where we were received by our Union comrades in the midst of demonstrations of admiration and joy. Here we had a splendid rest.

May 7.—This morning, after a more sumptuous breakfast than we had had for many days, we crossed the York River to Yorktown, where we encamped. We are now, as it may well be supposed, the "lions of the day." Nothing is too good for us. We have the freedom of the town, and the subject of our raid is the theme of private and public speculation.

In our travels we have captured and paroled over three hundred prisoners, burned five or six railroad bridges, destroyed all the ferries on our route, captured and demolished two wagon-trains, burned five or six depots of stores, destroyed one railroad train, besides stations and telegraph offices, and have torn several miles of track. We have taken over one hundred and fifty horses, some of them the finest in the country.

The following extract from the *Yorktown Gazette* will more fully explain the importance of our expedition:

> We have heard startling accounts of the prodigies of valour performed by Stuart's Cavalry in Virginia, and the bands of Morgan in the West. That they showed true valour, nice discretion, and great powers of endurance, we will not for a moment question. But the exploits of our cavalry, in the late expedition in the rear of Lee's army, surpasses anything ever achieved on this continent. Especially are the adventures of the Second New York (Harris Light Cavalry) and the Twelfth Illinois almost incredible. But they bear with them trophies that fully confirm the record of their daring.
>
> They penetrated within the outer lines of fortification at Richmond, to within less than two miles of the city, and captured prisoners and trophies there. They cut all the communications between that city and Lee's army, travelled two hundred miles, and lost only thirty men. Many of them have changed horses a

number of times on the route. Whenever theirs got tired, they laid hold of anything that came in their way that suited them better.

The contrabands flocked to them from every quarter. They would take their masters' teams from the plough and their best horses from the stables. Some of them were almost frantic with delight on the appearance of the Yankees. Over three hundred found their way to this place. Their services are all needed at this present time.

The following report of Brigadier-General King will be read with interest:

Yorktown, Virginia, May 7, 1863.

To Major-General Halleck:

Colonel Kilpatrick, with his regiment (the Harris Light Cavalry) and the rest of the Twelfth Illinois, have just arrived at Gloucester Point, opposite this post.

They burned the bridges over the Chickahominy, destroyed three large trains of provisions in the rear of Lee's army, drove in the Rebel pickets to within two miles of Richmond, and have lost only one lieutenant and thirty men, having captured and paroled upwards of three hundred prisoners.

Among the prisoners was an aid of General Winder, who was captured with his escort far within the entrenchments outside of Richmond.

The cavalry have marched nearly two hundred miles since the third of May. They were inside of the fortifications of Richmond on the fourth; burnt all the stores at Aylett's Station, on the Mattapony, on the fifth; destroyed all the ferries over the Pamunkey and Mattapony, and a large depot of commissary stores near and above the Rappahannock, and came here in good condition.

They deserve great credit for what they have done. It is one of the finest feats of the war.

Rufus King,
Brigadier-General Commanding Post.

Another print contained the following remarks: Two regiments of Stoneman's Cavalry, the Second New York (Harris Light Cavalry) and the Twelfth Illinois, after accomplishing the duty assigned them of cutting the railroads near Richmond, made their way through the country to this place. The boldness and success of their movements surpass anything of the kind ever performed in this country.

Various opinions are entertained with regard to General Stoneman's expedition as a whole, some believing it to have been a grand success, and others a conspicuous failure. The former look only at what was actually accomplished, the latter only at what they think might have been done. While all admit that the destruction of property and the severance of communications were a serious blow to the enemy, most persons agree that the general made a mistake in dividing his command. Had he kept his forces together he was amply sufficient to have broken all railroad and telegraphic connection between Lee and Richmond at least for a whole week, and he could have routed any cavalry force which could have been brought against him. As it was, by dividing his strength, he made each party too weak to effect very great damage, and exposed them to great danger of capture.

The following is a summary, in tabular form, as clipped from the *New York Herald*, of the work accomplished by General Stoneman's expedition:

Bridges destroyed	22
Culverts destroyed	7
Ferries destroyed	5
Railroads broken, places	7
Supply-trains burned	4
Wagons destroyed	122
Horses captured	200
Mules captured	104
Canals broken	3
Canal-boats burned	5
Trains of cars destroyed	3
Storehouses burned	2
Telegraph-stations burned	4
Wires cut, places	5
Depots burned	3
Towns visited	25
Contrabands liberated	400

In addition to the foregoing, large quantities of pork, bacon, flour, wheat, corn, clothing, and other articles of great value to the Confederate army, were burned or otherwise destroyed.

But it must be borne in mind that General Stoneman's grand raid and ride were only the background of a bloody tableau in the wilderness country around

CHANCELLORSVILLE.

The last days of April witnessed the stratagem and skill of General Hooker, in his advance upon the enemy's position. A feint of crossing his entire army to the south side of the Rappahannock below Fredericksburg completely deceived the enemy, who withdrew his forces from the upper fords of the river.

Three corps, commanded respectively by Generals Howard, Slocum, and Meade, had been sent up the river, but marched at a sufficient distance from the hostile southern bank to avoid all observation. Arriving at Kelly's Ford, they began to cross, though it was in the night, and the men were compelled to wade in water up to their armpits. The moon, which shone brightly, assisted them most of the night, but went down before the entire force had crossed, when crossing had to be suspended until morning. Pontoons were brought up and laid, and so the remainder of the infantry and the cavalry corps crossed pleasantly.

The column advanced towards the Rapidan, and Generals Howard and Slocum's commands crossed this stream at Germania Mills, and General Meade's at Ely Ford, below, and then all marched on roads which converge to the Chancellorsville House, a large brick edifice, which was used as a mansion and tavern, situated in a small clearing of a few acres, and which, with its few appendages of outbuildings, constituted the village known by that name. Other forces, including General Pleasonton, with nearly a brigade of cavalry, who guarded the flanks of the advancing columns, had crossed the river, and taken their position near Chancellorsville.

By this wily movement General Lee's position on the Rappahannock had been entirely flanked; and, flushed with incipient success. General Hooker followed his great captains, and in the evening of the thirtieth of April he established his headquarters in the historic brick mansion above described. So completely absorbed was our general with the brilliancy of his advance that, in the moment of exultation, he forgot the dangers of his situation, and issued the following congratulatory order:

Headquarters Army of the Potomac,
Camp near Falmouth, Virginia, April 30, 1863.
It is with heartfelt satisfaction that the commanding general

announces to the army that the operations of the last three days have determined that our enemy must either ingloriously fly or come out from behind his defences and give us battle on our own ground, where certain destruction awaits him. The operations of the Fifth, Eleventh, and Twelfth Corps have been a succession of splendid achievements.

By command of Major-General Hooker.

S. Williams, Assistant Adjutant-General

It would seem as if the general had overlooked the fact that his army had but eight days' supplies at hand; that a treacherous river flowed between him and his depots; that he was surrounded by a labyrinth of forests, traversed in every direction by narrow roads and paths, all well known to the enemy, but unknown even to most of his guides; and that many of his guns of heaviest calibre, and most needed in a deadly strife, were on the other side of the river.

General Lee had undoubtedly been outgeneralled by Hooker in this movement, but he appeared not to have been disconcerted. Leaving the Heights of Fredericksburg with a small force, he advanced towards Chancellorsville.

May 1.—The first collision between the contending forces took place today. General Sykes, with a division of regulars, was despatched at nine o'clock in the morning on the Old Pike to Fredericksburg. He was followed by a part of the Second Corps. Sykes had not proceeded far before he encountered Lee advancing, and a sharp contest ensued, with heavy losses on both sides.

The Rebels having the best ground, and being superior in numbers, compelled our men to fall back, which they did in tolerable order, bringing away everything but their dead and badly wounded. But the enemy followed our retreating column, though cautiously, and filled the woods with sharpshooters. They also planted their heavy batteries on hills which partially commanded the clearing around the Chancellorsville House. This gave them great advantage.

They were also greatly elated with the success which had crowned the first onset. This was Hooker's first misfortune or mistake. The first blow in such an engagement is quite as important as the last. This first movement ought to have been more powerful, and ought to have given to our men a foretaste of victory. But we had lost prestige and position which undoubtedly weakened us not a little. The night following passed quietly away, except that the leaders were laying their plans for future operations.

About eight o'clock on the morning of the second, it was reported that a heavy column of the enemy was passing rapidly toward our right, whither the Eleventh Corps had been stationed. This movement was hidden by the forests, though the road over which the column passed was not far from our front. A rifled battery was opened upon this moving column, which, though out of sight, was thrown into disorder, at which time General Birney made a charge upon them with such force as to capture and bring away five hundred prisoners. By successive and successful advances, by sunset our men had broken this column and held the road upon which they had been marching to some scene of mischief. But the evil was not cured, as other roads more distant and better screened were followed by the wily foe.

Just before dark Stonewall Jackson, with about twenty-five thousand veterans, fell like a whirlwind upon the Eleventh Corps, which he had flanked so cautiously and yet so rapidly that our German comrades were taken by surprise while preparing their suppers, with arms stacked, and no time to recover. It is not at all wonderful that men surprised under these circumstances should be panic-stricken and flee. Let the censure rest not upon the rout, but upon the carelessness that led to the surprise.

Whole divisions were now overwhelmed by the Rebel hordes, that swept forward amid blazing musketry and battle-shouts which made the wilderness resound; and a frantic stampede commenced which not all the courage and effort of commanding generals, or the intrepidity of some regiments could check, and which threatened to rout the entire army. This unforeseen disaster changed the whole programme of the battle and greatly disheartened our men.

However, the ground was not to be abandoned so ingloriously, and though our lines were broken, and the enemy had gained a great advantage, heroism was yet to manifest its grand spirit, and to achieve undying laurels. The sun had gone down, refusing to look upon this Union defeat and slaughter, but the pale-faced moon gazed with her weird light upon the bloody scene, while the carnage still continued.

With the disaster of the Eleventh Corps General Sickles, who was stationed in the front and centre of our lines, and had been preparing to deal a heavy blow upon the enemy, was left in a critical position. His expectation of assistance from General Howard was not only cut off, but he was left with only two divisions and his artillery to meet the shock of the advancing hosts. General Pleasanton, with his small force of cavalry, being under Sickles' command, was ordered to charge the proud columns of the enemy, with the hope of checking them until our batteries could be suitably planted.

Pleasonton, addressing Major Keenan of the Eighth Pennsylvania Cavalry, said, "You must charge into those woods with your regiment, and hold the Rebels until I can get some of these guns into position. You must do it at whatever cost."

"I will," was the noble response of the true soldier, who, with only about five hundred men, was to encounter columns at least twenty-five thousand strong, led by Stonewall Jackson! The forlorn charge was made, but the martyr leader, with the majority of his dauntless troopers, soon baptized the earth upon which he fell, with his life blood. But the precious sacrifice was not in vain. The Rebel advance was greatly checked, as when a trembling lamb is thrown into the jaws of a pursuing pack of ravenous wolves.

The two determined generals improved these dear bought moments in planting their own batteries, and getting in readiness also several guns which had been abandoned by the Eleventh Corps in its flight. All these guns were double-shotted, and all due preparation was made for the expected stroke. It was a moment of trembling suspense. Our heroes waited not long, when the woods just in front of them began to swarm with the advancing legions, who opened a fearful musketry, and charged toward our guns.

Darkness was failing; but the field where the batteries were planted was so level that the gunners could do wonderful execution. And this they did. The Rebel charge had just commenced when our guns simultaneously opened with a withering fire, which cut down whole ranks of living flesh like grass. As one line of embattled hosts melted away, another rushed forward in its place to meet the same sad fate. Three successive and desperate charges were made, one of them to within a few yards of the guns, but each was repulsed with terrible slaughter. In many places the dead were literally in heaps. Our resistance proved successful.

A little later in the night, and right in front of these batteries, fell Stonewall Jackson, mortally wounded by our scathing fire, as was at first supposed, but more likely by the fire of his own infantry, as one of their writers alleges. Speaking of Jackson, he says;

> Such was his ardour, at this critical moment, and his anxiety to penetrate the movements of the enemy, doubly screened as

they were by the dense forest and gathering darkness, that he rode ahead of his skirmishers, and exposed himself to a close and dangerous fire from the enemy's sharpshooters, posted in the timber.

So great was the danger which he thus ran, that one of his staff said: 'General, don't you think this is the wrong place for you?' He replied quickly; 'The danger is all over; the enemy is routed. Go back, and tell A. P. Hill to press right on.' Soon after giving this order General Jackson turned, and, accompanied by his staff and escort, rode back at a trot, on his well-known 'Old Sorrel,' toward his own men. Unhappily, in the darkness—it was now nine or ten o'clock at night—the little body of horsemen was mistaken for Federal cavalry charging, and the regiments on the right and left of the road fired a sudden volley into them with the most lamentable results.

Captain Boswell, of General Jackson's staff, chief of artillery, was wounded; and two couriers were killed. General Jackson received one ball in his left arm, two inches below the shoulder joint, shattering the bone and severing the chief artery; a second passed through the same arm, between the elbow and wrist, making its exit through the palm of the hand; a third ball entered the palm of his right hand, about the middle, and, passing through, broke two of the bones.

He fell from his horse, and was caught by Captain Wormly, to whom he said, 'All my wounds are by my own men.'

The loss of this heroic chieftain, this swift flanker and intrepid leader, was undoubtedly the greatest yet felt by either army in the fall of a single man. Some report that, on hearing of the sad fall of his chief captain, General Lee exclaimed, "I would rather have lost twenty thousand men!"

Admitting that the Rebels gained in this battle a great victory, its advantages were dearly purchased by the loss of Thomas Jonathan Jackson. About midnight a fierce charge was made by General Sickles' forces, which proved successful, enabling our boys to recover much of the ground formerly occupied by the unfortunate Eleventh Corps, and they brought back with them some abandoned guns and other valuable articles from the *débris*, which the Rebels had not time or disposition to disturb.

General Hooker then ordered this exposed position to be abandoned, and by daylight our lines were falling back in good order towards Chancellorsville, but were closely pursued by the enemy, who filled the woods. Several determined charges were made upon our retreating columns, which, however, were repelled mostly by the fire of our artillery, which mowed down hundreds as they rushed recklessly almost to the cannon's mouth.

But these batteries had been played and worked so incessantly for the last twelve hours, that ammunition began to fail, and General Sickles sent a message to Hooker that assistance must be granted him, or he would be compelled to yield his ground. The officer who brought the despatch, found General Hooker in a senseless state, surrounded by his hopeless attendants, while general confusion had possession of the headquarters. A few minutes previous to this a cannon-ball had struck the wall of the mansion upon which the general was incidentally leaning, the concussion felling him to the floor.

For some time he was supposed to be dead, but soon giving signs of returning consciousness. General Couch, who was next in rank, refused to assume command, and hence about one hour of precious time was lost. This was a fatal hour. Had General Hooker been able to receive Sickles' message, and ordered a heavy force to his assistance, it is thought that a great disaster could have been prevented, and probably a victory might have been gained.

But the golden opportunity, which is seldom duplicated in a given crisis or a lifetime, was lost; and the enemy, though somewhat disorganised and badly disheartened by our well-managed batteries, had time, during this lull, to recover strength. They then advanced again with such power as to compel our men to retire from Chancellorsville toward the Rappahannock, leaving the brick mansion a mass of ruins, made such by the fire of the enemy.

By noon General Hooker had recovered his consciousness sufficiently to order the movements of his troops. The fighting on his front was now nearly over, but his position was critical. General Sedgwick, who had been directed to cross the Rappahannock below Fredericksburg, with orders to advance thence against all obstacles until he could fall upon General Lee's rear, while the grand army engaged him in front, found it impossible to proceed as rapidly as was expected of him, and was finally repulsed with such slaughter and pursued with such vigour as to be compelled to recross the river, leaving at least five thousand of his men killed, wounded, and captured in the hands of the enemy.

No alternative seemed now left to the Army of the Potomac but to beat a retreat and recross the river. On the evening of the fifth, General Hooker held a council of war with his commanders, at which, however, nothing was decided upon; but in the night he took the responsibility of ordering all his forces to recross the Rappahannock, which they did in good order and without molestation; and thus ended the disastrous Battle of Chancellorsville, with a loss of about eighteen thousand men on each side, and our remaining troops returned to bivouac on their old camping-ground on the north bank of the river near Falmouth.

This retrograde movement was undoubtedly considered to be necessary in consequence of the impending storm, which set in about four o'clock of the afternoon of the fifth, and rendered the march and night exceedingly disagreeable. The river was swollen so rapidly as to set adrift several of our pontoons, and the act of recrossing, though orderly, was by no means pleasant. The storm was cold and violent, and the roads soon became so bad as to remind the boys of Burnside's unfortunate advance in January. It is supposed by some that the rain explains satisfactorily the conduct of the enemy, who seemed to make no attempt whatever to follow our returning troops.

While yet the rain was drenching our weary boys, on the sixth. General Hooker issued a congratulatory order to them and the country, in which are to be found the following characteristic passages:

> The Major-General commanding tenders to this army his congratulations on its achievements of the last seven days. If it has not accomplished all that was expected, the reasons are well known to the army. It is sufficient to say they were of a character not to be foreseen nor prevented by human sagacity or resources.
>
> In withdrawing from the south bank of the Rappahannock before delivering a general battle to our adversaries, the army has given renewed evidence of its confidence in itself and its fidelity to the principles it represents. In fighting at a disadvantage, we would have been recreant to our trust, to ourselves, our cause, and our country. Profoundly loyal, and conscious of its strength, the Army of the Potomac will give or decline battle whenever its interest or honour may demand. It will also be the guardian of its own history and its own honour.
>
> By our celerity and secrecy of movement, our advance and pas-

A FORAGING PARTY RETURNING TO CAMP

sage of the rivers was undisputed, and, on our withdrawal, not a Rebel ventured to follow.

The events of the last week may swell with pride the heart of every officer and soldier of this army. We have added new lustre to its former renown. We have made long marches, crossed rivers, surprised the enemy in his intrenchments, and, wherever we have fought, have inflicted heavier blows than we have received.

We have taken from the enemy five thousand prisoners and fifteen colours; captured and brought off seven pieces of artillery; placed *hors de combat* eighteen thousand of his chosen troops; destroyed his depots filled with a vast amount of stores; deranged his communications; captured prisoners within the fortifications of his capital, and filled his country with fear and consternation. We have no other regret than that caused by the loss of our brave companions; and in this we are consoled by the conviction that they have fallen in the holiest cause ever submitted to the arbitrament of battle.

This order, if not perfectly satisfactory to the country and to the authorities, was generally hailed with applause by the army, which recognised in its sagacious rendering of our difficulties and humiliations the meed of praise awarded where it was due.

General Lee's order respecting this campaign is also very modest and unique, and is worthy of a place in this record. In it he says:

With heartfelt gratification the general commanding expresses to the army his sense of the heroic conduct displayed by officers and men during the arduous operations in which they have just been engaged.

Under trying vicissitudes of heat and storm, you attacked the enemy strongly intrenched in the depths of a tangled wilderness, and again on the hills of Fredericksburg, fifteen miles distant, and, by the valour that has triumphed on so many fields, forced him once more to seek safety beyond the Rappahannock. While this glorious victory entitles you to the praise and gratitude of the nation, we are especially called upon to return our grateful thanks to the only Giver of victory for the signal deliverance He has wrought.

It is, therefore, earnestly recommended that the troops unite on Sunday next in ascribing to the Lord of Hosts the glory due

His name. Let us not forget in our rejoicings the brave soldiers who have fallen in defence of their country; and, while we mourn their loss, let us resolve to emulate their noble example. The army and the country alike lament the absence for a time of one (Jackson) to whose bravery, energy, and skill they are so much indebted for success.

The two great armies once more confronted each other from either bank of the river, as they had done during all the winter and spring months. On the seventh of May, President Lincoln visited the camp near Falmouth, conferred with his *generalissimo* on movements past and future, appeared pleased with the spirit and morale of the troops, and returned to Washington to continue his earnest toil for the nation's life and well-being.

During the month quite a depletion of the rank and file of the army took place, by the mustering out of large numbers of three months' and two years' men. And such had been the depressing influence of Chancellorsville upon the country, that the places of these men were not very easily filled. To the sagacious leaders in political and military circles this state of things was not a little alarming. But to the Rebel leaders the times were affording opportunities for grand schemes, and for the execution of movements most startling.

CHAPTER 11

From Yorktown to Falmouth

Long raids and general engagements or campaigns are usually followed by a few days of comparative rest. This is necessary both for animals and men. Vacancies which are generally made during such vicissitudes, in the staffs of commissioned and non-commissioned officers, have to be filled, and reorganisation takes place. This was the experience of the Army of the Potomac after its Chancellorsville campaign, as well as our own after our return from Richmond.

On the eighth of May, Kilpatrick's command left Gloucester Point in the morning, and, after crossing the York River, amid the cheers of General Keyes' command, we were provided with touts in an encampment within the fortifications of Fort Yorktown. Here was a fine opportunity for repose, which we were all in a condition to relish. Like the prince of poets, we could realise that

Weariness
Can snore upon the flint, when rusty sloth
Finds the down-pillow hard.

On the day following our arrival here, soldiers and citizens from the town were flocking into our camp in droves, from *réveille* till taps, eager to learn from us the particulars of our recent raid. Groups of attentive hearers could be seen in various parts of the grounds surrounding some of our talkative comrades who discoursed eloquently to them of the sufferings and fatigue, of the daring and danger, of the stratagem and endurance which attended the expedition. No little amount of yarn was spun, and not a little imagination was employed to paint the scenes as vividly as possible.

May 10.—A dress-parade was ordered at ten o'clock this morning, at which time a complimentary order to the regiment from the Secretary of War was read by the adjutant. The occasion was very interesting, and every man seemed to feel proud of himself, his deeds, and especially of his leader. In the afternoon our cup of delight was made to run over by the appearing of our paymaster with his "stamps," as the boys call the greenbacks. We received two months' pay. The usual scenes of pay-day were re-enacted, and the occasion passed away amid the untempered follies of some and the conserving wisdom of others.

The weather is warm and beautiful. Many of us are improving the opportunity of bathing in the York. This, though not a military, is certainly a very salutary, exercise, and one which we very much enjoy. Boat-rides are occasionally participated in, and lots of sport is found in raking the riverbed for oysters. "Two birds are here killed with one stone," for there is pleasure in catching, and a double pleasure in eating, these bivalvular creatures of the brine. Some days we live on little else but oysters—a diet which is very rapidly recuperating our overtasked powers.

Sunday, May 17.—This has been a beautiful day, and this evening a large meeting for religious services was held near the spot where Lord Cornwallis surrendered his sword to General Washington. The place seemed hallowed with the memory of those events; and it certainly ought to have witnessed the surrender of many rebellious hearts to the "King of kings and Lord of lords." The exercises of the meeting were conducted by the officers of the post, and were full of interest.

Wild and rude as soldiers often are, they generally attend with pleasure all religious services when they are pleasantly invited to do so. And I think no one ever beheld more attentive audiences than here. So great is the contrast between the spirit of such a meeting and the general tenor of our work, that the transition is relieving. Then there is so much in the life and character of a true soldier that suggests the experience and principles of a soldier of the Cross, that a versatile and interesting speaker in a religions assembly here finds ample illustrations from our everyday observations for the unfolding of Christian themes.

And yet the main influence of Christianity here lies back even of these statements; it is found in the ready response which memory brings from the fireside religion of our homes, and the early instructions of the Sunday-school and church. The "stirring up of our pure minds by way of remembrance," which is done so easily in the company of American soldiers, is one of the most potent elements of heroism and right discipline which can be found.

The history of this country borrows so much light from the cross which Columbus bore as an ensign, and planted here, from the prayers of the Pilgrim Fathers, and from the Christian devotion of Washington and others who laid the foundation of this great Republic, that a true American cannot be destitute of reverence for the religion of the Bible. Hence over us especially these religious assemblies cannot fail to exert a salutary influence. And yet we observe that not more than one regiment in five is provided with a chaplain, or with means of religious instruction.

To a certain extent this deficiency is supplied by the benevolent agents of the Christian Commission, who, however, are not able to fill the place of a faithful chaplain. But if it were not for these, many of our sick and dying would be utterly destitute of Christian influence, and our dead would be buried more like dogs than like Christian heroes. We fear that the government does not properly appreciate the importance of the chaplaincy in the army, and hence does not give sufficient inducement for true men to enter this difficult field of labour

Only a man of stalwart character is fit for the position—a man of physical, menial, and moral daring. And so far as our observations extend, with very few exceptions, this is the class of men who occupy the position of chaplains among us.

May 19.—Several days have been spent pleasantly within Fort Yorktown, and we are becoming somewhat eager for more lively experiences and scenes.

Variety's the source of joy below,
From which still fresh revolving pleasures flow.

During the day we abandoned Fort Yorktown, and Kilpatrick established a camp for the regiment in the old peach-orchard, famous for the battle which occurred within its limits during McClellan's Peninsular Campaign.

It is a lovely spot, which, however, shows signs of the conflict above referred to. There is scarcely a tree but presents marks of the bloody drama, in broken bark and splintered trunk, and in wounded branches which hang danglingly over our heads.

Raid to Mathews Court House

During the day a detail of the regiment, sufficient in number to mount all the serviceable horses, was ordered out in an expedition against Mathews Court House. A detachment of infantry and a battery of artillery accompany the cavalry, and Kilpatrick is in command of the entire force. The line of march is through a rich and beautiful region of country. Mathias County is a lovely peninsula, encompassed by the waters of the Piankatank River, on the north, the Chesapeake Bay, on the east, and Mob Jack Bay, on the south. The North River forms a portion of its boundary on the west, against Gloucester County, and nearly severs it from the mainland,

Kilpatrick was favoured with fine weather in his expedition, and returned on the twenty-second crowned with success. A multitude of slaves was liberated, hailing our forces everywhere as their friends and protectors. Large numbers of fine horses and mules, with which that country abounds, were also captured. No Rebel force of any importance was encountered, and the boys greatly enjoyed their visit to the well-stocked plantations of the wealthy farmers, many of whom had never before seen a Yankee.

May 24.—I was taken very suddenly ill during the night. Dr. Kingston came to see me at three o'clock, and so skilfully treated my case, that I was quickly relieved of pain. In three hours from the time the surgeon came to my quarters, I was well enough to be up and on duty, so that at six o'clock I was able to call the roll of my company as usual, and to attend to other duties.

The day after my illness I began to make out muster and payrolls for my company. This work was undertaken by all the first-sergeants of the regiment. But our task is unusually difficult, as nearly all our company-books and papers were captured by guerrillas at the commencement of the spring campaign, *Patience and perseverance* is our motto; and yet many times, as we endeavour to unravel the snarls and untie the knots, we find that the above virtues almost forsake us.

In the afternoon of May twenty-sixth we had mounted regimental drill, and this was followed by dress-parade. Our time is now devoted mostly to drilling, in preparation, as we all think, for some movement.

May 29.—Orders for an advance have at length reached us. At five o'clock this afternoon we struck our tents, broke camp, and crossed the York by ferry, halting for the night near Fort Keyes, at Gloucester

Point. There is much discussion among us as to the point of destination, but nearly all agree that we are to rejoin the Army of the Potomac. Soldiers seldom know the object of their movements. All we need is to receive the order or command, and we go, "asking no question for conscience' sake."

May 30.—We moved from Gloucester Point early in the morning, and made a forced march to the Piankatank River. The rising smoke announced to us that the bridge across this stream had been burnt before us. After considerable searching and sounding, a place so nearly fordable was found as to enable a portion of the command to cross over.

Others meanwhile constructed a temporary bridge over which they effected a crossing. Guerrillas are very numerous in these parts. One of our *vedettes* was fired upon and wounded by them early this, evening. All our attempts to capture such culprits are in vain. The forests are so dense, and ravines so deep and dark that a man acquainted with every secret nook and corner, can hide away in perfect security, after committing his depredations.

Sunday, May 31.—The Troy company is on picket duty today. A detachment from the company made a reconnaissance this morning beyond the outposts, and brought in two citizens of a suspicious character. They undoubtedly belong to the gang of bushwhackers that has hung upon our flanks and rear, and inflicted, the injuries we have sustained for the past few days. Rich supplies of bacon and corn, of sorghum and honey, are found along our path. The country has never been visited by Federal troops, and is as full of provisions for us as it is filled with consternation and alarm at our approach. We have spent the day in scouting the country.

June 1.—Our march was resumed at an early hour in the morning, and we advanced to Urbanna, a town on the Rappahannock. Here several important captures were made, including Colonel E. P. Jones and Captain Brown, of the Virginia militia. Here we spent the night pleasantly. During the night Kilpatrick managed to establish communication with our gun-boats on the Rappahannock, and in the morning early we were taken across on transports, protected by the gun-boats. After a short halt to feed our horses from the corn-ricks which dot the country, we resumed our march, and with the setting sun reached a place called Litwalton, where we bivouacked for the night.

June 3.—Today we had a very pleasant march through a pleasant country and with pleasant weather, Richmond Court House was reached for our bivouac tonight; but we left early in the morning of the fourth, and by good marching arrived at Port Conway at four o'clock p. m. Here we unsaddled our horses for the first time since leaving Yorktown, after the marches of six days.

June 5.—We reached Falmouth. Upon meeting our old acquaintances in the Army of the Potomac, cheers upon cheers were heartily vociferated for Kilpatrick and the Harris Light, and our march was a continual ovation.

The following quotations will show the consideration that was accorded to Kilpatrick's movements:

> Colonel Kilpatrick, with the Harris Light Cavalry and the Twelfth Illinois Cavalry, left Yorktown at twelve o'clock Friday night, reaching Gloucester Point at one a.m., and Gloucester Court House at half-past five a. m., Saturday, They left again at eight o'clock, and at four p, m, on the same day arrived at Saluda, leaving there at half-past four Monday morning, and reaching Urbanna at half-past six a, m., where the wharves were found to be partially destroyed by fire,
> The bridge on the Piankatank River, near Dragon Ordinary, had been destroyed by the citizens, and, as there were no fords, a squadron of the Twelfth Illinois swam their horses over the river, while another portion of Kilpatrick's command—the colonel and his staff-officers assisting—constructed a floating bridge of felled trees and fence-rails in about half an hour, over which the remainder of the cavalry crossed in safety.
> At Saluda the colours of the Twelfth Virginia Infantry were captured by the cavalry. From there the country was scoured for a distance of ten miles, resulting in the capture of horses, mules, and carriages, and in the emancipation of numerous slaves.
> Between Montague and Bowler's Ferry the Rebel pickets were driven in as far as the barricades which they had constructed of felled trees, within three miles of the ferry.
> Occasionally guerrilla skirmishing was encountered on the road; but there was no fighting with any considerable force of the Rebels, though they had infantry and artillery at Kings and Queens Court House and about two hundred cavalry at Bowler's Ferry.

A letter from Stuart was intercepted, addressed to a secessionist named Fontleroy, in Middlesex County, assuring him that he would have a sufficient force of cavalry in that neighbourhood by Sunday evening to relieve the anxiety of the people of the county and stop the raids of the Yankees.

Among the prisoners captured by Kilpatrick's cavalry was Captain Brown, of the Fifth Virginia cavalry, and the guerrilla, Colonel E. P. Jones. The only man wounded was Orderly-Sergeant Northrup, of Company G, Harris Light Cavalry, who was hit with a buckshot-charge fired by a bushwhacker.

The transports *Long Branch, William N. Frazier, Star,* and *Tallaca,* under the command of Lieutenant-Colonel Dickinson, of General Hooker's staff, conveyed the cavalry and the captured horses and mules across the Rappahannock from Urbanna to Carter's wharf, six miles higher up than the former place, and subsequently conveyed the contrabands to Aquia Creek.

The gun-boats *Freeborn, Yankee, Anacostia, Jacob Bell, Satellite, Primrose,* and *Currituck,* convoyed the transports up and down the river, and the *Jacob Bell* covered the landing at Carter's Creek. These vessels of the Potomac flotilla were under the command of Commodore Samuel Magaw.

There was a small force of infantry under Colonel Dickinson, being picked men; and the cavalry, with the aid of this infantry at Urbanna, despoiled the Rebels between Yorktown and the Rappahannock of nearly one thousand contrabands and about three hundred horses and mules, besides depleting their granaries and poultry-yards.

Colonel Kilpatrick, Colonel Dickinson, and Commodore Magaw, and those in their commands, are entitled to commendation for the energy exhibited, as is also the engineer corps of the Fiftieth New York, under Captain Folwell, which promptly repaired the bridge at Carter's wharf, Lieutenant-Colonel Dickinson, Captain John B. Howard, acting assistant-quartermaster, formerly of the Brooklyn Fourteenth, and other military gentlemen and civilians, rode out to Saluda, and were hospitably entertained at the residence of the Clerk of the Courts, who tendered his assurances of respect with generous plates of strawberries and cream.

From another periodical we clip the following:

We have an account of Colonel Kilpatrick's recent successful raid back from Gloucester Point, he crossed the country between the York and Rappahannock Rivers, making an extensive circuit through the garden-spot of Virginia—a section where our troops have never before penetrated. Colonel Kilpatrick made a large haul of negroes, horses, &c., and has arrived safely at Urbanna with them, he spread general terror among the Rebels. His forces were taken across the Rappahannock by our gun-boats, and proceeded at once to our lines.

A brief item from the *Troy Times* will complete the journal of this important event:

Colonel Kilpatrick is the hero of another great raid through the enemy's country. At the conclusion of Stoneman's raid, it will be remembered. Colonel Kilpatrick's command remained at Gloucester Court House. Last week he was ordered to again join the main army, and, on the thirtieth *ultimo*, he started on the march to Urbanna, on the Lower Rappahannock. He returned to the Army of the Potomac on the fifth instant, after travelling over a large extent of territory and destroying an immense amount of property.

A little rest was enjoyed at Falmouth. But our experience convinces us that the cavalryman must write history in haste if he would write as rapidly as it is made.

June 7.—The bugles sounded *réveille* at three o'clock a. m. "Boots and saddles" followed at four; "lead out" at four-and-a-quarter, and the column was in motion towards Warrenton Junction at four-and-a-half. We went *via* Catlett's Station, which place we reached at two o'clock p. m. Nearly every step of the march was on familiar ground, where we had passed and repassed many times. It seemed like meeting old friends, and nearly every object we saw suggested thoughts and experiences of the past.

At Warrenton Junction we rejoined the Cavalry Corps, now under the command of General Alfred Pleasonton.

June 9.—At two o'clock p. m. the whole Cavalry Corps moved from Warrenton Junction towards the Rappahannock. We are marching in two columns, one towards Beverly and the other towards Kelly's Fords. The Harris Light moves with the latter column. Two brigades of infantry under Generals Ames and Russell accompany the expedition, each with a battery of artillery.

Cavalry Fight at Brandy Station

Early on the morning of the ninth we arrived at the river, where it was evident we were not expected in force, for we found nothing but a strong picket-guard to contest our advance. A brief though brisk skirmish took place at the ford, but the Rebel pickets were soon driven back and our column began to cross over, the Harris Light being in the van. On reaching the south bank of the stream, the column was re-formed, and we advanced for some distance at a gallop.

The column at Beverly Ford, commanded by General Gregg, had been engaged since early in the morning, and the roaring of light arms and the booming of cannon clearly indicated to us that hot work was being done by our comrades below. It had been hoped that that column would be able to strike the enemy in flank at Brandy Station, in the early part of the day, giving us an opportunity to rake them furiously in front. Hence we were somewhat retarded in our movements, waiting or expecting the combinations and juxtapositions which had been planned. But, failing in this, at length we advanced towards the station, where, at ten o'clock, we engaged a regiment of Stuart's cavalry. As soon as we reached the field which they had evidently selected for the fight, we charged them in a splendid manner, routing them completely, and capturing many prisoners. Light artillery was used briskly on both sides.

By twelve o'clock Pleasonton's entire force had effected a union, after much severe fighting, on the left, and the engagement became general. The infantry fought side by side with the cavalry. There was some grand manoeuvring on that historic field, and feats were performed worthy of heroes.

One incident should be particularized. At a critical moment, when the formidable and ever-increasing hosts of the enemy were driving our forces from a desirable position we sought to gain, and when it seemed as though disaster to our arms would be fatal, Kilpatrick's battle-flag was seen advancing, followed by the tried squadrons of the Harris Light, the Tenth New York, and the First Maine. In *echelons* of squadrons his brigade was quickly formed, and he advanced like a storm-cloud upon the Rebel cavalry which filled the field before him.

The Tenth New York received the first shock of the Rebel charge, but was hurled back, though not in confusion. The Harris Light met with no better success; and, notwithstanding their prestige and power, they were repulsed under the very eye of their chief, whose excitement at the scene was well-nigh uncontrollable. His flashing eye now turned to the First Maine, a regiment composed mostly of heavy sturdy men, who had not been engaged as yet during the day; and, riding to the head of the column, he shouted, "Men of Maine, you must save the day! Follow me!"

With one simultaneous war-cry these giants of the North moved forward in one solid mass upon the flank of the Rebel columns. The shock was overwhelming; and the opposing lines crumbled like a "bowing wall" before this wild rush of prancing horses, gleaming sabres, and rattling balls.

On rode Kilpatrick with the men of Maine, and, on meeting the two regiments of his brigade, which had been repulsed and were returning from the front, the general's voice rang out like clarion notes above the din of battle, "Back, the Harris Light! Back, the Tenth New York! Re-form your squadrons and charge!"

With magical alacrity the order was obeyed, and the two regiments, which had been so humbled by their first reverse, now rushed into the fight with a spirit and success which redeemed them from censure, and accounted them worthy of their gallant leader. The commanding position was won; a battery lost in a previous charge was recaptured, and an effectual blow was given to the enemy, which greatly facilitated the movements which followed.

But the Rebel cavalry was greatly emboldened and strengthened by re-enforcements of infantry which were brought in railroad cars. We, however, continued to press them closely until six o'clock, when, by a grand charge of our entire force, we gained an important position, which ended the contest.

Heavy columns of Rebel infantry could now be distinctly seen advancing over the plains from the direction of Culpepper, to the rescue of their fairly beaten cavalry. But it was too late for them, for we had won a splendid victory, and had gained all the information of Rebel movements which we desired to obtain. Under cover of the night we recrossed the Rappahannock in safety.

The whole command had lost about five hundred men, and we brought over with us one hundred prisoners. In the early part of the engagement fell Colonel B. F. Davis, of the Eighth New York Cavalry, who was instantly killed. His loss was a subject of general lamentation. He had distinguished himself for great sagacity, wonderful powers of endurance, and unsurpassed bravery. He it was who led the cavalry safely from Harper's Ferry just before Miles' surrender of the place, and who, on his way to Pennsylvania, captured Longstreet's ammunition-train.

Among our wounded was Colonel Percy Wyndham. The enemy's killed included Colonel Saul Williams, of the Second North Carolina, and Lieutenant-Colonel Frank Hampton, of the South Carolina Cavalry. They acknowledge a loss of six hundred men.

From the Richmond *Sentinel* we clip the following account of the battle, by a Rebel Chaplain. The casualties of a single regiment may be regarded as an index of the general result:

Camp in Culpepper County,
June 10, 1863.

Tuesday, the ninth of June, will be memorable to General Stuart's command as the day on which was fought the longest and most hotly-contested cavalry battle of the war. At an early hour skirmishing commenced, and soon the commands of Hampton, the two Lees, Robinson, and Jones, were engaged along the whole Culpepper line, from Welford's Ford, on the Hazel, down to Stevensburg.

Each command acted nobly, and the Yankees were forced, after a fight of nearly twelve hours, to recross the river with great losses. We have to lament the loss of many gallant officers and privates, some killed and others permanently disabled. The forces under W. H. F. Lee, that worthy descendant of "Old Light Horse Harry," bore no mean part in the fray.

We have to regret the temporary loss of our general (W. H. F. Lee), who was wounded in the thigh, and the death of Colonel Williams (of our brigade), than whom a more elegant gentleman or braver soldier never lived.

Being connected with the Tenth Virginia Cavalry, under Colonel J. Lucius Davis, and, therefore, better cognizant of its conduct, it is not invidious to allude to it, though not claiming any superiority over other regiments, all of which did nobly. Early in the morning this regiment was dismounted for sharp-shooting, and, until ordered off, held its ground, though exposed to an incessant and galling fire from the Fifth United States Regulars, who were snugly ensconced behind a stone fence.

At this point many of the casualties in our regiment occurred. In the afternoon the Tenth, led by Colonel Davis, made a splendid charge on the Second United States Regulars, who, after a hand-to-hand conflict, broke and fled incontinently. Our General (Stuart), whose praise is not to be despised, paid a high compliment on the field to the Tenth for its conduct in holding Welford's Hill, and for its dashing charge.

I append a list of casualties:

Company A (Caskie Rangers), commanded by Captain Robert Caskie.—Killed: None. Wounded: Second Lieutenant, J. Doyle, slightly in head; Private, Eytel, in breast; English, in foot; Hubbell, in breast; Gill, in arm and shoulder; Wilson, in hip. Missing and taken prisoners: Privates Burton, Charles Childress, Joseph Childress, Fulcher, Hudnall and Parker.—Total, 12.

Company B, Captain W. B. Clements.—Killed: Corporal N. B. Ellis. Wounded: Privates Anderson Foster, severely in thigh; P. J. Cape, in thigh; H. Foster, slightly in foot R. P. Brewbaker, slightly in head; A. Caton, in hand.—Total, 6.

Company C, commanded by Lieutenant Richardson.—Killed: None. Wounded: Lieutenant N. Richardson, seriously through breast; Sergeant J. Mason, in leg; Corporal Brown, in arm; Privates J. B. King, slightly in thigh; W. B. Saw, seriously in hip; M. Potter, in hand. Missing: J. Shumate.—Total, 7.

Company D, absent on detached service.

Company E, commanded by Captain J. Tucker.—Killed: Private H. T. Bourgois. Wounded: Corporal F. S. Labit, in shoulder; S. H. Lamb, in hand. Missing: Sergeant Peter Smith (wounded and captured); Sergeant Stromburg (wounded and captured); Private Enoch Pelton.—Total, 6.

Company F, commanded by Captain J. H. Dettor.—Killed: G. Wescott. Wounded: Privates John White, in thigh; John E. Edge, in thigh; J. R. Giles, in arm; Sergeant J. Durret, arm.—Total, 5.

Company G, commanded by M. S. Kirtley.—Killed: None. Wounded: Corporal J. M. McConn, seriously in arm; Private Jonathan Shepherd, slightly in head. Missing: Private S. Hartley.—Total, 3.

Company H, commanded by Lieutenant S. K. Newham.—Killed: None. Wounded: Privates James O'Connor, mortally; M. Neff, seriously in leg. Missing: J. P. Martz, R. F. Koontz.—Total, 4.

Company I (Henrico Light Dragoons), commanded by Lieutenant J. H. T. McDowell.—Killed: Private Louis Ottenburg. Wounded: Sergeant S. L. McGruder, slightly in shoulder; Corporal J. C. Mann, slightly in leg; Privates Walter Priest, mortally in breast; George Waldrop, slightly in shoulder; B. J. Duval, slightly in head; W. T. Thomas, in shoulder slightly.—Total, 7.

Company K, commanded by Captain Dickinson.—Killed None. Wounded: Corporal J. L. Franklin, in right shoulder; Private J. M. Craig, head, left arm severely; R. V. Griffin, right shoulder severely; C. P. Preston, slightly in nose; W. T. Arrington, breast slightly; T. R. Gilbert, left arm slightly. Missing: Sergeant T. S. Holland; Privates E. A. Haines and S. R. Gilbert.—Total, 9.

Total killed, wounded, and missing, 59.

J. B. Taylor, Jr., Chaplain Tenth Virginia Cavalry,
W. H. F. Lee's Brigade.

Two important ends were reached by this advance, namely, first, a cavalry raid contemplated by Stuart, who had massed his forces near Culpepper, was utterly frustrated; and second, General Pleasonton ascertained conclusively that General Lee was marching his army northward, with the evident design of invading the Northern States. Indeed, it was a suspicion of such a movement that led General Hooker to order the reconnaissance.

The day following this glorious fight, in which the men of the North had proved themselves to be more than a match for the boasted Southern chivalry, and had gained a name which placed Pleasonton's command at the head of the world's cavalry forces, Pleasonton was made a Major-General, and Kilpatrick a Brigadier. Their stars were well-deserved and proudly worn.

During the day the Cavalry Corps moved to Warrenton Junction, leaving strong guards at the fords of the Rappahannock to prevent any crossing which might be attempted by the enemy.

June 11.—At two o'clock this afternoon General Gregg inspected our division. The day was beautiful, and the troopers made a splendid appearance.

To heighten the interest of the occasion, the colours captured by the Harris Light at Urbanna, and those taken by the First Maine in their memorable charge at Brandy Station on the ninth instant, were displayed amid the cheers of the enthusiastic cavalrymen, whose past deeds give encouraging promise for the future.

Sunday, June 14.—We are still encamped on the plains near Warrenton Junction. On the twelfth the regiment was inspected by Captain Armstrong, of Kilpatrick's staff. The following day we had an interesting mounted-drill. We cannot keep idle. This afternoon, at two o'clock, we received orders to prepare to move at a moment's notice. Cannonading is distinctly heard in the direction of Warrenton.

For several days it has been expected that General Lee, with his forces, would make his appearance on the banks of the Potomac, somewhere below Harper's Ferry. But as they have failed to do so, the inquiry is very general among us, "Where are they?" and, "What do they intend?" To work out the answer to such interrogations is generally the work of the cavalry; so that, when our orders for readiness to move were received, we saw before us a reconnaissance in force. We understand that already Rebel cavalry is raiding more or less in Maryland, and some exciting times are expected before long.

CHAPTER 12

Second Invasion of Maryland —Gettysburg

For nearly two days we were prepared to march, and awaiting orders, when at last they came. At about six o'clock on the morning of the sixteenth we took up our line of march, which was mostly along the railroad in the direction of Manassas. Having arrived at these celebrated plains, we struck off a little to the left towards Centreville, where we arrived at ten o'clock, weary with the long journey. Here we ascertained that General Hooker's headquarters are at Fairfax Court House, or in the vicinity, and that his army covers the approaches to Washington.

June 17.—After a refreshing night's rest, we were up early in the morning, and resumed our march at six o'clock, taking the Warrenton Turnpike. Kilpatrick has the advance of the corps. We soon crossed the memorable fields of the two Bull Run battles, passed the famous field of Groveton, and there deflecting to the right, and pushing forward rapidly, we arrived by noon in sight of the hills which partially surround the village of Aldie, on, the north side of the Bull Run Mountains. Kilpatrick had been directed to move through Aldie, and thence to and through Ashby's Gap, in the Blue Ridge, learn all he could of the enemy's movements, and, then returning, to rejoin the corps at Nolan's Ferry on the Potomac. Colonel Duffié, with his regiment, the First Rhode Island, was ordered to move throug Thoroughfare Gap, and to join Kilpatrick in Pleasant Valley beyond. These plans were laid with the presumption that no very heavy force of Rebels remained north of the Blue Ridge, and none at all north of the Bull Run Mountains. But this was eventually found to be a great mistake.

Bloody Battle of Aldie

James Moore, M, D., Surgeon of the Ninth Pennsylvania Cavalry, thus describes what occurred to Kilpatrick and his command at this place:

> Scarcely had his advance reached the town of Aldie, when it came directly upon the advance-guard of W. H. F. Lee. It was entirely unexpected. No enemy was supposed to be on the Aldie side of the Bull Run Mountains.
>
> The general rode to the front, ran his eye over the field for a moment, and then rapidly gave his orders. He had taken in the whole field at one rapid glance, and saw the important points that must be gained. The Harris Light Cavalry was directed to charge straight down the road, through the town, gain and hold the long, low hill over which runs the road from Middleburg. With anxious eye he watched the charge, on which so much depended, saw that it was successful, and quickly and resolutely pushed in one regiment after another on the right of the Harris Light, till the high hills far on the right of Aldie were gained.
>
> This fine disposition was made, and important position won, before the Rebel General Fitzhugh Lee could make a single effort to prevent it, although he had a division of cavalry at his back.
>
> He soon recovered, however, from the temporary surprise, and for two hours made most desperate efforts to regain the position lost. He struck the right, left, and centre in quick succession, while his battery of Blakely guns thundered forth their messengers of death.
>
> But all in vain! Kilpatrick's gallant men—the heroes of Brandy Station—met and hurled back each charge, while Randall's battery, ignoring entirely the Rebel guns, sent his canister and shells tearing through the heavy columns of the enemy.
>
> On this day Kilpatrick did wonders. He fought under the eye of his chief, and where bullets flew the thickest, and where the shock came the heaviest, there rang his cheering voice and there flashed his sabre. His own regiment, the Harris Light, had failed to meet his hopes on the plains of Brandy Station. This was known to the officers of that splendid organisation, and on that very morning they had petitioned their general for an opportunity to retrieve their reputation. The opportunity was

at hand.

A large force of the enemy occupied a strong position behind rail barricades encircling large stacks of hay. For a long time Rebel sharpshooters, from this secure position, had baffled every attempt to advance our lines on the left. The general ordered up a battalion of the Harris Light. Quickly they came! Addressing a few encouraging words to the men, and then turning to Major McIrvin, the officer in command, he said, pointing to the barricades: 'Major, there is the opportunity you have asked for. Go, take that position!'

Away dashed this officer and his men. In a moment the enemy was reached, and the struggle began. The horses could not leap the barricade, but the men dismounted, scaled those formidable barriers, and, with drawn sabres, rushed upon the hidden foe, who quickly asked for quarter.

Another incident occurred worth mentioning. Colonel Cesnola, of the Fourth New York Cavalry, had that morning, through mistake, been placed under arrest, and, his sword being taken from him, was without arms. But in one of these wild charges, made early in the contest, his regiment hesitated, Forgetting that he was under arrest, and without command, he flew to the head of his regiment, reassured his men, and, without a weapon to give or ward a blow, led them to the charge. This gallant act was seen by his general, who, meeting him on his return, said: 'Colonel, you are a brave man; you are released from arrest;' and, taking his own sword from his side, handed it to the colonel, saying: 'Here is my sword; wear it in honour of this day!' In the next charge Colonel Cesnola fell, desperately wounded, and was taken prisoner.

The Rebel general, being foiled at every point, resolved to make one more desperate effort. Silently and quickly he massed a heavy force upon our extreme right, and, led by General Rosser, made one of the most desperate and determined charges of the day. Kilpatrick was aware of this movement, and satisfied that his men, exhausted as they were, could not withstand the charge, had already sent for re-enforcements.

Before these could reach him the shock came. The First Massachusetts had the right, and fought as only brave men could to stem the tide that steadily bore them back, until the whole right gave way. Back rushed our men in wild confusion, and on came the victorious Rebel horsemen. the general saw, with anguish, his flying soldiers, yet in his extremity retained his presence of mind, and proved himself worthy the star he had won at Brandy Station.

Sending orders for the centre and left to stand fast, he placed himself at the head of the First Maine, sent to his assistance, and coolly waited till the Rebel charging columns had advanced within fifty yards of Randall's guns. He then shouted 'Forward!' and the same regiment that saved the day at Brandy Station was destined to save the day at Aldie. Rosser's men could not withstand the charge, but broke and fled up the hill. The general's horse was killed in the charge, and here the brave Colonel Doughty fell.

The general determined now to complete the victory, and, mounting a fresh horse, he urged on the First Maine and First Massachusetts, sent orders for his whole line to advance, and then sounded the charge. Lee struggled for a few minutes against this advance, and then ordered a retreat, which ended in a rout. His troops were driven in confusion as far as Middleburg, and night alone saved the remnant of his command.

This was by far the most bloody cavalry battle of the war. The Rebel chivalry had again been beaten, and Kilpatrick, who was the only general on the field, at once took a proud stand among the most famous of our Union cavalry generals. The fame of our cavalry was now much enhanced, and caused the greatest joy to the nation.

June 18.—General Pleasonton was anxious to press the Rebel cavalry back upon their infantry, to ascertain minutely their movements; hence, today, Kilpatrick was ordered to advance through the Bull Run Mountains, and to occupy Middleburg. Jaded as we were, as well as our horses, with the fearful yet glorious labours of the previous day, with mercury up to 98° Fahrenheit in the shade, and 122° in the sun, with an atmosphere unusually oppressive for Virginia, and through dust which many tramping hoofs made almost intolerable, we marched into Pleasant Valley. The outpost of the Rebel cavalry was met near the town, but they were driven from the streets, and we took possession of Middleburg.

About three o'clock in the afternoon a heavy wind arose, betokening rain, which began to fall about five o'clock, mingled with hail.

For this atmospheric change we had earnestly prayed. The heat had become so oppressive, and the roads so dusty, as to make our movements very unpleasant and disastrous to men and beasts, especially to the latter.

In this beautiful region of country we spent a few days very pleasantly, recruiting our strength and awaiting orders.

Cavalry Battle at Upperville

June 21.—The Cavalry Corps, with General Pleasonton at its head, moved, at eight o'clock this morning, in the direction of Ashby's Gap, in the Blue Ridge. We had not proceeded far before we encountered the Rebel pickets, which we drove steadily before us. Their strength, however, greatly increased as we advanced. Quite a large force contested our progress when we entered Carrtown, and from this place to Upperville the engagement was a little too heavy to be called a skirmish. Nevertheless, we pushed ahead without being seriously retarded until we reached Upperville.

Here our advance was met with great desperation, the enemy charging us handsomely, but with no great damage. When our forces had been properly arranged, and the right time had come, Kilpatrick was ordered to charge the town. with drawn sabres—weapons in which the general always had great confidence, and generally won success—and with yells which made the mountains and plains resound, we rushed upon the foe.

The fray was terrible. Several times did the Rebels break, but, being re-enforced or falling back upon some better position, again endeavoured to baffle our efforts. But they were not equal to the task, and we drove them through the village of Paris, and finally through Ashby's Gap, upon their infantry columns in the Shenandoah Valley. In these charges and chase we captured two pieces of artillery, four caissons, several stand of small arms, and a large number of prisoners.

It was my misfortune, in one of those desperate encounters, to have a favourite horse shot under me. But it was also my fortune to escape from the deadly missiles which filled the air, and from my fallen horse, unhurt. Another animal was soon provided for me from the captures we had made.

Our scouts, daring this engagement, had managed to gain an entrance into the Valley, where they ascertained that the Rebel army, in heavy columns, was advancing towards the Upper Potomac.

This fight was of sufficient importance to call forth from the commanding general the following official document:

> Headquarters Cavalry Corps,
> Camp near Upperville, 5.20 p. m., June 21.
>
> Brigadier-General S. Williams:
>
> General: I moved with my command this morning to Middleburg, and attacked the cavalry force of the Rebels under Stuart, and steadily drove him all day, inflicting a heavy loss at every step.
>
> I drove him through Upperville into Ashby's Gap.
>
> We took two pieces of artillery, one being a Blakely gun, and three caissons, besides blowing up one; also, upwards of sixty prisoners, and more are coming; a lieutenant-colonel, major, and five other officers, besides a wounded colonel and a large number of wounded Rebels left in the town of Upperville.
>
> They left their dead and wounded upon the field; of the former I saw upward of twenty.
>
> We also took a large number of carbines, pistols, and sabres. In fact, it was a most disastrous day to the Rebel cavalry.
>
> Our loss has been very small both in men and horses.
>
> I never saw the troops behave better, or under more difficult circumstances.
>
> Very heavy charges were made, and the sabre used freely but always with great advantage to us.
>
> A. Pleasonton,
> Brigadier-General.

The day following this decided victory by force of arms, and by the stratagem of scouts, who obtained all needful information as to the intentions of the enemy, the Cavalry Corps retired from Ashby's Gap and established its headquarters at Aldie. Our outposts are near Middleburg. We are now receiving some exciting news from Maryland and the North. It appears that Rebel cavalry was raiding through Maryland, destroying railroads and bridges, telegraph lines and depots, and making havoc on the Chesapeake and Ohio Canal as early as the fifteenth instant; and that General Ewell, with a corps of infantry, crossed the Potomac at Williamsport on the sixteenth, and advanced *via* Hagerstown towards Pennsylvania.

A sad and distressing alarm seems to have aroused the North. General Lee's advance thus far, excepting the repulses of his cavalry on his right flank, has been a perfect success. It is true that Washington, the glittering prize before him, has been protected by General Hooker's cautious movements. But this protection of the capital has consumed time and given the enemy a decided advantage in other quarters. He had already entered the Free States before we fairly understood his intentions.

Winchester, an important post in the Shenandoah Valley, guarded by General Milroy, was nearly surrounded by the advancing Rebel hordes, before our general even dreamed that he was in jeopardy. The few of our men who escaped from that garrison, were greatly demoralised, while about four thousand were made prisoners, and many heavy guns, small arms, wagons, horses, and stores of all kinds fell into the enemy's hands.

These blunders on our part and losses, together with the prowess and boast of the Rebel legions, gave the malcontents of the North, and political tricksters, a coveted opportunity to rail against the administration, and to weaken, as far as their influence could be felt, the confidence which had been reposed in it. The president was represented as an imbecile, utterly devoid of statesmanship. The army was berated with no measured terms. Every reverse of fortune was attributed to a want of brains and heart in the heads of departments. The Republic had certainly fallen upon dark days.

General Lee, undoubtedly, expected to make capital out of this state of things, and hoped that by winning a grand victory on Northern soil, so to cripple the administration and to demoralise the political party in power, that he could secure the aid and comfort of the opposing party, and thus compel the North to submit to any terms of peace which the anomalous Confederacy might dictate.

Notwithstanding the threatening posture of military affairs, and that the government was thoroughly alarmed and ordered out the militia of Maryland, Pennsylvania, New York, Ohio, West Virginia, and other States, the call being faithfully re-echoed by the governors of those States, the responses were comparatively faint and fell far short of the numbers which had been demanded. New York City alone responded generously. The uniformed and disciplined regiments there generally and promptly went to the contest, and appeared where they were needed. For this the governor of the State was publicly thanked by the Secretary of War.

June 25.—We are informed that our infantry and artillery, with small detachments of cavalry, are advancing through Maryland to meet and repel the invaders, who are reported to be crossing the Potomac in two heavy columns at Shepherdstown and Williamsport. Every department of the service seems to be in commotion, and great things are expected. A heavy rain set in early this evening.

At six o'clock on the morning of June twenty-sixth we broke camp at Aldie and advanced towards Leesburg, spending the night near this place. Most of our time has been spent in the saddle. This is becoming not only our seat, but also our bed and pillow.

Our corps commenced its march towards Edward's Ferry, on the Potomac, at five o'clock a. m. of June twenty-seventh. On our way to the ferry we crossed the famous battlefield of Ball's Bluff, where Colonel Baker and many of his gallant Californians became an early and costly sacrifice to the cause of the Union.

On reaching the river we found the two pontoon bridges over which already a large portion of our army had passed on before us. They had been much retarded by the heavy rains and mud. The approaches to the pontoons had been so trodden by the myriad feet of men and beasts, and cut by the heavy wheels of laden wagons and artillery, that we found the roads almost bottomless.

But as we had seen mud many times before, we moved forward undismayed, though somewhat retarded, and were soon on Northern soil. A somewhat strange feeling came over us on finding ourselves marching mainly towards the North Star to meet the enemy, whereas we had so long been accustomed to look and march only southward for this purpose.

Our march lay through a fine and fertile section of country. The vast fields of grain are ripening for the harvest, and their appearance indicates that thus far the labours of the husbandman have not been in vain. The peacefulness of the fields and flocks presents a striking contrast to the warlike preparations which are now being made for what must be the most decisive and bloody contest of the war. The rebellion seems to have risked its very existence in the coming conflict, which cannot be many days hence.

Determination and desperation seem foremost in the movement. On our side a solemn decision seems to be actuating the masses. We know that should the "Stars and Bars" be victorious again, and at this crisis of our national affairs, as they were at the two Bull Run battles, and at Chancellorsville, our "Stars and Stripes" will not only be shamefully humbled, but suffer cruel elimination. In such an event some of our stars must fall and some of the beams of our light must be obscured.

> But conquer we must, for our cause it is just,
> And this be our motto, 'In God is our trust.'
> And the star-spangled banner in triumph shall wave
> O'er the land of the free and the home of the brave.

Sunday, June 28.—All night long we were on the march, arriving in the vicinity of Frederick City early in the morning. The whole country for miles seems to be covered with soldiers. This is one of the most beautiful spots in the world. However, the city does not show the thrift and prosperity which are evidenced in Northern cities enjoying similar advantages. This is the capital of Frederick County, one of the richest in the State. Looking southward from the city we behold an almost interminable stretch of beautiful rolling land, nearly every inch of which is not only arable but richly productive.

On the east, at a distance of several miles, the eye rests upon a range of hills which sweep downward toward the Potomac, terminating in the lofty peak called Sugarloaf. Westward rises the loftier chain of the Catoctin, which is but a continuation of the Bull Run Mountains, severed by the river at Point of Pocks. All the highest peaks of these hills and mountains are now used for signal stations, where wave the signal flags by day and flash the signal fires by night. One seldom wearies in watching these operations, though he may not understand their significance.

Change of Commanders

This has been a day of much interest among us and of no little excitement—a day of changes and re-organisation. An exciting rumour was bandied from man to man this morning, that General Hooker was about to be relieved from the command of the grand army; and the day was only partly spent when the strange rumour resolved itself into the astounding truth.

The facts which led to this result may not be perfectly understood among us, but appear to be about as follows: On discovering that the enemy had actually invaded the Northern States, General Hooker requested the authorities to send him all the forces which could be spared from General Heintzleman's command in and about the Defences of Washington. This was done. But, having crossed the Potomac, General Hooker visited Harper's Ferry with its strong garrison, and immediately urged upon the government the importance of placing this force also under his command. Upon this subject there sprang up a sharp controversy between Hooker and Halleck. The latter rejoined to the former in these words:

> Maryland Heights have always been regarded as an important point to be held by us, and much expense and labour incurred in fortifying them. I cannot approve of their abandonment, except in case of absolute necessity.

General Hooker's reply to this shows him to have been in the right, and to have comprehended the relative importance of the position in question:

> I have received your telegram in regard to Harper's Ferry. I find ten thousand men here in condition to take the field. Here they are of no earthly account. They cannot defend a ford of the river; and, so far as Harper's Ferry is concerned, there is nothing of it. As for the fortifications, the work of the troops, they remain when the troops are withdrawn. This is my opinion. All the public property could have been secured tonight, and the troops marched to where they could have been of some service. Now they are but a bait for the Rebels, should they return. I beg that this may be presented to the Secretary of War, and his Excellency, the President.

Receiving no direct reply to this announcement, and goaded by the pressure of fast-moving events, our general yielded to do what many of us heartily condemn, by sending the following message:

> Sandy Hook, Md.,
> June 27, 1863.
>
> *Major-General H. W. Halleck, General-in-Chief:*
> My original instructions require me to cover Harper's Ferry and Washington. I have now imposed upon me, in addition, an enemy in my front of more than my numbers. I beg to be understood respectfully, but firmly, that I am unable to comply with this condition, with the means at my disposal, and earnestly request that I may at once be relieved from the position I occupy.
>
> Joseph Hooker, Major General,

Today came the order relieving General Hooker, who issued the following characteristic farewell address to the troops, many of whom were taken wholly by surprise, and all of them appeared greatly afflicted:

> Headquarters Army of the Potomac,
> Frederick, Md., June 28, 1863.
>
> In conformity with the orders of the War Department, dated June 27, 1863, I relinquish the command of the Army of the Potomac. It is transferred to Major-General George G, Meade, a brave and accomplished officer, who has nobly earned the confidence and esteem of the army on many a well-fought field. Impressed with the belief that my usefulness as the commander of the Army of the Potomac is impaired, I part from it, yet not without the deepest emotions.
>
> The sorrow of parting with the comrades of so many battles is relieved by the conviction that the courage and devotion of this army will never cease nor fail; that it will yield to my successor, as it has to me, a willing and hearty support. With the earnest prayer that the triumph of this army may bring successes worthy of it and the nation, I bid it farewell.
>
> Joseph Hooker, Major-General.

Such a change of *régime* on the eve of a great battle, with the command in the hands of one less known and trusted, at first seemed to threaten disaster. But the modest, earnest words with which the new commander framed his first order to the troops allayed all fears, renewed confidence, and greatly attached to him the hearts of his subordinates.

> Headquarters Army of the Potomac,
> June 28, 1863.
>
> By direction of the President of the United States I hereby assume command of the Army of the Potomac. As a soldier, in obeying this order—an order totally unexpected and unsolicited—I have no promises or pledges to make. The country looks to this army to relieve it from the devastation and disgrace of a hostile invasion.
>
> Whatever fatigues and sacrifices we may be called to undergo, let us have in view constantly the magnitude of the interests involved, and let each man determine to do his duty, leaving to an all-controlling Providence the decision of the contest.
>
> It is with just diffidence that I relieved, in the command of this army, an eminent and accomplished soldier, whose name must

ever appear conspicuous in the history of its achievements; but I rely upon the hearty support of my companions in arms to assist me in the discharge of the duties of the important trust which has been confided to me.

George G. Meade,
Major-General Commanding.

This change of commanders was followed by others in various branches of the service, not excepting the Cavalry Corps. Our force has been increased by General Julius Stahil's division, which has been employed for some time in the vicinity of Fairfax Court House, and along the line of the Orange and Alexandria Railroad. In the reorganisation, the corps, which continues under the efficient command of General Pleasonton, is arranged into three divisions, the First, Second, and Third, commanded respectively by Generals Buford, Gregg, and Kilpatrick. A more effective cavalry force was never organised on this continent, and probably on no other.

The Harris Light is assigned to General Gregg's division, which separates us, for the first time, from our former beloved commander. But we are not among those who desire to shirk responsibility for any such cause as this. After the division had been reorganised and reviewed, in the afternoon we took up our line of march to New Market. Some rain fell towards night, which laid the dust and allayed the heat. Men and horses are living well upon the rich products of the country. Upon such supplies we rely mainly, though our trains are not wholly destitute.

We are received with more or less enthusiasm and demonstrations of patriotism in nearly all the towns we visit, making a very striking contrast with our former receptions in cities and towns of Virginia. This gives our men additional courage, and nerves us for the conflicts impending.

June 29.—We have been in the saddle nearly all day, scouting the country in the neighbourhood of Westminster. On the morning of the thirtieth, about nine o'clock, the regiment entered this pleasant town, the citizens flocking from all directions to pay us their respects, and to show their devotion to the cause of the Union. After a short halt we advanced to Manchester.

On the first of July we marched to Hanover Junction, Pennsylvania where we met the enemy's cavalry under General John Jenkins, and, after a spirited skirmish, they were forced to retire.

The Pennsylvanians welcomed us with glad cheers, and showed their appreciation of our presence and services by driving several "huckster's wagons" into our midst, well laden with a great variety of eatables, which were donated to us by the good citizens of the surrounding country. It is true that some of the inhabitants made their gifts very sparingly and not without grudging, while others charged enormous prices for such articles as we were willing to purchase; but justice demands that we state that such inhospitable, unpatriotic, and niggardly souls were the exception.

While here we learned the particulars of important movements made by other portions of our cavalry. Kilpatrick, with his vigorous division, left the vicinity of Frederick on Monday; and, striking northward, he passed through Taneytown, reaching Littletown about ten o'clock at night, where he was received in the midst of great rejoicing.

A large group of children and young ladies, gayly attired, on the balcony of a hotel, waving handkerchiefs and flags, greeted their defenders with patriotic songs, while the heroic troopers responded with cheers which made the welkin ring. The command bivouacked in the vicinity of the village, where the citizens brought abundant forage for the horses, and the cavalrymen rested till mornings. The march was then resumed in the direction of Hanover.

The column, which was several miles in length, entered this beautiful town, and was passing through, while the citizens were regaling the men sumptuously from their bountifully provided larders, and interchanging friendly and patriotic greetings, neither party suspecting the presence of the enemy. Nearly one half the column had already passed through, when suddenly the quiet, social scene was disturbed by the opening of a Rebel battery concealed on a wood-crowned hill, and so posted as to rake a portion of the road upon which the Union forces entered the town.

This was immediately followed by a charge of Rebel cavalry, which had been drawn up in line of battle just behind a chain of hills which ran near and parallel to the highway. There they had quietly waited until the train was passing before them, with the hope that this might be captured or stampeded, and a glorious victory be won. General Stuart commanded in person, and the attack was certainly well planned. But Kilpatrick's boys were not to be disconcerted nor panic-stricken by any such or any other trap.

The main force of the charging column happened to be in the

rear of the Fifth New York, commanded by Major Hammond. Quick work was necessary. Rapidly moving out of the street into the open park near the railroad depot. Major Hammond drew his regiment in line of battle, and in nearly as short time as it takes to record it, charged with drawn sabres the Rebels, who then possessed the town. The charging columns met on Frederick street, where a fierce and bloody hand-to-hand contest ensued.

For a few moments the enemy made heroic resistance, but soon broke and fled, closely pursued. They rallied again and again as fresh regiments came to their aid, but they were met, hurled back, and pursued with irresistible onsets, which compelled them to retire not only from the town, but also behind the hills under cover of their batteries.

In less than fifteen minutes from the time the Rebels charged into the village they were driven from it, leaving the streets strewn with their dead men and horses, and the *débris* which always accompanies such a conflict. the dead of both parties lay promiscuously about the street, so covered with blood and dust as to render identification in some cases very difficult. The blue of the Union and the gray of Rebellion were almost entirely obliterated, and, in many instances, the contending parties mingled their blood in one common pool.

This work of destruction had but just commenced when Generals Kilpatrick and Farnsworth, who, though some miles distant at the head of the column when the booming cannon announced the bloody fray, arrived in hot haste and took personal charge of the movements. These were ordered with consummate skill, and executed with promptness and success.

Elder's battery, well posted on the hills facing the Rebels, and well supported, soon silenced the guns of the enemy, and drove him in the direction of Lee's main army. He was thoroughly punished for his audacious attack, and left many dead, wounded, and captured. The colours of the Thirteenth Virginia Cavalry were captured by a sergeant of the Fifth New York. About seventy-five prisoners, beside the wounded, fell into our hands, including Lieutenant-Colonel Payne, who commanded a brigade.

The particulars of his capture are worthy of historic record. In one of the charges made in the edge of the town, one of our boys, by the name of Abram Folger, was captured by Colonel Payne, and marched toward the rear. Just outside the town was a large brick tannery, the vats of which were not under cover, and close alongside of the highway. Folger was walking beside the colonel's orderly. As they approached the tan-vats he espied a carbine lying on the ground. Quick as thought he seized it, fired, and killed Payne's horse.

The animal, in his death-struggle, plunged over towards the vats, and Payne was thrown headlong into one of them, being completely submerged in the tan-liquid. Folger, feeling that the colonel was secure enough for the moment, levelled his piece on the orderly, who, finding that his pistol was fouled and hence useless, attempted to jump his horse over the fence, but not succeeding, surrendered. It happened, however, that Folger had expended the last shot in the carbine on the colonel's horse; but, as the orderly did not know it, it was just as well for Folger as though more ammunition had been on hand.

The recently-made prisoner was compelled to assist his colonel from the vat. His gray uniform, with white velvet trimmings, his white gauntlets, and his face and hair had received a brief but thorough tanning. Folger marched the two in front of him to the market-place in the centre of the village, where he delivered his captives to the authorities. In one hand the brave soldier-boy carried his empty carbine, and in the other a good strong stick. It was a most ludicrous and interesting scene. Folger was captured by Payne's command, in Virginia, the winter before this affair, and his feelings may be imagined at having so nicely returned the compliment.

The citizens of Hanover, who so nobly cared for our wounded in the hospitals during and after the battle, and assisted us in burying our dead, will not soon forget that terrible last day of June. Our brave boys, who, though taken by surprise, had so valiantly defeated the enemy, built their bivouac fires and rested for the night on the field of their recent victory. Stuart's cavalry was now losing caste, while our troopers were not only adding fresh laurels to their chaplet of renown, but also new fibres of vitality to the hearts and hands which loved and defended the sacred Tree of Liberty.

First Day at Gettysburg

General Buford, with his division, had moved from Frederick City directly to Gettysburg, the capital of Adams County, a rural village of about three thousand inhabitants, beautifully situated among the hills, which, though quite lofty, are generally well cultivated. The general found the borough very quiet, and passed through; but he had not proceeded far beyond before he met the van of the Rebel army under General Heth, of Hill's Corps.

Cavalry fight at Brandy Station, June 9th, 1863

The dauntless troopers charged furiously the invading hordes, and drove them back upon their supports, where our boys were driven back in their turn before overwhelming numbers. As Providence would have it, our infantry advance, under General James S. Wadsworth, marching from the village of Emmitsburg, hearing the familiar sound of battle, went into a double-quick, and, hastening through Gettysburg, struck the advancing Rebel column just in time to seize and occupy the range of hills that overlooks the place from the northwest, in the direction of Chambersburg.

General John F. Reynolds, a true Pennsylvanian, was in command of our entire advance, which consisted of the First and Eleventh Corps, about twenty-two thousand strong. As General Wadsworth was placing his division in position, General Reynolds went forward quite alone to reconnoitre, when he discovered a heavy force of the enemy in a grove not far distant.

Dismounting quickly he crouched down by a fence through which he sought to survey the force and its position by means of his field-glass, when a whistling ball from a sharpshooter's musket struck him in the neck. He fell on his face and baptized with his life-blood the soil which had given him birth. His untimely fall, especially at this crisis and almost in sight of his childhood's home, was generally lamented. His lifeless form was borne away to the rear just as the Rebels in heavy force advanced upon not more than one-third their number.

General Abner Doubleday had to assume command of our forces under this galling fire, having arrived with a portion of the First Corps, the remainder of which and the Eleventh Corps, not being able to join them until two hours of fearful destruction had gone on. Our feeble advance was compelled to fall quickly back upon Seminary Hill, just west of the village, and were pursued very closely, so much so that one portion of our line, seeing its opportunity, swung around rapidly, enveloping the Rebel advance and capturing General Archer the leader and about eight hundred prisoners.

On the arrival of the Eleventh Corps, General O. O. Howard, being the ranking officer present, assumed command, giving his place to General Carl Schurz. Our men, now emboldened by these fresh arrivals of helpers, and having alighted upon a fine commanding position, renewed the fight with spirit and wonderful success. This prosperous tide of things continued until about one o'clock p. m., when their right wing was assailed furiously by fresh troops, which proved to be General Ewell's Corps, which had been marching from York, directed by the thunder of battle.

Thus flanked and outnumbered by the gathering hosts, the Eleventh Corps, which was most exposed to the enfilading fire of the newly arrived columns, began to waver, then to break, and soon fled in perfect rout. The First Corps was thus compelled to follow, or be annihilated. The two retreating columns met and mingled in more or less confusion in the streets of the town, where they greatly obstructed each other, though the First Corps retained its organisation quite unbroken.

In passing through the town the Eleventh Corps was especially exposed to the fire of the enemy, who pressed his advantage and captured thousands of prisoners. Our wounded, who, up to this time, had been quartered in Gettysburg, fell into the enemy's hands, and scarcely one-half of our brave boys, who had so recently and proudly passed through the streets to the battle lines, had the privilege of returning, but either lay dead or dying on the well-fought fields, or were captives with a cruel foe. The number of killed and wounded showed how desperately they had fought, and the large number captured was evidence of the overwhelming numbers with which they had contended.

General Buford, with his troopers, covered our retreat, showing as bold a front as possible to the enemy, who, it was feared, would follow fiercely, as they were very strong and several hours of daylight yet remained. But doubtless fearing that a trap might be laid for them if they advanced too far, they contented themselves with only a portion of the borough, their main force occupying the hills which form a grand amphitheatre on the north and west. It would be difficult to refrain from saying, that those Rebel forces were prevented from advancing by some mighty unseen hand—the hand of Him who "watches over the destiny of nations."

Our feeble and decimated forces took possession of Cemetery Hill, south, of the town, and being re-enforced by General Sickles' Corps, they began to intrench themselves with earthworks and rifle-pits, to extend their lines to right and left, and to select the best positions for our batteries. This work was continued quite late into the evening, the broad moonlight greatly facilitating the operations.

General Meade, who had selected his ground for the impending battle along the banks of Pipe Creek, and who at one o'clock p.m. was at Taneytown when the news of the fight, and the death of the brave Reynolds at Gettysburg, reached him, despatched General Hancock to the scene of conflict to take command, and to ascertain whether Gettysburg afforded better ground than that which had been selected.

Hancock arrived at Cemetery Hill just as our broken lines were hastily and confusedly retreating from the village; our advance, however, had already taken this commanding position and was making some preparation for resistance. The newly arrived general began at once to order the forces which had been engaged and others which were occasionally arriving. He ordered the occupancy of Culp's Hill on our extreme right, and extended the lines to our left well up the high ground in the vicinity of Round Top, a rocky eminence about two miles from Gettysburg, and nearly equi-distant from the Emmitsburg and Taneytown roads.

The line having been made as secure as possible, Hancock wrote to Meade that the position was excellent. His despatch had scarcely gone, when he was relieved by General Slocum, a ranking officer, and so, leaving the field, Hancock hastened to report in person to his chief the condition of things at Gettysburg. On arriving, Meade informed him that he had decided to fight at Gettysburg, and had sent orders to the various commands to that effect; then together they rode to Gettysburg, arriving about eleven o'clock at night.

All night long our forces were concentrating before this historic village, where they were all found on the morning of the second of July, except the Sixth Corps, General Sedgwick's, which did not arrive until two o'clock in the afternoon, after marching nearly all the previous night.

Second Day's Fight

Until three o'clock all was quiet along the battle lines, except an occasional picket or sharpshooter's fire. However, there had been considerable manoeuvring. On our left General Sickles, in his eagerness for a fight, had advanced his corps across the Emmitsburg road, and on a wood-crowned ridge in the immediate vicinity of the main portion of the Rebel army. General Meade, in his inspection of the lines, remonstrated against the perilous position which Sickles had taken the liberty to gain. He, however, intimated that, if desired, he would withdraw to the ridge which Meade had justly indicated as the proper place where our forces would be better protected, and would be able to cover Round Top, a point which it was considered essential to retain.

General Meade thereupon expressed his fear to Sickles that the enemy would not permit him quietly to retire from the trap in which he had placed his foot; and the last words had scarcely fallen from his lips, when the Rebel batteries were opened with fearful accuracy and at short range, and the infantry came on with their fierce charging yell. General Longstreet was in command.

With so long and strong lines of infantry in his front, which lapped over his flanks on either side, and a fearful enfilading fire from the heavy batteries on Seminary Hill, Sickles and his brave men were torn, shattered, overwhelmed, and with terrible loss and in great confusion, fell back to the ridge from which he ought not to have advanced. In the struggle the Rebels made a desperate attempt to reach and possess Round Top, which they came near doing before General Sykes, who had been ordered to advance and hold it, had gained the elevation. But their failure to possess this coveted prize proved a great disaster; for before they could withdraw their charging columns across the plain between Round Top and the ridge where Sickles stood at the beginning of the fray, they were attacked by General Hancock with a heavy force, and driven almost like chaff before the wind. Their loss was terrible. At the close of this encounter our lines stood precisely where General Meade desired they should be before the fight commenced, with Round Top fully in our possession and now strongly fortified with heavy artillery and good infantry support.

On our right General Ewell had succeeded in pushing back some portions of our lines under Slocum, who occupied Culp's Hill, and some of our fortified lines and rifle-pits were occupied by the Rebels. Night came on to close the dreadful day. Thus far the battle had been mostly in the advantage of the Rebels. They held the ground where Reynolds had fallen, also Seminary Ridge, and the elevation whence the Eleventh Corps had been driven.

They also occupied the ridge on which Sickles had commenced to fight. Sickles himself was *hors de combat*, with a shattered leg which had to be amputated, and not far from twenty thousand of our men had been killed, wounded, and captured! The Rebels had also lost heavily; but, as they themselves believed, they were the winners.

General Lee, in his official report, says:

> After a severe struggle, Longstreet succeeded in getting possession of and holding the desired ground. Ewell also carried some of the strong positions which he assailed; and the result was such as to lead to the belief that he would ultimately be able to dislodge the enemy. The battle ceased at dark. These partial suc-

cesses determined me to continue the assault next day.

During these days of deadly strife and of unprecedented slaughter, our cavalry was by no means idle. On the morning of the first, Kilpatrick advanced his victorious squadrons to the vicinity of Abbottstown, where they struck a force of Rebel cavalry, which they scattered, capturing several prisoners, and then rested. To the ears of the alert chieftain came the sound of battle at Gettysburg, accompanied with the intelligence, from prisoners mostly, that Stuart's main force was bent on doing mischief on the right of our infantry lines, which were not far from the night's bivouac.

He appeared instinctively to know where he was most needed; so in the absence of orders, early the next morning he advanced to Hunterstown. At this point were the extreme wings of the infantry lines, and as Kilpatrick expected, he encountered the Rebel cavalry, commanded by his old antagonists, Stuart, Lee, and Hampton. The early part of the day was spent mostly in reconnoitring; but all the latter part of the day was occupied in hard, bold, and bloody work.

Charges and counter-charges were made; the carbine, pistol, and sabre were used by turns, and the artillery thundered even late after the infantry around Gettysburg had sunk to rest, well-nigh exhausted with the bloody carnage of the weary day. But Stuart, who had hoped to break in upon our flank and rear, and to pounce upon our trains, was not only foiled in his endeavour by the gallant Kilpatrick, but also driven back upon his infantry supports, and badly beaten.

In the night, Kilpatrick, after leaving a sufficient force to prevent Stuart from doing any special damage on our right, swung around with the rest of his troopers to the left of our line, near Round Top, and was there prepared for any work which might be assigned him.

Friday, July 3.—The sun rose bright and warm upon the blackened corpses of the dead, which were strewn over the bloody earth; upon the wounded who had not been cared for, and upon long glistening lines of armed men ready to renew the conflict. Each antagonist, rousing every slumbering element of power, seemed to be resolved upon victory or death.

The Last Effort

The fight commenced early by an attack of General Slocum's men, who, determined to regain the rifle-pits they had lost the evening before, descended like an avalanche upon the foe. The attack met with a prompt response from General Ewell. But after several hours of desperate fighting, victory perched upon the Union banners, and with great loss and slaughter the Rebels were driven out of the breastworks, and fell back upon their main lines near Benner's Hill.

This successful move on the part of our boys in blue was followed by an ominous lull, or quiet, which continued about three hours. Meanwhile the silence was fitfully broken by an occasional spit of fire, while every preparation was being made for a last, supreme effort, which, it was expected, would decide the mighty contest. The scales were being poised for the last time, and upon the one side or the other was soon to be written the "*Mene, Mene, Tekel, Upharsin.*" Hearts either trembled or waxed strong in the awful presence of this responsibility.

At length one o'clock arrived; a signal-gun was fired, and then at least one hundred and twenty-five guns from Hill and Longstreet concentrated and crossed their fires upon Cemetery Hill, the centre and key of our position. Just behind this crest, though much exposed, were General Meade's headquarters. For nearly two hours this hill was ploughed and torn by solid shot and bursting shell, while about one hundred guns on our side, mainly from this crest and Round Top, made sharp response.

The earth and the air shook for miles around with the terrific concussion, which came no longer in volleys, but in a continual roar. So long and fearful a cannonade was never before witnessed on this continent. As the range was short and the aim accurate, the destruction was terrible. But the advantage was decidedly in favour of the Rebels, whose guns were superior in number to ours, and of heavier calibre, and had been concentrated for the attack. A spectator of the Union army thus describes the scene:

> The storm broke upon us so suddenly, that soldiers and officers—who leaped, as it began, from their tents, or from lazy *siestas* on the grass—were stricken in their rising with mortal wounds, and died, some with cigars between their teeth, some with pieces of food in their fingers, and one at least—a pale young German, from Pennsylvania—with a miniature of his sister in his hands. Horses fell, shrieking such awful cries as Cooper told of, and writhing themselves about in hopeless agony.
> The boards of fences, scattered by explosion, flew in splinters through the air the earth, torn up in clouds, blinded the eyes of hurrying men; and through the branches of trees and among

the gravestones of the cemetery a shower of destruction crashed ceaselessly. As, with hundreds of others, I groped through this tempest of death for the shelter of the bluff, an old man, a private in a company belonging to the Twenty-Fourth Michigan, was struck, scarcely ten feet away, by a cannon-ball, which tore through him, extorting such a low, intense cry of mortal pain as I pray God I may never again hear. The hill, which seemed alone devoted to this rain of death, was clear in nearly all its unsheltered places within five minutes after the fire began.

A correspondent from the Confederate Army thus describes this artillery contest:

> I have never yet heard such tremendous artillery-firing. The enemy must have had over one hundred guns, which, in addition to our one hundred and fifteen, made the air hideous with most discordant noise. The very earth shook beneath our feet, and the hills and rocks seemed to reel like a drunken man. For one hour and a half this most terrific fire was continued, during which time the shrieking of shell, the crash of fallen timbers, the fragments of rocks flying through the air, shattered from the cliffs by solid shot, the heavy mutterings from the valley between the opposing armies, the splash of bursting shrapnel, and the fierce neighing of wounded artillery-horses, made a picture terribly grand and sublime, but which my pen utterly fails to describe.

Gradually the fire on our side began to slacken, and General Meade, learning that our guns were becoming hot, gave orders to cease firing and to let the guns cool, though the Rebel balls were making fearful havoc among our gunners, while our infantry sought poor shelter behind every projection, anxiously awaiting the expected charge. At length the enemy, supposing that our guns were silenced, deemed that the moment for an irresistible attack had come.

Accordingly, as a lion emerges from his lair, he sallied forth, when strong lines of infantry, nearly three miles in length, with double lines of skirmishers in front, and heavy reserves in rear, advanced with desperation to the final effort. They moved with steady, measured tread over the plain below, and began the ascent of the hills occupied by our forces, concentrating somewhat upon General Hancock, though stretching across our entire front.

Says a correspondent of the *Richmond Enquirer*:

Just as Pickett was getting well under the enemy's fire, our batteries ceased firing. This was a fearful moment for Pickett and his brave command. Why do not our guns reopen their fire? is the inquiry that rises upon every lip. Still, our batteries are silent as death! And this undoubtedly decided the issue—was God's handwriting on the wall. The Rebel guns had been thundering so long and ceaselessly that they were now unfit for use, and ceased firing from very necessity.

"Agate," correspondent of *The Cincinnati Gazette*, gives the following graphic description of the struggle:

> The great, desperate, final charge came at four. The Rebels seemed to have gathered up all their strength and desperation for one fierce, convulsive effort, that should sweep over and wash out our obstinate resistance. They swept up as before: the flower of their army to the front, victory staked upon the issue. In some places they literally lifted up and pushed back our lines; but, that terrible position of ours!—wherever they entered it, enfilading fires from half a score of crests swept away their columns like merest chaff. Broken and hurled back, they easily fell into our hands; and, on the centre and left, the last half hour brought more prisoners than all the rest.
>
> So it was along the whole line; but it was on the Second Corps that the flower of the Rebel army was concentrated; it was there that the heaviest shock beat upon, and shook, and even sometimes crumbled, our lines.
>
> We had some shallow rifle-pits, with barricades of rails from the fences. The Rebel line, stretching away miles to the left, in magnificent array, but strongest here—Pickett's splendid division of Longstreet's corps in front, the best of A. P. Hill's veterans in support—came steadily, and as it seemed resistlessly, sweeping up. Our skirmishers retired slowly from the Emmitsburg road, holding their ground tenaciously to the last. The Rebels reserved their fire till they reached this same Emmitsburg road, then opened with a terrific crash. From a hundred iron throats, meantime, their artillery had been thundering on our barricades.
>
> Hancock was wounded; Gibbon succeeded to the command—an approved soldier, and ready for the crisis. As the tempest of fire approached its height, he walked along the line, and re-

newed his orders to the men to reserve their fire. The Rebels—three lines deep—came steadily up. They were in point-blank range.

At last the order came! From thrice six thousand guns there came a sheet of smoky flame, a crash, a rush of leaden death. The line literally melted away; but there came the second, resistless still. It had been our supreme effort; on the moment we were not equal to another.

Up to the rifle-pits, across them, over the barricades—the momentum of their charge, the mere machine-strength of their combined action, swept them on. Our thin line could fight, but it had not weight enough to oppose to this momentum. It was pushed behind the guns. Right on came the Rebels. They were upon our guns—were bayoneting the gunners—were waving their flags over our pieces.

But they had penetrated to the fatal point. A storm of grape and canister tore its way from man to man, and marked its track with corpses straight down their line! They had exposed themselves to the enfilading fire of the guns on the western slope of Cemetery Hill; that exposure sealed their fate.

The line reeled back—disjointed already—in an instant in fragments. Our men were just behind the guns. They leaped forward upon the disordered mass; but there was little need of fighting now. A regiment threw down its arms, and, with colours at its head, rushed over and surrendered. All along the field smaller detachments did the same. Webb's brigade brought in eight hundred: taken in as little time as it requires to write the simple sentence that tells it. Gibbon's old division took fifteen stand of colours.

Over the fields the escaped fragments of the charging line fell back—the battle there was over. A single brigade, Harrow's (of which the Seventh Michigan is part), came out with fifty four less officers, and seven hundred and ninety-three less men, than it took in! So the whole corps fought; so, too they fought farther down the line.

It was fruitless sacrifice. They gathered up their broken fragments, formed their lines, and slowly marched away. It was not a rout; it was a bitter, crushing defeat. For once the Army of the Potomac had won a clean, honest, acknowledged victory.

General Pickett's division was nearly annihilated. One of his officers recounted, that, as they were charging over the grassy plain, he threw himself down before a murderous discharge of grape and canister, which mowed the grass and men all around him, as though a scythe had been swung just above his prostrate form.

During the terrific cannonade and subsequent charges, our ammunition and other trains had been parked in rear of Round Top, which gave them splendid shelter. Partly to possess this train, but mainly to secure this commanding position, General Longstreet sent two strong divisions of infantry, with heavy artillery, to turn our flank, and to drive us from this ground. Kilpatrick, with his division, which had been strengthened by Merritt's Regular brigade, was watching this point, and waiting for an opportunity to strike the foe. It came at last. Emerging from the woods in front of him came a strong battle-line followed by others.

Death of General Farnsworth

To the young Farnsworth was committed the task of meeting infantry with cavalry in an open field. Placing the Fifth New York in support of Elder's battery, which was exposed to a galling fire, but made reply with characteristic rapidity, precision, and slaughter, Farnsworth quickly ordered the First Virginia, First Vermont, and Eighteenth Pennsylvania in line of battle, and galloped away and charged upon the flank of the advancing columns.

The attack was sharp, brief, and successful, though attended with great slaughter. But the Rebels were driven upon their main lines, and the flank movement was prevented. Thus the cavalry added another dearly-earned laurel to its chaplet of honour—dearly earned, because many of their bravest champions fell upon that bloody field.

Kilpatrick, in his official report of this sanguinary contest, says:

> In this charge fell the brave Farnsworth. Short and brilliant was his career. On the twenty-ninth of June a general; on the first of July he baptized his star in blood; and on the third, for the honour of his young brigade and the glory of his corps, he yielded up his noble life.

Thus ended the Battle of Gettysburg—the bloody turning-point of the Rebellion—the bloody baptism of the redeemed Republic. Nearly twenty thousand men from the Union ranks had been killed and wounded, and a larger number of the Rebels, making the enormous aggregate of at least forty thousand, whose blood was shed to fertilize the Tree of Liberty.

In the evening twilight of that eventful day General Meade penned the following interesting despatch to the government:

Headquarters Army of the Potomac,
Near Gettysburg, July 3, 8.30 p. m.

To Major-General Halleck, General-in-Chief:

The enemy opened at one o'clock p. m., from about one hundred and fifty guns. They concentrated upon my left centre, continuing without intermission for about three hours, at the expiration of which time he assaulted my left centre twice, being, upon both occasions, handsomely repulsed with severe loss to them, leaving in our hands nearly three thousand prisoners. Among the prisoners are Major-General Armistead, and many colonels and officers of lesser note. The enemy left many dead upon the field, and a large number of wounded in our hands. The loss upon our side has been considerable. Major-General Hancock and Brigadier-General Gibbon were wounded.

After the repelling of the assault, indications leading to the belief that the enemy might be withdrawing, an armed reconnaissance was pushed forward from the left, and the enemy found to be in force. At the present hour all is quiet.

The New York cavalry have been engaged all day on both flanks of the enemy, harassing and vigorously attacking him with great success, notwithstanding they encountered superior numbers, both of cavalry and artillery. The army is in fine spirits.

George G. Meade,
Major-General Commanding

On the morning of the Fourth of July, General Meade issued an address to the army:

Headquarters Army of the Potomac,
Near Gettysburg, July 4.

The commanding general, in behalf of the country, thanks the Army of the Potomac for the glorious result of the recent operations. Our enemy, superior in numbers and flushed with the pride of a successful invasion, attempted to overcome or destroy this army. Utterly baffled and defeated, he has now withdrawn from the contest.

The privations and fatigues the army has endured, and the heroic courage and gallantry it has displayed, will be matters of history to be ever remembered.

Our task is not yet accomplished, and the commanding general looks to the army for greater efforts, to drive from our soil every vestige of the presence of the invader.

It is right and proper that we should, on suitable occasions, return our grateful thanks to the Almighty Disposer of events, that, in the goodness of His providence. He has thought fit to give victory to the cause of the just.

By command of   Major-General Meade.
S. Williams, A. A.-General.

It is fitting we should close this chapter with President Lincoln's brief yet comprehensive announcement to the country:

Washington, D. C, July 4, 1803, 10 a. m.
The President of the United States announces to the country, that the news from the Army of the Potomac, up to ten o'clock p. m. of the third, is such as to cover the army with the highest honour—to promise great success to the cause of the Union—and to claim the condolence of all for the many gallant fallen; and that for this he especially desires that on this day, "He whose will, not ours, should ever be done," be everywhere remembered and reverenced with the profoundest gratitude.

Abraham Lincoln.

CHAPTER 13

Retreat of the Rebels from Gettysburg

The victory at Gettysburg, though purchased at so dear a price, when announced to the people, produced a deep and widespread joy, which contributed to make the Fourth of July doubly memorable. The gallant behaviour of our men furnished a theme for general exultation, and the removal of the threatened disaster foreshadowed in the pompous and successful invasion, made every true American breathe more freely.

But the work of the soldier was not yet done. The feet of the invaders were still upon free soil; and though his ranks had been thinned by desertions, and by unprecedented casualties in battle, and he had been thwarted in all the important *minutiæ* of his plan, he was still formidable, and compelled to fight with desperation, if attacked, to prevent utter destruction.

Some apprehension that the enemy was at least contemplating a speedy retreat was entertained during the night that followed the third bloody day. General Pleasonton, chief of cavalry, urged General Meade to advance in force upon the beaten foe, alleging that they were not only greatly weakened by their losses, but undoubtedly demoralised, in consequence of repulse and probable scarcity of ammunition. To ascertain positively what could be of these probabilities, Pleasonton was directed to make a reconnaissance toward the Rebel rear.

Accordingly, several detachments of cavalry were thrust out on different roads, where they rode all night. General Gregg, on our right, went about twenty-two miles on the road to Chambersburg, and returning early on the morning of the fourth, reported that the road was strewn with wounded and stragglers, ambulances and caissons, and general *débris*, which indicated that the enemy was retreating as rapidly as possible, and was passing through a terrible season of demoralisation.

The testimony of the mute witnesses of disaster was corroborated by that of the many prisoners which easily fell into Gregg's hands. Other expeditions, returning later in the day, had similar reports to render of what they had seen and heard. And now came the time for energetic cavalry movements. While our infantry was resting, or engaged in burying our own and the Rebel dead within our lines, the cavalry was despatched to do all possible damage to the retreating and demoralised Confederate columns.

Kilpatrick, having assembled his old and oft-tried division on the plain at the foot of Round Top, on the morning of the fourth, discoursed to them eloquently for a few moments on the interests of the times. He assured his men that their noble deeds were not passing by unnoticed, nor would they be unrequited, and that they were already a part of a grand history. He trusted that their future conduct would be a fair copy of the past. But his pathetic and patriotic accents had scarcely died upon the ear of his brave command, when the shrill bugle-blast brought eager men and grazing horses in line of march. Orders had been received by Kilpatrick to repair as swiftly as possible to the passes in the Catoctin Mountains, to intercept the enemy now known to be flying southward at a rapid rate.

The command had gone but a short distance when rain began to fall in torrents, as is usually the case after great battles, especially when artillery of heavy calibre is used. But through mud, in places to the horses' bodies, through brooks swollen enormously, and through the falling floods, the troopers pressed forward to the accomplishment of their task. About five o'clock p. m. Kilpatrick reached Emmitsburg, where he was joined by portions of General Gregg's command, including the Harris Light, which had been kept mostly in reserve during the conflicts of the past few days. Thus re-enforced, this intrepid leader marched directly towards the Monterey Pass, arriving at the foot of this rocky defile in the mountains in the midst of pitchy darkness.

As was anticipated, a heavy Rebel train was then trying to make its escape through the gorge, guarded by Stuart's Cavalry, with light artillery. This artillery was planted in a position to rake the narrow road upon which Kilpatrick was advancing. But the darkness was so intense that the guns could be of little use, except to make the night terribly hideous with their bellowings, the echoes of which reverberated in the mountain gorges in a most frightful manner.

To add to the horrors of the scene and position, the rain fell in floods, accompanied with groaning thunders, while lightnings flashed from cloud to cloud over our heads, and cleft the darkness only to leave friend and foe enveloped in greater darkness in the intervals of light. By these flashes, however, we gained a momentary glimpse of each other's position, and as we dashed forward in the gloom, we were further directed by the fire of the artillery and the desultory fire of the cavalry.

Surgeon Moore gives the following account of this affair:

> We do not hesitate in saying, and have good reason to know, that had any want of firmness on the part of the leader, or any indecision or vacillation appeared, and a mischance occurred, this splendid command would then and there have been lost.
>
> But with unflinching and steady purpose, bold bearing, and a mind equal to the emergency, the general rode to the head of the column, reassured his frightened people, and, notwithstanding the intense darkness that hid friend from foe, made such skilful dispositions, and then attacked the hidden foe with such impetuosity that he fled in wild dismay, leaving his guns, a battle-flag, and four hundred prisoners in the victor's hands.
>
> The pass was gained, and Pennington's and Elder's guns were soon echoing and re-echoing through the mountain defiles. The artillery opened thus on the flying columns of the routed foe, who, with wagons, ambulances, caissons, and the *débris* of a shattered army, were rushing in chaotic confusion down the narrow mountain road, and scattering through the fields and woods on the plains below.

All night long Kilpatrick and his successful followers were gathering the spoils of their evening work. Wagon after wagon was overtaken, captured, and destroyed, while hundreds of prisoners were easily captured. This daring exploit placed Kilpatrick in advance of the Rebel army, giving him a fine opportunity to obstruct their pathway of retreat, and to destroy whatever could be of any use to them. Had he not been cumbered with so many prisoners, it is not in the power of anyone to estimate the damage he would have done. In his official report he says:

> On this day I captured eighteen hundred and sixty prisoners,

including many officers of rank, and destroyed the Rebel General Ewell's immense wagon-train, nine miles long.

It should be stated that these wagons were mostly laden with the ripened and gathered crops of Pennsylvania and Maryland, and with the plunder of private and public stores, including dry goods and groceries of every variety and quality. None who saw it will ever forget the appearance of that mountain road the day following this night's foray.

Stuart, who was ingloriously defeated at Monterey, retired towards Emmitsburg with about fifty prisoners that he had captured during and after the fight. He then moved southward until he struck an unfrequented road which leads over the mountain *via* Wolfe's Tavern. By this turn he avoided immediate contact with our cavalry. But about five o'clock p. m., as he was about to debouch into the valley, Kilpatrick, who was watching for him as a cat does a mouse, attacked him with artillery and fought him till dark. This fight occurred near Smithburg, whence the prisoners in Kilpatrick's hands were sent to South Mountain, guarded by the Harris Light.

Darkness having put an end to the contest, Kilpatrick marched through Cavetown to Boonsboro', where he bivouacked for the night. Stuart, it was ascertained, marched till about midnight to the small town of Leitersburgh, where he rested his worn and wearied command. His condition was really pitiable.

A large number of his men were mounted on shoeless horses, whose leanness showed that they had made many a long march through and from Virginia. Or, as was the case with a large proportion of them, they had fat horses, which were stolen from the fields and stalls of the invaded States, but, being entirely unused to such hard and cruel treatment as they were now receiving, were well-nigh unserviceable. Lameness and demoralisation were prominent characteristics among animals and men.

July 6—This morning, at an early hour, Kilpatrick's crowd of prisoners were turned over into the hands of General French, and then his command marched to Hagerstown, taking possession of the place in advance of Stuart, whose approach about eleven o'clock was met with determined resistance, and, at first, with great success. A heavy battle was fought, in which Kilpatrick's men showed their usual prowess and strength. Had not Rebel infantry come to the aid of his cavalry, Stuart would have suffered a stunning blow. For several hours the contest was wholly between cavalry and light artillery. Charges of great daring and skill were made. One reporter says:

> Elder gave them grape and canister, and the Fifth New York sabres, while the First Vermont used their carbines.

In one of those charges, made in the face of a very superior force, Captain James A. Penfield, of the Fifth New York, at the head of his company, had his horse killed under him, and, while struggling to extricate himself from the animal, which lay upon him in part, he was struck a fearful blow of a sabre on the head, which came near severing it in twain. Thus wounded, with blood streaming down upon his long beard and clothes, he was made a prisoner. In a similar charge the gallant Captain Ulric Dahlgren lost a leg, though not his valuable life.

It appeared as though the Rebels were afforded an opportunity to avenge themselves in part for the shameful losses which they had sustained in this very place by the strategic operations of a Union scout, by the name of C. A. Phelps, during the incipient step of the invasion. We will let the scout relate his own story, which is corroborated by a signal-officer, who, from one of the lofty peaks of the mountains, witnessed the exciting denouement. The scout proceeds to say:

> I was very anxious to learn all about General Stuart's force and contemplated movements, and resolved to see the general himself or some of his staff-officers, soon after he entered Hagerstown.
> Accordingly I procured of a Union man a suit of raglings, knocked off one boot-heel to make one leg appear shorter than the other, and put a gimblet, a tow-string, and an old broken jack-knife in my pockets. My jewellery corresponded with my clothes. I adopted the name of George Fry, a harvest-hand of Dr. Farney, from Wolfetown, on the north side of the mountain, and I was a cripple from rheumatism.
> Having completed arrangements with Dr. Farney, Mr. Landers, and other Union men, that they might be of service to me in case the Rebels should be suspicious of my character, I hobbled away on my perilous journey, and entered the city by leaping the high stone wall which guards it on the north side near the depot. This occurred just as the town-clock struck one.
> It was a clear, starlight night, and the glistening sabres of the sentries could be seen as they walked their lonely beat. Scarcely had I gained the sidewalk leading to the centre of the town

when the sentry nearest me cried, 'Halt! who goes there?'
'A friend,' I replied.
'A friend to North or South?'
'To the South, of course, and all right.'
'Advance, then,' was the response. On reaching him, he asked me what could be my business at this hour of the night. I told him I had come in to see our brave boys, who could whip the Yankees so handsomely, as they had done especially at Bull Run and Chancellorsville. We tell at once to the discussion of the war-questions of the day.
In the midst of our colloquy up came the officer of the guard on his 'grand rounds,' who, after probing me thoroughly, as he thought, with many questions, finally said, 'Had you not better go with me to see General Stuart?'
'I should reelly like ter git a sight of the gin'ral,' I quickly replied, 'for I never seen a reel gin'ral in all my life.'
I was soon in the presence of the general, who received me very cordially. I found him to be a man a little above the medium height, and fine looking. His features are very distinct in outline, his nose long and sharp, his eye keen and restless. His complexion is florid and his manners affable. I told him who I was and where I lived when at home.
'Wolfetown!' exclaimed the general, 'have not the Yankees a large wagon-train there?' I told him they had; and then, turning to one of his staff-officers, he said, 'I must have it; it would be a fine prize.'
I noted his words and determined, if I possessed any Yankee wit, to make use of it on this occasion,
'Gin'ral,' said I, '*you all* don't think of capterin' them are Yankee wagons, do you?'
'Why not? I have here five thousand cavalry and sixteen pieces of artillery, and I understand the train is lightly guarded.'
I saw that he had been properly informed, and I told him they came there last evening with twelve big brass cannon and three regiments of foot-soldiers, and if he was to try to go through the gap of the mountain they would shoot all the cannon off right in the gap, and kill all his horses and men. The general smiled at my naive answer, and said I had a strange idea of war if I thought so many men would be killed at once, and added that I would not be a very brave soldier, I replied that many

times I had felt like going into the Confederate Army, but my rheumatism kept me out.

After a while the general concluded not to try the train, and I was heartily glad, for he would have taken at least two hundred wagons easily, as they were guarded by not more than three hundred men.

He then gave orders to have the main body of his cavalry move towards Green Castle; and I distinctly heard him give orders to the major to remain in town with fifty men as rearguard, and to send on the army mail, which was expected there about six the next evening. I made up my mind that it would be a small mail he would get, as I proposed to myself to be postmaster for once.

After seeing the general and his cavalry move out of town, I went directly for my horse, which I had concealed in a safe place some distance from the city, meanwhile surveying the ground to see which way I could best come in to capture the mail, and determined to charge the place on the pike from Boonsboro', and made my arrangements to that effect.

I got a Union man, by the name of Thornburgh, to go into the town and notify the Union people that, when the town-clock struck six p. m., I would charge in and capture the Rebel mail, at the risk of losing my own life and every man with me. I had now but eight men, two having been sent to General Stahel with despatches.

I then returned to Boonsboro', and found my men waiting for me. I told them my intentions, and offered to send back to his regiment any man who feared to go with me. But everyone bravely said he would not leave me, nor surrender without my order. I then ordered them to bring out their horses, and we were soon on the road.

It was a moment of thrilling interest to us all, as we approached Hagerstown, and lingered to hear the signal-strokes of that monitor in the old church-tower. At the appointed time (we had already entered into the edge of the town), with a wild shout we dashed into the streets, and the major and his fifty braves fled without firing a shot.

We captured sixteen prisoners, twenty-six horses, several small-arms, and a heavy army mail, which contained three important despatches from Jeff. Davis, and two from the Rebel Secretary of War to General Lee. All this substantial booty we safely carried within our own lines, without the loss of a man or a horse.

Many thanks are due to Dr. C. R. Doran and Mr. Robert Thornburgh, for their kind and timely assistance, and also to Misses Susie Carson and Addie Brenner, who did so much for the comfort of our brave men. I still have in my possession some choice flowers, preserved from a bouquet presented to me by Miss Carson the evening we captured the Rebel mail; and though the flowers have faded, the good deeds done by the giver will ever grow bright through coming time.

All honour to the brave Union ladies.

In these same streets, where Captain Briggs with his telescope witnessed the successful charge of the scouting party, raged the battle hotly on the sixth of July. But, as the Rebel infantry was advancing with heavy artillery to the aid of Stuart's cavalry, Kilpatrick was sorely pressed, and, at length, compelled to retire. His ears were now saluted with the sound of artillery in the direction of Williamsport, and a messenger arrived with the intelligence that General John Buford, who had advanced through the South Mountain Pass, was now attempting to destroy Lee's immense supply train, which was packed near Williamsport, and not very heavily guarded.

Kilpatrick desired no better work than to assist his brave comrade, and he at once hastened down the main road, and soon joined Buford in the work of destruction. These combined commands were making fearful havoc in the Rebel commissary and quartermaster stores. Many wagons were burned, and the whole train would have shared the same fate had not the united infantry and cavalry of the enemy come down upon us in overwhelming force.

But we were not to be driven away very suddenly nor cheaply. Long and desperately we contended with the accumulating forces, until darkness came on, when we found ourselves completely enveloped by the foe. Nothing but splendid generalship and true bravery on the part of our officers and men saved us from capture and destruction. Some of our number were made prisoners, but our losses were very small considering the amount of depredations we had committed, and the great danger to which we were exposed.

As it was, the commands were successfully withdrawn from their hazardous position, and through the darkness of the night we crossed

Antietam Creek, and bivouacked in safety on the opposite bank. Several prisoners were captured from the Rebels during the fights of the day. They were mostly from Alabama and Louisiana regiments; and they state that their army is all together, and well on its way to the river. They speak doubtfully of Lee's recrossing the Potomac.

July 7.—Our cavalry is in the vicinity of Boonsboro', and is acting mostly on the defensive. The enemy in force is in our front, and an attack is momentarily expected. At six p. m. "to horse" was sounded throughout our camps; and, after waiting two hours in rain, ready for a move, orders were received to return to our quarters. Rain is now falling in torrents, accompanied with fearful thunderings and lightnings.

Unpleasant as it is, we welcome its peltings, hoping that the storm will raise the Potomac above the fording mark, and thus give Meade an opportunity to attack Lee before he has time to recross the river into Virginia. We know that his pontoons at Falling Waters have been totally destroyed by our cavalry and by the high water, and that the only ford available is at Williamsport, and hence we welcome the falling floods. Many of us have to lie down in water, which, however, is not very cold. But the night is very tedious

July 8.—The sun came out bright and warm this morning, enabling us in a few moments to dry our drenched blankets and garments. The roads, however, abound in mud, and the streams are enormously swollen. Early in the day our pickets were driven in along the Antietam, and the enemy advanced with such force that by noon the plains around Boonsboro' were the scene of a furious cavalry engagement.

CAVALRY BATTLE AT BOONSBORO'

Dr. Moore, from whose excellent reports we have before quoted, gives the following graphic description of this cavalry duel

> Buford had the right and Kilpatrick the left. The movements of the cavalry lines in this battle were among the finest sights the author remembers ever to have seen. It was here he first saw the young general (Kilpatrick), and little thought that one day the deeds he saw him perform he would transmit to paper and to posterity. Here, all day long, the Rebel and the Union cavalry-chiefs fought, mounted and dismounted, and striving in every manner possible to defeat and rout the other.
> The din and roar of battle that, from ten a. m. until long after dark, had rolled over the plains and back through the moun-

tains, told to the most anxious generals of them all, Meade and Lee, how desperate was the struggle—Stuart and his men fighting for the safety of the Rebel army, Buford and Kilpatrick for South Mountain's narrow Pass.

Just as the setting sun sent his last rays over that muddy battlefield, Buford and Kilpatrick were seen rapidly approaching each other from opposite directions.

They met; a few hasty words were exchanged, and away dashed Buford far off to the right, and Kilpatrick straight to the centre; and in less than twenty minutes, from right to centre, and from centre to left, the clear notes of the bugles rang out the welcome charging, and with one long, wild shout, those glorious squadrons of Buford and Kilpatrick, from right to left, as far as the eye could see, in one unbroken line, charged upon the foe. The shock was irresistible; the Rebel line was broken—the routed enemy confessed the superiority of our men as they fled from the well-fought field, leaving their dead and dying behind them; and our heroic chiefs led back their victorious squadrons, and, while resting on their laurels, gave their brave, wearied troops a momentary repose.

Thus far our cavalry had done much to obstruct the retreat of the Rebel army, and had inflicted incalculable losses of men and materials. But the pursuit of our main army was not correspondingly vigorous. Two pretty good reasons may be assigned for this seeming incompetency or want of energy. The first reason is found in the fact that scarcely more than a brigade of infantry had been kept in reserve during the great and destructive battle of Gettysburg, while the three days of struggle had well-nigh exhausted our entire strength.

Rest was therefore greatly needed, and a general engagement was to be guarded against. It should also be remembered that nearly one fourth of our entire army was *hors de combat*. The second reason may be found in the heavy rains which fell, "impeding pursuers," as one writer says, "more than pursued, though they need not." But the retreating army has this advantage; it usually chooses its own route, which it can generally cover or hide by means of stratagem, so that it requires time as well as study to effectually pursue. Perhaps a third reason for our tardiness of pursuit should be presented.

Does it not appear to be an overruling act of Providence? Had General Meade advanced, as it seems he might have done with the resources at his command, against the demoralised, decimated, and flying army, with its ammunition quite exhausted, and a swollen river, unfordable and bridgeless, between it and safety, Lee could not have escaped annihilation. But the public sentiment of the country, though forming and improving rapidly, was not yet prepared for such a victory. We needed to spend more treasure, spill more blood, sacrifice more precious lives, to lift us up to those heights of public and political virtue, where we could be safely entrusted with so dear a boon. We were not then prepared for peace, that sovereign balm for a nation's woes.

The tardiness with which our movements were made enabled the enemy to reach a good position near Hagerstown, which he began to fortify in such a manner as to cover his crossing. Meantime we understood that successful efforts were made to rebuild the bridge at Falling Waters.

General Meade, in his official report, gives the following account of his pursuit:

> The fifth and sixth of July were employed in succouring the wounded and burying the dead. Major-General Sedgwick, commanding the Sixth Corps, having pushed the pursuit of the enemy as far as the Fairfield Pass and the mountains, and reporting that the pass was very strong—one in which a small force of the enemy could hold in check and delay for a considerable time any pursuing force—I determined to follow the enemy by a flank movement, and, accordingly, leaving McIntosh's brigade of cavalry and Neil's brigade of infantry to continue harassing the enemy, I put the army in motion for Middletown, and orders were immediately sent to Major-General French, at Frederick, to reoccupy Harper's Ferry, and send a force to occupy Turner's Pass, in South Mountains.
>
> I subsequently ascertained that Major-General French had not only anticipated these orders in part, but had pushed a cavalry force to Williamsport and Falling Waters, where they destroyed the enemy's pontoon bridge, and captured its guard. Buford was at the same time sent to Williamsport and Hagerstown. The duty above assigned to the cavalry was most successfully accomplished, the enemy being greatly harassed, his trains destroyed, and many captures of guns and prisoners made.
>
> *July 10.*—This morning, at five o'clock, the cavalry advanced from Boonsboro', passed through Keedysville, and crossed the Antietam

about ten o'clock. At twelve o'clock we engaged the enemy at Jones' Cross Roads. The Harris Light led the advance, dismounted. The Rebels were driven three consecutive times from as many positions which they had chosen. Their resistance was by no means strong nor determined. Before night Buford moved his command to Sharpsburg, on the extreme left of our lines, and Kilpatrick advanced to a position on the extreme right, in the vicinity of Hagerstown, where he covered the road to Gettysburg.

On the eleventh only picket skirmishes occupied the time. But on the twelfth Kilpatrick, supported by a brigade of infantry under the command of Brigadier-General Ames, of Howard's Corps, advanced upon the enemy near Hagerstown, drove them from their works, and then out of the streets of the city, and took permanent possession. This successful movement greatly contracted our lines, and brought our forces into a better position. At the close of this enterprise, as we are informed, General Meade called a council of war, at which was discussed earnestly and long the propriety of attacking the enemy.

Notwithstanding the anxiety of the chief commander to advance and reap fully the fruit of Gettysburg, five of his corps commanders, out of eight, argued against the measure, and as Meade did not desire to assume the grave responsibility of a movement against such protests, no move was immediately attempted.

This statement may modify the condemnatory judgments which were formed against General Meade, and may prepare our minds rightly to interpret General A. P. Howe's report of the general pursuit. In narrating its spirit and progress, he says:

> On the fourth of July it seemed evident enough that the enemy were retreating. How far they were gone we could not see from the front. We could see but a comparatively small force from the position where I was. On Sunday the Fifth and Sixth Corps moved in pursuit. As we moved, a small rearguard of the enemy retreated. We followed them, with this small rearguard of the enemy before us, up to Fairfield, in a gorge of the mountains. There we again waited for them to go on. There seemed to be no disposition to push this rearguard when we got up to Fairfield. A lieutenant from the enemy came into our lines and gave himself up.
>
> He was a Northern Union man, in service in one of the Georgia regiments; and, without being asked, he unhesitatingly told

me, when I met him as he was being brought in, that he belonged to the artillery of the rearguard of the enemy, and that they had but two rounds of ammunition with the rearguard. But we waited there without receiving any orders to attack.

It was a place where, as I informed General Sedgwick, we could easily attack the enemy with advantage. But no movement was made by us until the enemy went away. Then one brigade of my division, with some cavalry, was sent to follow after them, while the remainder of the Sixth Corps moved to the left. We moved on through Boonsboro', and passed up on the pike-road leading to Hagerstown.

After passing Boonsboro' it became my turn to lead the Sixth Corps. That day, just before we started. General Sedgwick ordered me to move on and take up the best position I could over a little stream on the Frederick side of Funkstown. As I moved on, it was suggested to me by him to move carefully. 'Don't come into contact with the enemy; we don't want to bring on a general engagement.'

It seemed to be the current impression that it was not desired to bring on a general engagement. I moved on until we came near Funkstown. General Buford was along that way with his cavalry. I had passed over the stream referred to, and found a strong position, which I concluded to take, and wait for the Sixth Corps to come up.

In the meantime General Buford, who was in front, came back to me, and said, 'I am pretty hardly engaged here; I have used a great deal of my ammunition; it is a strong place in front; it is an excellent position.'

It was a little farther out than I was—near Funkstown. He said, 'I have used a great deal of my ammunition, and I ought to go to the right; suppose you move up there, or send up a brigade, or even a part of one, and hold that position.'

Said I, 'I will do so at once, if I can just communicate with General Sedgwick; I am ordered to take up a position over here, and hold it, and the intimation conveyed to me was, that they did not want to get into a general engagement; I will send for General Sedgwick, and ask permission to hold that position, and relieve you.'

I accordingly sent a staff-officer to General Sedgwick with a request that I might go up at once and assist General Buford, stating that he had a strong position, but his ammunition was giving out. General Buford remained with me until I should get an answer. The answer was, 'No; we do not want to bring on a general engagement.'

'Well,' said I, 'Buford, what can I do?'

He said, 'they expect me to go farther to the right; my ammunition is pretty much out. That position is a strong one, and we ought not to let it go.'

I sent down again to General Sedgwick, stating the condition of General Buford, and that he would have to leave unless he could get some assistance; that his position was not far in front, and that it seemed to me that we should hold it, and I should like to send some force up to picket it at least.

After a time I got a reply that, if General Buford left, I might occupy the position. General Buford was still with me, and I said to him, 'If you go away from there I will have to hold it.'

'That's all right,' said he, 'I will go away.' He did so, and I moved right up. It was a pretty good position when you cover your troops. Soon after relieving Buford, we saw some Rebel infantry advancing. I do not know whether they brought them from Hagerstown, or from some other place. They made three dashes, not in heavy force, upon our line to drive us back. The troops that happened to be there on our line were what we considered, in the Army of the Potomac, unusually good ones. They quietly repulsed the Rebels twice, and the third time they came up they sent them flying into Funkstown.

Yet there was no permission to move on and follow up the enemy. We remained there some time, until we had orders to move on and take a position a mile or more nearer Hagerstown. As we moved up we saw that the Rebels had some light fieldworks—hurriedly thrown up, apparently—to cover themselves while they recrossed the river. I think we remained there three days; and the third night, I think, after we got up into that position, it was said the Rebels recrossed the river.

Sunday, July 12.—I had the misfortune to be kicked off my pins last night, just before we were relieved at the front. Approaching my sorrel pony from the rear, in a careless manner—for he could not see me until I got within short range—he raised his heels very suddenly, and, without ceremony, planted them in my breast, laying me, not in the most gentle manner, flat upon the ground. Medical aid is considered necessary today, as I am suffering not a little. But, as the accident was purely the result of my own folly, I hope to endure my pains with becoming patience.

Today I found the following despatches in some Northern paper, and I record them to show what contradictory reports will often find their way into the public press concerning men and measures:

> Mountain-House, near Boonsboro' July 9.
> There has been no fighting this morning. The fight of yesterday, near Boonsboro,' was between Generals Buford and Kilpatrick's cavalry and Rebel infantry, principally on the bushwhacking style. Our troops fell back early in the day, but subsequently reoccupied the ground. Artillery was most effectually used on both sides in this engagement.
> There is no truth in the reported death of General Kilpatrick.

> Boonsboro' July 9, 8 p. m.
> There have been no active operations on our front today. After the cavalry fight of yesterday the enemy drew in their forces towards Hagerstown, and formed a line on elevated ground from Funkstown on the right to the bend of the river below Williamsport on the left, thus uncovering the Shepherdstown crossing. Scouts and reconnoitring parties report that Lee is entrenching his front and drawing from his train on the Virginia side, and making general preparations for another battle. It is contradicted, tonight, that we have a force on General Lee's line of retreat in Virginia.

July 13.—All has been quiet along our lines today. The army, being pretty well rested by this time, is waiting impatiently for the command to advance. Our position is also a good one, though not better than that of the enemy. We have every reason to believe that the Rebel army is still on the north bank of the Potomac. The recent rains have raised the river above the fording mark. However, Lee will undoubtedly fall back into Virginia if he finds a good opportunity. During the latter part of the day General Meade finally decided to assault the position of the invaders.

FALLING WATERS

Very much to the delight of the rank and file of the army, orders were promulgated to the effect that a strong and simultaneous advance must be made early on the morning of the fourteenth. Preparations were immediately begun.

Kilpatrick and his cavalry were sent out on picket, and advanced as near the enemy's lines as it was prudent. Not many hours of the night had passed away when Kilpatrick discovered certain movements which indicated that the enemy was leaving his front. Prepared as he was to attack them by the morning light, he was ready to follow up any movement which they might make. Hence, at three o'clock on the morning of the fourteenth, his advance-guard moved forward upon the retiring enemy.

While information of this unexpected movement of the enemy was despatched to General Meade, Kilpatrick advanced towards Williamsport with his usual rapidity and power, driving and capturing everything before him. Informed by citizens that the rearguard of the retreating army had but a few moments before started from the river, he followed closely in their tracks, and struck them at Falling Waters, where, after a brilliant and sharp conflict, he bagged a large number of prisoners. Many a poor fellow never reached the long-looked-for Virginia shore.

General Meade then sent the following despatch to Washington:

Headquarters Army of the Potomac,
July 14, 3 p. m.

H. W. Halleck, General-in-Chief:
My cavalry now occupy Falling Waters, having overtaken and captured a brigade of infantry, fifteen hundred strong, two guns, two caissons, two battle-flags, and a large number of small-arms. The enemy are all across the Potomac.

George G. Meade, Major-General.

Later in the day he sent the following:

Headquarters Army of the Potomac,
July 14, 8.30 p. m.

Major-General Halleck, General-in-Chief:
My cavalry have captured five hundred prisoners, in addition to those previously reported. General Pettigrew, of the Confederate army, was killed this morning in the attack on the enemy's rearguard. His body is in our hands.

G. G. Meade, Major-General.

These despatches were afterward denied by General Lee in a letter to his authorities, as follows:

> Headquarters Army of Northern Virginia,
> July ,1803.
>
> *General S. Cooper, Adjutant and Inspector-General C. S. A.:*
>
> General: I have seen in the Northern papers what purports to be an official despatch from General Meade, stating that he had captured a brigade of infantry, two pieces of artillery, two caissons, and a large number of small-arms, as this army retired to the south bank of the Potomac on the thirteenth and fourteenth instant.
>
> This despatch has been copied into the Richmond papers; and, as its official character may cause it to be believed, I desire to state that it is incorrect. The enemy did not capture any organised body of men on that occasion, but only stragglers, and such as were left asleep on the road, exhausted by the fatigue and exposure of one of the most inclement nights I have ever known at this season of the year. It rained without cessation, rendering the road by which our troops marched toward the bridge at Falling Waters very difficult to pass, and causing so much delay that the last of the troops did not cross the river at the bridge until one a. m. on the morning of the fourteenth.
>
> While the column was thus detained on the road a number of men, worn down with fatigue, laid down in barns and by the roadside, and though officers were sent back to arouse them as the troops moved on, the darkness and rain prevented them from finding all, and many were in this way left behind.
>
> Two guns were left on the road; the horses that drew them became exhausted, and the officers went back to procure others. When they returned, the rear of the column had passed the guns so far that it was deemed unsafe to send back for them, and they were thus lost. No arms, cannon, or prisoners were taken by the enemy in battle, but only such as were left behind, as I have described, under the circumstances. The number of stragglers thus lost I am unable to state with accuracy, but it is greatly exaggerated in the despatch referred to.
>
> I am, with great respect, your obedient servant,
>
> R. E. Lee, General.

This was evidently an attempt, on the part of the Rebel leader, to disparage our victories and to wipe out of his record, with a sort of legerdemain, the disgraceful and disastrous denouement of his invasion. In the following important statement General Meade confirms his position by incontestable facts, and shows how the matter stood:

Headquarters Army of the Potomac,
Aug. ——, 1863.

Major-General Halleck; General-in-Chief:

My attention has been called to what purports to be an official despatch of General R. E. Lee, commanding the Rebel army, to General S. Cooper, Adjutant and Inspector-General, denying the accuracy of my telegram to you, of July fourteenth, announcing the result of the cavalry affair at Falling Waters.

I have delayed taking any notice of Lee's report until the return of Brigadier-General Kilpatrick, absent on leave, who commanded the cavalry on the occasion referred to, and on whose report from the field my telegram was leased. I now enclose the official report of Brigadier-General Kilpatrick, made after his attention had been called to Lee's report. You will see that he reiterates and confirms all that my despatch averred, and proves most conclusively that General Lee has been deceived by his subordinates, or he would never, in the face of the facts now alleged, have made the assertion his report claims.

It appears that I was in error in stating that the body of General Pettigrew was left in our hands, although I did not communicate that fact until an officer from the field reported to me he had seen the body. It is now ascertained, from the Richmond papers, that General Pettigrew, though mortally wounded in the affair, was taken to Winchester, where he subsequently died. The three battle-flags captured on this occasion, and sent to Washington, belonged to the Fortieth, Forty-seventh, and Fifty-fifth Virginia regiments of infantry.

General Lee will surely acknowledge these were not left in the hands of stragglers asleep in barns.

George G. Meade, Major-General Commanding

Kilpatrick, in his letter of explanation, referred to in the above despatch, gives the following graphic account of this last scene in the great drama of the invasion:

Headquarters Third Division Cavalry Corps,
Warrenton Junction, Va., Aug.——

To Colonel A. J. Alexander, Chief of Staff of Cavalry Corps:

Colonel: In compliance with a letter just received from the headquarters of the Cavalry Corps of the Army of the Potomac, directing me to give the facts connected with the fight at Falling Waters, I have the honour to state that, at three a. m. of the fourteenth *ultimo*, I learned that the enemy's pickets were retiring in my front. Having been previously ordered to attack at seven a. m., I was ready to move at once.

At daylight I had reached the crest of hills occupied by the enemy an hour before, and, a few minutes before six, General Custer drove the rearguard of the enemy into the river at Williamsport. Learning from citizens that a portion of the enemy had retreated in the direction of Falling Waters, I at once moved rapidly for that point, and came up with this rearguard of the enemy at seven-thirty a. m., at a point two miles distant from Falling Waters.

We pressed on, driving them before us, capturing many prisoners and one gun. When within a mile and a half of Falling Waters, the enemy was found in large force, drawn up in line of battle on the crest of a hill, commanding the road on which I was advancing. His left was protected by earthworks, and his right extended to the woods on our left.

The enemy was, when first seen, in two lines of battle, with arms stacked within less than one thousand yards of the large force. A second piece of artillery, with its support, consisting of infantry, was captured while attempting to get into position. The gun was taken to the rear. A portion of the Sixth Michigan Cavalry, seeing only that portion of the enemy behind the earthworks, charged.

This charge was led by Major Webber, and was the most gallant ever made. At a trot he passed up the hill, received the fire from the whole line, and the next moment rode through and over the earthworks, and passed to the right, sabring the Rebels along the entire line, and returned with a loss of thirty killed, wounded, and missing, including the gallant Major Webber, killed.

I directed General Custer to send forward one regiment as skirmishers. They were repulsed before support could be sent them, and driven back, closely followed by the Rebels, until checked by the First Michigan and a squadron of the Eighth New York. The Second brigade having come up, it was quickly thrown into position, and, after a fight of two hours and thirty minutes, routed the enemy at all points and drove him toward the river. When within a short distance of the bridge, General Buford's command came up and took the advance. We lost twenty-nine killed, thirty-six wounded, and forty missing. We found upon the field one hundred and twenty-five dead Rebels, and brought away upward of fifty wounded. A large number of the enemy's wounded were left upon the field in charge of their own surgeons. We captured two guns, three battle-flags, and upward of fifteen hundred prisoners.

To General Custer and his brigade, Lieutenant Pennington and his battery, and one squadron of the Eighth New York Cavalry, of General Buford's command, all praise is due.

Very respectfully, your obedient servant,

J. Kilpatrick, Brigadier-General.

In his official report of operations from the twenty-eighth of June, when he assumed command of the Third division, Kilpatrick says:

In this campaign my command has captured forty-five hundred prisoners, nine guns, and eleven battle-flags.

Never before, in the history of warfare, has it been permitted to any man commanding a division to include, in a report of about forty-five days' operations, such magnificent results.

As the last foot of the invaders disappeared from the soil where they had never been successful, our gallant boys built their bivouac fires and rested themselves and their weary animals near the scene of their recent victory.

The telegraph lines, which had so often been burdened with news of disaster, now sang with joyful intelligence from all departments of our vast armies. Gettysburg was soon followed by Vicksburg, then Port Hudson, the names being emblazoned upon many a glowing transparency, to the honour of the heroes who had planned, and the braves who had fought, so successfully and well. The news was welcomed with salutes of artillery and bonfires in most of the Northern cities and villages, while the whole mass of our people was jubilant and rejoicing.

On the fifteenth the president issued a proclamation of Thanksgiving, in which he recognised the hand of God in our victories, and called upon the people to "render the homage due to the Divine Majesty for the wonderful things He has done in the nation's behalf, and to invoke the influence of His Holy Spirit to subdue the anger which has produced, and so long sustained, a needless and cruel rebellion." In the midst of these rejoicings we end our chapter.

CHAPTER 14

Kilpatrick's Gunboat Expedition

This sudden and masterly movement of the Rebels was a cutting surprise to General Meade, and a source of mortification and chagrin to all. Gloriously successful as we had been, it was evident that hesitation and indecision had greatly detracted from our laurels. We had won a world-renowned victory, but we had failed to reap all the legitimate fruits which our situation placed within our reach.

General Lee had been terribly punished, but his escape was quite marvellous. One writer says:

> When his shattered columns commenced their retreat from Gettysburg, few of his officers can have imagined that they would ever reach Virginia with their artillery and most of their trains.

And though their trains were severely handled and greatly injured, yet the old Rebel army of Northern Virginia, with nearly all its artillery, made its exit from soil too sacred to freedom for a Rebel victory. Their losses, however, had been immense, and they were only too glad to escape in a manner very unlike the audacious way in which they had advanced but a few weeks previous into the Northern States.

It now became the policy of our leader to follow the fugitives as closely as the changed circumstances of affairs would permit, and to give the Rebels no rest, while he endeavoured to press them determinedly, and watched them by means of scouts and signal-stations with a jealous eye.

There is, however, a limit to the endurance which men and horses are capable of, and, beyond this, the overtaxed powers give way, and exhausted nature claims her rights. Few there are, except those who have had experience, who know how much privation the brave soldier and his general suffer in the toils of the field, on the rapid march, the hasty bivouac, the broken slumbers, the wakeful watchings, and the scanty fare.

It must be remembered, also, that our army had made many forced marches, describing in its route a line somewhat resembling the circumference of a great circle, as a careful survey of the map of movements will show; while the route of the enemy, who had several days the start of us, was more like the diameter of that circle.

Our cavalry had not only fought and defeated the Rebel cavalry on many sanguinary fields, but it had met the serried lines of their infantry also, as at Gettysburg, where the brave Farnsworth fell. Owing to this fatigue of our forces, our pursuit of the enemy was not as vigorous, it would seem at a cursory glance, as it should have been.

As soon as it was ascertained that the Rebel army was in full retreat, a force of our cavalry was sent across the Potomac at Harper's Ferry, bivouacking, the night of the fourteenth of July, on Bolivar Heights. Early the next morning we advanced on the Winchester Turnpike as far as Halltown, where we deflected to the right on the road to Shepherdstown. We had not proceeded far before we encountered the enemy's cavalry under Fitzhugh Lee, with which we were soon involved in a spirited contest.

At first our troopers were worsted and driven back a short distance. But, having found a good position, we rallied, and repulsed several desperate charges, inflicting heavy losses, until the Rebels were glad to give up the game, and consequently retired. Colonel Drake (First Virginia) and Colonel Gregg were among the Rebel slain, while on our side the highest officer killed was Captain Fisher, of the Sixteenth Pennsylvania. The fighting was done principally on foot.

While these things were transpiring, Kilpatrick moved his division from Falling Waters to Boonsboro' by way of Williamsport and Hagerstown. Sad evidences of the recent battles and marches, in dead animals and general *débris*, were seen all along the way. Having reached our bivouac near Boonsboro', our men and horses came to their rations and rest with a wonderful relish.

During the day we have been reading of the murderous riots made in Northern cities, especially in New York, where men in mobs have ostensibly leagued against the authority of the government. The bloody accounts are stirring the rank and file of our army terribly. A feeling of intense indignation exists against traitorous demagogues, who are undoubtedly at the bottom of all this anarchy. Detachments from many of the old regiments are now being sent North to look after Northern traitors. this depletion of our ranks we cannot well afford, for every available man is needed in the field.

Many of our regiments are much reduced. The Harris Light now musters but one hundred men fit for duty, scarcely one tenth the number with which we entered upon the campaign. Our horses are also much used up. Hundreds of them have been killed and wounded in battle, and not a few have "played out," so that they are utterly unserviceable. The author of these records has worn out completely two horses since he had a second horse shot under him in the cavalry fight near Upperville.

Upon the sixteenth of July, just as that peculiar tint of sky and atmosphere which mark it to be about four o'clock of a summer morning in the South, had begun to disturb the lighter sleepers in our camp, a command most welcome to the trooper, that of "boots and saddles," rang out clearly on the air, and the response coming with unusual alacrity, before daylight had fully dawned we were fairly on our way to Harper's Ferry. Revisiting Rhorersville, and crossing Crampton's Gap upon the way, we struck the Potomac at Berlin, where the division was subdivided, a portion of it moving on Harper's Ferry to bivouac for the night, which it did amid the ruins of the destroyed Government Hospital.

By this time pontoons had been laid at both Berlin and Harper's Ferry, and the important work of crossing a large force was in progress of successful accomplishment. The passage of a stream of any magnitude by a force of this size is always a matter of great difficulty, impeded as it must be, even under the most favourable circumstances, by many obstacles, and occupying a great deal of time; yet, when the movement is one on the advance, its very boldness lends it attractiveness, and inspires the men with renewed confidence, and it is at such a time they most keenly feel, that,

To every man upon this earth
Death cometh soon or late—
And how can man die better
Than facing fearful odds,
For the ashes of his fathers
And the Temples of his Gods;

*And for the tender mother
Who dandled him to rest,
And for the wife who nurses
His baby at her breast?*

With the exception of the bustle and activity incident to this transportation, everything is quiet, and the "busy note of preparation," however warlike may be its purpose, assumes a pacific aspect now. We are receiving a new issue of clothing, too; and our ranks, while losing somewhat of their veteranly appearance, have certainly gained much in cleanliness and comfort by the change. The fact is, that many of us, like the followers of Falstaff, began to look almost as "ragged as Lazarus," and without the chance the fat knight promised his men, of "finding new linen on every hedge." Their re-equipment, therefore, could not fail to be popular.

This agreeable surprise was followed by another. The first sergeants were commanded to make out the pay-rolls of the Harris Light, and, with the exception of a report that Lee was falling back on the Rappahannock, nothing farther of note occurred until Sunday, the 19th inst. On the afternoon of that day, while gentle hearts in many a great city and quiet hamlet were sending up to the throne of the Great Creator prayers for the safety of the soldier and the success of the cause, our cavalry crossed the river at Sandy Hook and advanced into the interior of Virginia.

Our progress at first was far from rapid, for scarce a breath of air was stirring, and the red glare of a Southern sun made the march weary and oppressive. We were therefore glad when the day came to an end, and it was ten o'clock on the following morning before we resumed our march and advanced to Leesburg, where man and horse enjoyed for a time both rations and rest, enabling the regiment towards the decline of the day to resume its journey and bivouac at night upon the grassy banks of a stream which, notwithstanding its homely name, Goose Creek, possessed many substantial attractions for the weary troopers and their tired steeds.

Daylight brought with it renewed activity, for by this time our entire cavalry force was being rapidly advanced towards the Rappahannock, and by way of Gum Spring and Centreville we that day reached Manassas Junction.

The march was not altogether unaccompanied with some evidences of insubordination, though the cause that called this dangerous spirit forth was one of a very trivial character. All along the line of march, blackberries were discovered to be growing in great abundance, and our "children of a larger growth" "went for them" (to use their own expression) without permission from their officers, and with true military *vim*.

For this breach of discipline, General Gregg was compelled to dismount several of the men, and ordered them to trudge along on foot. To the civilian this punishment may seem disproportioned to the offence; but in an army, in time of war, the slightest infraction of discipline may become a precedent, dangerous in the extreme.

A command would soon be totally demoralised, unless the first tendency to unsoldierly conduct was not checked; and though at times discipline may seem severe, yet, especially with a force recruited to meet the exigencies of a particular conflict, and made up of all ranks and races of people, it is absolutely necessary.

"I am surprised," said Condorcet to Lafayette, seeing him enter a room in the uniform of a private of the National Guard, of which he had so recently been the commander; "I am surprised, General, to see *you* in that dress."

"Not at all," replied Lafayette, "I was tired of obeying, and wished to command. In the *Gardes Nationale*, the men direct and the officers obey."

This spirit led the celebrated body referred to, to exerciser a right of individual judgment in the matter of obeying or disobeying their leaders, and it was not until it withered into blind obedience beneath the iron will of the Great Napoleon, that victory once more perched upon the eagles of France. A similar demoralisation in the Prætorian Guard brought about the decline of Rome, and so it must always be, for discipline makes an army—the want of it constitutes a mob.

The advent of another day found us near Gainesville, and in crossing the old battlefield of Bull Run we fell in with Scott's "nine hundred," among whom were several old acquaintances. A number of these were personal friends of my own, and from my native State and county, St. Lawrence, New York, and of course these were warmly welcomed. The meeting was recognised by us all as a happy event, but, as it turned out, it was very near being the proximate cause of my capture by the enemy.

Even in the midst of the endearments of home it is by no means an easy task to separate from those who have been the schoolmates and companions of our boyhood; even then scenes and incidents of "the happy days of yore" come trooping up before the imagination, peopling the dim arches of the memory with bright reminiscences of the past, until we hate to separate from the friendly magicians, the sight of whom has evoked their presence.

How doubly difficult, then, does the parting seem, when the meeting takes place in one of those intervals of a soldier's life which show him the dull monotony of a camp behind and the red glare of battle before him—intervals which may, for aught he knows, be, both for his friends and himself, but a bridge of moments at the end of which lie their open graves.

In the present case it was indeed difficult, and for a time the author lived again among the "soft humanities" of his boyhood, to the utter exclusion of the sterner obligations and responsibilities of the hour. The position of myself and friends was upon the flank of Scott's Regiment, so that until we reached Catlett Station I did not discover the important fact that my command, debouching from the main column at Manassas Junction, had gone on towards Gainesville, that being their destination.

I therefore found myself cut off from the regiment, and in anything but an enviable position, and the sudden realisation of the unpleasantness of my position at once brought me to myself. How to extricate myself, was the important question. To reach my regiment by the usual road *via* Manassas would compel me to ride twenty-five good miles; but by describing the arc of a circle, I could cross the country, economize considerable time, and save my already tired horse some weary miles of travel.

I determined, therefore, upon taking the latter course; so making warm but hasty *adieux* to my companions, I turned my horse's head towards, and rode as rapidly as possible in the direction of, Gainesville. Over hill and dale, for about eight miles, my good horse carried me in right gallant style, and I was congratulating myself on the rapidity with which I was lessening the distance I had to travel in this, G. P. R. James' "solitary horseman" sort of style, when I thought I perceived still further cause of self-gratulation in the approach of what seemed, to all appearance, a detachment of Federal Cavalry.

The reader may therefore judge of my chagrin, when I found, as I did in a very few moments, such a preponderance of gray uniform in the advancing force, as to convince me that I was within rifle-range of a body of Mosby's Guerrillas. This was falling out of the frying-pan into the fire, with a vengeance. The slightest effort to reverse my course would inevitably draw the enemy's fire, and to advance was equally sure to produce a similar result, but the latter course at least held out one advantage; namely, that if I did escape their bullets I would have at least a chance to push on to my regiment and reach it before being reported as absent.

A single instant's reflection, therefore, convinced me that of the two inevitable evils I must encounter, the latter was the least, and I determined at once to encounter it.

Without, therefore, paying the slightest attention to the Confederate leader's mandate to "halt," I dug the spurs into my faithful horse, and dashed straight through that portion of the partisan band which seemed to my eye least compactly massed, exchanging shots with them in my passage, but not of course stopping to mark the result. A loud yell announced their disappointment, and half a dozen of the bushwhackers started after me in hot pursuit, amusing themselves meanwhile by discharging as close to my person as the speed of the chase permitted the contents of a most heterogeneous assortment of carbines, shotguns, and old-fashioned horse-pistols.

With such odds against me, and concluding that in this case discretion was the better part of valour, I used my spurs to the best possible advantage. At the expiration of probably ten minutes, however, I ascertained that one of my pursuers had considerably outdistanced his companions, and was rapidly gaining upon me. I therefore suddenly wheeled round in my saddle, and ere he had recovered from his astonishment at the movement, gave him the contents of my revolver, thereby bringing him to the ground.

The others by this time seemed either discouraged by the now evident superior speed of my horse, or else they thought the game not worth so long a chase, or possibly they were afraid of not being able to rejoin their main body; at all events they gathered round the body of their fallen comrade, and followed me no further, so that after all my mishaps I was lucky enough to quietly drop into my proper position in my regiment, and nothing being said about my absence, was soon jogging along with my companions in arms, in the ordinary routine way.

When in camp or on the march even trivial circumstances are welcomed as breaking the monotony of the days, but the twenty-third of the month brought to us that most welcome of all events, the arrival of a large mail, which contained letters for nearly all. In the hurry and rush of an active campaign like that which we had just passed through in Pennsylvania and Maryland, postal regularity is almost impossible of attainment, and even the most vigorous and well-directed efforts of the Government to secure it fail, so that army mails are greatly delayed, sometimes even for weeks together.

The result is that, when the post does arrive, it is hailed with a delight that is almost frantic. The post-boys are cheered as soon as seen, in wending their way from camp to camp, and in the present instance the plethoric condition of the burdens they bore made the hurrahs louder and longer, until the very welkin rang again.

Who shall write the romance of an army mail? How the magic pen of him who but the other day, as now it seems, was laid away to sleep with the other mighty dead in the Abbey Church of Westminster, could have quickened such a theme! What an arabesque of wonders he could have spun, and yet not o'erdrawn the simple truth a single jot!

Why, the very faces of the men, as each receives his special parcel, are instinct with suggestion. Here a veteran, upon whose bronzed features the "shadowed livery of the burning sun" glows lurid as a picture of Murillo's—telling the story of many a weary march and murderous battle—trembles like a puny girl at the sight of a letter, the black border of which is but a foreshadowing of the blacker news within; there a stripling draws himself up with the pride of all the Cæsars, to hide the blush that mantles his cheek when his gaze falls upon a tiny missive, bearing his name in tracery so fine that only a woman's hand could have inscribed it there; while within a stone's throw of these another hurtles curses forth, at some written news of wrong or shame, and still others laugh or cry, or move silently away to sorrow or rejoice according to their several messages and natures.

Upon the morning following mail-day, that is to say, on the 24th of July, in the year of grace *a.d.* 1863, heavy cannonading was heard in the direction of White Plains, and this lasted throughout the day. In explanation of the fact, we subsequently learned that General Meade, being misled by the erroneous reports of certain of his scouts, expected to bring on a general engagement with the enemy at Manassas Gap, at which place General Buford found the Rebels apparently in force.

The commander-in-chief therefore directed the army to be massed upon that point. The Third Corps, under General French, which had occupied Ashby's Gap, was sent forward to support Buford, and the whole of the First Division, commanded by General Hobart Ward, pushed through the Gap, driving the enemy before it, a movement which was attended by about equal loss to both parties. In this advance the celebrated Excelsior Brigade, under the leadership of General F.B. Spinola, added new brilliancy to its already splendid record, by making three heroic charges up the frowning steeps where the Rebels were strongly posted.

In these charges General Spinola was twice wounded, but seemed to lose sight of his personal injuries in the joy inspired by his successful achievement. The next day, the 25th, the army pushed forward as far as Front Royal, but found no enemy. They then, for the first time, discovered that they had been engaging only a portion of Lee's rear-guard, and not, as they had imagined, his main body, and that, having accomplished the object of that astute general, their late opponents had slipped away in the trail of their main army southward.

In consequence of this erroneous movement, General Meade's army lost full two days in time, and when we again reached the banks of the Rappahannock, we once more found our wily foe, facing us in a threatening attitude upon the opposite shore.

The hour of noon brought orders to the Harris Light to proceed upon a recognisance to Thoroughfare Gap, so off we dashed, reaching our objective point in good time, and without accident to man or beast. From the heights beyond the Gap, creeping along like a huge serpent, in the direction of Warrenton, we saw the wagon train of the Eleventh Army Corps, that being a portion of the force which had moved on Manassas Gap in expectation of a battle.

After this we saw nothing more that is worthy of record, and ere the passage of another day the whole body of Cavalry (the second squadron of our regiment under Captain O. J. Downing having joined ns at Gainesville), went into bivouac at Warrenton. The first duty to which we were assigned was to relieve the First Virginia Calvary, which had been previously detailed to picket Catlett's Station. An inspection of horses followed in the morning, resulting in the condemnation of a large number, as being utterly unserviceable, and these veterans were started off towards Washington to be replaced by better ones. Such changes are of frequent occurrence, for raids and forced marches tell terribly upon the poor quadrupeds, and, to be effective, troopers need thoroughly efficient mounts.

The twenty-seventh of July, were I a Greek, should be marked with a white stone, for upon that day I was honoured by being placed in command of a company. Owing to the great loss in officers sustained by the army in our late campaigns, that day found many of the companies of our regiment without commissioned officers, and their places had to be filled from the enlisted men.

The company to which I was assigned had not felt the direct influence of shoulder-straps for over three months. Upon the afternoon I assumed command, a detachment was sent out upon a foraging expedition with instructions to patrol near Bristersburg. Our duties for the most part, since the Battle of Gettysburg, have been of a similar nature; picketing, scouting and recruiting, filling up the measure of our diurnal operations. This kind of work is very wearing, on account of its sameness, but it is not for a soldier to choose his duties but to perform them.

On the 29th, the entire brigade to which my regiment was attached was moved to within three miles of Warrenton, and then countermarched to the old camp, and upon the last day of the month it advanced quite up to Warrenton, at which point General Meade for that day established his headquarters, but the next moved them still further to Rappahannock Station.

By this time, the Dog Star, which, in the month of July, begins to rage in the Southern States, was carrying that rage to an almost intolerable height, and several of our men had been sun-struck, so that when we left Warrenton we moved very slowly, bivouacking at night not far from New Baltimore.

The next day the Harris Light had more picket duty to perform, but at this place found it neither difficult nor dangerous; and so we pursued the "even tenor of our way" until the third of this, the last of the summer months, a day that found the Harris Light at Thoroughfare Gap, encamped in an orchard like Barbara Freitche's, with "*apple and peach-tree fruited deep,*" and the long lines of our infantry stretched out in full view away down the Rappahannock to Fredericksburg, now held by the Federal troops.

As far as the eye could reach, our cavalry pickets, too, were to be seen, and vast as seemed the expanse of country they had to guard, their great numbers made the duty comparatively light. My own regiment, of course, had to take its turn in the patrol, at times being placed along the Manassas Gap Railroad, and again, moving from the camp to the picket reserve. In this way the hours went slowly but surely by, to *join the unrecorded syllables of time before the Flood,* until Sunday, the third instant, upon which day Major E. F. Cook, a deservedly popular officer, who had for some time been absent from the regiment, returned and took command. No officer in the regiment had a greater number of warm personal friends than he, and his return was the occasion of general rejoicing.

This quiet Sabbath having passed away, and Monday having come, we struck tents, and separating into several detachments, moved upon White Plains and Middleburg from different directions. These points had been occupied for some time prior to this by Mosby's Guerrillas, but they studiously kept themselves beyond the reach of our carbines, and we failed to bring them to an engagement.

It is true that now and then they attacked our pickets, and some lively skirmishing was the result, but they did not seem disposed to come to close quarters with our main body. The thirteenth brought me another change of position, the adjutant having detailed me to act as sergeant-major in place of Sergeant Temple, assigned to the command of a company. This was the result, again, of the scarcity of commissioned officers with the regiment. A few of the absent were out on detached service, while many others during the lull of army operations had asked and obtained leave of absence, and were visiting their friends in the North.

As far as military movements were concerned at that time, we experienced a dead calm, and might have easily imagined ourselves a huge picnic party, rusticating for the benefit of our several healths, had not the pleasing delusion been rendered impossible by the fact that marauding bands every now and then attacked our outposts, occasionally disturbed our lines of communication, and even at times severed temporarily the links which connected us with our bases of supply.

Up to the fourteenth, not an event occurred out of the usual course of camp and picket duty; but on that day we had a modest sort of sensation in the fact that a detachment of the regiment commanded by Captain Griggs, taking advantage of an opportunity with which fortune favoured him, made a gallant dash upon a portion of Mosby's band, capturing thereby three men and twenty-seven horses. Most of the latter bore the familiar brand, U. S., and the saddles were evidently of Northern make, facts which indicated that in their seizure we were simply taking our own again.

The day following this skirmish, at ten o'clock, a.m., the regiment moved from Thoroughfare Gap, and taking New Baltimore and Greenwich in the way, reached Hartwood Church at eight o'clock that night. At Warrenton Junction a considerable halt was made, for the purpose of drawing rations and forage, and while we were there,

Henry E. Davies, newly promoted to the coloncey of the regiment, joined us, and took command. His promotion and his arrival among us were subjects of equal satisfaction to both officers and men.

There was not a man in the regiment who did not appreciate his worth and admire his daring, and his warmest friends were those who had the good sense to value courage and recognise the advantages of thorough discipline in fitting men for the art of war. Our camp at Hartwood Church was in the immediate vicinity of General Kilpatrick's headquarters, and it so remained all that day, and the next, and the latter proving an eventful day to me, for it brought me an order made by our new colonel, appointing me second lieutenant.

This promotion was not less gratifying to my feelings than was my first upward step in the ranks, for, after being promoted to the position of corporal, it became my ardent ambition to be deemed worthy of a place in front of the line; and now, having passed through the various grades of non-commission, I could not but feel gratified that my elevation was due to no extrinsic influence, but had been fairly earned by earnest effort while serving in the old Troy company in which I first enlisted as a private. Before I had time to grow warm in my new lieutenancy, I was assigned to the command of Company "M," the captain and first lieutenant of which were both absent upon detached service.

Late in the evening I received orders to report, with my company, at an early hour next day, to Captain Meade, division quartermaster. At five o'clock on the morning of the eighteenth we made our bow to the captain, who despatched us as an escort or guard to a train from Hartwood to Warrenton Junction.

During the march we made an exciting clash upon a band of guerrillas who were in ambush for us, expecting to make some captures. But they were disappointed, for we were not only prepared to resist them, but would have captured them but for the superior fleetness of their horses. After accomplishing the work we were sent out to do, and resting one night, we returned to the regiment.

August 22.—This is my natal day. I find myself twenty-two years of age. I am not surrounded on this anniversary, as in former years, by the friends of my childhood. But memories of the past come trooping up in such vivid lines, as to make the day one of deep interest.

August 28.—My company, which forms a part of Captain Mitchell's battalion, is doing picket-duty at present with the battalion on the

Rappahannock between Banks and United States Fords. My company is at the captain's headquarters, and acts as grand guard.

Sunday, August 30.—Today I accompanied the division and brigade officers of the day in their visit to and inspection of the pickets along the Rappahannock. Our ride was very pleasant. Captain Barker, of the Fifth New York Cavalry, dined with Captain Mitchell and myself. He is a lively companion; was in the hands of Mosby last Spring; and has a fund of amusing and interesting incidents of army-life with which to enliven his conversation.

On the last day of August, Captain Mitchell was ordered to report to the regiment at Hartwood Church, with his reserves. The pickets are to remain on the river until attacked by the enemy or recalled by orders from division headquarters.

Cavalry Gunboat Expedition

September 4.—To break the monotony of picketing and to subserve the cause of freedom, a most novel scheme was lately undertaken, known as Kilpatrick's Gunboat Expedition. The object was to destroy a portion of the Rebel navy anchored in the Rappahannock, near Port Conway, opposite Port Royal. This peculiar kind of warfare, which required genius and dash, was waged by the troopers with complete success, and they returned to their bivouac fires to enliven the weary hours with stories of their long march down the river, and their destructive charge upon the gunboats of the enemy. The expedition set out about two o'clock on the morning of September first.

Doctor Lucius P. Woods, Surgeon-in-Chief of the First Brigade, Third Division, gives the following interesting description of the above raid in a letter to Mrs. Woods:

> I returned yesterday after a three days' expedition after gunboats! We all laughed at the order sending cavalry after such craft, but I am happy to say that the object of the expedition was accomplished. We left camp at two o'clock a. m., marched all day and all the following night, till three o'clock next morning, when we made a furious charge upon Rebel infantry. They ran so fast as to disarrange the general's plan of attack. The morning was so dark that we could not see one rod in advance.
>
> We captured twelve or fifteen prisoners, and General Kilpatrick gave orders in their hearing to have the whole command fall back, stating that the gunboats would be alarmed and the ex-

pedition be a failure. The general took particular pains to allow half the prisoners to escape and to get across the Rappahannock.

After falling back two miles, we were counter-marched toward the river, near which we were formed in line of battle. We sat there on our horses waiting for daylight. Then the flying artillery of ten guns, supported by the old Fifth New York and First Michigan, dashed at a full run down to the river-bank, wheeled into position, and gave the Rebels a small cargo of hissing cast-iron, which waked them up more effectually than their ordinary morning-call.

They soon came to their senses, and for half an hour sent over to us what I should think to be, by the noise they made, tea-kettles, cooking-stoves, large cast-iron hats, etc. But our smaller and more active guns soon silenced theirs, and drove the gunners away, when we turned our attention to the boring of holes in their boats with conical pieces of iron, vulgarly called solid shot.

I am sure I can recommend them as first-class augers, for they sank the boats in time for all hands to sit down to breakfast at half-past nine o'clock. The repast consisted of muddy water, rusty salt-pork, and half a hard cracker, termed by us "an iron clad breakfast." We were absent from camp three days, and had only nine hours' sleep.

Further interesting particulars were given in a New York daily, as follows:

> The expedition under General Kilpatrick, sent out a few days since to recapture, in conjunction with the navy, the gunboats *Satellite* and *Reliance*, which recently fell into the hands of the Rebels, was, so far as the cavalry is concerned, successful.
>
> On Tuesday evening General Kilpatrick arrived on this side the river, at Port Conway, and brilliantly dashed upon the enemy's pickets under Colonel Low. The Rebels did not even make a show of resistance, but rushed into a number of flat-boats in the wildest confusion, and landed safely on the opposite bank. If they had made a show of light, they would have most likely been captured.
>
> After the escape of the enemy. General Kilpatrick waited two hours for the cooperation of the navy, which is understood to

The Cavalry Bivouac

have been agreed upon.

The vessels did not arrive, and General Kilpatrick ordered a battery to open fire upon the gunboats *Reliance* and *Satellite*. This was done at the distance of six hundred and fifty yards. The enemy immediately abandoned the gunboats—very fortunately for themselves, for only a few moments elapsed before the *Satellite* was in a sinking condition, and the *Reliance* rendered useless. Both boats were completely riddled by shot and shell. The force under Kilpatrick consisted of cavalry and two batteries of artillery. The *Satellite* is sunk, and the *Reliance* so completely disabled as to be beyond hope of being repaired by the Rebels.

On our return from Port Conway we passed, through Falmouth, where we halted a short time. It was pleasant to survey the scenes of former labours and conflicts. Much alarm appears to have been created among the Rebels by our gunboat disturbance. A large force of Rebel cavalry can be distinctly seen approaching Fredericksburg on the Telegraph Road, and more or less commotion prevails across the river. From Falmouth we marched directly to Hartwood Church. On arriving here. Captain Mitchell's battalion was ordered back to its old position on picket, to relieve the infantry which took our places before the expedition to Port Conway.

September 5.—We continue on picket near United States Ford. This morning the regiment was mustered in for pay by Major McIrvin, who is temporarily in command, Colonel Davies having been placed in command of a brigade.

At ten o'clock a. m. I received my commission of second lieutenant. It was brought from the headquarters of the regiment by the bugler of Company "H." It dates from the cavalry fight at Aldie, which occurred on the seventeenth of June.

On this line of pickets we have continued uninterruptedly for a week. On the seventh, Colonel Davies, with his assistant adjutant-general, visited our post. It was very gratifying to Captain Mitchell and myself to receive the colonel's compliments for promptness and vigilance in our work, especially as he has the reputation of never bestowing praise where it is not deserved.

I rode down to Lieutenant Temple's picket-reserve, at Richard's Ferry, on the eighth. I found the lieutenant in excellent humour, but decidedly opposed to picketing as a permanent occupation. We were, however, consoled with the hope of relief ere long.

In the afternoon the brigade officer of the day called at the bivouac of the "grand guard," and expressed himself as being highly pleased with the disposition and management of the pickets. The enemy's pickets confront ours at all the fords of the river, and appear in heavy force.

For some time past we have understood that General Lee's headquarters are at Orange Court House, while his infantry occupies the south banks and bluffs of the Rapidan. Stuart occupies Culpepper Court House, and pickets and patrols the territory between the Rapidan and the Rappahannock, a region shaped much like an old-fashioned harrow.

September 13.—An advance of the Union army was ordered yesterday by its chief, in which the cavalry was to take a prominent part. Orders were issued accordingly last evening, and every needed preparation made for our work. At an early hour this morning the entire cavalry corps was on the march. In order that the enemy might not be prematurely warned of our design, the several commands were ordered to make as little noise as possible.

Consequently the bugle-calls were dispensed with, and commanders made use of their voices, and in some instances the orders were conveyed from rank to rank in a whisper. The three great divisions of the corps were to cross the river as follows: Gregg's, at Sulphur Springs; Buford's, at Rappahannock Bridge; and Kilpatrick's, at Kelly's Ford.

Brandy Station No. 3

At six o'clock the Harris Light plunged into the river at Kelly's Ford, leading the advance. A strong detachment of Stuart's cavalry, consisting of pickets and reserves, opposed our crossing with dogged pertinacity, but finally, yielding to our superior numbers and to the deadly accuracy of our carbines, gave way. He then advanced in the direction of Brandy Station. The farther we advanced the stronger grew the ever-accumulating force of the enemy, who disputed every inch of ground with great stubbornness.

On arriving near the station we found the enemy in strong force, with artillery posted on the surrounding hills. We saw clearly that a third cavalry fight was destined to be fought on this historic field, and we began to make preparations for the onset. It was my fortune to lead the advance company in the first charge. Three men and four horses were killed and wounded in this company by the first discharge of the enemy's artillery, whose fire was terribly accurate.

But we had not been fighting long before the other divisions joined us. At their approach great enthusiasm among our boys prevailed. Before our combined force the enemy was swept from those plains like chaff before the whirlwind. They fled in the direction of Culpepper, a naturally strong and now fortified position, where we knew we must soon encounter the Rebel chivalry *en masse* upon their chosen field.

Fight at Culpepper Court House

From Brandy Station General Pleasonton directed Kilpatrick to make a detour *via* Stevensburg, in order to operate as a flanking column upon the enemy at the proper time. With the First and Second divisions Pleasonton pushed straight on to Culpepper, driving the enemy before him without much resistance until within about a mile of the town. Here our advance was effectually checked.

A fearful duel now took place with varying fortunes. For some time the enemy baffled all our efforts to dislodge him from his strong position, and our men began to look wishfully for the flankers, when lo! Kilpatrick's flags were seen advancing from the direction of Stevensburg, and his artillery was soon thundering in the enemy's flank and rear. Under this unexpected and well-directed fire, that portion of the enemy which had kept our main column at bay fell back in confusion into the town; and, before they had time to re-form their broken lines, the Harris Light, Fifth New York, First Vermont, and First Michigan, led by General Custer, dashed upon the "Johnnies" in the streets, throwing the boast of the chivalry into a perfect rout.

Many prisoners were captured, more or less material of war, and three Blakely guns. The Rebels retreated hastily in the direction of Pony Mountain and Rapidan Bridge, whither they were closely pursued by our victorious squadrons. The day following this brilliant advance Pleasonton occupied all the fords of the Rapidan, extending his pickets on our right as far forward as the Robertson and Hazel Rivers.

The way having been thus prepared by his heroic *avant-couriers*, General Meade advanced the Army of the Potomac across the Rappahannock, and took his temporary residence in Culpepper.

On the fifteenth, Kilpatrick's division advanced from Culpepper to Raccoon Ford on the Rapidan. Colonel Davies' brigade supported a battery of artillery a short distance from the ford from one till four p. m. The shelling from the enemy's batteries was terrific. Their position was admirable on the high bluff south of the ford, and the range was just right for execution. Their artillery was of a heavy calibre, and supported by infantry. They were finely screened by earthworks, while our forces were almost entirely exposed, and protected only here and there by a little knoll. In the unequal duel which took place, two of our guns were dismounted and disabled, while several artillerymen and horses were killed. It was not at all practicable for us to attempt a crossing.

Before night we retired from the ford, and the divisions took up their headquarters, Gregg's, at Rappahannock Bridge; Buford's, at Stevensburg; and Kilpatrick's, on the extreme right, at James City.

September 16.—Today we are picketing the fords of the Robertson River, a branch of the Rapidan. At five o'clock p. m. the Fifth New York pickets were attacked and driven to within a few rods of their reserve; but being re-enforced by ourselves, who were ordered to relieve them, the enemy was compelled to retire hastily, and we reoccupied the line which was taken up by the Fifth in the morning.

At ten o'clock in the night I received orders to take four men and communicate with Major McIrvin at Newman's Ford, two miles above our post on the Robertson. This was by no means an easy task, as the wilderness country was almost wholly unknown to us, and the Rebel pickets in this quarter had not been sounded.

Through the darkness, however, I advanced with my men as cautiously as possible, and yet at several points along our line of march we drew the fire of the Rebel pickets. At length we espied a force of cavalry approaching us, which proved to be a detachment under Major McIrvin on their way to the ford. We challenged one another simultaneously, each supposing the other to be an enemy. The major was on the point of ordering his command to fire upon me, when I recognised his voice and quickly gave him my name. The discovery was timely, and mutually enjoyable.

September 17.—The enemy advanced his picket lines this morning across the river, pushed ours back with considerable precipitancy, when a general skirmish occurred along the lines for a distance of about two miles. Captain Hasty was chief in command of our skirmishers. I assisted him, riding my sorrel pony, the only horse on the skirmish line, as all the men fought dismounted. At nine o'clock Colonel Davies arrived with his brigade and took command. The Rebels were not able to withstand our accumulated power, and rapidly retreated across the river, enabling us to re-establish our lines where they were before the onset.

Picket-firing is very common. "Give and take" is the game we play, and sometimes the blows are as severe as they are unexpected. The cavalry is almost constantly on duty, scouting, patrolling, and very often fighting. Thus we are kept ever in motion.

The only relief for our excessive labours is our good living. Seldom are soldiers permitted to live in a country of which it may be said as emphatically as of this, that it *flows with milk and honey*. The numerous flocks of sheep and herds of cattle in the neighbourhood are made to contribute the basis of our rations, while the poultry-yards, larders, and orchards are made to yield the delicacies of the season. The country abounds with sorghum, apple-butter, milk, honey, sweet potatoes, peaches, apples, etc.; so that kings are not much better fed than are the cavaliers of this command.

September 19.—The weather is becoming cold and wet. Yesterday this brigade retired from the Robertson to the vicinity of Stevensburg, where we bivouacked in the pine woods.

Henry E. Davies, Jr., formerly Colonel of the Harris Light, and for some time past in command of the First brigade of Kilpatrick's division, was congratulated today by his friends upon his promotion to brigadier-general. No promotion was ever, more fitly made, and the "star" never graced a more perfect gentleman or more gallant soldier. The general feeling in the command is, long may he live in the service of his country and for the honour of her flag.

Sunday, September 20.—This morning very appropriate and solemn funeral services were held, conducted by Chaplain Edward P. Roe, in honour of the officers and soldiers of the Harris Light, who were killed in our recent advance to, and skirmishes along, the Rapidan and Robertson Rivers.

IMPORTANT RECONNAISSANCE AND RAID

On the morning of the twenty-first, at daybreak, an important movement was commenced by Generals Kilpatrick and Buford, while General Gregg remained on the picket lines. The object of the advance was mainly to reconnoitre the position and strength of the enemy, and at the same time to do all the mischief we could. We made a forced march directly upon Madison Court House, meeting but little opposition. The tired troopers rested themselves and their animals at night, preparatory to another early advance.

September 22.—We were early in the saddle, with our steps turned southward in the direction of Orange Court House. The two divisions advanced upon different but nearly parallel roads. We had not proceeded far before messengers from General Buford informed us that, by a rapid movement across the country between the two roads, Kilpatrick might intercept a brigade of the enemy's cavalry, which Buford was engaging and pursuing.

The Harris Light had the advance of the division, and we soon came in contact with the retreating Rebel force in a dense oak forest, through which we were compelled to approach the pike by a wood road, which was so narrow as to necessitate our moving in columns of twos. Upon gaining the main road we found the entire force of the enemy advancing with skirmishers deployed, and A battery of light artillery in position, which instantaneously opened upon us with grape and canister. The situation of our regiment was extremely critical and embarrassing.

Engagement at Liberty Mills

Generals Kilpatrick and Davies were at the head of the column, and by them we were ordered and encouraged to present a bold front and make a desperate resistance, in order to give the division time to file out of the forest and to get into a fighting position along the road. At this juncture I was in command of the first company of the first squadron, and consequently was ordered to cross the pike, and to check the advance of the enemy in that quarter, while the balance of the regiment was to hold the pike and a small opening to the left.

We had barely time to deploy as skirmishers, when the Rebel commander, Seeing that his only hope of escape from the trap we were laying for him lay in a quick and decisive charge, came down upon us like an avalanche, crushing through the force that was on the road, and sweeping a clean path for his escape. The resistance of the regiment, however, was so desperate that the killed and wounded from both sides strewed the hotly-contested ground in every direction.

Not more than twenty minutes elapsed from the time we first saw the enemy before the contest was decided; and yet, in this brief period of time, the Harris Light lost several of its most gallant officers and many of its bravest men. Our loss was principally in wounded and prisoners, while that of the enemy was in killed and wounded.

By this sudden and unexpected charge of the enemy upon the

force on the pike, myself and company were completely cut off from our main column. For one whole hour we were entirely enclosed within the lines of the Rebel cavalry. It is true that they had about all they could do to take care of themselves, and yet they might have bagged and gobbled our small force.

But by swift and careful movements we succeeded in eluding the vigilance of the Rebels, and finally made our exit from their lines unhurt, and with much valuable information which we had obtained. As soon as possible I reported to General Kilpatrick, who was much surprised at seeing me, having come to the conclusion that myself and men were already on our way to "Richmond!"

The forces of Stuart were ultimately routed and fell back from Liberty Ford, near which the fight occurred, upon their infantry reserves at Gordonsville.

My escape from the toils of the enemy was regarded as almost miraculous. General Davies sent an aid to me with his compliments, inviting me to his headquarters, where he expressed his surprise at my safe return, and complimented me for the dexterity, wisdom, and success of my movements.

The day following this engagement and adventure our forces returned to the vicinity of Culpepper, where we spent a few days in comparative rest—rest which we all needed and greatly enjoyed.

September 25.—I received an order this afternoon from Major McIrvin, commanding the regiment, directing me to take command of Company "H," which is without a commander.

On the twenty-sixth the paymaster made his appearance among us, much to the satisfaction of the command. Owing to the continuous movements of the cavalry corps, and its generally exposed condition, no opportunity has been afforded the government to pay us for the last six months. Very little money was in the regiment, even officers as well as men being pretty well reduced. The paymaster's "stamps" were more than usually acceptable.

September 28.—Four companies, namely, B, F, H, and M, commanded by Captain Grinton, were ordered on picket today along the Hazel River. One half of this force occupies the picket line, the other half patrols the country. The captain commands the post, and I have the special charge of the pickets. We do not want, at present, for fresh meat and vegetables. We live almost entirely from the country, and we live well. Our bill of fare is varied and rich forage for our horses is also abundant on all the neighbouring plantations. Picketing under these circumstances is more like a picnic than anything else which we can remember.

October 8.—We are still in *statu quo,* picketing on the Hazel River. However, yesterday Captain Mitchell relieved Captain Grinton in command of the post. The reserve companies fell in line to hear the orders of the War Department, concerning veteran volunteers. They produced quite an excitement among us. The three years' enlistment of a large portion of the army is nearly expired, and the government, in its anxiety to avail itself of the experience of the veteran troops to the end of the conflict, is now offering extra inducements, in the way of furloughs and bounties, to secure the reenlistment of these men to the end of the war.

The orders propounded to us meet with universal favour, and the cry runs like wild-fire from rank to rank, "let us go in, boys!" This will be an element of great power.

A citizen-youth, of manly bearing, who professes loyalty to our cause, came to our pickets today, and from thence to headquarters, bringing information of a Rebel plan to surprise our picket lines tonight. We will give them a warm reception if they undertake the execution of their scheme. A regiment of infantry, and one squadron of cavalry arrived before dark, and are in readiness for the night's entertainment. The pickets are doubly strong, and are under special orders to be vigilant,

October 9.—The enemy did not venture an attack last night, but doubtless contented themselves with the maxim that *discretion is the better part of valour.* Possibly they were informed of our preparation for them. Spies and informants are numerous and active on both sides.

Lieutenant Houston and Privates Donahue and Pugh were captured this morning while scouting just beyond the pickets. Much activity is manifested on our front. Indeed, it is quite generally understood among us that General Lee is taking the initiatory steps of a flank movement upon us. Our scouts so report, and the suspicious movements of the pickets and forces before us corroborate the information.

Chapter 15

Capture of the Author

Early in the morning of October tenth the enemy, a heavy force, came down upon our pickets along the Robertson River, driving us back in haste and occupying the fords. The flank movement of General Lee was fully understood. He had crossed the Rapidan, advanced to Madison Court House, and was lapping around our right wing, threatening it with destruction. Quick work on our part was now necessary. Swift messengers from officers high in command brought orders to retire with promptness, but in good order, if possible.

Our boys, in many instances, were compelled to leave uneaten and even untasted their palatable preparations for breakfast of roast lamb, sweet potatoes, fine wheat bread, milk honey, etc., etc., to attend to the stern and always unpleasant duties of a retreat, with the enemy pressing very closely upon us.

Sharp skirmishing took place at the river, and the successive crack of carbines afforded the music of our march to James City, where the conflict deepened into a battle, which raged with fury and slaughter. The enemy, conscious of having outgeneralled us in this instance, and having at least a temporary advantage, was bold and defiant. He was met, however, with corresponding vigour. Those contesting legions, which had so often measured sabres in the fearful charge and hand-to-hand encounter, again appealed to the God of battle, and wrestled with Herculean strength for the mastery. Night came on at length to hush the strife, and the weary men and horses sought repose from the bloody fray.

October 11.—With the first pencillings of the morning light we took up our line of march toward the Rappahannock. Skirmishing continued nearly every step of the way. On the Sperryville pike to

Culpepper we were closely pursued and heavily pressed. At Culpepper the corps separated. Gregg, who had come by way of Cedar Mountain, passed out on the road to Sulphur Springs. Buford moved in the direction of Stevensburg, leaving Kilpatrick alone on the main thoroughfare along the railroad line.

Kilpatrick, accompanied by Pleasonton, had scarcely left Culpepper, when Hampton's Legions made a furious attack upon his rear-guard, with the hope of breaking through upon the main column to scatter it, or of so retarding its progress that a flanking column might fall upon him ere he could reach the safe shore of the Rappahannock. Our infantry, which yesterday occupied this ground, had retired, leaving the cavalry to struggle out of the toils of the enemy as best it could.

Gallantly repelling every attack of the enemy, our command moved on, without expending much of its time and material, until opposite the residence of Hon. John Minor Botts, where a few regiments suddenly wheeled about, and, facing the pursuing foe, charged upon them with pistols and sabres, giving them a severe check and an unexpected repulse. On arriving at Brandy Station Kilpatrick found himself in a most critical situation, with an accumulation of formidable difficulties on every hand, which threatened his annihilation.

Buford, who had been sharply pursued by Fitzhugh Lee's division over the plains of Stevensburg, had retired more rapidly than Kilpatrick, and, unaware of his comrade's danger, had suffered Lee to plant his batteries on the high hills which commanded Kilpatrick's right, while the Rebel troopers, in three heavy lines of battle, held the only route by which Kilpatrick could retreat.

Lee's sharpshooters also occupied the woods in the immediate vicinity of Kilpatrick's columns, where they were making themselves a source of damage and great annoyance. To increase the danger of the situation, Stuart, by hard marching, had swung around to Kilpatrick's left, and had taken possession of a range of hills, planted batteries, and was preparing to charge down upon the surrounded division below.

This was a situation to try the stoutest hearts. Nothing daunted, however, by this terrific array of the enemy, Kilpatrick displayed that decision and daring which have ever characterized him as a great cavalry leader, and he proved himself worthy of the brave men who compose his command. His preparation for the grand charge was soon completed. Forming his division into three lines of battle, he assigned the right to Davies, the left to Custer, and, placing himself with

Pleasonton in the centre, he advanced with unwavering determination to the contest. Having approached to within a few yards of the enemy's lines on his front, he ordered his band to strike up a national air, to whose spirit-stirring strains was joined the blast of scores of bugles ringing forth the charge.

With his usual daring Davies was foremost in the fray, leading his command for the fourth time on this memorable field. To his men he had addressed these stirring words:

> Soldiers of the First Brigade! I know you have not forgotten the example of your brave comrades, who, in past engagements here, were not afraid to die in defence of the 'old flag.'

Custer, the daring, terrible demon that he is in battle, pulled off his cap and handed it to his orderly, then dashed madly forward in the charge, while his yellow locks floated like pennants on the breeze. Pennington and Elder handled their batteries with great agility and success, at times opening huge gaps in the serried lines of the enemy.

Fired to an almost divine potency, and with a majestic madness, this band of heroic troopers shook the air with their battle-cry, and dashed forward to meet the hitherto exultant foe. Ambulances, forges, and cannon, with pack-horses and mules, non-combatants and others, all joined to swell the mighty tide. Brave hearts grew braver, and faltering ones waxed warmer and stronger, until pride of country had touched this raging sea of thought and emotion, kindling an unconquerable principle, which emphatically affirmed every man a hero unto death. So swiftly swept forward this tide of animated power, that the Rebel lines broke in wild dismay before the uplifted and firmly-grasped sabres of these unflinching veterans, who, feeling that life and country were at stake, risked them both upon the fearful issue.

Kilpatrick thus escaped disaster, defeated his pursuers, captured several pieces of the enemy's artillery, and presented to the beholders one of the grandest scenes ever witnessed in the New World.

> *By Heaven! it was a splendid sight to see,*
> *For one who had no friend or brother there.*

No one who looked upon that wonderful panorama can ever forget it. On the great field were riderless horses and dying men; clouds of dust from solid shot and bursting shell occasionally obscured the sky; broken caissons and upturned ambulances obstructed the way, while long lines of cavalry were pressing forward in the charge, with their drawn sabres, glistening in the bright sunlight. Far beyond the scene of tumult were the quiet, dark green forests which skirt the banks of the Rappahannock. The poet Havard, in his *Scauderberg* has well described the scene:

> *Hark! the death-denouncing trumpet sounds*
> *The fatal charge, and shouts proclaim the onset.*
> *Destruction rushes dreadful to the field*
> *And bathes itself it: blood: havoc let loose,*
> *Now undistinguish'd, rages all around;*
> *While Ruin, seated on her dreary throne,*
> *Sees the plain strewed with subjects, truly hers,*
> *Breathless and cold.*

The Rebel cavalry, undoubtedly ashamed of their own conduct and defeat, reorganised their broken ranks, and again advanced upon Kilpatrick and Buford, whose divisions had united to repel the attack. For at least two long hours of slaughter these opposing squadrons dashed upon one another over these historic fields. Charges and countercharges followed in quick succession, and at times the "gray" and the "blue" were so confusedly commingled together, that it was difficult to conjecture how they could regain their appropriate places.

Quite a number of prisoners were made on both sides. It was a scene of wild commotion and blood. This carnival continued until late at night, when the exhausted and beaten foe sank back upon safer grounds to rest, while our victorious braves, crowned with undying laurels, gathered up their wounded and dead companions, and, unmolested, recrossed the Rappahannock.

October 12.—Today a portion of our infantry was thrown across the Rappahannock. They advanced by a forced march to reconnoitre as far as Brandy Station, where they met the enemy in force and engaged him in a sharp contest. They returned, however, without serious loss. Our main army is retreating toward Washington.

On the evening of the thirteenth, while bivouacking near Bealeton Station, a serio-comical scene diverted for a time the attention of our officers and men. By a strange accident an ammunition wagon took fire, which caused the rapid explosion of its contents. Shells flew and burst in every direction, and the apparent musketry was terrible. The consequence was a wide-spread alarm, which brought every trooper to his horse ready to engage the foe, who was supposed to have made a furious onset. Great merriment and relished rest followed the discovery of the cause of disturbance, especially as no one was seriously hurt.

Since our last reconnaissance to Brandy Station, Stuart has been very active, following our rear very closely, and committing all the depredations possible. In his hands have fallen many stragglers, who, it is true, were of very little use to us, but who would count as well as true men in the Rebel lists of exchanges of prisoners. Some of Stuart's performances were exceedingly hazardous, as the following well-described narrative from a well-known pen will clearly show:

> Stuart, with two thousand of his cavalry, presided our rear so eagerly that, when near Catlett's Station, he had inadvertently got ahead, by a flank movement of our Second Corps, General Warren acting as rear-guard, and was hemmed in, where his whole command must have been destroyed or captured had he not succeeded in hiding it in a thicket of old field-pines, close by the road whereon our men marched by: the rear of the corps encamping close beside the enemy, utterly unsuspicious of their neighbourhood, though every word uttered in our lines, as they passed, was distinctly heard by the lurking foe.
>
> Stuart at first resolved to abandon his guns and attempt to escape with moderate loss, but finally picked three of his men, gave them muskets, made them up so as to look as much as possible like our soldiers, and thus drop silently into our ranks as they passed, march awhile, then slip out on the other side of the column, and make all haste to General Lee, at Warrenton, in quest of help. During the night two of our officers, who stepped into the thicket, were quietly captured.
>
> At daylight the crack of skirmishers' muskets in the distance gave token that Lee had received and responded to the prayer for help, when Stuart promptly opened with grape and canister on the rear of our astounded column, which had bivouacked just in his front, throwing it into such confusion that he easily dashed by and rejoined his chief, having inflicted some loss and suffered little or none.

Battle of Bristoe

The above manoeuvre was a great and unexpected or unsought risk, which, however, did not prove disastrous to the authors, but which might not again be ventured with similar results. A performance resembling it somewhat was enacted by the Rebels, but with very different issue. Early in the morning of the fourteenth A. P. Hill's corps left Warrenton, with orders to strike our rear at Bristoe Station. They moved up the Alexandria Turnpike to Broad Run Church, where they deflected on the road to Greenwich, and soon after struck our trail just behind the Third Corps, and eagerly pursued it.

They were busy picking up stragglers and making some preparation for an attack upon our unsuspecting corps, when about noon General Warren's Second Corps, which was still behind, and bringing up the rear, made its appearance on the *tapis*, and materially changed the programme of the scene. Hill, finding himself nicely sandwiched or trapped by his own indiscretion, turned away from the retreating Third Corps, to fight, and, if possible, drive back the advancing Second.

Warren's surprise in finding an enemy in force before him was not less than Hill's in finding one behind him; but it took Warren only about ten minutes to adjust himself to this unexpected position of affairs, when his batteries opened with such precision and effect, aided by the musketry of his infantry, that the Rebels fell back in much greater haste than they had advanced, leaving six of their guns in our hands and multitudes of dead, wounded, and prisoners. Five of the captured guns, still serviceable, were at once seized and used against the disappointed foe with telling power.

One historian says;

> Our loss in killed and wounded was about two hundred, including Colonel James E. Mallon, Forty-second New York, killed, and General Tile, of Pennsylvania, wounded; that of the enemy was probably four hundred (besides prisoners), including Generals Posey (mortally). Kirkland, and Cooke, wounded, and Colonels Ruffin, First North Carolina, and Thompson, Fifth North Carolina Cavalry, killed.

This Bristoe fiasco was a stunning blow to the Rebel pursuit, and greatly checked their incursions.

But our soldiers held the field so lately won only until dark, and "then followed the rest of the army, whose retreat they had so effectually covered."

General Meade continued his retreat to Centreville, and then, seemingly ashamed—as well he might be—of his flight, would have retraced his steps and pushed back the insolent foe, but he was prevented from executing his plans by a heavy rain-storm, which began on the sixteenth. While he was awaiting the arrival of pontoons to enable him to recross Bull Run, which was enormously swollen, the enemy, after some daring skirmishes along his front, and some feints of attack, retreated quite rapidly, completely destroying the Orange and Alexandria Railroad from Manassas Junction to the Rappahannock.

A more thorough work of destruction was never witnessed. Scarcely a tie even remained. The ties were generally heaped together, and set on fire, and the rails were laid upon the heaps cross-wise. As the middle of the rails became heated, the ends lopped down, forming a graceful bow. They were thus effectually ruined. In many instances the rails thus heated were twisted around the trees. The road and the telegraph lines and posts were utterly demolished.

For a few days the Harris Light was bivouacking near Sudley Church, and the cavalry was picketing, scouting, and patrolling on either side of Bull Run; and, on one occasion, while endeavouring to ford the swollen stream, several men and horses were drowned.

October 18.—Today Kilpatrick advanced with his division, which consists of Custer's and Davies' brigades, to within a half-mile of Gainesville, where we bivouacked for the night. A terrific rain-storm raged nearly all night, making our condition very uncomfortable, and rendering the going impracticable, except upon the turnpikes. At this time of the year these night-storms in Virginia are very cold, and the sufferings of men mostly unsheltered, as we were, are beyond description. On such a night one will naturally recall such passages as the following, from Byron's *Childe Harold*:

> The sky is changed, and such a change! oh, night,
> And storm, and darkness, ye are wondrous strong,
> Yet lovely in your strength, as is the light
> Of a dark eye in woman! far along
> From peak to peak, the rattling crags among.
> Leaps the live thunder! not from one lone cloud,
> But every mountain now hath found a tongue,
> And Jura answers through her misty shroud.
> Back to the joyous Alps, who call to her aloud!
> And this is in the night: most glorious night!
> Thou wert not sent for slumber! let me be
> A sharer in thy fierce and far delight,—
> A portion of the tempest and of thee!

It is true that the poet, looking out upon the storm and listening to its mutterings from his comfortable studio, may call such a night "glorious," and may find in it depths of inspiration and delight; but to us poor soldiers it seemed more appropriate to take up Shakespeare's lines:

> The tyranny of th' open night's too rough
> For nature to endure

While everyone felt to say,

> The gathering clouds, like meeting armies,
> Come on apace.—Lee's *Mithridates*.

All night long our pickets along Cedar Run were confronted by Stuart's pickets, though no disposition to fight us was manifest in the morning. Dripping with wet and somewhat stiffened with cold, we were ordered in battle array early in the morning, and the command, about two thousand strong, advanced toward Buckland Mills. The Rebel pickets were quickly withdrawn, and their whole force slowly and without resistance retired before us. With some degree of hesitation, yet unconscious of imminent danger, we advanced on the main turnpike toward Warrenton.

Our advance-brigade had just passed New Baltimore, when Fitz-Hugh Lee, who had surprised and cut his way through a small detachment of our infantry at Thoroughfare Gap, then had swiftly swung around our right by an unpicketed road, fell upon our rearguard at Buckland Mills, and opened upon our unsuspecting column with a battery of flying artillery. At this signal Stuart, who had hitherto retired before us quietly, now turned about and advanced upon us in front with terrible determination.

Thus unexpected troubles were multiplying around us. Scarcely had we time to recover our senses from the first shock of attack upon our rear and front, when General Gordon, with a third division of cavalry, until now concealed behind a low range of hills and woods on our left, appeared upon the scene, and advanced upon our flank with a furious attack, which threatened to sever our two small brigades and to annihilate the entire command. We were now completely surrounded by a force which greatly outnumbered our own.

This was a critical situation; but "Kil" (as the general is familiarly styled among us) seemed to comprehend it in a moment. All thought and effort now centralized into a plan of escape from the snares which the enemy had laid for us, and into which we had too easily thrown ourselves. Kilpatrick is supposed by some to have unnecessarily exposed himself, in which he suffered his first defeat, though escaping with a remarkably small loss.

Quickly ordering his force to wheel about, he led them back in a determined charge upon Lee's columns and artillery, now planted on the banks along Cedar Run. This timely order, executed with masterly skill, saved his command from utter disaster, and justified his course. As it was, however, he lost nearly three hundred men, including quite a number who were drowned in the creek while endeavouring to escape. The scene was one of great confusion and distress.

The Author's Capture

By the sudden evolution of the command, when the order was first executed, the Harris Light, which was in front, while advancing, was thrown in the rear, and was thus compelled to meet the desperate charges of the enemy in pursuit, and to defend itself as best it could from fire on the flank. Having reached a slight elevation of ground in the road, we made a stand, and for sometime checked the advancing columns of the Rebels by pouring into their ranks rapid and deadly volleys from our carbines and revolvers.

Stuart, who commanded in person, saw clearly that the quickest and almost only way to dislodge us was by charging upon us, and, consequently ordering the charge, he came with a whole brigade amid deafening yells. Our men stood firmly, almost like rocks before the surging sea. We were soon engaged in a fierce hand-to-hand conflict with the advancing columns.

In Byron's *Corsair* we find a description of the scene:

Within a narrow ring compressed, beset,
Hopeless, not heartless, strive and struggle yet,—
Ah! now they fight in firmest file no more,
Hemmed in—cut off—cleft down—and trampled o'er,
But each strikes singly, silently, and home,
And sinks outwearied rather than o'ercome,
His last faint quittance rendering with his breath,
Till the blade glimmers in the grasp of death.

At this important juncture my faithful horse was shot under me, and we both fell to the ground. Meanwhile our little party, outnumbered ten to one, was hurled back by the overpowering shock of the Rebels, who rode directly over me. Injured somewhat by the falling of my horse, and nearly killed by the charging squadrons, which one after another trod upon me, I lay in the mud for some time quite insensible. How long I lay there I cannot tell; but when I returned to consciousness the scene had changed.

I was in the hands of a Rebel guard, who were carrying me hastily from the hard-fought field. My arms had been taken from me, and my pockets rifled of all their valuables, including my watch. I was unceremoniously borne to the vicinity of an old building, where I met a number of my comrades, who with me had shared the misfortunes of the day. And thus ended three years and more of camping and campaigning with the Harris Light.

What I saw and endured, thought and experienced, during a little more than a year among the Rebels, in several of their loathsome prisons, may be found recorded in a volume I published in 1865, entitled *The Capture, Prison-Pen, and Escape.*

The capture—Cavalry fight at Buckland's Mills

The Capture, Prison-Pen and Escape

Contents

Preface	239
Enlistment and Service in the Field	243
The Capture	248
Libby Prison	255
In the Hospital at Libby	261
Return From the Hospital	274
Imprisonment at Danville, Virginia	291
At Macon, Georgia.—"Camp Oglethorpe"	298
Savannah, Georgia,—"Camp Davidson"	311
At Charleston, "Under Fire"	318
Roper Hospital, Charleston	330
Removal to Columbia	338
Columbia, South Carolina—"Camp Sorghum"	342
The Escape From Columbia[1]	357
The Escape—Following the Rebel Army in Georgia	382
Recaptured by a Rebel Picket	393
The Escape From Sylvania, Georgia	404
Homeward Bound	419
At Millin—"Camp Lawton"	423

Salisbury Prison	428
At Andersonville—"Camp Sumter"	433
Appendix	448

We speak that we do know, and testify that we have seen.

To
THE WIDOWS, CHILDREN, FATHERS,
MOTHERS, BROTHERS, SISTERS, FRIENDS, AND
SURVIVING COMRADES
OF THE THOUSANDS OF BRAVE MEN
WHO LEFT THE PLEASURES AND COMFORTS OF HOME,
ABANDONED CHERISHED ENTERPRISES
AND BUSINESS SCHEMES
FOR THE PURPOSE OF SERVING THEIR COUNTRY,
AND WHO HAVE BEEN CAPTURED BY THE ENEMY
WHILE IN THE FAITHFUL PERFORMANCE OF
THEIR DUTY, AND GONE DOWN TO UNTIMELY GRAVES
THROUGH UNPARALLELED SUFFERINGS,
IS THIS VOLUME MOST RESPECTFULLY DEDICATED
The Author.

Hallow ye each unmarked grave,
Make their memory sure and blest;
For their lives they nobly gave
And their spirits are at rest.

Preface

The following pages are offered to inquiring minds with the hope that they may throw some light upon the inhuman treatment we received in Southern Prisons.

They do not pretend to give a complete history of prison-life in the South—only a part. Others are contributing sketches for the dark picture, which at the best, can but poorly illustrate the fearful atrocities of our brutal keepers.

The multiplied woes of the battlefield, the sufferings of the sick and wounded in hospitals which the Federal Government has established, might almost be considered the enjoyments of Paradise, when compared with the heartrending and prolonged agonies of captives in Rebel stockades.

Sad and painful as it seems in the former case, there are a great variety of mitigating circumstances which tend to soothe the feelings as we contemplate them. Their sufferings are of comparatively short duration, surrounded as they are by these who never tire in their efforts to provide comfort and relief. Members of the numerous humane societies can visit them and attend to their wants; but in the latter case they have passed the boundary which bars them from all these things.

We are even led to conclude, by the usage which we have received at the hands of our captors, that it was their deliberate intention to maim, and there by render us completely unfit for future service. They have seen us, with apparent satisfaction, become so much reduced in clothing as to have scarcely rags for a covering; they have condemned us to hunger and thirst, pain and weariness, affliction and misery in every conceivable form, so that thousands of our unfortunate fellow-beings have anxiously awaited the approach of the King of Terrors as the arrival of a welcome friend that had come to bring them a happy release.

In the absence of much information on this subject, it is impossible for me to give an exact account of the number of deaths in Rebel prisons. Still, if we consider the statements of several who have reduced their calculations to figures, we may arrive at a more correct conclusion than we otherwise should. Robert H. Kellogg, sergeant-major, 16th Connecticut Volunteers, who was at Andersonville and Florence, says the deaths at the latter place were twelve *per cent*, per month. Mr. Richardson, correspondent of the *New-York Tribune*, says it was thirteen *per cent*, at Salisbury for the same time. There were 13,000 deaths at Andersonville. Mr. Kellogg affirms that one-half of his regiment captured, died in about seven months.

Let us suppose that the prisoners will average 25,000 from January 1, 1862, to January 1, 1865, and the deaths to be nine *per cent*, per month, or 2,250; then multiply by thirty-six mouths, and we have 81,000 deaths. Had we been provided with such clothing, shelter, and food as the laws of health absolutely require, it is probable that there would not have been more than one-eighth of the actual number of deaths.

Hence, we conclude that 70,875 have fallen victims to inhuman treatment. My figures with regard to the number of prisoners and the percentage of deaths may be too large; but allowing that my estimates are nearly right, the awful carnage of the battlefield has not exceeded the frightful mortality of the prison-pen. Whether the Rebels have intentionally murdered our unfortunate soldiers or not, I leave the reader to decide.

I had no thoughts of publishing a book until several weeks after my escape. I kept a diary and journal from the time of my capture. Upon reading portions of it to some of my friends, they persuaded me to amplify, and put it in a readable form.

The rough manuscript was, for the most part, written during my imprisonment at Columbia, sitting on the ground, and writing on my knee. Captain Kelly, 1st Kentucky Cavalry, brought a part of that manuscript through the lines by concealing it in the crown of an old regulation hat, which he wore during his escape. I smuggled the remainder through in the lining of my jacket.

The Appendix is principally the work of Robert J. Fisher, late captain 17th Missouri Volunteers, being taken from his lithograph, entitled the *Libby Prison Memorial*. To these, as well as those friends who have expressed an interest in the work, and in various ways aided in

promoting it, my sincere thanks are tendered.
   Willard W. Glazier.
   Albany, N.Y., November 12, 1865.

The principal Rebel prisons, and where they were located.

Libby, Richmond, Virginia.

Castle Thunder, Richmond, Virginia.

Danville, Pottsylvania County, Virginia.

Belle Isle, in James River, near Richmond.

Macon, Georgia, known south as Camp Oglethorpe.

Savannah, Georgia, known south as Camp Davidson.

Andersonville, Sumter County, Georgia, known south as Camp Sumter.

Millin, Burke County, Georgia, known south as Camp Lawton.

Charleston, South Carolina.

Columbia, South Carolina, known south as Camp Sorghum.

Blackstone, South Carolina.

Florence, Darlington County, South Carolina.

Salisbury, Rowan County, North Carolina.

Raleigh, North Carolina.

Goldsborough, North Carolina.

Charlotte, North Carolina.

Tyler, Smith County, Texas.

Cahawba, Dallas County, Alabama.

Chapter 1

Enlistment and Service in the Field

The first Battle of Bull Run had just been fought, July 21, 1861, and our proud, confident advance into "Dixie" checked, and turned into a disastrous rout. The unwarlike enthusiasm of the country, which hoped to crush the Rebellion with seventy-five thousand men, had been temporarily chilled. It was chilled, as the first stealthy drops of the thunder-gust chill and deaden a raging fire, which breaks out anew when the tempest fans it with its fury, and contrives to burn in spite of a deluge of rain. The chill had passed and the fever was raging. From the great centres of national life, a renovating public opinion had gone out, which reached, in its greatness and universality, the farthest hamlet on our frontier.

Every true man had met the emergency at his own fireside, in consultation with his family, and the Rebellion was just as surely doomed as when Grant received the surrender of Lee's army. In a wider sense, the country had risen to meet the emergency, and Northern patriotism, now thoroughly aroused, was sweeping everything before it. The cry was, everywhere, "To arms!" and thousands upon thousands were answering to the generous call of our President.

It was under such circumstances that I enlisted, as a private soldier, at Troy, New York, on the 6th day of August, in a company raised by Captain Clarence Buel, for the Second Regiment of New York Cavalry, "Harris Light."

I need make no elaborate mention of the emotions or motives which induced me to enter the service; they will be readily conjectured by all loyal hearts.

The Harris Light Cavalry was organised by J. Mansfield Davies, of New York, as colonel, and Judson Kilpatrick, of New Jersey, as lieutenant-colonel.

Up to this time it had been no part of the policy of the Government to increase the cavalry arm of the service. General Scott had trusted entirely to infantry, and his example was still potent. Bull Run, however, had demonstrated the efficiency of cavalry, and the Government began to change its views. To match the famous "Black Horse Cavalry" of Virginia, it was determined to raise a cavalry force in the North, and as Senator Ira Harris, of New York, took an active part in securing the enlargement of this branch of the army, a brigade was formed in honour of his name.

The regiment to which I belonged was denominated the Harris Light Cavalry, and was composed of men from New York, New Jersey, Connecticut, Vermont, Pennsylvania, and Indiana. It was originally intended for the regular army, and was for some time known as the Seventh U. S. Cavalry; but the regular cavalry having been reduced to six regiments, we were assigned to New York, as she had contributed the largest number of men to the organisation.

During the latter part of August, the regiment was ordered to Washington, and after a month's drill crossed the Potomac, and encamped in front of the enemy at Munson's Hill.

McClellan was in command, and all was quiet on the Potomac until spring. The winter was spent in drilling, and the discipline at that time imparted to the army was of great service in after campaigns. Our regiment was encamped at Arlington Heights, on the Rebel General Lee's plantation.

March 3, 1862, began the grand advance of the Army of the Potomac, which resulted in the capture of the "Quaker guns" at Centreville. In this campaign the Harris Light was, for a time, body guard to General McClellan. The army then fell back to its old position, and shortly after the main portion of it was embarked for the Peninsular Campaign. General McDowell was left in command of Northern Virginia, with a small force designed more particularly for the defence of Washington, although they did good service in harassing the enemy still remaining in their front.

About the first of April, he advanced with the small force left in his command, Colonel—afterwards General—Bayard being in command of the cavalry, which at that time consisted of the Second New York and the First Pennsylvania Cavalry, the former being the regiment to which I belonged. Several days were spent in feeling the front of the enemy, and finding their exact location. Reconnoitring was the principal order for a time. Each side had to become familiar with the changed circumstances of the situation, and neither seemed disposed to take a hasty step which might prove advantageous to the other. This cautious policy was broken in upon by the apparently reckless daring of General—then Colonel—Kilpatrick. The enemy were strongly intrenched at Falmouth Heights, and he asked permission to surprise them in the night time. After much persuasion leave was granted, and, at the head of our small regiment of cavalry, he undertook the work.

As we approached the works in the darkness, to within hearing of the Rebels, he shouted, to his officers,—

"Bring up your artillery in the centre, and infantry on the left!"

"Well, but, Colonel," said an honest, but rather obtuse captain, "we haven't got ——"

"Silence in the ranks!" shouted Kilpatrick.

"Artillery in the centre, and infantry on the left!"

The Rebel pickets caught and spread the alarm, and the heights were carried with little opposition.

The early part of the summer was spent almost entirely in raiding. Expeditions were sent in every direction, but more especially towards Richmond. Many railroads were destroyed, and large quantities of commissary stores. In this way the cavalry found enough of both war and romance.

About the first of July, General Pope was put in command of the troops in Virginia, and soon after fought the battle of Cedar Mountain. A battalion of our regiment was body-guard to McDowell during the fight.

The campaign on the Peninsula having been concluded, McClellan re-embarked his troops for Washington, while Lee left his fortifications around Richmond, and soon confronted Pope on the old Bull-Run battle-ground. Just before this, while Lee was bringing his army northward, occurred the first cavalry fight at Brandy Station, in which the Harris Light lost heavily.

After the second Bull Run battle, the cavalry covered the retreat to Washington, checking the advance of the Rebels, and covering the flanks and roar of our army. This necessitated continual fighting with the enemy's cavalry and with the vanguard of their infantry.

By the almost continual skirmishing of the summer campaign our numbers were sadly depleted; and we were at this time ordered to Hall's Hill, eight miles from Washington, to recruit our wasted ranks.

The first of November we again moved to the front, and picketed the advance, under General Bayard, until the Battle of Fredericksburg, in the early part of December.

In this disastrous engagement, General Bayard was killed, and Burnside, with his whole army, forced to recross the river. Winter quarters were soon after established, and the two armies passed the winter in watching each other across a narrow river. The cavalry remained at the extreme front, doing picket duty along the north bank of the Rappahannock.

About the first of April, 1863, preparations were made for another movement. The cavalry were sent on a raiding expedition in the direction of Warrenton. At this place the Harris Light gave the famous Black Horse Cavalry a few scares. Our company of less than a hundred men rode into the town, and as they did so, about two hundred of the gallant black knights rode out at a break-neck pace, on the opposite side.

During the winter, Hooker had taken command of the army, and great preparations were made for a vigorous campaign. On the 27th, the army again crossed the river, and for several days the great battle of Chancellorsville raged. At this time General Stoneman had command of the cavalry. He had turned the enemy's position at Chancellorsville, while the battle was being fought, and cut off their communications in the rear.

While Stoneman was thus engaged, Colonel Kilpatrick galloped entirely around Lee's army, and passed within the second line of fortifications around Richmond, from there across to Yorktown, and returned with a swoop in time to be at the second fight at Brandy Station, on the 9th of June. This was the largest as well as the most stubbornly contested cavalry fight of the war.

Lee at this time was advancing up the Shenandoah Valley, and our cavalry, under General Pleasanton, was guarding the supply train in the rear of our army, and fighting the Rebel General Stuart through the gaps in the Blue Ridge Mountains.

During this advance were fought the battles at Aldie, Middleburg, and Upperville,—all severe contests, in which "the Harris Light" lost heavily.

Immediately after was fought the Battle of Gettysburg. During this engagement the cavalry were harassing the Rebel rear, and taking care of Stuart's cavalry. On the night of the 4th of July our cavalry captured General Longstreet's entire wagon train, laden with the ripe crops of Pennsylvania and Mary land, and guarded it safely, together with fourteen hundred prisoners, in spite of Stuart's most vigorous efforts to effect a recapture.

During the retreat of Lee, Gens. Kilpatrick and Stuart were almost daily in conflict. The battles of Boonsboro, Williamsport, and Hagerstown, were fought, and in fact the cavalry was constantly engaged until we made the final charge on Lee's rear, as he was crossing the Potomac at Falling Waters on the 14th of July.

Our army then slowly followed the great Rebel raider, until he halted on the south bank of the Rapidan. Skirmishing was kept up till late in the fall, when the movements mentioned in the next chapter were inaugurated, which to me resulted in capture.

CHAPTER 2

The Capture

In the early part of October, 1863, the Army of the Potomac, resting from its arduous work of the summer campaign, was encamped on the north bank of the Rapidan.

From April till September the contending armies had been almost constantly engaged, each endeavouring to strike the telling blow that was to drive its enemy back upon Richmond or Washington. The public feeling, both North and South, had been wrought up to its highest pitch. General Meade was thought equal to the emergency by the loyal ones, and many prayers ascended daily for him and his noble army.

Six months had now been consumed, and apparently without any decisive result. Active preparations were in progress for a renewal of the struggle. Reconnoissances were made, and orders were confidently expected from General Meade to advance; but just on the eve of our forward movement, intelligence was received that Lee had very suddenly withdrawn the main force of his army, which had been confronting us along the line of the Rapidan, and was making a rapid flank movement, threatening the occupation of the plains of Manassas before General Meacle could reach them. Swift messengers, from officers high in command, brought orders to retire with promptness, but in good order, if possible. My regiment was called in from picket duty on the morning of October 9th, and ordered to join the division at James City, at which place we had an engagement with the Rebel cavalry on the following day.

The battle raged with fury and slaughter until eight o'clock p. m., when the firing ceased, and the contending legions sought repose from their work of death. The main body of our cavalry retired a short distance from the field, leaving only a light skirmish line at the front, and at an early hour on the morning of the 11th we took up march for the Rappahannock, acting is rear-guard of the army. Skirmishing was continued at almost every step of the march. On the Sperryville Pike to Culpepper, the Rebels pressed us vigorously. At this point the cavalry corps separated, Buford with his division falling back by way of Stevensburg, Gregg by Sulphur Springs, leaving Kilpatrick on the main thoroughfare along the rail road by Brandy Station.

Kilpatrick had but just moved out of Culpepper when Hampton's division of cavalry made a furious attack upon the Harris Light acting as rear-guard, with the apparent hope of breaking through upon the main column and dispersing it or of delaying it, so as to enable a flanking column to intercept our retreat.

Gallantly repelling every attack the command moved on until within sight of Brandy Station, when it was discovered that General Fitz Hugh Lee hold the only road upon which it was possible for Kilpatrick to retire. Stuart at the head of another column of Rebel cavalry, aided by artillery well posted, threatened our left. The right was exposed to a galling fire from the enemy's sharp shooters, while behind us were Hampton's legions predicting speedy destruction to their retiring foe.

This was a situation to try the stoutest hearts. Nothing daunted by this formidable disposition of an enemy very superior in numbers, Kilpatrick displayed that decision and daring which have ever characterized him as a great leader of cavalry, and proved himself worthy to lead the brave men who composed his command. Forming his division into three lines of battle, he assigned the right to General Davies, the left to General Custer, and placing himself in the centre, advanced with terrible determination to the contest.

Having approached to within a few hundred yards of the enemy's lines, Kilpatrick ordered his band to strike up some national airs, to whose spirit-stirring strains was joined the blast of scores of bugles ringing forth the charge. Brave hearts became braver, and if the patriotism of any waxed cold, and the courage of any faltered, they here grew warmer and stronger until pride of country had touched the will, and an uncontrollable principle had been kindled that emphatically affirmed the man a hero until death. Fired with a love for the cause in which they were engaged, this band of invincible troopers shook the air with their battle cry and dashed forward to meet their unequal foe.

With his usual daring, General Davies was foremost in the fray, and led his command for the fourth time on this memorable field.[1] His words of encouragement were, "Soldiers of the First Brigade, I know you have not forgotten the examples of your brave comrades who in past engagements were not afraid to die here in defence of the old flag."

The Rebel lines broke in wild dismay before the uplifted sabres of the unflinching veterans, who, feeling that they had nothing but life to lose, risked it, with a vengeance, upon the fearful issue. Kilpatrick thus escaped disaster, defeated his pursuers, and presented to the beholders one of the grandest sights ever witnessed on the Western Continent.

By Heaven! it was a goodly sight to see,
For one who had no friend or brother there.

No one who looked upon that wonderful panorama can ever forget it. On the great field were riderless horses and dying men, clouds of dirt from solid shot and exploding shells, long dark lines of cavalry dashing on to the charge, with their drawn and firmly grasped sabres glistening in the light of the declining sun; while far beyond this scene of tumult were the dark green forests skirting the north bank of the Rappahannock. Kilpatrick's division soon afterward joined that of Buford, and with their united forces they engaged the enemy in a series of brilliant charges which materially checked his pursuit, and at night we crossed the Rappahannock in safety.

The cavalry continued its retreat, acting as rear guard to the infantry, to the old field of Bull Run, where it was expected a third battle would be fought.

October 12.—The cavalry corps moved from Rappahannock Station at two o'clock p.m. A portion of our infantry recrossed the Rappahannock at an early hour in the morning, and made a forced march to Brandy Station, where a spirited engagement took place. The movement seems to have been made with a view to deceiving the enemy.

October 13.—Left Bealton at two a. m. While the regiment lay bivouacked at that place, an artillery caisson took fire by accident, causing a rapid explosion of its contents. The consequence was a wide-spread alarm which brought every trooper to his horse, prepared to resist the foe, who was supposed to have made a furious onset.

October 15.—Near Sudley Church. The army continued its retreat

---

1. First Brandy Station was fought August 20th, 1862; second, June 9th; third, September 12th; and fourth, October 11th, 1863.

on the 14th, until late in the afternoon, when a general halt was ordered and preparations made for battle. At early dawn on the morning of the 15th the thunder of our artillery at Bristoe announced General Meade's intentions, and opened an engagement which resulted in a disastrous repulse to the enemy, and effectually checked his advance, which had thus far met with but little opposition.

October 16.—The Harris Light was relieved from picket at twelve o'clock m., and moved with the brigade to Bull Run bridge. Kilpatrick's division ordered out at three o'clock p. m. to make a reconnoissance in force. A terrific rainstorm ensues. Several men and horses drowned while fording Bull Run.

October 17.—"Boots and saddles" at nine a. m. Ten o'clock, supporting a battery. Shelled the Rebel skirmishers and drove them back two miles toward Gainesville.

October 18.—Kilpatrick's division was ordered in pursuit of the enemy at four o'clock p. m. Skirmishing was kept up vigorously with the Rebel cavalry from Newmarket to Gainesville. The Harris Light acted as advance-guard, and picketed the front until late in the evening, when we were relieved by the Fifth New York Cavalry.

October 19.—Kilpatrick resumed march at daybreak. The Rebel cavalry, under Stuart, retired without opposition, until our advance had passed New Baltimore on the Warrenton pike, when Fitz Hugh Lee, who had surprised and cut his way through our infantry at Thoroughfare Gap, fell upon our rear guard at Buckland, and opened with his artillery. At this signal General Stuart, who had hitherto been very quietly retiring, now turned and charged us in front. The Rebel General Gordon made a furious attack upon our left flank, threatening to separate the two small brigades which composed Kilpatrick's division. This was a critical situation, but "Kil.," ever equal to the emergency, ordered his whole force to wheel about and charge the columns of Lee.

The Harris Light, having been in front while advancing, now became the rear guard, and by this movement we were compelled to meet the desperate charges of the enemy in pursuit; having reached a little rise of ground we made a stand, and for some time checked the advance of the Rebels by pouring into their ranks deadly volleys from our carbines and revolvers. General Stuart, who was at the head of his command, saw clearly that he could only dislodge us by a charge, and ordering it lead a brigade in person. Our men stood firm and were

The capture—Cavalry fight at New Baltimore

soon engaged in a hand to hand conflict with the advancing columns of the foe.

At this juncture my horse was shot under me, and our little party, outnumbered ten to one, was hurled back by the overpowering force of the Rebels, their whole command riding over myself and horse.

Being severely injured by the fall of my horse, and by the charging squadrons that passed over me, I was insensible for several moments, and on becoming conscious, found that I was being carried hastily from the scene of action under a Rebel guard. My arms had been stripped from me, my pockets rifled, and watch taken.

Once a prisoner, I was taken to a spot near an old building where a number of others, equally unfortunate, were being guarded.

Here we witnessed an amusing exhibition of "Rebel bravery." The woods were full of skulkers, and in order to make a show of having something to do, each and all were sedulously devoting themselves to guarding the prisoners. Corporals and sergeants and privates in succession had charge of us, and each in his turn would call us into line, count us in an officious manner, and issue orders according to his liking; until some sneak of higher rank came along, when he assumed command, and said in a tone of authority to the others, "Your services are very much needed at the front; go and do your duty like men."

This was often said with chattering teeth and anxious glances in the direction of our cavalry.

Thus we passed under the notice of one coward after another, each styling himself "Assistant Deputy Provost Marshal," until evening, when we were marched to Warrenton and lodged in the county jail.

While at Warrenton most of the prisoners were robbed of their clothing and watches, and in fact everything which could have been of the slightest value to our captors.

One of these "chivalrous gentleman," whose "vaulting ambition generally o'erleaped itself," demanded my hat, overcoat, and boots, when the following conversation ensued:—

Reb. Here, Yank, hand me that hat; yes, and come out of that overcoat and them boots too, you damned son of a ———.

Fed. The articles you demand are my personal property, and you have no right to take them from me.

Reb. We have authority from General Stuart to take from prisoners whatever we damned please.

Fed. I doubt your authority, sir; and if you are a gentleman you will not be guilty of stripping a defenceless prisoner.

Reb. I will show you my authority, you damned Blue Belly (drawing his revolver). Now take off that coat, or I will blow your brains out.

Fed. Blow away, then; it's as well to be without brains as without clothing, at this season of the year.

Johnny Reb was not quite disposed to fire upon me, and giving his head a shake rode off, thinking, no doubt, that he could supply his wants in another direction without wasting his ammunition.

In the morning before sunrise we started for Culpepper. It was one of the severest tramps of my life. The weather was exceedingly hot, and the distance not less than thirty miles. Our guard was mounted, and evinced but little sympathy for our unfortunate condition as we endeavoured to keep pace with them. Their great haste was owing to the fact that General Lee had been defeated at the battle of Bristoe and was in full retreat for the Rapidan, our army in pursuit. None, save those who have been in the cavalry service, know how to sympathize with a dismounted cavalier if compelled to march on foot. Our sufferings were indescribable; curses and threats long and loud were freely indulged in by the guard because we could not walk faster. Six of our number fell by the wayside before we reached Culpepper from utter exhaustion. I thought of several plans for escape during the day, but the guard were old soldiers and watched us closely. We were guarded in a large public building at Culpepper during the night and remained in town all the next day.

Late in the evening we left Culpepper on a train for Rapidan Station, on the Rapidan River. Here the bridge was down, and we were obliged to march to Orange Court House, a distance of six miles. Thoroughly demoralised by the tramp from Warrenton to Culpepper, it was constant pain to make our way. The boys will long remember that short march. The next morning we left Orange Court House by rail for Gordonsville, at which place we remained until three o'clock on the morning of the 23rd of October. The guards became intoxicated on very bad whiskey, and were very abusive. Cursing and threatening, and levelling their muskets at prisoners, finally relieved them from duty, and their places were filled by others. At three o'clock a. m. we started for Richmond, to be consigned to the tender mercies of Libby Prison.

CHAPTER 3

Libby Prison

At eight o'clock on the morning of Friday, October 23rd, we arrived in Richmond. The streets were filled with people whose countenances betokened anxiety concerning the result of the terrible struggle that had just terminated in Northern Virginia.

Immediately after our arrival at the depot we were hurried from the cars and marched through some of the principal streets to Libby Prison.

As we passed along, our ears were greeted with an innumerable number of questions and observations, the general character of which may be inferred from the following: "How are you, Blue Bellies?" "Why didn't you all come into Richmond with your arms on?" "What did you'uns all want to come down here and run off we'uns niggers, and burn our houses for?"

Mrs. Johnny Reb remarked: "If these are the officers of the Yankee army, what must the privates be?"

Another sensitively delicate matron, as if taking her cue from the former remark, chimed in with a tragic shudder: "Oh, what a pity it is that our noble sons should be murdered by such miserable "Vagabonds!"

The usual Southern epithets for Federal soldiers were vigorously applied, hence we were not surprised when jested at as "hirelings," "mudsills," "Northern vandals", etc.

A troop of boys followed in our rear, hooting, hallooing, and calling us names; and, really, as is generally the case, they said smarter things than the older ones.

After a walk of little more than a mile, we were halted in front of a large three-storey brick building, dark and frowning, and from the north-west corner of which hung a small sign which tells to the passer by, that "Libby & Son, ship chandlers and grocers," have called attention to this point, as the one where their business was transacted, and where those persons must repair who were interested in bargains particularly associated with their vocation. I confess I did not like the idea of being a "ship chandler" just then; but Rebel bayonets were powerful arguments, and so we all entered the prison, and were informally introduced to Major Turner and disciples, of whom I shall speak at more length in the following pages. By his order, our clothing was carefully examined.

All money was taken from us, and, in short, we were very quickly divested of everything which could excite either the curiosity or avarice of a Rebel. It was not the intention to leave anything that might minister to our comfort or pleasure. Yankee ingenuity, however, as is generally the case, was more than a match for Rebel cupidity. Many valuables were retained by slyly passing them to those who had been examined, while the attention of the guard was elsewhere. In this way I saved my journal.

After this most disgraceful robbery was concluded we were taken to the rooms occupied by the prisoners, and, as we met them, were amazed at their cries of "Fresh fish," "Close up," "Where were you captured?" "What army do you belong to?" "Give him air," etc. They did not abate their zeal in the use of the above expressions until several moments after our entrance. I soon learned that it was the universal custom to treat all new comers in the same manner. This was a sort of initiation, and the more graciously it was endured the better.

There was a melancholy pleasure in meeting several officers of my own regiment. Glad to have their fellowship and cheer, but sad to meet them in such undesirable circumstances.

Upon entering the prison the officers were separated from the enlisted men, and we were not after that permitted to be near enough to them to engage in conversation.

We soon found friends, and became domesticated in our new abode. With the Yankee tendency to organisation, the prisoners divided into messes of twenty each. I was notified in due time that I would be considered a member of "Mess Number Twenty-one," and was at once made acquainted with my new duties. In our mess each man in turn did the cooking for an entire day. In that close, suffocating room, burning corn-meal for coffee and making rice soup over the smoking, broken stove, was indeed extremely disagreeable. The prison days were exceedingly long,—and yet our turns for cooking seemed

Libby Prison

to recur with unpleasant frequency.

October 28.—We are beginning to get accustomed to prison life. I presume we shall fall into the habit of enjoying ourselves at times. *How use doth breed a habit in a man.* Have gathered some facts with regard to the place which must be our home for God only knows how long.

The Libby Prison is an old and somewhat dilapidated building, belonging to the estate of John Enders. Before the war it was used by Libby & Son as a storehouse; but now it is used by Southern fiends—I cannot countenance a milder term—as a den of torture for such as may be so unfortunate as to fall into their hands. There are but few windows, and these small and carefully secured by iron grates. The sentinels are stationed in front of the windows, outside of the building, with orders to fire upon the first man who attempts to look out. We are here huddled together, like sheep in a slaughter-house, awaiting the approach of those monsters, eager to destroy us by any mode of torture The rooms are filthy and unfurnished. There are no chairs or bunks, and but few have blankets.

They do not even furnish us with a necessary allowance of wood. We receive nothing but our rations; a meagre allowance, at the most. Yes, we do receive something else, *viz.*, execrations and curses without measure. Previous to our becoming the occupants of this abode, the sentinel in front of one of the windows fired at a prisoner confined in the room now occupied by us, the one for whom the shot was intended observing the motions of the guard, instantly dodged, and thus escaped unharmed. But the ball, passing through and into the room above, there selected its unconscious victim, and without a moment's warning, launched him forth, prepared or otherwise, to appear before that God who knows every thought and purpose of the hearts of men.

The commandant of the prison is Major Thomas P. Turner, of the C. S. A. He was formerly a student at West Point; but it is generally understood among the prisoners that he was expelled from that school for forgery. He was subsequently made captain in the Rebel service, and, for efficiency as a great Yankee destroyer, has recently been promoted to the rank of major. We come in contact with Major Turner more than with any other of the prison authorities. He is a man whose character may easily be gathered from his countenance; for the hoof-prints of appetite have made a lasting impression there. The utter depravity of the man seems to have gained a full and complete expression in every lineament of his countenance.

To one who comprehends the sublime capabilities of the human soul, there is something inconceivably terrible in its perversions. Look at it as it comes, pure and plastic, from its Maker; look at it in the maturity of its development, as it stands before the world stained and hardened.

The higher and nobler the purpose to which a life may be devoted, the darker and deeper the infamy into which it may be plunged.

There is nothing so loathsome and so much to be feared, as a human soul grown powerful in sin, and left to be racked and twisted by the machinations of the evil one and the sinful promptings of human nature. Demons grown from germs that might have produced angels;—rank developments, drinking in the healthful stimulants of life, and reproducing them in hideous forms of vice and crime;—

Souls made of fire, and children of the sun,
With whom revenge is virtue.

Such, I conclude, is the character of the man in question. It seems as though he has no feelings of humanity. He is, in fact, prepared for any crime that could enlist the evil passions of our nature. He uses every means at his command for annoying the prisoners. So atrocious are his deeds, that the stings of conscience give him no rest day or night. He fancies that the prisoners are plotting to take his life, and has changed his quarters from the prison to a building across the street.

October 29.—There is at present much sickness in the hospital. A large number of the prisoners, captured during the fall campaign, are suffering most severely from their wounds. As the Rebels are utterly regardless of the sufferings of those under their charge, here the spirit of vengeance and brute ferocity is manifested in its most malignant form. The treatment that our officers, wounded and sick, receive at the hands of the "Southern chivalry" is most brutal. It would chill the blood of him not entirely bereft of human feelings to witness such usage of even the dumb beasts of the forest.

November 7.—Today there is an interval in the uneasiness of the prisoners. A flag-of-truce boat is in. It is now thought and earnestly hoped that something will be done to relieve the sufferings of our prisoners, both here and on Belle Isle; yet, what the result will be time only can reveal. It is expected that Colonel Wm. Irvine, of the Tenth New York Cavalry, will be assistant commissioner of exchange.

If we remain long in prison there is a disagreeable lesson for us to learn. Rumours are constantly afloat, and it is so hard to believe that they are not true, that there is a strong desire to trust that we may be soon released. Our wishes are constantly suggesting means for their own accomplishment. And yet it is not well to suffer ourselves to be aroused by these exciting hopes. Such unsatisfied expectations, ending as they do in depression of spirits and disgust of our surroundings, will have a deteriorating effect upon our health. We must grow into the luxury of indifference. Experience must teach us the lesson. That hard schoolmaster must lash us, until our nerves will remain quiet even underneath the stroke.

There is no room for philosophy. It is not enough to say to ourselves, "it is not best to trust these rumours." The mind rebels. It will trust them. We cannot control our rampant thoughts. Fancy will run wild, and dwell on distant scenes of pleasure and comfort from which we are excluded. While she feasts, we are starving. The spirit is strong, but the flesh is weak,—and when the strong spirit returns from its wanderings, weak and weary, how much more weary is the weak flesh that takes it home.

Such struggles must we engage in until we sink into a kind of stupor, which scarcely cares whether life or death be our portion. There is something of the animal in this lethargy, which makes it disagreeable to contemplate. It is natural for man to hope, and when he has outlived hope, he has outlived his manhood likewise.

Chapter 4

In the Hospital at Libby

November 8.—For some days my health had been failing, and when at "sick call" the Rebel sergeant called out, "Fall in, sick!" a friend gave me the assistance of his arm, and I appeared before the prison surgeon.

With something like the business air with which a grocery clerk would address a country customer, came the rapid questions, "What do you want? Where are you sick? How long have you been so? Have you taken any medicine?"

Then turning to the sergeant, "Take this man to the hospital," ended the examination.

Once in the hospital, I was not long in being subjected to its peculiar influence. There was the ominous stillness, only broken by a choking cough or laboured groan; there was the chilling dread, as though one were in the immediate presence of death and under the ban of silence; there was the anxious yearning—the almost frantic yearning—which one feels in the contemplation of suffering which he is powerless to alleviate. And worse than all, soon came that hardened feeling which a familiarity with such scenes necessitates.

It is nothing more or less than a charnel house! We are constantly in the midst of the dead and dying. I am well aware that in time of war, on the field of carnage, in camp, where the pestilential fevers rage, or in the crowded prisons of the enemy, under such circumstances human life is but little valued. Yet there are moments amidst all these scenes, when the awful reality seems to force itself upon the mind of every man with power that cannot be resisted.

Prevailing Diseases

Scurvy, chronic diarrhoea, and fever, are the prevailing diseases here, and from their baneful effects scores of our brave men are dying daily.

It is well known that scurvy originates from an exclusive diet of salt rations and corn bread. Its most effectual cure is a change to vegetable food, vinegar, or some other acid. Its first symptoms are eruptions on different parts of the body. Soon it locates—generally in the ankles. Here large sores begin to form similar to the first appearance of boils. These deepen and spread. The limbs become swollen. If not checked, it soon covers the whole body, and and the flesh actually rots away and falls off the bones. It generally proves fatal by attacking the glands of the throat. These swell enormously, and the patient is often strangled. Sometimes it locates in the mouth; in this case the gums become softened and the teeth drop out.

How human beings could keep their unfortunate fellows in prison, tormented by such maladies, where they could not or would not afford them the means of relief, must remain forever a problem in "secession ethics."

Rebel Surgeons

November 9.—The prison surgeons appear to be gentlemen, and treat us with some little consideration. To be sure, we are not very exacting, and consider ourselves remarkably fortunate if not subjected to positive abuse; still, much credit is due to many of the medical men of the South. They seem disposed to make the best possible use of the means placed at their disposal, and even remonstrated with the Rebel authorities for withholding those medicines and comforts without which a hospital is not a hospital.

There were exceptions to this rule, as I learned from those who were old residents of the prison when I arrived. Some of them have been tyrannical and abusive. Our own surgeons are permitted to be among the sick, and this is a great comfort. Their prescriptions are filled, so far as the prison dispensary has a supply.

November 11.—I arose this morning weak and weary. To sleep during the night was impossible; coughed severely at intervals. Pneumonia is making serious work among the sick. Many, reduced to extreme weakness by fevers and diarrhoea, are attacked with it, and cough their lives away. The climate seems favourable to the development of pulmonary diseases.

Hospital Rations

Our rations in the hospital consist of one small slice of bread for breakfast, for dinner a table-spoonful of rice and a very small piece of meat, and for supper the same allowance as for breakfast.

The hospital connected with Libby is a room about forty feet by one hundred and twenty. It is filled to its utmost capacity, while many cannot get admittance, and so die at their quarters in the upper rooms. In addition to this are many other hospitals in different parts of the city, besides those on Belle Island.

November 15.—I am still very weak, but think my health is improving. Some boxes, sent by our Sanitary Commission, have been opened for the benefit of the sick. It was my good fortune to get some pickles with the vinegar about them. This has had the effect of checking the scurvy, and I am in a fair way to recover.

In spite of the distressing circumstances that surround us, we yet, occasionally, find something to laugh at. A cheerful heart and a smiling face are better antidotes to disease than all the nostrums in the calendar; but they are more rare in southern hospitals than even medicines. He who makes us laugh is a real benefactor. It is generally considered that when a man goes to the hospital, he goes there to die. On this supposition a poor fellow, whose waggery is irrepressible, as he was brought into the hospital today, called out with as loud a voice as he could muster, "Hello, fellers, I've got leave to die, too."

The sickest could scarcely repress a smile, and all felt as though they had received a tonic.

Exchange Rumours

The medical gentlemen in the prison are on their high-heels. The Rebs. tell them that they are soon to be exchanged. Anxiety, hope, fear, and what not, have a strange effect upon them. They are well nigh insane.

November 23.—The prospect of an immediate exchange having vanished, there seems to be no hope, for at least one or two months to come. We can with but slight certainty predict the future, This is true, under favourable circumstances; but in these times of doubt and uncertainty, we truly know not what a day may bring forth.

November 25.—The exchange of surgeons has finally been accomplished, and there is now a general feeling of joy within the walls of Libby. Although we are still destined to remain, yet it is a source of joy to know that some of our number are afforded the opportunity of leaving these execrable walls.

Major Turner issued the order for surgeons to fall in, early in the morning. There was a general rush among the prisoners to send some word to their friends at home by the liberated. The medical gentlemen were very obliging, but had to be on their guard. They were carefully searched before leaving, and if anything contraband was discovered, it was understood that it would not only be taken, but the bearer be detained.

Where only one or two were going, they would read the letters sent home by the prisoners, and if nothing objectionable was found, let them pass. In this instance, however, they had no time for so minute an inspection, and necessarily detained everything. But they were outwitted by many little expedients. Almost every button on the coats of those going home, contained a good-sized letter written on tissue paper. These buttons could be easily taken apart. The soles of their shoes and boots were loosened and papers put between them. The crowns of hats and caps were ripped apart, filled with letters, and sewed together again. Every device was resorted to that offered a prospect of success.

The chief thing desired by the prisoners was, that their friends might learn the secret of communicating with them without the knowledge of the Rebel authorities. One wrote to bid friends to hold his letters to the fire, that the writing might become visible. Another directed a box to be sent him with greenbacks hidden in a roll of butter, or in a piece of cheese, or inside a pickle in a bottle of vinegar.

What we most expect, however, is that the surgeons will make such representations to the authorities at Washington as will bring about a general exchange. Situated as we are, we cannot see why this cannot be readily accomplished. Surely prisoners ought not to be subjected to such treatment in a Christian land, and Church and State be powerless to help them. Truly we looked for more consideration at the hands of our Christian brethren and fellow-countrymen.

Our present condition seems more like a cruel dream of the old barbarous times than a reality of the nineteenth century in civilized America.

Received the *Richmond Sentinel* this morning from a friend upstairs, who conveyed it to me through the keyhole. This keyhole is in an unused door which has been nailed up and the lock removed, leaving this means of communication exposed, and as it has gradually grown larger with use, it is of some service to us.

"OLD NEWSBOY BEN"

Every day a jolly old negro goes along past the prison crying,

"Great tallyraphic news in de papers! Mighty news from de Army of Northern Virginy! Great fightin in de Souf-west!"

It is astonishing how the cry thrills us. It has a *home sound*, and we forget for the moment that we are prisoners in the land of Secessia. These papers we have, at times, been permitted to purchase at prices ranging from twenty-five cents (two bits) to one dollar.

Here we get the southern accounts of the war, with customary embellishments. Whenever they are full of bluster, *braggadocio*, and abuse, we know it has been going ill with the Rebels. When the tone is mild and reasonable and conciliatory, we have reason to believe that things go on swimmingly with them. Thus we interpret their accounts, as gypsies interpret dreams.

November 26.—This is Thanksgiving day. We may feel—and indeed are—thankful that our condition, bad even as it is, is no worse.

Under the very worst circumstances allotted to mortals, we can still imagine something worse, and ought to be thankful. The Scotch divine, who was subject to gout and rheumatism, used to thank the Lord, when suffering with the former that it was not the latter; when the latter got hold of him, he was thankful that he had not both at once; and when both seized him at once, he was more thankful than ever that he had not the toothache at the same time.

Still, we make no very special point of being thankful. There are no chaplains with us, and no religious exercises have been held. There is no danger of its being turned into a day of feasting; for our stinted allowance will not admit of that. Major Turner allowed an issue of the remaining few of our private boxes this morning, which have been in his possession for the past two months. They were all broken open, and were generally stripped of everything which could be of any use to us. They were plundered by the common soldiers of the regiment doing guard duty here, under the eyes and with the permission of the prison authorities. Were we among barbarians, such treatment would be nothing more than we might reasonably expect. But among civilized men, who acknowledge that a God of justice rules among the nations of the earth, with the name of Christian ever on their lips, it is not endurable!

This day calls to mind some days of thanksgiving instituted by Rebels. What they had to be thankful for, nobody knows. Yet these same men, who deliberately starved and froze our unfortunate soldiers, would lift their hands to Heaven with as much fervour as a dying saint, thankful perhaps that the strength and means had been given them to torment their fellow-men. Thankful that their armies were occasionally successful in their strife against the best and freest and most liberal government on earth. Thankful that the chains were tightening on the limbs of the bondman. Thankful that a fierce and cruel aristocracy were triumphing over the equal rights of the people; at least so they thought as they turned their blood-stained palms heavenward. And they thanked God for these results. A greater mistake was never made, as we confidently believe.

If history thanks God for these seemingly retrograde movements of freedom, I question whether the Rebels of the present day will join in the *pean*.

November 27.—Brings us a mail from the North. I was so fortunate as to receive two letters. They were indeed like *cold water to a thirsty soul*. No one can appreciate the value of a bit of paper crossed with familiar lines and home thoughts until they receive it under such circumstances. The reception of these letters, however, is an unusual occurrence; for we are seldom permitted to correspond with our friends; and then only under the most cruel restrictions. Our letters are limited to six lines of ordinary note paper, including date, signature, and address. They are carefully criticised by the Rebel authorities, and no information concerning our true condition is allowed to be sent.

Every scheme that could be divined to outwit the Rebels has been resorted to, and successful to some extent; for General Dow and many other prisoners have learned the secret of writing with "invisible ink," which is nothing more than a solution of soda or *saleratus*. This leaves no impression on the paper until it is heated, when it becomes quite distinct, and may be easily read. But this secret was at length discovered; it occurred in this wise: A captain, writing to a fair and undoubtedly very dear friend, could not brook to be limited to only six lines, when he had so much to communicate; so, resorting to this mixture, he completely filled the sheet with "soft and winning words;" and then, fearing lest his fair *dulcenea* would not discover the secret, added,—

"Now, my dear, read this over, and then bake it in the oven and read it again."

This was too much. The Rebels thinking that if the letter would improve by baking it might be well to improve it at once, accordingly held it to the fire. This brought to light four closely-written pages of the tenderest and most heart-rending sentiment.

The hard-hearted wretches were not in the least affected by the soul-stirring appeals, but threw it into the fire. Since then our correspondence has been carefully scrutinized, and will doubtless in the future be subjected to all manner of tests.

GENERAL NEAL DOW,

of Maine, is the highest in rank of the officers confined here. He makes no very imposing appearance; wears an old red skull-cap, which gives him the appearance of a Turk, and minds his own business. The Rebels, in particular, find him very reticent. He seems to have a perfect contempt for traitors, and scarcely ever speaks to them. They, in turn, hate him very much worse than they do the devil. Several times during his imprisonment they refused to exchange on direct application from our government.

The general has not recovered from his Maine-law proclivities by any means. He very often discourses to us from his corner on the subject of temperance, and sends home his thrusts with all his former vigour.

He is also something of a wit. The prison is alive with vermin, and so is the general. One day while sitting on his blanket searching his clothes, an officer said to him, "What, general! are you lousy?"

"No," said the general, "I ain't, but my shirt is."

Many of his letters, written to friends in the North, with invisible ink, have been published; but his literary labours are at an end for the present at least.

November 28.—Some of our senior officers have complained to the prison authorities in relation to our rations, but to no purpose. You might as well approach a granite rock, with expectation of receiving sympathy; for they are perfectly hardened to all feelings of humanity, and are only delighted with the intensity of our sufferings.

We are becoming accustomed to the sensations of hunger. A continual gnawing at the stomach has become chronic, and is little regarded, yet is surely having its legitimate effects on our health and constitutions.

The ravages of death are spreading most fearfully among our enlisted men on Belle Island, and in the various hospitals of the city.

BURIAL OF THE DEAD

The burial of the dead is a very business-like affair. As fast as men die they are carried out to the "dead house" and piled up, much as bags of corn would be, until there are enough for a load, when the keeper calls out to the prison carter, "A load of dead Yankees! Drive up your mule." The carter then drives up, and takes in his load with as much unconcern as though he were drawing wood or other articles.

Escape of Dead Yankees

At first there was no such officer as "dead-house keeper," but it was noticed that somehow the dead Yankees often came up missing—concluding to bury themselves, or get along without burial; and after this the dead were under surveillance, as well as the living.

Escaping was a regular trade. The first move was to play sick, and get into the hospital. The next move was to bribe, or otherwise influence, the hospital steward, who was generally a Federal soldier, and get them to agree to do the "carrying out." The next move was to get so sick that the Rebel surgeon would say, "he must die." The last performance of the sick man was to die in agony, and be carried to the dead house. His future movements were not very well understood, but somehow the corpse was never seen more. Ingenuity was tasked to the utmost to devise means of escape. Yankee brass was almost invariably more than a match for all obstacles.

A Rebel Surgeon Outwitted by a Yankee Tailor.

A major, whose name I have forgotten, made his escape a short time before I entered the hospital, and deserves a medal for it. He had been a tailor before entering the service, and as the Rebels had a high opinion of Yankee handicraft, the prison surgeon sent him his coat to be remodelled after a northern pattern.

The work was made to last until about dusk, when the tailor soldier put on the surgeon's coat, and taking with him a friend as hospital steward, coolly walked out into the street, and neither of them were heard of again until they reached the Federal lines.

November 29.—More letters reached us today, bringing to me the sad news of the death of a sister. Oh, how inexpressibly sad do such tidings strike the heart. In the very midst of death, I am permitted to drag out a weary life, while dear ones in a land of health and plenty are struck down by the fatal shafts. Her death occurred on the 20th of October, the day after my capture. Just as I was thrust into prison and doubly bound to the grovelling discomforts of earth, she was released from the prison-house of clay, and received, I trust, into the joyous freedom of Heaven.

Our lives are all in the hands of him "who doeth all things well." He appoints us a period of existence, and appoints a moment to depart. All other influences are subordinate to his will.

What can preserve our lives—or what destroy?
An angel's arm can't snatch us from the grave—
Legions of angels can't confine us there.

Bragg's Defeat

November 30.—The Rebels are now smarting under the severe defeat of General Bragg, and although desirous of keeping us in ignorance of our success, yet we have been able to gather nearly all of the particulars. It seems that General Hooker, on the 24th, succeeded in carrying, by assault, the northern slope of Lookout Mountain, while General Sherman, co-operating with him, crossed the river at the mouth of the South Chickamauga. After meeting an obstinate resistance, he at last succeeded in capturing the northern extremity of Missionary Ridge. Owing to the combined success of Hooker and Sherman, the enemy abandoned Lookout Mountain during the night, retiring toward Chickamauga.

Early the next morning the battle was commenced with renewed energy by General Sherman, who made an assault upon the enemy at the northern end of Missionary Ridge. But our troops met with a severe repulse. The field was hotly contested with varied fortune until three o'clock in the afternoon, when General Grant, by hurling two columns against their centre, forced them back, and gained possession of the ridge. The enemy, once routed, retired rapidly toward Dalton, Ga., being hotly pressed by our forces as far as Ringold. The Rebels admit a loss of six thousand prisoners, seven thousand stand of small arms, and upwards of fifty pieces of artillery. They regard this as one of the severest defeats that they have sustained since the war began.

Many jokes were perpetrated on General Bragg, as a result of his defeat. In telegraphing an account of the battle to the Confederate government he had been extremely laconic and quite as unsatisfactory, merely stating that "his left centre had been badly pressed by the enemy."

Some of the prisoners had improvised a minstrel troupe, of which Adjutant P. O. Jones was manager. All the tables had been moved to one side of the cook-room to serve as a stage, and the performance was announced to come off at a certain hour. When the time arrived no Jones was to be found. An hour or two after he came in, and was severely taken to task for his absence, when he turned to the spectators, and with an air of injured innocence said, "I tell you, gentlemen, I have the best excuse in the world for my absence. My left centre was badly pressed by the enemy, and I was compelled to retire."

December 1.—The weather is extremely cold, and the sufferings of the prisoners in the upper rooms are indescribable, owing to the want of blankets and clothing. There are no fires, and, as yet, there is but little prospect of their being furnished with stoves. Many of our men on Belle Island are dying daily from exposure. Large numbers of the prisoners have no blankets, and are poorly clad. They are compelled to walk during the night-time to keep from freezing.

Position of the Armies

This morning we obtained the *Richmond Enquirer* through one of our guards. It is thought that General Meade will soon come in contact with General Lee. Both armies are now drawn up in line of battle, on opposite sides of Mine Run. The Rebels seem to be greatly alarmed at the critical state of affairs, and we are most deeply interested in the result of the movement, which we earnestly hope may, in addition to the defeat of General Lee and the capture of Richmond, release us forever from these filthy dungeons.

Plans for Escape

I have been communicating with Lieutenant S. H. Tresouthick, Eighteenth Pennsylvania Cavalry, through the keyhole, nearly all day, with regard to various plans of escape. All I have to do is, to go to the head of the stairs and push a paper through the keyhole when no Rebel officers are near, and it will be carried to the man to whom it is directed.

To give somewhat of a correct idea of the plans proposed, I will give a short description of the different rooms in the prison. There are three stories besides the basement. Each floor is divided into three rooms fifty feet by one hundred and twenty. The basement is similarly divided, and is used as a cook-room and store-house. The hospital room is on the first floor above the basement, and the room corresponding to this, on the next floor above, is the one occupied by Lieutenant Tresouthick. There are sinks built on the outside of the building at the same height as each story, and running the whole length of the prison.

Tresouthick first proposed that he should feign sickness and get into the hospital, and I in the meantime should, with a saw-backed knife, cut a board out of the sink large enough to let us through.

After an investigation, it was found that our opening would let us through directly opposite the guard, whom we had no means of passing; consequently, this plan had to be given up.

I then proposed that he should get into the hospital as before arranged, and I would manage to get a piece of rope eight or ten feet long, and then some dark, rainy night we would steal down into the basement, the outside doors of which are not locked till ten o'clock p.m., and await our opportunity.

When the sentinel's back is turned we will rush past him on either side, and with the rope trip him down, hoping to be beyond the reach of his musket before he can fire.

This plan seems to suit the lieutenant, and we must wait for his admission to the hospital. He commenced to be slightly sick two or three days ago, he tells me.

Decembers 3.—This morning I read the *Richmond Sentinel,* which was passed to me through the previously-described keyhole by friend Richardson. General Meade is reported to be retiring in the direction of Fredericksburg. The object of the movement is not understood here.

Belle Island

A small portion of the clothing sent on by our government is now being issued to the enlisted men on Belle Island. Colonel J. M. Sanderson, of our service, is permitted to make the issue. The prisoners are in a state of utter destitution, and the clothing cannot be distributed without guards; the poor boys, having been so long destitute, and having almost perished for the want of sufficient covering, now rush upon the party making the issue, and take such articles as they need. There is no way of keeping them in restraint, but by military force. There is much misery here, caused by a disregard of justice. Could all the corruption and consequent suffering be known, it would be a dark spot upon the annals of American history.

Tresouthick's illness progresses finely, and we have hopes of being able to take advantage of it soon. He has only to present himself before the surgeon a sufficient number of times, and insist that he is very sick, in order to be admitted to the hospital, as we think.

December 8.—The weather is a little more mild today, and I find my health gradually improving. The greater portion of my time is now occupied in reading *Napoleon and his Marshals.* I make it a daily practice to read the *Bible,* and to commit a portion of St. Matthew.

Amusements

There are games of amusement among us, which I sometimes participate in; the most popular are chess, checkers, dominoes, and cards. This evening I had a game of chess with Lieutenant Carter, formerly of Baltimore.

Games of all kinds are vigorously plied to pass away time. Looking into any of the large rooms, you may see a party in one corner playing chess on a board marked out on the floor, with chess men made of beef bones. In another corner, a group are playing checkers in the same manner, with buttons and wooden men. Others are huddled together around a set of dominoes, which they are rattling with considerable vigour.

Everywhere, and at all times, you may see the inevitable greasy cards; and euchre, whist, and bluff, go the rounds in rapid succession.

Here a group of lawyers are holding a moot-court, with a grave judge opposite, and a panel of duly-sworn jurymen sitting on the floor along the sides. Acres of valuable land have changed hands under, their decisions. Horses have been adjudged to belong here and cows there, and dogs anywhere and everywhere. Nearly every man of the number has failed in business, and a large *per cent*, have been divorced; and lastly, judge and jury have unanimously decided, that they all be sent home without a moment's delay, times without number.

Debating clubs are settling important questions in different parts of the room, and youthful orators are constraining prison-life to give grace to their gestures and fluency to their tongues.

Finally, from some distant corner, may be heard the winning words of the gospel. An old gray-haired man, it may be, is telling an attentive company of younger men how precious the religion of Christ is to him in the midst of his sufferings. Hymns are sung, prayers are offered, and souls are refreshed.

Many are indifferent to all these things, and are sleeping on the floor.

In this way the time is passed, and in infinitely more ways, which the ingenuity of idle men will suggest.

Getting into the hospital is no easy matter, but Tresouthick is sicker than he was, and has good hopes.

An Escape and Its Consequences

December 12.—Last night Captains Anderson and Skelton made their escape by bribing the guard. Skelton had been wounded, under

Grant, before Vicksburg, and captured. A few days after, he made his appearance in Libby, with a patch over his eye and a green cap drawn over his head, smoking a cigar as complacently as though nothing had happened. A ball had entered his eye and come out behind his ear. Although bright as ever, he feigned dullness, and so was retained in the hospital. Anderson was just admitted, and with all the money they could muster they bribed a guard to let them out.

This morning at roll-call two bunks were empty, but after the sergeant had gone down one tier, two men left their bunks, and went to those of Anderson and Skelton, so their absence was not observed. When the surgeon came, however, he missed Skelton at once, as he was "a very noticeable man." The alarm was immediately given; but, as yet, nothing has been heard of the escaping party.

But little wood has been issued; and our hitherto scanty rations have been reduced as a punishment for the escape of Anderson and Skelton. It seems to be an established custom with Major Turner to punish all the prisoners for the escape of a single man from his number; and we now expect the most cruel exposure to cold and hunger for several days to come.

CHAPTER 5

Return From the Hospital

The exit of Anderson and Skelton has exasperated the prison authorities terribly, and most of all because their success was due to the treachery of their own guards. Thus our prospect of an escape has vanished, and we must take our chances with the others in the upper rooms. It has had a decided effect on Tresouthick's "health," however. He is much better today, and will probably recover much faster than he got sick.

December 26.—There has been much excitement today concerning an exchange of prisoners. Captain Sawyer of the First New Jersey Cavalry has received a letter from Major Mulford, our Commissioner of Exchange, in which prospects of an exchange of all the prisoners confined are mentioned. There are many conflicting opinions and warm discussions. It is rumoured that thirty officers and five hundred men are already declared exchanged. There seems to be much hilarity among the prisoners; yet I fear, as has been too often the case, we shall be disappointed. True, we cannot but feel great anxiety for our release; yet such reports have been so often afloat, that I can place but little confidence in anything that may be said in relation to this subject.

Sawyer has come to be our best authority on exchange, and expresses his opinions with all the bombast and assurance of a Wall-street broker. This is the Captain Sawyer, who, with Captain Flynn of the Fifty-first Indiana Infantry, was sentenced to be shot in retaliation for two Rebel officers tried and shot by Burnside, in Kentucky, for recruiting within the Federal lines.

Flynn was a modest man, and bore his notoriety commendably. Sawyer did a great deal of talking, and made himself a mark for many rich jokes. The prisoners often remarked that they would give a thousand dollars to be shot as Sawyer was.

Hostages Destined for Salisbury

A short time since twenty-four captains were ordered down to Major Turner's office to draw for the chances of going to Salisbury, N. C. Three were to be chosen as hostages for some Rebel officers confined in the penitentiary at Alton, Ill. The lots fell on Captains Julius L. Litchfield of the Fourth Maine Infantry, Edward E. Chase, First Rhode Island Cavalry, and Charles Kendall of the Signal Corps. Last night they were ordered out and sent to their destination, where they are sentenced to hard labour.[1]

December 31.—This day closes up the old year, and soon, if life is spared, we shall enter upon the duties of the new; and what shall be the issues of the coming year none of us can tell. There is an air of sadness observable on the countenances of many, while others, thinking of the festivities of other days, on the occasion of this anniversary, seem desirous of celebrating as they were wont to do in the more peaceful days of yore. Many are making preparations to have a dance in the "cook-room" this evening. Evening advances, and with its onward march the dance ensues. For a time the prisoners seemed to forget that they were securely enclosed within these inhospitable prison walls. The merriment and hilarity still continued till the old year passed away to return no more.

Some, apparently disgusted with the reckless merriment, collected in groups, and sang in full chorus, national songs, till the old year was gone. "The Star-Spangled Banner," "Red, White, and Blue," "Rally Bound the Flag, Boys," etc., pealed through the long rooms with terrible emphasis, and when the chorus,—

The Union forever,—hurrah, boys, hurrah!
Down with the traitors and up with the stars,
While we rally round the Flag, boys, rally once again!
Shouting the battle-cry of Freedom!

was reiterated again and again, with significant beating of feet, it seemed as if the very roof must give way before the accumulated volume of sound.

Some, as quietly as they might, in the midst of so much noise, watched the old year out, according to custom, with prayer and religious songs. All made a "watch-night" of it, for sleep was out of the

---

1. We afterwards learned that they refused to work, and were never compelled to.

INTERIOR VIEW OF LIBBY PRISON

question.

Some time ago a contribution was taken up among the prisoners, of the little money they had kept concealed from the prison authorities, and some musical instruments purchased. A bass-viol, violin, and banjo, compose our orchestra—besides a bushel or more of "bones."

These were on "extra duty" during the whole night, and certainly tended to cause us to forget our aches and privations. Such jollification the Rebels allowed, I suppose, because they happened to be in good humour, or had amusements of their own to attend to.

THE NEW YEAR IN LIBBY.

January 1, 1864.—Another year has been ushered in to mark an important period in the world's history. Its records will, ere long, be fixed by the historian, and posterity shall know the successes and defeats, the trials and sufferings, of the present eventful epoch.

Some little attempt has been made by the cooks to give us a "New Year's dinner," although no extra rations have been issued. For instance, instead of simply boiled rice and corncakes, they have given us rice soup, or rice-water and gruel; rice pudding, that is, boiled rice mixed with cornmeal and water; corn-meal pudding, which is meal-batter mixed with boiled rice; then we have had boiled rice and cornbread, pure, unmixed, *à la Libby*. Thus we have had unity, or at least duality, in the midst of variety—which is an excellent thing.

January 2.—The following is the daily allowance of rations issued to us by the prison authorities: About three-fourths of a pound of corn-bread, one gill of rice, one-half pound of beef, and a very little salt. On such rations we are left to live or die. Groceries can be purchased of the prison commissary at the following rates:—

Potatoes, per bushel,	$40
Onions, " "	50
Wheat bread, 6 oz. loaves,	1
Butter, per lb	10
Lard, " "	8
Sugar, " "	6
Coffee, " "	10
Tea, " "	12
Eggs, per doz.,	6

At the above prices the prisoners may purchase the necessaries of life by disposing of their clothing, rings, and anything else of value which it may be their good fortune to possess.

Punishment for Singing Our National Songs

January 24.—It has all along been our custom to go down to the cook-room occasionally, for a promenade, there being more room for exercise there than in our own quarters. It is a great relief to walk without being constantly compelled to exercise care lest you step on someone. I went down last evening for a walk, and there found about sixty prisoners marching around the room at double-quick, in column of fours. I fell in with them, and all commenced singing "Star-Spangled Banner," "Rally Round the Flag, Boys," etc.

This had continued for some time, when the door leading into the street suddenly opened, and a squad of armed Rebels filed in. Major Turner was at their head, and quickly crossing the room and placing himself at the door leading upstairs to prevent any of us from escaping from the room, he began, "Now then, you damned boisterous scoundrels, I'll teach you to begin your cursed howling in this building again. I want you to understand that you mustn't drive people crazy out in the streets with your villainous Yankee songs."

Then, turning to the guards—"Take your stations about these damned rascals, and shoot the first man that dares to stir out of his tracks, and relieve each other till further orders."

To us again: "Now, damn you, you will stand here till twelve o'clock tonight; and make a bit of noise or move from your places, at your peril."

He then ordered us into line, and marched us to the north end of the cook-room, where we were kept till the appointed time.

The fires went out early in the evening, and it was very cold. Some managed to get blankets from their friends above, but the guards soon put a stop to such transactions. One man from above called down to a friend, through a knot-hole in the floor, and asked him if he wanted a blanket. The guard heard him, cocked his gun, and aimed at the hole; but a call from below gave the man warning, and he was away. So much for singing national songs. But patriotism will find vent somehow, in spite of Rebel vengeance.

The Jews, during their captivity, hung their harps on the willows, and complained bitterly when they were asked to sing their native songs. Union prisoners seem to be affected very differently.

John Morgan, the Rebel Guerrilla, Visits Libby

January 25.—John Morgan, the famous Rebel raider, visited the prison today. His popularity is very great just at present. Major Turner, and a large company of Confederates, accompanied him through the rooms.

As they approached the end of the room occupied by General Dow, they naturally expected him to recognise them, or otherwise show some signs of life; but the stern old general did not for a moment raise his eyes from the book he was reading, until the last Rebel had passed, when he gave one contemptuous glance at them, and continued his reading.

Morgan is a large, fine-looking officer; wears a full beard, and a Rebel uniform trimmed with the usual amount of gold braid.

The Great Yankee Tunnel

February 11.—Sometime ago twenty-seven of our number commenced digging a tunnel with a view to making an escape. We were a regularly organised company of "sappers." Colonel Thomas E. Hose, Seventy-seventh Pennsylvania Volunteers, conceived the plan, and the work was carried on under his supervision. None were admitted into the secret but the workmen.

Colonel Rose was well prepared to superintend the work, for he had served in the Mexican war, was taken prisoner by the Mexicans, and after a short confinement escaped, by tunnelling from the prison a sufficient distance to be clear from the guards. He had served his apprenticeship, and was now prepared to manage and direct.

The Plan of Operation:—

is as follows: There is in the basement a small unoccupied room, which has been closed ever since our arrival here; and we soon discovered that the prison authorities had no use for it, and never entered it. In this room a chimney starts, which runs up through the cook-room, and so to the top of the building. The first operation was to make an opening into this chimney from the cook-room, which opening was hidden by some slop-barrels. These barrels our own soldiers were of course obliged to empty, so that there was no danger of detection at this point. Through this opening a ladder was entered one night, and carried on down to the ground. This ladder had been brought into the prison by the Rebels for the purpose of raising a flag on the building. Inquiry was made concerning it, a few days after it was taken, but as no one knew anything about it, it was inferred that it was taken for fuel.

At the foot of the ladder another opening was made through the chimney wall leading into the, underground basement-room. By removing a few stones from the wall of this room, we were in a situation to commence the work of tunnelling

Conveniences for Performing the Work

The only implements in our possession for performing the work, were an old trowel and half of a canteen. The arduous labour was commenced with the fragment of a canteen, but with this, the progress was so slow, that the most patient were almost disheartened. Fortunately for us, a mason came in to repair the prison walls, and going to dinner before he had finished his work left his trowel, which in his absence most mysteriously disappeared. To him it may have been of but little account, to us it was a Godsend. With the aid of this implement, we were able to make more rapid progress, were greatly encouraged, and worked night and day with ceaseless energy.

Two of our number were kept in the tunnel almost constantly. One, by a vigorous use of the trowel and canteen, would advance slowly on, placing the dirt in an old blanket, which the other would convey out of the tunnel into a corner of the basement-room whence the tunnel started. The work was entirely screened from the Rebel authorities, as they never had occasion to visit this apartment, and the aperture in the chimney was carefully concealed. We at length succeeded in digging underground, until we had passed beyond the line of sentinels stationed about the prison, and then worked our way to the surface, leaving a passage just large enough for one man to crawl through at a time.

The outer end of the tunnel was in a small unfrequented lot, adjoining a small building in which boxes sent from the North were stored. This was a fortunate circumstance, as the Rebel guards used to skulk about this building at night, for the purpose of plundering the boxes; and on the night of the escape, the sentinels about the prison saw every man who came out, but supposing they were Rebels, only whispered to each other, "The fellows are going through the Yankee boxes mighty fast tonight." These whisperings were distinctly heard by some of our men.

The tunnel was made ready for our exit on the night of February 9th. It was about sixty-five feet in length.

Each Man Determined to be First Out

The company of sappers had entered into an arrangement that they should make their exit first, and inform the others just as they were going out; but each man had a particular friend whom he wished to notify, and as we were seen packing our clothing, it soon became suspected that something unusual was in the wind. Curiosity, once on the alert, soon discovered the secret, and then all were jubilant with the hope of escape, and commenced packing up. But egress was so slow that it soon became evident to the cool calculator, that at the best but a comparatively small proportion of our number would be fortunate enough to take their departure from Libby, before daylight would forbid any further efforts to breathe the free air of heaven.

In order to get down the chimney, as well as along the tunnel, it was necessary to strip naked, wrap our clothing into a bundle, and push this on before us. As soon as it was seen that only a few could possibly get out, many, and in fact, most, became selfish, and thought only of furthering their own wishes; all rushed for the mouth of the tunnel, each man seeming determined to be first out. By this movement, the organisation formed by the working party was broken up, and the workmen who were to have had the first opportunity for escape, were not more favourably situated than those who never had borne a hand in the digging.

At the mouth of the tunnel were hundreds most eagerly waiting their time. Through the intense anxiety, there was a rush and a crowd, each one being eager to improve the earliest opportunity. Muscle was the "trump-card," and won all the victories. The weak had to step aside, or rather, they were pushed aside without any apology. No respect was shown to rank or justice. A long-armed second lieutenant had no hesitancy in taking hold of a pair of shoulders that wore eagles and pushing them out of the way. There was no standing aside for betters.

The aged did not receive that deference which unfortunate gray hairs are accustomed to be shown. Mere physical force was the test of championship. Those poor, weak ones, who got help to gravitate to the outskirts of such an eager, crowding mass, just as surely as the light kernels will find their way to the top of a shaken measure of wheat, thought, as they felt themselves being crowded farther and farther from the opening,—

Oh, 'tis excellent
To have a giant's strength, but it is tyrannous
To use it like a giant!

I made several efforts to assert what I supposed my rights, but, as I had not at that time much muscle to back my claims, they were not recognised, and thus I spent the whole night without avail in this bootless struggle for freedom. One prisoner, a Lieutenant Randolph, of the Regular Army, had much difficulty in getting through.

In digging the tunnel, we had encountered a green root which could not be broken, and we had no means to cut it away. It projected from the ground above, and, as the lieutenant was a large man, caught him as he was passing, and held him fast. There was a man before him and one behind, who almost entirely excluded the air; and before he could be helped from his unfortunate situation, he was nearly dead. He, however, got through, and made his way safely to our lines.

Some of the outsiders in this struggle, who despaired of accomplishing anything by strength, had recourse to strategy. There had been considerable noise during this contest for freedom, and the guards were expected to make their appearance at any moment. The outsiders, taking advantage of this apprehension, went to the farther end of the long building, and in the darkness made a racket with the pots and kettles, which sounded very much like the clashing of fire-arms; while some of their number in the crowd sang out, "Guards! guards!"

THE STAMPEDE

In an instant every man was gone from the tunnel, and there was a frantic rush for the single stairway, by about five hundred men. Such a struggling and pressing I have never elsewhere seen or participated in. We neither walked up nor ran up, but were literally lifted from our feet, and pushed in a mass along up the passage, and made our entrance through the door at the head of the stairs as though we had been shot from a cannon, the most of us not stopping until we struck the wall on the opposite side of the room. While this was going on, the scamps who had given the alarm were quietly passing out of the tunnel.

The ruse was soon discovered, however, and in a few minutes there was as great a jam at the mouth of the tunnel as ever. But so eager and unthinking were we, that within half an hour the same dodge was played on us again, and there was another stampede up the stairs.

This continued till morning, when the opening in the chimney was covered, and we went to our quarters. Here a "count" was made, to discover how many had made their escape, when it was found that one hundred and fifteen were missing. Arrangements were at once made to account for their absence, and certain men were designated to cross the room slyly during roll-call, and be counted twice.

Roll-Call

For some reason the authorities were late that morning, and did not make their appearance till about ten o'clock. In calling the roll the men at tempted to cross the room, but were discovered, and so the count came one hundred and fifteen short. The Rebels thought there must be a mistake, and so counted again, but with the same result. Still they thought there must be some mistake, and joked little Ross, the prison clerk, who was none of the brightest, because he could not count a thousand Yankees. This time we were marched from one room to another, and counted one by one, but in every way there were one hundred and fifteen men missing. We of course were as much surprised as the Rebels. They next sent for Major Turner, and he counted us two or three times, but with equally unsatisfactory results. He asked us where they had gone and how they got out, but not a man knew.

The escape was at once made public, and the papers were filled with it, and the most effectual means were used to secure their recapture.

The Guard in Castle Thunder

The authorities were terribly exasperated, and at first arrested the guard and threw them into Castle Thunder, thinking, as a matter of course, that they had been bribed. This set the guards to thinking, and one of them recollected that he had seen a great number of men in the lot near the Yankee boxes. Latouche, the prison adjutant, hearing of this just before night, went and found the opening. Next, they questioned the prisoners as to where in the building it began, but could get no satisfaction; and not until after a long search, did they find the opening in the chimney.

They were really pleased with the shrewdness of the scheme, and were loud in their praises of Yankee ingenuity. Guards were placed over each end of the tunnel, and it was on exhibition for a while. Crowds have been to see the "Great Yankee Wonder," as they call it.

Recapture of Prisoners

February 12.—Twelve of the escaped prisoners were brought in today, and thrown into the cells. Poor fellows! they look crestfallen enough.

February 13.—Sixteen more of the escaped prisoners were brought in and placed in close confinement. Their rations have been greatly reduced, and many of them have been thrown in irons.

Major Turner allowed an issue of boxes today, which have been in his hands for the past two months. The scoundrel had given our government the assurance that all private boxes sent on to the prisoners would be immediately distributed; but in this case there is not even "honour among thieves." Most of the boxes were plundered under the eyes of the prison authorities; and those that were issued were robbed of their most valuable contents. These are doubtless the boxes the guards saw their comrades robbing on the night of the escape.

Twenty more of the escaped prisoners have been brought in during the day.

March 8.—Some of the guard, more communicative than discreet, have been led to disclose all they know concerning Kilpatrick's raid. It seems, from what we can learn, that an expedition has been organised for the purpose of releasing the prisoners at Richmond. We have heard the dull booming of artillery at intervals during the day, which proves that our troops are already engaging the enemy in the fortifications. The prisoners are all on the *qui vive*, anxiously awaiting the result; and how anxiously! When, since the commencement of the war, has there been so much at stake? Richmond to be gained or lost, and with it the freedom of thousands of brave men, incarcerated in filthy dungeons, and dying of starvation!

To be ready for an emergency, we have organised ourselves into regiments, appointed officers, and made all necessary preparations for co-operating with our troops in case of a release, as they will undoubtedly be prepared to supply us with arms. If we are suffered to remain here, we hope, in a measure at least, to aid in our release.

Hopes and Fears

The day wears away, and still no change in the situation that we can learn. Night comes, and the welcome sound of artillery has ceased, and the prisoners are earnestly asking, "Is it a repulse, or has darkness put an end to a conflict destined to break forth with renewed energy in the morning?" The Rebels seem as much in doubt as ourselves, and equally desirous of information. It is a comfort to hear the opinions of others under the circumstances, whether we accept those opinions or not.

March 12.—During the last few days, since the battle, we have learned some of the particulars, from Rebel sources, concerning the fate of General Kilpatrick's expedition.

It seems that at Frederick's Hall, Colonel Dahlgren, with about five hundred men, was detached, with orders to move by the way of Louisa Court House, while Kilpatrick, with the main body, moved on Ashland, thus threatening Richmond with two columns, destroying all government property on their line of march. But a misfortune, which a military commander in an enemy's country is so liable to meet with, thwarted one of the best conceived and most daring plans of the war.

Colonel Dahlgren had employed a negro, as guide, who betrayed him by leading in the direction of Gouchland. When Dahlgren discovered his mistake, he ordered the negro to be executed for his perfidy, and, changing his course, commenced marching rapidly upon Richmond; but the Rebels were now well informed of the movement, and were on the alert.

Death of Colonel Dahlgren

On his return, Colonel Dahlgren destroyed the Dover flouring mills and several private flouring establishments. He also materially injured the James River Canal; but in attempting to cross the river he was surprised by a large force of the enemy in ambush, who fired upon him, killing himself and scattering his party by the first volley.

Kilpatrick, deprived of the valuable services of Dahlgren, and having also to contend against an enemy who were receiving large reinforcements from Pickett's brigade at Bottom Bridge, acted the wise part, and retired during the night in the direction of Mechanicsville.

The advantages gained from the expedition seem to consist wholly in the large destruction of Rebel property, and also in cutting the communication between Lee's army and Richmond. The enemy captured a few prisoners, and, of course, claimed a decided victory.

Rebel Mode of Treating Raiders

The prisoners captured from the raiding party are treated with the greatest inhumanity. The Rebels evidently have not exhausted all their resources of cruelty upon us; for we are well used in comparison. Officers, enlisted men, and negroes, are crowded together in filthy cells, and not allowed to communicate with the other prisoners. Their rations are much less than ours, and even of a poorer quality; no indignity so great as not to be offered them. A Rebel sergeant brings their meals to them, and then orders them to sit down alternately with the negroes. Many men have done this by chance, or from choice it maybe, and thought nothing of it but to be compelled to sit in such a manner by Rebel orders, for the purpose of affording amusement to idle lookers-on is something more than an American's pride can endure with equanimity.

They are not allowed to leave the room, and instead of going to the sink, are compelled to use an open tub which stands in one corner of the room. The object seems to be to impose a sense of disgrace on the men, and subject them to the ridicule of their own comrades, if possible, as well as that of the Rebels.

The reasons which they assign for this inhuman and uncivilized system of torture, is the destruction of public and private property during the raid, for which they hold them responsible.

The cell in which the raiders are confined is discreetly underneath my room; of course, every device is used to open communication with them, that we may get a true history of their treatment, and also for the purpose of alleviating their sufferings as much as lies within our power. We have succeeded, by the aid of a saw-backed knife, in cutting a small hole through the floor, which we have kept carefully concealed.

The authorities are in the habit of inspecting the floors continually to see that nothing is wrong. The hole opens through the ceiling of the cell, just over a large beam only a few inches below it. This prevents their seeing it from below, while the raiders, by climbing upon a table, can place a tin plate on the beam, and receive whatever is put down to them. To prevent their seeing it from our room above, we insert the piece that was sawed out, and plaster it over well with the vile black soap issued to us.

Through this hole we have furnished them with a share of such rations as have been issued to us. Some of our number were discovered by the Rebels while communicating with them, and, as a punishment for this offence, have been transferred to their cell. Henceforth, this was made the penalty for any such attempt; but its only effect was to warn us to be more cautious in the future.

The Prison Undermined

March 15.—Immediately after Kilpatrick's raid, the prison authorities set to work to undermine the building. The small basement-room from which the tunnel commenced, has been filled with a sufficient quantity of powder, and now the Yanks, are prepared for h—ll, as they graphically express it. This is said to be in the event of our attempting to escape, or of a release being attempted by raiding parties. The whole transaction is in perfect harmony with their ideas of civilized warfare.

Such a plan of wholesale murder evinces a state of moral depravity on the part of the authorities at Richmond, to which we challenge the historian to find a parallel in the records of any civilized nation. Can such a people, that will perform acts of this description without apparent shame or conscious self-abasement, be entitled to be called by the mild term "enemies"? None but the blackest of traitors could resort to such an expedient.

Trains have been laid from this room to various guard-posts, where they can be fired at a moment's notice. Major Turner himself has given us to understand that if any more attempts are made at our rescue, the prison will be blown to atoms.

March 20.—Sixty of our number were paroled today, and taken to City Point for the Confederate officers brought down by the Federal authorities; they are to be exchanged. Major McIrvin, of the old regiment, is one of the fortunates. The prisoners are in excellent spirits, and are universally afflicted with "exchange on the brain." Three boat loads have now been permitted to return to God's country, including many of our enlisted men from Belle Isle.

Belle Boyd

A few days ago, the famous Belle Boyd, a Rebel spy, who was at one time captured by Kilpatrick and sent on to Washington, came through the prison. We received no warning of her approach, and were employed, as usual, looking for live stitches in the seams of our clothing. Some were sitting on the floor, with their shirts off; others were giving their last pair of pantaloons a careful scrutiny, while others had dispensed with both these articles, and were performing ablutions at the bath trough. She bore herself with becoming dignity, however, and seemed to look on all, "in the calm light of mild philosophy."

March 22.—The officers captured during Kilpatrick's raid are still confined in the cell with negroes and the officers of coloured troops, who have always been treated as felons.

I came very near being detected this morning by Sergeant Briggs, while attempting to administer to their wants through the previously-described hole in the floor. I had stationed pickets about the building to warn me of the approach of the authorities, but the sergeant happened to be in the small room occupied by General Scammon, at the time I opened the hole, and hence was not seen by the men on the alert for him. Upon leaving the general's room, the sergeant passed within six feet of the place where I was so busily engaged in putting down cornbread and burnt-meal coffee, that I did not notice his approach. Several prisoners, however, who were watching, stepped between us, and thus fortunately saved me from sharing the fate of those whose sufferings I was endeavouring to alleviate.

Prisoners From Plymouth

April 25.—Our number has been increased to day by the arrival of several "fresh-fish," captured recently at Plymouth, N. C. Having been in comfortable quarters at that point ever since their enlistment, they feel the privations and hardships of prison-life much more than prisoners in general. Long, fatiguing marches, and the hardships of many campaigns have somewhat prepared the most of us for still greater endurance; and then we have discovered many expedients for getting along, which only a long experience can make available.

It was quite amusing to see how the "Pilgrims" regarded their "position." Having prepared their first rations in Libby, which, however poor they might be, their long march had made acceptable to them, they remarked that there was no suitable place for taking their meals, and were not a little embarrassed at the merriment the remark produced among the old prisoners, who had long since ceased to consider where they should eat, but what?

The want of bunks, and chairs too, gave them equal solicitude. They are trim-looking fellows, and when we look at our own tattered garments and haggard faces, it seems a pity that they must be reduced to a similar condition.

Through the new arrivals, we are enabled to learn some news from our armies, and the particulars of the fight in which they were captured. It appears that they were overpowered at Plymouth, and, after repelling several desperate charges, Were compelled to surrender. Brigadier General W. H. Wessels was in command of the post, and was among the captured. The general is an old man and looks worn. The Rebels give him credit for desperate courage at Plymouth. He made no surrender, but was actually captured behind the intrenchments, by an overwhelming force.

April 26.—Weather cold and disagreeable. No wood allowed in the upper rooms. Suffering in tense. Our men on Belle Island are being removed to Georgia. Exchange stock low.

The Guerrilla, Moseby

Passed through the prison today. He is about twenty-eight or thirty years of age; has a slight figure, straight hair, and a smooth face, except the upper-lip, which is hidden by a faded German moustache. He recognised many officers whom he himself had captured, and pleasantly remarked that he was glad to see them here. Very little attention was shown him, as we regard it a disgrace for any man to accompany a Rebel through the building.

April 28.—Exchange stock up. It is said there is another boat in with prisoners from the North. The terms for a general exchange are said to be agreed upon, and Aiken's Landing is to be the place of transfer.

April 30.—The prisoners are very despondent today. The rumours of the 28th inst. appear to have had no foundation. The feelings occasioned by our disappointment can be better imagined than described, but imagination, even in her most extravagant flights, can but poorly picture the horrors of this prison life. Our constant experience is *hope deferred*, and yet, *the miserable have no other medicine, but only hope*! and we must continue to hope on.

May 6.—There was great excitement in the city during the day concerning war matters. General Lee was reported to have been defeated, and to be falling back to the fortifications. Several regiments passed through town in the afternoon, on their way to the front. It was evident that there must be some truth in the rumour, for at eleven p.m. we were notified by Major Turner to be ready to leave the prison at a moment's notice.

At twelve o'clock the adjutant's clerk, Mr. Ross, began calling the roll. As his name was called each prisoner passed from the cook-room, through the door opening on Gary Street, and filed down between two lines of guards, closing up to those who had preceded him, and receiving, as he took his place in the ranks, a "corn dodger," which we were told must satisfy hunger until another issue could be made. I could not help rejoicing at my exit from the walls of Libby, for I felt that our condition could be made no worse, while a change of base might present opportunities for escape.

Farewell to Libby

A few of the prisoners were inclined to be despondent, and seemed to indorse the old maxim of *better bear those ills we have, than fly to others that we know not of*. We did not leave Gary Street until the dawn of day, when we moved down to the first bridge and crossed over the "James" to Manchester, where we were packed into cattle-cars, and started for the South. Our place of destination was not known, but was supposed to be some point in Georgia.

CHAPTER 6

Imprisonment at Danville, Virginia

On the morning of May 7th, just at daylight, we left Richmond, and reached Danville about ten o'clock the same evening. It was a long, tedious ride of a hundred and forty miles. Being badly crowded in rough box-cars, it was anything but a pleasant trip. Several of our number effected an escape from the train during the first part of the night.

My old friend Barse jumped from his car while in motion. Twenty shots or more were fired at him by the guard, and he dropped on the ground. The Rebels boasted that "the damned Yank, would never escape again," and were so well satisfied of it that they did not think it worthwhile to stop the train. We afterwards learned that he got off with a slight flesh wound, but was subsequently recaptured and brought back to prison.

Many others attempted to release themselves in various ways. Some succeeded, through the aid of saw-backed knives, in hacking holes in the sides of the cars, and then, at the earliest opportunity, made their way out.

The party with whom I was confined were engaged in this manner, but, unfortunately, our work was discovered before its completion; and thus the scheme was exposed. We were not, however, easily discouraged; for what idea will not awaken itself in the mind of man when destined to a loathsome-imprisonment?

New Plans For Escape

No sooner was our work discovered, and guards stationed near it, than we began to concoct a new plan for escape; which was to disarm the stupid guard by removing the caps from their guns, and then to dash past them at the first convenient opportunity.

We succeeded in rendering one gun useless; but the guard carrying the other, being on the alert, it was impossible to uncap it, and, consequently, we very reluctantly abandoned our cherished project, and turned to think, or perchance to dream, of "prison pens," "bare feet," "corn dodgers," and "deadlines."

After reaching Danville we spent a sleepless night in our crowded position in the cars, and were removed at an early hour in the morning to the military prisons at this post. These prisons consist of three large brick buildings, on the east side of the town.

Previous to our transfer to this place, they were occupied by enlisted men. Near the centre of the second floor of one of the prisons, my messmates, Lieutenants Nyce and Richardson of the old regiment, and myself, have chosen a small spot, which we call our portion of the room.

Military Importance of Danville

Danville is situated at the terminus of the Richmond and Danville Railroad, one hundred and forty miles south-west of the former place, and four miles from the southern boundary of the State. It can be easily defended, and is, without doubt, one of the strongest natural positions south of Richmond. It has a population of about two thousand inhabitants.

Our daily allowance of rations at this prison is as follows: One loaf of corn bread, weighing about three-fourths of a pound; one-half pound of bacon, and one pint of soup. No other varieties.

This is about fifty *per cent*, better than we had at Richmond. Such as it is, there is enough to sustain life. We are fired upon by the guard for the offence of looking out of the windows, as was the case at Libby.

In this, and many other respects, I cannot see that we have gained by the change; for we meet the same stamp of men here that we left at Richmond. In some respects our condition is worse. Especially is there great suffering for want of room. It is impossible to find a place to sleep without disturbing someone. In order to economize space, we have yielded to the necessity of—

Sleeping Spoon-Fashion

At the best, large numbers are compelled to sit up till morning, and then take the places others have vacated.

In spite of the annoyance there is something comical in our situation. We pack ourselves down to rest as a housewife would pack her silver spoons to lay them away; and when any one gets tired of lying on any given side, he sings out, "Spoon to the right!" or, "spoon to the left!" as the case may be, and all turn in the direction indicated by the speaker.

If a man has occasion to leave his place during the night, he is sure to find it filled when he returns; and he will not even know who is the trespasser, unless he has taken the precaution to count and number his place from the wall. Thus he is never sure of cursing the right one.

There is no military force at this point except the prison guard, which is commanded by Major Moffat, who also acts as commandant of the post.

News From the Army

We learn by rumour that there has been a pretty severe engagement between Grant and Lee since the 7th inst. It is generally inferred, by the uneasiness of the Rebels, as well as their disposition to curtail our privileges, that "Uncle Bob," as they familiarly call General Lee, has come off second best.

May 11.—We have already commenced a large tunnel, and, should we remain here long enough, will give the Rebels another subject for reflection. The study of plans of escape is our constant employment under whatever circumstances we are placed. The mind naturally reverts to the army, to home, and friends; and we are willing to risk anything to secure a release from confinement.

Could we but hear from our army, or were we permitted to receive letters, it would be some satisfaction; but even this small favour is denied us.

The papers are vigilantly excluded, but rumour brings us the news that General Averill is making a raid in this direction. This, with the fact that a day's rations have been issued, and the manifest uneasiness of the Rebels, lead us to believe that we will soon be removed to some point in Georgia, out of the possible reach of Yankee horsemen.

We are all in high glee over the possibilities of a release. Groups are collecting, and talking over the chances of success. Were so many children assembled together in anticipation of a day of jubilee, the scene could not be more wild.

The "Star-Spangled Banner" has just been struck up, and all join heart and soul in singing it.

Greensboro , N. C., May 12.

At four o'clock in the morning we bade farewell to Danville, after a stay of four days, and were again set in motion toward the South. We think travelling very beneficial to health; and one not acquainted with the Rebel mode of treating prisoners might be inclined to think that they are disposed to favour us in this respect; for we do not seem destined to remain in one place any great length of time.

It has been a damp, chilly day. Our circumstances (and we, also, doubtless) have been very disagreeable. The cars leaked badly, and the rain was driven in fiercely by the wind.

Meeting Conscripts for Lee's Army

The Rebels are apparently very much alarmed at the state of affairs in Northern Virginia. We met conscripts almost every hour on their way to join Lee's forces.

A more motley, ill-looking lot of men could not have come together, if they had done so by design. They were going in squads of ten, twenty, fifty, or more, as the case might be, "across lots to join Uncle Bob's army in Virginny." Some had hats, and some caps; some coats, and some none. All were armed more or less, always according to their own fancy, or "what they happened to have in the house." Shotguns, rifles, old rusty swords, long knives, horse-pistols, carbines, and broken jack-knives, bid fair to damage their owners much more than anyone else. It is very questionable whether many of them ever swelled Lee's ranks to any great extent,

After a ride of twenty-four miles by rail, we were compelled to leave the cars and march on foot to within eight miles of Greensboro'. The roads were muddy, and our tramp by no means pleasant; for our long imprisonment and scant rations have rendered us completely unfit for a walk of half a mile even. We suffered much in attempting to keep pace with the guard, who urged us forward at the point of the bayonet, cursing and threatening most fearfully all those that fell by the way from weakness and utter exhaustion. No chances of escape were offered, as the guards were very vigilant.

An Attempt to Escape.

When we were again put into the cars, I attempted to hide behind a log and feign sleep, but was discovered, and after sundry kicks allowed myself to be awakened. By this time the cars were filled, and as the prisoners claimed that their cars could hold no more, there seemed to be no room for me, which of course I did not much regret. The officer in command, however, undertook to find me a place, and as the doors were all closed, without further trouble ordered me to make my entrance through a small window near the top of one of the cars. This I was assisted to do by a bank which happened to be alongside of the train just at that point. There were objections from within, however, the men crying, "There is no room in here," but Rebel bayonets were urgent outside, and in I plunged without any definite prospect of touching bottom.

As the fates would have it, I landed on the head of Lieutenant Colonel G. C. Joslyn, Fifteenth Massachusetts. There was much howling, in which, I think the lieutenant-colonel did not participate. In the *mêlée* my few effects were scattered about the car, and I very soon found my level among the others.

There's a divinity that shapes our ends,
Rough-hew them as we will.

Charlotte, N. C., May 13.

Leaving Greensboro', early in the morning, we reached Charlotte late in the afternoon, and were marched under heavy guard to the Commons; where we were told that an issue of rations would be made before leaving the place.

On learning that there were Yankee prisoners in town, the citizens came out in large numbers. Many approached the guard line, and endeavoured to converse with us, but were forced back at the point of the bayonet. Finding that we could not converse with them, we concluded to entertain them with some music; accordingly we struck up the "Star-Spangled Banner," "Rally Round the Flag, Boys," etc.

After each singing, we could see white handkerchiefs waving in the breeze, showing that we were among loyal people who hailed again their country's stirring airs. These demonstrations so exasperated the guard that they sent a detail to drive the "damned tar-heels," as they style the North Carolinians, off the field. All through North Carolina we saw unmistakable evidence of Union feeling, and they manifested their loyalty in a bold and defiant manner.

As night approached, the guard was doubled, which satisfied us that we should remain during the night. Many plans of escape were discussed, all feeling satisfied that if we could once pass the guard, great assistance would be rendered us by the loyalists of North Carolina.

Columbia, S. C., May 14.

We left Charlotte, under very exciting circumstances, at one o'clock this morning.

The night being dark, and the soil light, many of the prisoners dug holes in the ground and there buried themselves, hoping thus to escape the vigilance of the guard, when we should be marched from the field to the cars. Unfortunately, however, the scheme was exposed by one of the guards, who accidentally stumbled into a hole, in the bottom of which he beheld a live Yankee.

Struck with astonishment, he shouted, "Oh, my God! captain, here be one Yank, bury heself in de ground!" A great excitement was the natural consequence. A general search ensued. Torch-lights were used, and the trees and ground thoroughly inspected. This investigation brought to light several holes of a similar character, each having deposited therein a Federal prisoner.

The guards were very angry, and went about shouting, "Run them through!" "Pick up the damned hounds!" etc.; but their captain, a good-natured sort of a man, said, "No, no; the damned Yankees have a right to escape, if they can. I'd do the same myself. I'll risk their getting away from me." But in spite of his confidence, quite a number were left behind in these pits. As many as thirty men had thus buried themselves in the ground.

Our liberties were immediately curtailed, and we were hurriedly driven into the cars and set in motion towards the South. Reached Columbia, South Carolina, late in the afternoon, and were given to understand that after a brief halt we should move on to Macon, Georgia.

Augusta, Ga., May 15.

After leaving Columbia, we pushed on without any incident of importance, being closely guarded, and reached Augusta at six o'clock p. m. We were immediately turned over to the city militia, a motley crowd of cowardly ruffians, who seemed to think that to be soldierly they must abuse defenceless prisoners on the simplest pretext. It has been generally remarked, that the most cruel soldiers are those who have done their fighting at home.

The suffering caused by close confinement was intense. We were not permitted to leave the filthy cars after our unfortunate adventure at Charlotte.

A son of Governor Bradford, of Maryland, was provost marshal of the city. This graceless youth afterwards led a band of guerrillas to his father's residence, and plundered his own home.

Between Augusta And Macon, Ga., May 16.

About eight o'clock in the morning we started for Macon, halted on the way, and several of our number made their escape. Lieutenant Kellogg of the Fifth Michigan Cavalry climbed up into a water-tank, and was unfortunately left behind when the train moved on. Several days afterwards, however, he was recaptured, and made one of our number again. During the whole night we moved slowly on towards Macon.

Chapter 7

At Macon, Georgia.—"Camp Oglethorpe"

May 19, 1864.—We reached Macon at eight o'clock on the evening of the 17th. Two long files of sneaking, stay-at-home Georgia militia extended from the cars to the prison pen, and between them we were marched into "Camp Oglethorpe."

On our arrival at the front gate whom should we find but the veritable Major Thomas P. Turner, fiend incarnate, from Libby Prison. This human monster stood at the gate to count us as we passed in. To his great chagrin forty-seven of our original number were missing, all of whom had escaped from the cars. He drew us up in line, and informed us of the prison regulations, especially that any man would be shot who approached the "dead line." He soon afterward returned to Richmond. His object in coming to Macon was, I presume, to give the authorities some instruction in regard to the treatment of Federal prisoners, and they showed themselves apt scholars.

The Prison Pen takes its name from Gov. Oglethorpe, of Georgia. It is about eighty rods east of the city, and covers an area of a little more than two acres. The enclosure is surrounded by a stockade fence about fifteen feet high, near the top of which projects a platform on which the guards are stationed. Within the stockade, at a distance of fifteen feet from it, is the dead-line, extending entirely around the camp. This consists of an ordinary picket fence three and a half feet high. In many prison pens of the South it is only a line of stakes, with sometimes a single board attached. Camp Oglethorpe was made expressly for our reception, and had never before been occupied.

Macon is situated on the Ocmulgee River in the central part of the State, about four hundred and fifty miles from Danville, our last place of imprisnment. It is finely located, has a population of about ten thousand, and is at present one of the most stirring and important towns in the South. It is one hundred and sixty miles from Augusta, and one hundred miles from Atlanta. Two daily newspapers, the *Macon Confederate* and *Telegraph*, are published here.

Since leaving Richmond my health has been very poor; caused, doubtless, by the various changes to which we have been subjected. Besides, the cars in which we were transported were extremely filthy, and as they were kept constantly closed, the air was very impure. The heat, also, is getting to be intense during the day, and its effects are telling on the strength of the men.

May 22.—Our daily allowance of rations at this pen is as follows: Cornmeal, one pint; bacon, one-fourth of a pound; rice, one ounce; peas or beans, one ounce; salt, one tablespoonful for four days.

We have no cooking utensils except a few iron skillets. The beans furnished here are wholly unfit for use. The rations issued are about one-half of what we really need.

The mortality here, as also at Andersonville, is fearful. Men are hopelessly pining away, while their friends are powerless to help them. It is sad to see a friend and comrade dying in such a shameful manner, while we ourselves have only to expect a similar fate.

New Arrivals

On the morning of the 20th one hundred and seven officers from Grant's army arrived, to take up their abode in the prison pen. Among them are Generals Shayler and Seymour. As soon as the "fresh-fish"[1] arrived the cry ran through the camp, and a general rush was made for the gate. An eager group surrounded each man, and our appearance was quite as strange to them as theirs to us. Generally their first question was, "Are you Federals or Confederates?" there being little in our appearance to make the question unnecessary.

The process of initiation was very disgusting to most of them. While some would be seriously asking questions concerning their capture and listening to their pitiful story, others would call out, "Take your fingers out of his haversack"; "Keep that louse off him"; "Give him air," etc. All this affected them strangely at first, but soon came to be an old story. They brought very welcome news concerning the

---

1. The first six months of prison life, an officer is called a "fresh-fish;" the next four months, a "sucker;" the next two months, a "dry cod"; the balance of his time a "dried herring", and after exchange, a "pickled sardine."

movements of our armies.

There are at present about twelve hundred of our officers confined here, four hundred of whom were captured since the commencement of the campaign in front of Richmond.

Firing Upon a Prisoner

Early on the morning of the 22nd, Lieutenant H. P. Barker, First Rhode Island Cavalry, was fired upon by one of the sentinels—a boy not more than fourteen years of age. The youth missed his aim, however, and his ball buried itself in a tree a little beyond. The lieutenant is quite an old man. Looking across the intermediate space, to the boy, he coolly said,—

"Young man, what are you shooting at?"

"I am shooting at you, you damned old cuss," was the reply.

"And what are you shooting at me for?"

"Because you had your hands on the dead-line," said the boy.

At this moment two other guards came up, and one of them taking the boy by the collar and shaking him thoroughly, demanded,—

"What are you shooting at that prisoner for, you damned little whelp?"

The boy replied, "Because he had his hands on the dead-line."

The guard shook him again, and told him he was a liar, as the man was not within twenty feet of the dead-line, and then called the corporal of the guard, who marched the precocious monster away. If any punishment was administered to him, we never heard of it.

I was lying within ten feet of Lieutenant Barker when the shot was fired, and am certain that he was at least thirty feet distant from the fatal line.

Tunnelling the Narrow Path to Freedom

May 29.—This morning we received notice from Captain W. Kemp Tabb, present commandant of the prison, that in the future, all prisoners not in ranks at roll-call, will be shot down by the sentinels on the guard line.

We have also received orders to take our boards and blankets from the ground. The probable reason of this vigilance is, that they have discovered several tunnels which we had commenced, and were carrying forward as fast as possible.

Our plan of operations was as follows: We have been allowed to build ourselves small sheds, to afford a shelter from the burning sun, of some refuse boards that were lying about; and under these sheds we have made bunks to sleep on. A bunk was selected in a shed as near the dead-line as possible, and under this bunk we sunk a hole or "well," as it was termed, straight down to the depth of five or six feet. From the bottom of this well the tunnel extended out under the stockade. But one man could dig at a time, and as the work was very fatiguing, we relieved each other often. The dirt was brought to the mouth of the tunnel in meal sacks which had been stolen from the ration wagon.

Two or three were detailed to carry off the dirt to the sinks. We usually commenced operations after ten o'clock in the evening, and continued until nearly daylight. Upon leaving the tunnel, a board was fitted in about a foot from the surface, and then dirt was swept over so as to obliterate all traces of the digging.

From sixteen to twenty days were thus required to finish the narrow road to liberty. Fires were built by the guard at short intervals, between the dead-line and stockade, completely encircling the camp, so that the tunnels had to be carried a great distance, in order to have the place of egress as safe as possible.

If the work could have been completed, we should have chosen some dark and stormy night to remove the slight cap of earth, at the outer extremity of the subterranean channel, and then stealing out cautiously, so as not to attract the attention of the vigilant sentinel, we would have made for the woods and swamps.

Those who had done the digging were to have had the first opportunity to pass out, and then as many more were to go, as could get through the tunnel before daybreak.

Our plan was a good one, and we felt confident that it would prove a perfect success until the eve of its completion, when either some cowardly traitor in our midst, or a detective sent in by the authorities, exposed the scheme, and thus blighted our brilliant prospects.

Unpleasant Consequences

The result of this attempt to reach "God's country," is a reduction of rations, and a resort to every restriction which could possibly be conceived by a Rebel.

While in Libby, I imagined that the deeds of villainy were well-nigh exhausted,—I had thought that the catalogue of crime was nearly filled by the Confederate miscreants, but alas! you have only to see the heartlessness and the intrigues of the authorities here,—you have only to witness the suffering, the frenzy, and the fever, and you will then say, that these are the deeds of pitiless monsters.

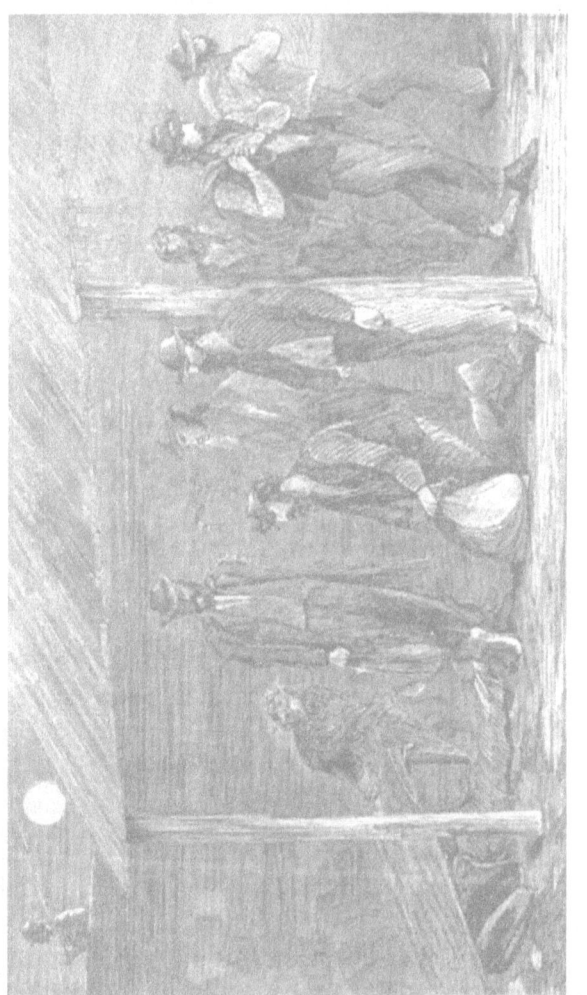

Tunnelling the narrow path to freedom

A short time since, Captain Irich, Forty-fifth New York, sent a watch and chain by Captain Tabb, to be sold for not less than four hundred dollars. Sometime afterward Tabb was seen wearing the chain, and upon being questioned, said he had sold them for two hundred dollars, and the chain had been given to him. Irich thereupon demanded either the property or the four hundred dollars, threatening to expose the whole affair if they were not given up.

For this offence he was bucked several hours—but the articles were restored.

Irich was a German, and splendidly posted in military tactics, besides being a line swordsman. When we were being marched into Camp Oglethorpe, Tabb had given an unmilitary order, and Irich corrected him, when the infuriate Rebel ordered him to keep silent, threatening with drawn sabre to split his head open. Irich, with a little stick in his hand, dared him to strike a blow, and the braggart was forced to put up his sword, amid the jeers of the citizens standing about. This may have been the reason for the severity of the punishment in the affair of the watch.

Religious Meetings

Prayer meetings, or religious meetings of some kind, are held almost every evening; and if the prayers of prisoners can avail, our president will be wise as Solomon, and our armies universally successful. Captain Tabb had heard that it was customary to pray for the president and the generals of our army, and one evening during service came in to put a stop to it. While he was issuing his orders in one corner of the room to Chaplain White, Fourth Rhode Island Battery, Chaplain Dixon, Sixteenth Connecticut, stepped forward and offered a prayer. The fearless and devout man prayed for the president and his advisers, Generals Grant and Sherman; that treason might be crushed, and the Stars and Stripes once more wave over our common country. Tabb heard him through, and then walked out remarking, "Damned smart prayer, but it won't answer the purpose." No further attempts were made to curtail the freedom of prayer. Large numbers have been converted, of those who had all their lives been regardless of such matters.

June 12.—Some days ago Captain Tabb was relieved of command by Captain Geo. C. Gibbs. On the 10th fifty officers were sent to Charleston to be put under fire of our siege-guns. These included all the general officers, together with the highest in rank of the field officers. Among them were Generals Scammon, Wessells, Seymour, Shayler, and Heckman, who were shortly after exchanged.

A Prisoner Shot

At eight o'clock on the evening of the 11th Lieutenant Otto Grierson, Forty-fifth New York Volunteers, was shot through the body and mortally wounded by a sentinel on the stockade.

It is asserted by the sentinel, that the lieutenant was in the act of making his escape, by crawling up the creek to the "dead-line," preparatory to passing under the stockade; but those who were nearby, and saw the affair as it occurred, said that he was not in the creek at all, and that he was at least sixteen feet from the "fatal line."

The lieutenant was at the spring where we are accustomed to bathe, and while there for that purpose, was murdered by the wretch, whose name we have not yet learned. We shall mark him if we are ever permitted to catch a glimpse of his cowardly phiz in daylight. I had just left the spring with water, previous to the discharge of the sentry's musket.

The wounded lieutenant was carried to the hospital, but never spoke after he was shot. Some of our number called upon Captain Gibbs, the prison commandant, informed him of the facts, and requested an investigation, but were turned away with no satisfactory answer, or rather with the understanding, that we need not expect anything in that direction. But the villain who perpetrated the deed was promoted to a sergeant, and given a furlough, for his fidelity and promptness in the execution of orders. These facts we learned from members of his own regiment.

Thus goes another of our number, murdered in cold blood at the hands of a traitor.

Practical Infamy of Rebels

June 22.—Captain Gibbs proposes to allow us the privilege, as he is pleased to term it, of choosing delegates to solicit of the authorities at Richmond an opportunity to visit our enlisted men at Andersonville, for the purpose of reporting their condition to our authorities at Washington.[2]

The fact is, if the truth were known, the Rebels seem desirous of placing a weapon in the hands of the "peace party" at the North,

---

2. The representations they propose to make are, "that the awful suffering of our men in southern prisons is caused by a change of climate and the hopelessness of exchange."

whereby the cause of the Unionists may be defeated.

Confederate officers and citizens are allowed to visit us frequently. They represent to us, and would gladly have us believe, that they are doing all in their power to make it comfortable and agreeable for us.

They repeatedly affirm that the non-exchange of prisoners is due entirely to the fault of our government. In short, they are very anxious to have us send a deputation to Washington, for the purpose of placing before President Lincoln and the administration the horrid condition of our men in southern prisons, and to ask an immediate general exchange of prisoners, claiming, as a matter of course, that they are doing all they possibly can for us.

In accordance with their entreaties, we have held a meeting, but the result is quite unsatisfactory to the Rebels; for we have most firmly resolved never to become agents in advancing the interests of the southern cause, even though our sufferings be increased a hundredfold.

I am perfectly satisfied that there has been no time since the beginning of the war when the enemy could not have given their prisoners an abundance of cornmeal and bacon, were they so disposed; and from observation I know that they could have furnished lumber, to provide us with more comfortable quarters. With such facts, glaring and palpable as they are, we will be a party to no transaction which can possibly aid in furthering their base designs.

Discovery of Tunnels

The camp was searched today by order of the prison commandant, and the three tunnels which have been in process of digging for the past fifteen days were discovered. Had it not been for this misfortune, many of us would have bid farewell tomorrow night to this field of suffering.

Doubtless, some detective from the outside exposed the scheme. Never was I more disappointed than in this misfortune; for our plan was a good one. The tunnels were large, and it was estimated that nearly, if not quite all of the prisoners could pass through them in a single night.

We had looked forward with the deepest anxiety to what we felt assured would be the happy termination of our labours; but alas! when it seemed that we were about to reap the promised reward, like the mirage, it vanished in the distance.

As a result of the discovery the following order has appeared on the Prison Bulletin:—

C. S. Military Prison,
Macon, Ga., June 22, 1864.

Special Orders,
No. 6.

Sentinels are instructed to shoot down all prisoners, in the future, who are seen moving about camp after taps.

Geo. C. Gibbs, Captain Commanding.

The guards appear delighted to receive orders of such a character, and seem to find real consolation in having the privilege of firing upon us on the most trivial pretext. A thirst for blood seems to characterize them. They have all their lives long been taught that the blood of niggers and Yankees was made to be spilled when occasion requires, and they never hesitate to put the teaching into practice. Hereafter all who leave their bunks at night to go to the sinks or elsewhere, do so at the peril of their lives.

Scurvy is now becoming fearfully prevalent in our midst. Chronic diarrhoea is also sweeping off its victims most fearfully. It is almost impossible to get treatment for either. Large numbers, who are afflicted with the former disease, may be seen every day burying themselves up in the ground, as the earth has a tendency to check its frightful ravages.

Much to my disgust, I find that this loathsome disease has again got hold of me. I have been hoping that it would pass me by in its visitations, but it is unquestionably present in my limbs. I attended sick-call this morning, and was prescribed for by the surgeon the first time since we left Richmond. I shall not make any effort to get into the hospital, for I am confident that it is much better to remain in camp, among my friends, where they can administer to my wants, than to go where the prisoner can expect but little sympathy, or anything else that might have a tendency to rid him of disease or recruit his wasted strength.

It is not strange that the term "hospital" has become synonymous with death; for but few who enter it ever come out alive. When a man is seen leaving camp in a blanket, it is thought that he is past help; and if he is fortunate enough to return to his fellows, it is considered an exceptional case.

Deaths have been very frequent since the warm weather came on. Many have gone to their long homes since our arrival here. We call it being "exchanged"; and it certainly is a happy transformation from so much misery and wretchedness on earth to a life of eternal joy in the bright realms above. We cannot sigh for such, but only rejoice that their cares and misfortunes are ended. It almost makes one long to go, when we think that their sufferings and trials are over, and it is not wonderful that they should murmur in their last moments,—

> *I would not live alway —I joy in the trust,*
> *That when this frail form shall return to the dust,*
> *My spirit shall rise on the wings of thy love,*
> *To seek its true home in the mansions above.*

Fourth of July in Prison

We had several roll-calls in the morning. The prison authorities seemed very fearful that we would attempt a general escape. Immediately after the roll-calls a large meeting was organised. Captain Todd, Eighth New Jersey Infantry, displayed a small silk flag four by six inches, which had been presented to him by Miss Paradise of Jersey City, and which had thus far escaped the vigilance of southern relic seekers. The miniature "Star-Spangled Banner" was hailed with rounds of cheers, which showed that they came from loyal hearts.

We then adjourned to the large building occupied by the general and field officers, where Chaplain Dixon, Sixteenth Connecticut Volunteers, opened the exercises with prayer. Captain Ives, Lieutenant Ogden, First "Wisconsin Cavalry; Captain Lee, Fifth Michigan Cavalry; Lieutenant Kellogg, Chaplain Whitney, One Hundred and Fourth Ohio; Chaplain Dixon, and Lieutenant Colonel Thorp, First New York Dragoons, then followed with speeches and toasts, interspersed with national songs, while far above our heads, attached to a long pole was the emblem of freedom, the "Red, White, and Blue."

Although in prison, and held here by those who ought always to have regarded the people of the North with brotherly kindness, who never should have raised the recreant hand of treason against the government established by our common fathers and sealed with their blood, there was still a universal feeling that the day which sealed our liberties should be observed with suitable ceremonies. All felt that, live or die, survive or perish, we would give a hearty support to those Stars and Stripes—the banner of the free—that had so long waved over our heads, and for which we are now suffering every indignity and privation.

We had every reason to believe that the Rebels would not object to the celebration of the day that proclaimed us victorious over the

British Lion, and brought freedom to them, as well as to us; but in this we were mistaken. Whilst we were listening to a spirited oration from Colonel Thorp, the commandant of the prison, Captain Gibbs, deemed it necessary, in the exercise of his little authority, to march a regiment of troops into the enclosure and order the assemblage to disperse. Having no possible alternative, the order was, of course, complied with.

The meeting was conducted in a quiet and orderly manner; the animus of the speaking was generally national, and nothing but Rebel tyranny could object to it.

Colonel Thorp having been for some time past in command of the interior of the prison, by virtue of his position as senior officer, was relieved from duty by the following order:—

C. S. Military Prison,
Macon, Ga., July 4, 1864.

Special Orders,
No. 9.
1. Lieutenant Colonel Thorp is relieved from duty as senior officer of prisoners, for a violation of prison rules, and Lieutenant Colonel McCrary will again assume that position.
2. The same order and quiet will be observed on this day as on any other.
3. A disregard of this order may subject offenders to unpleasant consequences.

Geo. C. Gibbs, Captain Commanding.

July 6.—Heat intense. No rain since the early part of last month. I am suffering with chronic diarrhoea at present, but shall not endeavour to get into the hospital while I have a friend left in camp.

July 7.—I am no better today. Have not tasted of my rations since the 5th.

July 8.—Crawled down to the creek in the forenoon, near which I lay until evening.

A fellow-prisoner recommended me to chew white-oak bark for my complaint, and has persuaded me to try the experiment. He has very kindly placed three pieces of the said bark at my disposal, which he stripped from an old tree that stands within the enclosure.

July 9.—I am very weak today: cannot walk without assistance. Am inclined to think that chewing bark will not effect a cure in my case.

Brass buttons being in great demand with the Rebels, I pulled the remaining few from my old coat yesterday, and sold them to one of the guards for ten dollars, and with that sum purchased five loaves of wheat bread, which will last me six or seven days, if used sparingly.

I have not touched my cornmeal for a long time, my stomach being entirely too weak to endure such coarse diet, and the consequence is, I am reduced to a mere skeleton. I think the flour bread will have the effect of checking the diarrhoea, or at least of recruiting my strength. I should have disposed of the buttons long ago, had I not thought that a day of greater need might come.

The Rebels have a perfect passion for Federal buttons, and often pay extravagant prices for them. Buttons are very scarce in the Confederacy, and many are reduced to the necessity of wearing wooden ones. Occasionally a fine joke is played upon the guards. Not long since a modest, rather green little Confederate came into the prison asking, "Has any of you 'uns got any brass buttons to sell? I've got four on the back of my jacket, and I'll give eight dollars for four more to put on the front."

One of the prisoners conceived an idea at once, and replied, "Well, corporal, I'll try and find you some." Then giving the wink to some of his companions, who immediately engaged the Reb. in conversation, he slipped round behind him, and cut the four buttons from the back of his jacket, and soon returned, saying,—

"Here, corporal, how do you like the looks of these?"

The corporal was suited, of course, and after considerable bantering paid the sum of nine dollars in Confederate scrip for them and went his way rejoicing.

July 16.—My health is improving. Friends have been very kind during my illness, and are still untiring in their efforts to keep me in the land of the living. It is affirmed by the authorities, that there will be a general exchange of prisoners on the 24th of the present month. The "fresh-fish" are troubled with an affliction known to the old prisoners as "exchange on the brain."

July 27.—Six hundred prisoners were counted out of the enclosure this evening; their destination is supposed to be Charleston, where they will doubtless be placed under fire of our guns on Morris Island, as were the field officers sent thither during the early part of last month. This is a most singular method of defending a besieged city against its enemies, and illustrates, to some extent, the character of a people that would like to be "let alone," while attempting to establish a government in accordance with their own chivalrous notions of justice, equality, and State rights.

July 28.—The second six hundred were counted out of the pen late in the afternoon. As his name was called, each prisoner stepped between the dead-line and stockade, where we expect to remain until morning, when it is generally understood that we will be shipped to the coast.

All the old prisoners are in line, and we shall leave Camp Oglethorpe in charge of a hundred prisoners from Sherman's army, who were brought in yesterday.

CHAPTER 8

Savannah, Georgia,—"Camp Davidson"

We left Macon at four o'clock a. m. of July 29th, guarded by a battalion of the Fifth Georgia Reserves, and reached Savannah at six o'clock the same evening, the distance being about one hundred and fifty miles. It soon became apparent that the Rebel authorities were moving us from necessity. Their hurried and excited manner indicated that all was not well. Artillery was being rapidly hurled into position, the troops were on the alert, and every preparation made to defend the place; but as for ourselves, we could only hope that through their misfortune we might find an opportunity for escape: and the reader may imagine our disappointment when we learned afterwards, from one of the guards, that our cavalry, under General Stoneman, cut the road at Griffin Station only thirty minutes after we had passed. To think that freedom had come almost within our grasp, and yet eluded us, tended only to add bitterness to our hard lot. General Stoneman attacked Macon, but was repulsed, and himself with a detachment of his command were captured. One hundred prisoners, or more, who had not been removed, were hurried down into a swamp, and guarded during the fight.

SAVANNAH

Is situated at the mouth of the Savannah River, on the eastern coast of Georgia. It is unsurpassed by any other city in the State in its business facilities, and also in its neatness and regularity. In a military point of view, it stands next to Charleston in importance. Its population at present is about twenty thousand, including a large number of refugees. The inhabitants are generally suffering from the most abject poverty. At present there is a perfect stagnation in business; but one can easily judge its past enterprising spirit by the unmistakable marks of its former prosperity.

Our camp is in the eastern part of the city, near the Marine Hospital, which was built and formerly used by our government.

Pulaski's monument stands within plain view. This is a fine structure, about forty feet in height.

There are about four thousand Rebel troops doing garrison duty in the city. The nearest Union troops are at Fort Pulaski, located at the entrance of the harbour, on the South Carolina shore. They are in such close proximity to the Rebel forces that if we could but escape the vigilance of our guard we should be almost certain of reaching the Federal lines in safety.

Camp Davidson, our present Prison Pen, takes its name from Captain H. H. Davidson, who was its first commandant. It is surrounded by a stockade and dead-line, and does not differ materially from the pen at Macon. Quite a number of large, moss-covered live-oak trees are growing within the enclosure, which will furnish a refreshing shade from the oppressive noonday sun.

Kind Treatment at Savannah

So great is the contrast between our treatment here and at other places, that we cannot but feel that fortune has certainly smiled kindly upon us for once.

This is truly the oasis in the desert of our prison lives. The authorities have issued tents and cooking utensils to us, and seem inclined to alleviate suffering as far as lies within their power. We have pitched our tents in regular order, so that the camp has quite a military appearance.

Our senior officer, Colonel Miller of New York, acts as commandant of the interior, and all requests and complaints are made through him to the prison authorities. He also superintends the issuing of rations and policing of the camp. It is fortunate for us that our guard, the First Georgia Volunteers, have been prisoners of war, and have learned what we had a right to expect, from the magnanimous treatment they themselves have received from the Federal government. And then Nature is kind to us; we are enabled to bear our sufferings more cheerfully than at first. Scenes which at home would chill the blood and destroy all peace of mind, have become so commonplace with us that we look upon them unmoved; 'tis a dangerous experiment to place one constantly amidst the misery and sufferings of others, with no power to alleviate them.

At Richmond, Danville, and Macon, the authorities adopted a course, which they believed would forever render us unfit for further military duty. Their means were starvation, close confinement in filthy dungeons, and cruel treatment. The slightest pretext was sufficient to increase its severity. Evidently, at Savannah they have not yet learned the usual method of ridding the Confederacy of its enemies.

The troops here have all seen service, and there is nothing like the adventures of the battlefield and the mutual sufferings there experienced, to teach soldiers humanity towards each other. Whenever attempts are made to escape, they give us to understand that they would do the same themselves, under like circumstances, but are still compelled to punish such infractions of prison discipline. They politely ask our pardon for inspecting our quarters, and in a manner as gentlemanly as possible, remove our blankets from the floors of the tents in their search for incipient tunnels, etc. All this is very gratifying, and tends to remove the bitter hatred which former brutality had engendered.

These Georgia boys will be long remembered, and may look for the utmost kindness and consideration from us, if chance ever reverses our situations.

Our rations, though barely sufficient to sustain what little vitality we have left, arc of a better quality than we have received before, since our capture. The following is our daily allowance: Cornmeal, one pint; fresh beef, one pound; rice, one gill; salt, one ounce, for four days.

Sutlers are allowed to sell to us in camp; but having been robbed of our money and nearly all our valuables when captured, we are generally very poor customers. We gradually find ourselves dispossessed of whatever remains to us of value, such as rings, pocket-knives, watches, etc., which we succeeded in concealing from our captors.

These souvenirs of the past were disposed of to purchase the necessaries of life, which we could have at the following prices: Flour, four dollars per quart; onions, three for a dollar; potatoes, forty-eight dollars per bushel; bread, two dollars per loaf; butter, ten dollars per pound; eggs, six dollars per dozen; milk, three dollars per quart.

At such prices we, of course, soon wasted away what we chanced to have; and this done, these land sharks ceased their visits, and we had to again content ourselves with what the Rebel government saw fit to furnish.

Brick Ovens

The authorities have been kind enough to make an issue of brick, with which to build ovens. We raise them about two feet from the ground. The brick are arranged in an oval form, and strongly cemented together with mortar made of clay, which is very adhesive, and serves as a good substitute for lime and mortar.

We use these ovens principally for baking our cornbread, which is prepared by stirring the meal and cold water together. When baked, this bread is as heavy and almost as hard as the iron skillet used in baking it. Still it is far preferable to that produced by the usual method of cooking.

It is rumoured that the first six hundred prisoners sent from Macon, attempted to disarm the guard, and take the train between this place and Charleston. The attempt seems to have proved a failure, as the guard had assistance from some temporary troops stationed along the railroad.

It may seem strange that men will incur such risks in the hope of regaining their freedom, when they know full well the bitter consequences of an unsuccessful effort.

Violent attempts, when they prove abortive, always render them liable to be shot down without mercy. Stealth and strategy are the prisoners only weapons, and they are always more safe and more effective than force.

Tunnelling

August 22.—Tunnelling, as a means of escape, has become quite an institution. A tunnel was commenced some days ago from a well which we had dug and abandoned for this purpose. None but the working party were in the secret; and they themselves sworn not to divulge our plans. Tools were frequently brought in for cleaning the camp, and we managed to keep some of these generally for a day or two, until a search was instituted for them, when they were left exposed in some other part of the camp for the Rebels to find.

Our Scheme Exposed by a Cow.

This tunnel was about two and a half feet in diameter and four feet below the surface. The soil is sandy, and the digging was carried on rapidly. When some distance beyond the stockade, it was brought to the surface, and a very small hole made through the sward. Through this a reconnoissance was made, and the first thing discovered was a pair of gray legs pacing along only a few inches from the opening.

The hole was immediately closed and the tunnel pushed farther on, with the intention of carrying it beyond the second line of sentinels, which, it thus appeared, had been established.

The work was progressing finely when, in the afternoon, a cow, passing over the tunnel, broke through, and was unable to extricate herself. The Rebels, seeing her in difficulty, came to the rescue, and thus discovered our work.

The tunnel was filled up at once, the camp carefully inspected, and the most severe penalties threatened in case of any further attempts to escape.

That poor, stupid cow had brought to light by mere chance, what Rebel scrutiny had failed to discover. There were no blessings for the cow that day at least, not within the stockade.

Joy Without, Death Within the Stockade

August 26.—This has been a gala-day for the Rebels at this point. A picnic has been given to the Rebel troops stationed here, by the ladies of Savannah. It was held a short distance from our camp so near that our ears have been greeted by lively music, joyous peals of laughter, and happy voices.

How many sacred memories of other days did this scene recall! Freedom, certainly, seemed a precious gift to them. It will be doubly so to us if we are ever permitted to regain it; and hence, in the future, we may be compensated for our present loss. But to many of us the day has been as sad within the stockade as seemingly joyous without.

One of our number, Captain McGinnis, died this morning. He had a large number of friends among the prisoners, and was held in high esteem for his many noble qualities; but the severity of prison life had done its work, and he was gone; and we were desirous that one so brave and noble as he had proved himself to be should have, at least, a decent burial. Therefore we appointed a committee to wait upon the commandant of the camp, Colonel Wayne, to request that we might be permitted to give the captain a decent burial; but received from him the response, that the captain "was nothing but a damned Yankee, deserving to be buried like a dog, and so he should be."

We expected little more, as Colonel Wayne is a cruel person, and would consider it beneath his dignity to confer a Christian favour, or even give a respectful reply. Although an excellent military officer, he has no just claim to the title of a "man," and his very appearance indicates as much. Fortunately for us, he is an exception among the officers of his command, and it is only justice to them to state that they universally despise him.

Kindness of Ladies

We were greatly surprised this evening upon receiving a note from ladies in the city, informing us that they had learned with pain of Colonel Wayne's answer to our petition, and that they themselves have purchased a burial lot unbeknown to the colonel, where the captain's remains will be suitably interred under their direction. Thank God for this dear womanly act!

A short time since, Lieutenant Pierce Horn of the First Georgia, came into our quarters, asking if we had any men from Troy, New York. Having enlisted in that place myself, I informed him of the fact, and held a very pleasant conversation for an hour. He informed me that he had, some years ago, attended Union College, Schenectady, New York, and also the Troy Polytechnic Institute. He was opposed to secession in the outset, but when his State chose to go, he had no alternative but to go with her. His father is a large Georgia planter.

August 30.—An exchange of army chaplains and surgeons has been effected; and those held as prisoners at this point are to take passage North on the next flag-of-truce boat, and will leave this place for Charleston on the four o'clock p. m. train. The wildest enthusiasm prevails among them. An exchange from close, confinement in the hands of an enemy, to perfect freedom among one's friends is certainly a sufficient cause for exultation and joy.

The D.D.s and M.D.s are now the great centre of attraction with the prisoners. Crowds have been collecting around them all day, with some message for their friends at home, which they promise sacredly to deliver. They will be sadly missed by us; for they were untiring in their labours while here.

September 1.—Heavy cannonading has been heard in the direction of Charleston all day. The atmosphere is damp, and the heavy booming of Gilmore's "swamp angel" has been distinctly brought to our ears.

Have been amusing myself during my stay here, in studying geometry. As a matter of review it does very well, but I question whether much progress could be made in any new department of study. Samuel Johnson, I think it was, who, when he suspected that his brain might be softening, used to turn to mathematics as a test. If we were tried by such a standard, I fear many of us might find ourselves candidates for a lunatic asylum.

September 11.—Exchange stock above par. It is rumoured that we are to be sent to Charleston in the morning for exchange, but few are inclined to invest. The general impression is that if we are removed at all, it will be to share the fate of our fellow-officers, who were sent thither from Macon. It is not with pleasant feelings that we anticipate a removal. Our treatment here has been kind and even generous, in many instances, and it is feared that an exchange can only be for the worse. Dreading greater hardships, we leave Savannah with regret.

CHAPTER 9

At Charleston, "Under Fire"

Late in the evening of September 11th, without warning or explanation other than our own hopes and fears suggested, we received the order "pack up,"—a generic command which had no very literal significance under the circumstances, and yet it necessitated some little compliance.

A prisoner without shoes for his feet or coat for his back, with one hat and one shirt and no blanket, will yet be thankful for a little time in which to pack up. If he is a Yankee, he has become the owner of some personal property, though his bondage have been on Sahara's barren desert; and then there are souvenirs of home that his tact and tenderness have retained in spite of Rebel surveillance; and he must take with him relics of his dark, gloomy prison home. This passion for relics is all prevailing among northern soldiers.

If a Yankee boy were incarcerated in the sulphurous dungeon of Tartarus, the chances are ten to one that he would bring away with him on his release a piece of brimstone at least, though he had to burn his fingers in getting it, and Cerebrus would be more than usually alert, if he didn't get half a dozen hairs from his tail. Attention to these relics, farewells to the various scenes of suffering and want, and especially the subject of rations, required a considerable time.

From our stock of cornmeal we had to make "pones," or cornmeal cakes, enough for the journey; these were baked in the skillets before mentioned, one skillet serving for twenty men. As soon as "marching orders" were received there was a vigorous rush for the skillets, of course, and "De'il take the hindermost," found a practical illustration. Those who failed to be first, strove to be second, by exacting a pledge from No. 1, that he would give them the skillet when he was through with it; those who failed to be second would fain content themselves with being third, and so on up the scale.

Sometimes differences of opinion arose with regard to the relative position of certain parties on the "skillet" schedule, and mild knock-downs resulted, which placed both at the foot of the list.

Men will fight for their "rights" even when staring death in the face in a southern prison. Had they all been sentenced to be hung, they would doubtless have "stood on the order of their going," and insisted on the precedence of rank.

Baking the "pones" occupied the greater part of the night, and on the morning of September 12th at six o'clock, we were marched out of Camp Davidson by our old guard, the Second Georgia Regulars.

There is something sad about leaving even a "Prison Pen" after a long and familiar acquaintance. Fibres of attachment will spring from the heart to fasten on the most loathsome objects where circumstances of necessity and mutual suffering make the soil mellow. I felt stealing over me something of those hopeless emotions which brought Byron's sad and subdued *Prisoner of Chillon* to say:—

My very chains and I grew friends,
So much a long communion tends
To make us what we are;—even I
Regained my freedom with a sigh.

Only ours was not freedom, but rather something worse than the worst bondage. We were to be taken to Charleston and placed under the fire of our own batteries, for the enemy seem to think that we may be the means of saving the besieged city from the doom which inevitably awaits it. Of course they affirm that this is retaliation, but with the North retaliation has ever been looked upon as a sad extremity, and to be exercised only when no other resource remains for restraining the excesses of its foes. With the Rebels, the slightest pretext has been sufficient to cause the most wanton destruction of life.

After leaving our camp at Savannah, we were turned over to the City Battalion which guarded us through town.

We remained for a number of hours in the dusty streets of the city, under the scorching heat of the sun, when we were ordered into cattle-cars, weary and sick at heart, yet not entirely despondent, for there is

No grief so great, but runneth to an end,
No hap so hard, but will in time amend.

One of our number having obtained permission from the nearest guard, under the plea of necessity, stepped out of his car at the first station, when he was immediately fired upon by several others. The prisoner only saved his life by dodging under the car. Even while there, the commanding officer of the guard rushed up with boisterous curses and discharged his revolver at the defenceless victim without asking a word of explanation. The prisoner was dragged from under the car and thrown back among his fellows. And yet these men, who could thus murderously fire on a defenceless prisoner guilty of no offence, were constantly talking of their honour and their "chivalry." Their deeds will publish their true characters long after their words are forgotten.

A run of ten or twelve hours brought us to Charleston. The citizens turned out in crowds as we marched down Coming Street, and, as usual, we listened to the stereotyped Billingsgate of the Southern chivalry. We were entirely satisfied that *"familiarity breeds contempt,"* as we listened to their coarse comments on the "damned Yankees," "northern blue-bellies," "baboons," "Lincoln's monkeys," etc. Many, on the other hand, in the interval of our short halts, expressed sincere regrets at our unfortunate situation, and, rather quietly, to be sure, assured us of their faith in the ultimate triumph of the government. It was rather surprising to find so many of this class in the cradle of secession. There were just enough of them to save from utter ruin that treason-polluted city.

Our destination was Charleston jail-yard, the grand receptacle of all Union prisoners in Charleston. It is situated in the south-eastern portion of the city, and in plain view of Morris Island, on which our batteries were planted, which did such fearful execution.

Charleston Jail and its Inmates

The jail is a large octagonal building of four stories, surmounted by a tower forty feet in height. On the right is the large Bastille-shaped work-house, where a part of the prisoners were confined.

The gallows is located at the south side of the jail, and the fragment of a tent which I occupied was directly in front of it. This is the nearest we ever came to hanging, so far as I could learn,—unless it be the necessary suspense of our situation.

Our quarters were in the yard, and the whole enclosure was surrounded by a massive wall of masonry sixteen feet in height. Everything was in the most filthy condition conceivable, having been occupied for a long time by prisoners and convicts, without ever having

Jail-yard, Charleston, South Carolina

been cleaned. We were unable to obtain even the necessary tools from the authorities, to do this work ourselves. Its sanitary condition was such, that it seemed impossible for us to remain there long without suffering from some foul and malignant disease. The ground was literally covered with vermin. A fellow-prisoner has said that he thought it the "nastiest, dirtiest, filthiest, lousiest place he was ever in."

We were without shelter. Fragments of tents were still standing, but afforded no protection from the sun or storm, for the prisoners who were confined there before us, many of whom were from Andersonville, were in such a destitute condition upon their arrival, that they cut the tents to pieces to make themselves clothes to wear.

The ground floor of the jail was occupied by civil convicts; the second storey, by Rebel officers and soldiers under punishment for military offences; the third storey, by negro prisoners; and the fourth, by Federal and Rebel deserters.

It is a fine compliment to the good sense of the Rebels, that the deserters from either side were treated with the same severity. They seemed to consider that none but those who deserved the severest punishment would be guilty of deserting the Federal army to go over to them; and so they placed them side by side with deserters from their own ranks, and subjected them to the same privations.

It must have been consoling to the cowards and sneaks, who deserted the Stars and Stripes, to receive such close attention. Sometimes they ventured down from their fourth storey to mingle with the Federal soldiers in the yard. Under such circumstances nothing could restrain the prisoners from working a general onslaught, and the miserable slinks did well if they got back to their "sky-lot" with whole heads. This righteous indignation of suffering soldiers was a natural out-cropping of that heroic determination which kept their patriotism burning brightly in the midst of their untold sufferings.

Many of the negro prisoners in the jail were captured at our assault on Fort Wagner. I had a conversation with Sergeant Johnson (coloured), Company F, Fifty-fifth Massachusetts Infantry; he was a full-blooded negro, but possessed of no ordinary degree of intelligence; he gave me an interesting history of the captivity and trial of the negro prisoners! Soon after their capture they were informed, that they were to be tried by a civil commission on a charge of having abandoned their masters and enlisted in the United States Army, and if found guilty, they were told that they might make up their minds to stretch hemp.

And why should they not be found guilty? to be sure, nearly all were from the North and had always been free; but they knew full well that this court was formed, not to subserve the ends of justice, but to convict, for the Rebels had sufficiently illustrated their method of dealing with negro prisoners, that is, when they deigned to receive them as such, instead of murdering them in cold blood, in order to convince their comrades of the narrow chances for life, should they unfortunately fall into the hands of an enemy.

A Friend

The sergeant told me that they were surprised to find a friend in a relative of Ex-Governor Pickens of South Carolina. The governor himself was true to Southern principles, having been elected to the legislature of his State by the nullifiers in 1832, and being among the foremost to urge his State out of the Union in 1860; but this friend to the oppressed remained firm in the cause of his country, and bravely loyal as the sequel will show. He came to them and offered unrecompensed to plead their cause before the sham tribunal that was to decide their fate. When he first revealed his intention to act in their behalf, he was regarded as an impostor, a government detective, whose only object was to learn their history; that is, to ascertain if they had been slaves, to whom they had belonged, and under what circumstances they had left their masters.

But he persisted, and gave them money to purchase little necessaries (for nothing but cornmeal was issued to them, and this in very small quantities), and left them with the promise that he would soon return, and report the progress of his investigations; but when he came, he found them still doubting, and unwilling to place confidence in him; but, calling them together, he related that before the war he himself was a slaveholder, and was known and respected throughout his State. But at the commencement of this intestine strife, having proved true to the "old flag," his property had been swept from him, calling him traitor, and an abolitionist, and that now he was an outcast among his friends, and in constant danger of being assassinated.

Genuine Patriotism

He also told them that he knew that this must be his fate, from the first, if he remained true to his convictions; but that, having counted the cost, it was as nothing when weighed in the balance against truth; and he was now prepared to do his work thoroughly and unhesitatingly, regarding only as friends those who were true to the cause of their country.

By this means he gained their confidence, for there is a higher language than the written. It is seen in the mute dropping of the tear, in the trembling of the lip, in the flashing of the eye, in the melody of the voice. The tones of sympathy and friendship cannot be successfully counterfeited. Deceivers may impose on those whose perceptions have been dulled by the conventionalities and allowed hypocrisies of society; but the quick-sighted instincts of the child of nature will readily detect the fraud. They listen to the words of a man, and then look into his eyes to interpret his meaning; and this decision cannot be revoked. And when this language shall become as universally studied and understood as the written language which we speak, then shall the divine command, *Thou shalt not lie*, never be violated on account of the inability of mankind to deceive us with their words.

As the sergeant related to me how untiring were the efforts of this friend during their prolonged and doubtful trial, in combating error with firm, convincing truth, in proving their innocence, even under laws that were made but for white men, he seemed at times to be completely overcome by his feelings, so unused was he to sympathy or kind words; but when their trial was once over, and their innocence established, they returned to jail, to be regarded as prisoners of war.

The Last Visit

It was after their return to the jail that their friend and advocate visited them for the last time. Their emotions were uncontrollable, and they seemed unable to give even a faint expression of their gratitude to him who had sacrificed so much for them. Their admiration for this devoted friend of the Union was so great, that the mere mention of his name is sufficient to bring tears to the eyes of these swarthy sons, who have thus far had so little to be grateful to us for.

This young man, who thus came forward to defend innocent and unfortunate men, was to them, and is to us "nameless"; but his memory will be green in their simple hearts until their black faces go down to the grave. The gratitude of the humblest of our fellow-men is a treasure the true heart will cherish.

This stranger died shortly after. Whatever may have been his previous life, he carries with him in the act of unselfish philanthropy a gift that is dear to Heaven.

Negro Melodies

At the close of day the negro prisoners made a practice of getting together in the jail, and singing their plaintive melodies till late in the evening. The character of their songs was usually mournful; and it was often affecting to listen to them—always embodying, as they did, those simple, child-like emotions and sentiments for which the negro is so justly celebrated. The harmony and rich melody of their voices are rarely surpassed. Indeed, this seems a special gift to them. This very fact gives the surest promise of their future elevation and refinement. No race so delicately sensitive to the emotional can be essentially coarse and barbarous.

One song, which appeared to be a special favourite with them, was written by Sergeant Johnson, whom I have before mentioned. He intended it as a parody on "When this cruel war is over." I give the song as he furnished it to me.

1

When I enlisted in the army,
Then I thought 'twas grand,
Marching through the streets of Boston
Behind a regimental band.
When at Wagner I was captured,
Then my courage failed;
Now I m lousy, hungry, naked,
Here in Charleston jail.

Chorus. *Weeping, sad and lonely—*
Oh! how bad I feel;
Down in Charleston, South Car'lna,
Praying for a good 'square meal'

2

If Jeff. Davis will release me,
Oh, how glad I'll be;
When I get on Morris Island
Then I shall be free;
Then I'll tell those conscript soldiers
How they use us here;
Giving us an old corn-dodger—
They call it prisoner's fare.

3

We are longing, watching, praying,
But will not repine
'Till Jeff. Davis does release us,

And sends us 'in our lines'.
Then with words of kind affection,
How they'll greet us there!
Wondering how we could live so long
Upon the dodgers fare.

Chorus. *Then we will laugh long and loudly—*
Oh, how glad we'll feel,
When we arrive on Morris Island
And eat a good 'square meal'

The negroes sang this song with a great deal of zest, as it related to their present sufferings, and was just mournful enough to excite our sympathy.

A small portion of the present inmates of the jail-yard were removed here from Andersonville; and I have listened with pain and perfect horror to the history of their past treatment. Future generations will stand aghast in view of the unheard of and pitiless deeds of men, steeped in infamy their foul and barbarous usage of our unfortunate soldiers.

At Andersonville large numbers were crowded into a small space, where the ground was literally alive with vermin. During the heat of day, by watching closely in the warm sand, you could perceive a constant motion among the particles; so alive was it with lice. On such ground as this, the men were closely crowded together, without shelter, and with fare which a Rebel surgeon himself declared, "would produce disease among swine."

Awful Condition of the Hospital

The hospital was in the most wretched condition; no one left the pen, however feeble he might be, who had any friend to attend to his wants, for the only advantage gained by leaving the stockade, was a shelter from the scorching rays of the sun, but this was counterbalanced by being brought in such immediate contact with so many afflicted with the most foul and offensive diseases.

The men were placed upon the ground, nothing underneath them, and usually without covering, while the nights were so chilling as to keep the poor fellows quaking with cold until the sun appeared again to warm them, and then followed the other extreme, the intense heat which rendered the sufferings of those intolerable whose blood was almost quenched with burning fevers.

The Rebel surgeons seemed to give them little or no care.

So filthy and obnoxious, so infested with vermin, and so loathsome had this den of living death be come, that it was indeed impossible for a person of good health to endure it long.

While such a state of things existed, it is not strange that the mortality among them was fearful. Each day the dead were carried away by scores, their places to be again filled by others, who in all probability would soon share the same fate, for none but those who were so low as to be past cure were ever looked at by the surgeons, and nearly as many died within the pen, without ever receiving any medical treatment, as in the hospital.

A fearful responsibility certainly rests somewhere, and men who could thus wantonly murder so many helpless and innocent men, are almost as much to be pitied for their moral depravity as the prisoners for their bodily suffering, and yet these martyrs to the cause of "Liberty and their Country," never murmured against the government, always believing that it was powerless to help them, or else that it did not understand their true condition.

I have noticed scarcely a prisoner from Andersonville, who was not more or less affected by some disease contracted there, so that we now see the truthfulness of what they say proven by their physical condition.

One poor fellow, who was lying in the jail-yard when we arrived, recognised in one of our number his former captain. In a feeble voice, he addressed him as such, but the poor prisoner was so tattered and emaciated, and blackened by disease and exposure, that the captain did not recognise him. A faltering, broken explanation located him in his memory, and they took a melancholy pleasure in rehearsing their mutual and individual experiences. The dying man was too far gone to need assistance had any been possible, and all the captain could do was to lie down by his side during the long, cold night that followed, and close his lifeless eyes in the morning.

A Thunder-Storm

September 20.—I find myself weak and exhausted this morning, with blood feverish and my system racked with pain, the result of yesterday's suffering; for it was one of the most wretched days that I have passed since my capture.

Nothing could have been more lovely than the morning, but the sky was soon overcast with dark clouds, and one of the most fearful thunderstorms broke forth that I have ever witnessed, followed by a severe and drenching rain, which continued during the day and night. We were without shelter, or wood to build fires, and were obliged to exercise constantly to keep from chilling.

Refused Admission to the Jail

At night, as there were no signs of the storm abating, we sent a committee to wait upon the jailer, to obtain permission, if possible, to go inside the jail, as there were a number of unoccupied cells, but were refused admission without a reason being given.

Before morning the yard became flooded with water some four or five inches deep, and with our garments drenched and our limbs benumbed with cold, we were compelled to walk through this flood, in order to keep the blood in circulation.

There were a few small out-houses connected with the jail, formerly used as sinks, and which were in the most loathsome and filthy condition; yet into these a small portion of the prisoners crowded themselves, and were partially protected from the storm, but suffered almost as severely from the obnoxious vapours, as we from the drenching rain.

Our situation called to mind the experiences of persons whose minds had become weakened by a necessitated abode on some desert island, whose manhood had been lost by an unbroken familiarity with forest solitudes and savage beasts, whose natures had been almost changed by the wind and spray and shell-fish diet of some bleak ocean-rock; and I wondered, since the influences in the outer world are so potent for good or evil, what must be the effect upon us, whose vision cannot extend beyond the dismal walls which surround this abode of misery. The monotony, too, is only relieved by a "jail," a "work-house," and the whizzing, bursting shells.

September 22.—Heat oppressive. Heard from the members of my regiment who are confined in Roper Hospital. They are making an effort to have Richardson and myself transferred to that building, which is a far better place than the jail-yard, although it is quite as much exposed to shot and shell.

The naval officers are in excellent spirits at present, having learned by the last flag-of-truce boat that terms for a special exchange of all naval prisoners have been agreed upon.

Shelling is kept up vigorously. From sixty to a hundred huge, smoking two-hundred-pounders convey Federal compliments daily to the cursing city.

It is a singularly noticeable fact, that every Charleston paper, in its report of "damage done the city" by our batteries, never chronicles the loss of a white person; but in every morning edition we notice the name of some "poor negro," whose life has been taken by the "cruel barbarity of the d——d Yankees."

CHAPTER 10

Roper Hospital, Charleston

September 29.—Today is an eventful one for Richardson and myself. Our rations being entirely gone, we started in quest of something to eat, after taking our usual morning bath. We succeeded in finding a friend who had a little cornmeal left, and who willingly shared it with us.

Hastening back to our quarters, we converted it into mush, and sat down fully prepared to do ample justice to the dish, when a cry was heard, "All those whose names are called will prepare to go to Roper Hospital immediately."

We listen, but our names are not called; we wait and wait for the next list to be read. It seems evident that we are destined to remain in the jail-yard, when, to our great surprise, we hear the welcome voice of Major E. F. Cooke, of the old regiment, who has at last succeeded in persuading the authorities to remove us from this hell on earth. How we start! How eagerly do we grasp his extended hand! He tells us to "pack up," which requires but a moment, as our wardrobe is very scanty, and our equipments few. Passing through the heavy doors of the jail, it seemed as though a new life had sprung up within us. We felt free, although the Rebel bayonets still surrounded us. We were taken before the Rebel commandant, to whom we gave the following parole:—

Charleston, S. C., C. S. A.,
September —, 1864.

We, the undersigned, prisoners of war, confined in the city of Charleston, in the Confederate States of America, do pledge our parole, individually, as military men and men of honour, that we will not attempt to pass the lines which shall be established and guarded around our prison-house; nor will we, by letter, word, or sign, hold any intercourse with parties beyond those lines, nor with those who may visit us, without authority. It is understood by us that this parole is voluntary on our part, and given in consideration of privileges secured to us, by lessening the stringency of the guard, of free ingress and egress of the house and appointed grounds during the day, by which we secure a liberty of fresh air and exercise grateful to comfort and health.

Hereby we admit that this, our parole, binds us in letter and spirit, with no room for doubt or technicality of construction, and its violation will be an act of lasting disgrace.

Signed:

After signing this we were marched under guard through the gateway of "Roper" into the beautiful garden of the hospital. How great the change! Here we are comparatively free. Here all seem better contented. We are assigned quarters on the third-floor *piazza*: the hard floor seeming a luxury, and the place itself a paradise, compared to that worse than grave Charleston jail-yard.

September 30.—Sixty shells and solid shot of very heavy calibre were thrown into the city today, many of which exploded in what is commonly called the:

Burnt District

It covers about one-third of the city, and was burnt during the early part of the year, having been set on fire by the explosion of shells thrown from our batteries on Morris Island.

This part of the city has been deserted by all except the negroes, who, whenever there is a cessation of shelling for a short time, flock here in great numbers to save rent. But a few shell dropped into the streets will soon disperse them, although they are easily tempted back again. And after a few days of quiet, they may be seen trudging around with bundles on their backs, looking for the most favourable location, often taking up their quarters in the dwellings of the former notables. Before the siege the poor negroes could only gain admission by the back entrance, where, with hat in hand, they awaited the orders of "massa."

Well, truth is stranger than fiction, and the city, built by the hard labour of slaves, now holds them as her principal occupants.

SHELLS A SUBJECT FOR DISCUSSION

As the shells from our batteries came screaming over our heads we took them as the subject of numerous and warmly-contested discussions. Some, for an argument, claimed that a shell is entirely harmless in its progress through the air if it does not explode before reaching a point directly overhead; others asserted that it must be past sufficiently far to make an angle of forty-eight degrees with the horizon before all danger is over. There are many absurd notions afloat with regard to the explosion of shells. Pictorial papers represent them as exploding while sweeping through the air, and the fragments flying in all directions. Soldiers return from the army, and tell of small shells entering men's heads, exploding just as they were passing through, and so scattering brains and skulls to the four winds of heaven.

The laws of physics will teach us that if a shell is moving through the air with a velocity greater than that which its explosion is capable of giving to the fragments, none of them can possibly fall back of the place of explosion. If the velocities here spoken of should be exactly equal, the pieces of the shell on the side next the mortar would be just stopped by the explosion, and so would fall perpendicularly to the ground, while those on the side opposite the mortar, being propelled by two forces (that of the mortar and that of the explosion), would necessarily be thrown a great distance for ward.

The pieces at right angles to the direction of motion would be thrown at right angles to this direction if the velocities were equal; if not equal they would move obliquely backwards or forwards according to the velocities, making the hypotenuse of a parallelogram. The explosion of shells over large bodies of water will thoroughly test these conclusions; and observations made under such circumstances prove them to be correct. If a shell explodes when moving rapidly over a body of water the pieces all strike the water several rods in advance of the place of explosion,—some more, some less,—the puff of smoke still remaining to mark the spot. Some move obliquely forward, some strike nearer and some farther from the place of explosion. It would not be difficult to tell from the striking location of any fragment whether it was at the north, south, east, or west side of the shell at the instant of explosion. If a shell is stationary, or moving very slowly, the pieces of course fly in all directions.

Groups of prisoners collected from time to time for the purpose of discussing this and various other subjects in which we had a direct, though unpleasant interest. Hours were spent thus, whilst every fifteen or twenty minutes we could see the smoke and hear the explosion of "Foster's messengers," as we called them, which came to us in the shape of screeching, tearing, death-dealing, two-hundred pound shells; and, although we were completely isolated from the outer world, yet these "terrible despatches" seemed ever welcome. They told us of the untiring perseverance of our forces on Morris Island.

So correct was their aim, so well did the gunners know of our whereabouts, that shells burst all around in front, and often flew screeching directly overhead without injury to us. When the distant rumbling of the "swamp-angel" was heard, and the cry "Here it comes!" resounded through our prison house there was a general stir. Sleepers sprang to their feet, the gloomy forgot their sorrows, conversation was hushed, and all started to see where the messenger would fall. Perhaps it would burst in mid air; perhaps fall crashing through the roof of some dwelling, converting it quickly from a stately mansion to a heap of smoking ruins.

The sight, at night, was truly beautiful. We traced along the sky a slight stream of fire, similar to the tail of a comet; followed its course until, "*whiz, whiz,*" came the little pieces from our mighty two hundred pounders, like "grape-shot," scattering themselves all around, and assuring us, in unmistakable language, that our soldiers were still battling for the cause of freedom inviolate.

October 1.—Yellow fever is raging fearfully in the city at present. Five shells from our batteries fell in the burnt district today. It was amusing to witness the flocks of negroes, who came running from the buildings which they have occupied since the commencement of the siege clear of rent charges, the owners being too timid to remain in that locality. The coloured people are often driven out in this manner, but invariably return after the shelling, to enjoy their threatened haunts.

Sisters of Charity

Confined as we are, so far away from every home comfort and influence, and from all that makes life worth living for, how quickly do we notice the first kind word, the passing friendly glance! Can any prisoner, confined here, ever forgot the "Sisters of Charity?" Ask the poor private, now suffering in those loathsome hospitals, so near us, if he can forget the kind look, the kind word given him by that "Sister," while burning with fever or racked with pain? Many are the bunches of grapes, many the sip of its pure juice, does the sufferer get from her hands. They seem—they are ministering angels; and while all around us are our avowed enemies, they remain true to every instinct of womanhood. They dare lift the finger to help, they do relieve many a sufferer.

All through the South our sick and wounded soldiers have had reason to bless the Sisters of Charity. They have ministered to their wants, and performed those kind womanly offices which are better to the sick than medicine, and so peculiarly soothing to the dying. These noble women have tended their sick beds when the other professedly Christian ladies of the South looked on in scorn, and turned away without even a kind word. They have done what some were too bitter and cruel to do; they have done what others did not dare to do. They were somehow permitted to bestow charities wherever charities were needed, without fear or molestation. Their bounties were bestowed indiscriminately on Federal and Rebel sufferers, and bespoke a broad philanthropy, unlimited by party or church or nation. Many a poor soldier has followed them from ward to ward with tearful eyes, and remembered the poet's lilies:—

> *Woman! Blest partner of our joys and woes!*
> *Even in the darkest hour of earthly ill,*
> *Untarnished yet, thy fond affection glows,*
> *Throbs with each pulse, and beats with every thrill!*
> *When sorrow rends the heart, when feverish pain*
> *Wrings the hot drops of anguish from the brow,*
> *To soothe the soul, to cool the burning brain,*
> *Oh, who so welcome, and so prompt as thou!*
> *The battle's hurried scene, and angry blow,*
> *The death-encircled pillow of distress,*
> *The lonely moments of secluded woe—*
> *Alike thy care and constancy confess,*
> *Alike thy pitying hand and fearless friendship bless.*

Were other denominations in the South as active in aiding us as the Catholics have been, I might have some faith in Rebel Christianity.

October 2.—Several shells passed directly over us this afternoon, a fragment of one striking the west end of the building.

October 3.—Our batteries have shelled the city vigorously during the past forty-eight hours. Many explosions very near us. No casualties among the prisoners.

Yellow Fever

The Rebel captain commanding this prison, and his adjutant, died last night with yellow fever. Many prisoners have been swept off by the same within the past few days.

October 4.—Heard from our enlisted men continued on Charleston Race Course. Starvation, exposure, and the frightful ravages of yellow fever are sweeping them off by the score.

October 5, eight a. m.—Orders are issued to "pack up" once more. We are to leave Charleston. The Rebel authorities ostensibly claim that they are removing us from the ravages of yellow fever. In view of the fact that we were brought here to be murdered by our own guns, this assertion seems doubtful,—and in view of the fact that it is no longer for their interest to keep us here it appears more doubtful. It seems scarcely credible that Louisianans should invoke the yellow fever upon our armies, and South Carolinians remove them from under its influence.

We were taken to Charleston to save the city from the shells of our batteries on Morris Island. The result proved that our gunners there could fire over and about our prison, and scathe the blackened city as fiercely as ever. In addition to this, General Foster placed an equal number of Rebel officers on government transports in front of his works, which effectually prevented them from firing upon him. It was for their interest, under these circumstances, to take steps to get these Rebel officers removed. These facts place their humanity in rather bad odour.

Farewell to Charleston

We bade the cruel city farewell without a regret. It has long been the abode of outrage and injustice. We expected no mercy at its hands, and have received none. The seething, almost conscious, shells from our island batteries are paying the respects of the North and northern men to this now desolate source of treason and discontent. We leave you to your fate, thankful that our presence, even as prisoners, has not mitigated your punishment.

The following verses were composed by Lieutenant J. Ogden, First Wisconsin Cavalry, and will fittingly close the chapter on Charleston:—

Charleston, South Carolina.

1

Oh, thou doomed city of the evil seed,[1]
Long nursed by baneful passion's heated breath!
Now bursts the germ, and lo, the evil deed
Invites the sword of war, the stroke of death!
Suns smile on thee, and yet thou smilest not;
Thy fame, thy fashion are alike forgot.
Consumption festers in thy inmost heart;
The shirt of Nessus fouls thy secret part.

2

Lo, in thy streets—thy boast in other days—
Grim silence sits, and rancorous weeds arise!
No joyous mirth, nor hymns of grateful praise,
Greet human ears nor court the upper skies;
But deadly pallor, and a fearful looking for
The hand of vengeance and the sword of war.
Thy prayer is answered, and around, above,
The wrath of God and man doth hourly move.

3

Thy foes are in thy heart, and lie unseen;
They drink thy life-blood and thy substance up;
And though in pride thou usest to sit a queen,
Justice at last commands the bitter cup.
The blood of slaves upon thy skirts is found;
Their tears have soaked this sacrilegious ground.
The chains that manacled their ebon arms
Now clank about thine own in dread alarms.

4

Thy sanctuaries are forsaken now;
Dark mould and moss cling to thy fretted towers;
Deep rents and seams, where straggling lichens grow,
And no sweet voice of prayer at vestal hours;
But voice of screaming shot and bursting shell,
Thy deep damnation and thy doom foretell.
The fire has left a swamp of broken walls,
Where night-hags revel in thy ruined halls.

5

Oh, vain thy boast, proud city, desolate!

---

1. The doctrine of State Rights as taught by John G. Calhoun.

Thy curses rest upon thy guilty head!
In folly's madness, thou didst desecrate
Thy sacred vows, to holy Union wed.
And now behold the fruit of this thy sin:
Thy courts without overrun, defiled within;
Gross darkness broods upon thy holy place;
Forsaken all, thy pride in deep disgrace.

6

Wail, city of the proud palmetto-tree!
Thy figs and vines shall bloom for thee no more!
Thou scorn'dst the hand of God, that made thee free,
In driving freemen from their native shore.
Thy rivers still seek peacefully the sea,
Yet bear no wealth on them, no joy for thee.
Thy isles look out and bask beneath the sun,
But silence reigns—their Sabbath is begun!

7

Blood! BLOOD is on thy skirts, oh, city doomed!
The cry of vengeance hath begirt thee round;
Here, where the citron and the orange bloomed,
God's curse rests on the half-forsaken ground!
Thy treason, passion-nursed, is overgrown—
Thy cup of wrath is full, is overflown.
Repent, for God can yet a remnant save,
But traitors and their deeds shall find the grave!

     Hospital, Charleston, S. C., Sept. 25, 1864.

Chapter 11

Removal to Columbia

Early on the morning of October 5th, Captain Mobly of the Thirty-second Georgia Volunteers gave us notice to prepare to remove to Columbia, the capital. In an hour's time we were securely packed in cattle-cars, ready for a start. These cattle-cars deserve a little notice. They were not exclusively cattle-cars, but were used to convey Union prisoners as well. One day they would be loaded with cattle, which did not tend to improve their sanitary condition to any great extent; the next day without any policing—they would be filled with barrels of sorghum molasses, a few of which would be smashed; and the next day fifty or sixty Yankees would be crowded into each of them, to be jumbled over a southern railroad a hundred miles or more.

Ye who pursue pleasure in splendid coaches along our northern railroads, think of this, and estimate the luxury of a trip from Charleston to Columbia under such circumstances. Our guard was the Thirty-second Georgia Volunteers, to whom too much credit cannot be given for their uniform kindness and, courtesy.

The Georgia troops seemed to be by far the most civil and gentlemanly of the southern army. They were the most respectable in appearance, most intelligent and liberal in conversation, and most fully recognised the principle that a man is a man under whatever circumstances he may be placed, and is entitled to humane treatment. They very generally addressed the prisoners as "gentlemen."

It is refreshing to find occasion to notice something commendable in those who were so almost universally tyrannical and cruel.

Our journey was marked with no features of peculiar interest, as the country through which we passed was a barren and sandy tract, with no vegetation to meet the weary eye, save occasionally a small patch of cotton, and sometimes sugarcane growing by the roadside.

We were about fourteen hours on the way, and arrived at Columbia, in the midst of a terrific rain storm, without food, blankets, or a necessary amount of clothing. We were compelled to vacate our quarters in the cars, and take up with such as were provided us by the Confederate officers in command, to wit: none at all.

We were closely guarded, and one of our number, Lieutenant H. L. Clark, Second Massachusetts Artillery, received a serious wound in the back by a bayonet in the hands of one of the sentinels, for attempting to take a small loaf of bread offered him joy a sympathizing citizen.

We remained in an open field on "Bridge Street" during the night, suffering from hunger, without blankets, tents, or any conveniences for comfort, at the mercy of the elements, with four pieces of artillery trained upon the ground which we occupied.

It was just before this that Alexander H. Stephens, their Vice-President, inaugurated his peace movement, and the Rebels expressed great anxiety for a knowledge of the result. They were anxious for peace, and hoped the movement would terminate in a settlement of their difficulties on a basis satisfactory to the interests of the southern people. Ever loud-mouthed and boastful, they still had misgivings as to the result, and eagerly caught at any prospect of a settlement.

Columbia

This capital city of the first State to raise the dark hand of treason against the American Union, has a population of from twenty to thirty thousand inhabitants, and is one of the finest in the State. It's handsomely situated on the Congaree River, one hundred and twenty-five miles from the sea, covering a gentle slope of ground which overlooks the surrounding country for a distance of from twenty to thirty miles, and it is equidistant from Charleston and Wilmington, North Carolina, on the line of the South-Carolina Central Railroad.

It is regularly laid out, its streets crossing each other at right angles; some are wide and planted with handsome trees, among which are found the Palmetto, which is familiar to all, as it was represented upon the first flag raised as a signal of war in opposition to the laws of our country.

Except in the busy, commercial parts of the town, the houses are surrounded with gardens, crowded with shrubs and flowers of all kinds; each establishment being generally encircled with hedges of hawthorn, interspersed with a luxuriant growth of roses.

The dwellings, which stand amid these beautiful pleasure grounds, are built of many different forms. Those of wood are usually painted white.

To the Southerner, this lovely place, during the war, has been one of perfect safety. It being the farthest of any from the lines of our advancing armies, and free from attack by our ever-watchful navy, many have flocked here from all parts of the Confederacy, where they might be beyond the reach of the dread sounds of war.

The Confederate government, influenced by the thought of impending danger, moved its treasury from the city of Richmond to this place, fearing that the Union army might make an inroad into its capital, and destroy its worthless currency.

The public buildings are of magnificent structure. The Capitol, or State House, occupies a commanding position near the centre of the town. The grounds adjoining are adorned with beautiful walks and avenues.

The military academy, court house, and its church edifices are built in splendid style. With all the beauty and magnificence combined to make these buildings grand to look upon, there yet remains connected with their history the memory of the dark deeds perpetrated within their walls, which resulted in the secession of the Palmetto State from our great and glorious Union. Here it was that the first steps were taken, which placed South Carolina foremost in the ranks of those States which afterwards adopted the ordinance of secession.

Although co-operation had been urged by many leading men of the South, among whom were Mr. Rhett, long conspicuous in the councils of the State, and Mr. Trenholm, afterwards a member of the Confederate cabinet, yet the fiery devotees of slavery forced their opinions, and controlled the public feeling, until a convention was called, which met on the 20th of December, 1860, when South Carolina launched forth upon a sea, above whose tranquil bosom brooded a pent-up storm, dark and tremendous, which, when it burst forth from its deathly silence, drenched her soil with the blood of her own sons, and scathed and blackened her as with fire from heaven, carried all away who had embarked upon its alluring surface, and dashed in one final wreck the frail structure upon which this unrighteous and unjust government was to be formed.

She entered upon a struggle which has devastated her lovely fields and finest cities, depopulated many of her most flourishing towns, and reduced her inhabitants to poverty, degradation, and despair.

By this deed, thousands of America's honoured sons, while battling nobly for the maintenance of right, have been sacrificed—making the fields of the South run red with blood.

But it has terminated in the complete overthrow of the foundation upon which these southern leaders attempted to rear their government, and in the destruction of that evil which had so long stained our nation's honour. Oh, Columbia! the pride of the South, thou hast passed through the fierce and bloody struggle without sharing in the general ruin which follows the footsteps of war. Although many of your hearth-stones have been made desolate, your beauty and magnificence yet remain.

May your people profit by the sad lot of other cities, and no longer invite destruction by fanning the flames of treason, and urging its cruel champions onward.

As soon as the storm had abated, which raged violently from the time we reached Columbia, cornmeal and sorghum molasses were issued to us in small quantities, and then we were moved from our camp on Bridge Street to the south side of the Congaree, about two miles from the city, and, like Nebuchadnezzar of old, turned out to grass.

Sorghum cane grows in large quantities in South Carolina, and from it a kind of molasses is made which entirely outdoes the blackest and dirtiest cane molasses. Cornmeal cakes and sorghum molasses will act as a cathartic on the strongest stomach, and to one already afflicted with chronic diarrhoea they were about as nourishing as a steady diet of Epsom salts.

CHAPTER 12

Columbia, South Carolina—"Camp Sorghum"

An attempt was made yesterday by the authorities to persuade us to take our paroles, in order that we might enjoy the privileges of an open field. We were threatened with confinement in some old tobacco houses in case we did not comply with their wishes; but we sternly refused to accept their base proposition, and utterly disregarded their threats, knowing that our condition could be made no worse by the change.

It may seem strange to some that these paroles were not accepted. Our reasons for not accepting them were these:

1st. They prevented our escaping, and this was the thought nearest our hearts.

2nd. We thought the punishment threatened rather more endurable than our condition when not under punishment.

They stated that they would confine us in some old tobacco houses, if we did not comply. Now, we considered confinement in any kind of a building more desirable than lying on the ground, without covering, during the damp chilly nights, exposed to the wind and storm.

For some reason unknown to us, we were not removed from this place into the tobacco houses; but a guard and "dead-line" were established; and in the open field, with no covering save the broad canopy of heaven, our band numbering upwards of fifteen hundred men was obliged to remain.

After many unsuccessful attempts to get a newspaper, I at last, by bribing one of our guards, secured a copy of the *South Carolinian*, a weekly sheet published in the city, from which I learned the position of the Union army under the gallant Sherman.

A Day of Joy

October 8.—This day was one of joy and thanks giving. Our hearts were made glad, and our hopes brighter, by the receipt of clothing, and many other articles of comfort sent to us from the North by that ever-beneficent organisation, the Sanitary Commission.

Those of our number who were the most needy were supplied with such articles as the authorities saw fit to allow them, which to some degree alleviated their sufferings, and made life somewhat sweeter. It was my happy lot to get a towel and an undershirt. The last-mentioned article was of great value to me, as more than three months had passed since I had had a change. Notwithstanding the distribution of clothing, many were without shoes, stockings, shirts, and coats—dying by inches for want of some protection from the inclement weather. They submitted to their fate, however trusting in the government and the ability of their country to save them before they finally perished.

The Test Election

October 16.—Our prison pen had been remarkably quiet for six or eight days, nothing having transpired among the prisoners to cause any excitement, and we were fast falling into a state of melancholy sadness, when, in view of the approaching presidential election, it was suggested that we vote upon the subject ourselves. The idea was approved by most of our number, as. it was also by the Rebels; for they wished to get an expression of the prevailing sentiment among us, that they might the better judge of the feeling that pervaded the people of the North. There were men among us from every State in the Union, and they naturally inferred that a vote in our camp would be an index of the vote at the North. Accordingly they urged the thing on, and promised to publish the result in the city papers,—though when they saw what the result was, they hastily changed their minds, and no mention was made of our election.

Many warm and even violent discussions had taken place for a number of days among the prisoners, and political spirit ran so high that they could not wait till election day. The vote was taken by States at the quarters of the senior officer of each State, and the results sent in to the general office. Written ballots were used which were handed to the officer, and by him deposited in an old meal bag, which served as a ballot-box. A bulletin-board and telegraph-office were established, and sham telegrams were published from the different States, especially New Jersey.

I cast my vote for Abraham Lincoln, as did my messmates, Hampton and Richardson, deeply regretting that it was my sad lot to be denied the privilege of doing so where it might count for some good. At six o'clock p. m. the counting was finished, the result being ten hundred and twenty-four votes for Lincoln, and one hundred and forty-three for McClellan.

This was the expression of feeling and opinion among men who had been deprived of all the common comforts of life, half starved, with nothing but dirty rags hanging to their emaciated limbs to protect their bodies from the cold, wasting away by hunger and exposure, yet would not favour a peace degrading to their country's honour.

Cheer upon cheer arose from our feeble voices, and resounded through our prison yard, upon the announcement, making the McClellanites, who had been very confident of the success of their candidate, look crestfallen and disappointed.

The Confederates understood the significance of the re-election of Mr. Lincoln full well. They knew it would be impossible to free themselves from the serpent into whose coils they had been drawn; but that they must fight for a cause that originated in sin, that was nurtured in iniquity, and that must perish in infamy and disgrace.

The Rebel officers had continually misrepresented the Federal administration to the prisoners; and as we had no means by which to refute the arguments of these wily secessionists, except the firm confidence in our government, our souls were filled with joy and gladness by this favourable result of our *impromptu* election.

The song of war shall echo through the mountains
'Till not one hateful link remains
Of slavery's lingering chains;
'Till not one tyrant treads our plains,
Nor traitor lips pollute our fountains.

An Escape

October 18.—Our camp was today thrown into a state of wild excitement, owing to the escape of three prisoners, who ran the guard and made towards "God's country." Several shots were fired at them as they passed the outer line, but without doing them any injury, and they passed out in safety. The entire guard was aroused. The men flew to arms, the artillerymen to their guns. The Rebel officers, calling loudly to their men to fall in, could be distinctly heard at my quarters, making me tremble for the fate of the brave men who, risking life, were trying to make their escape from this den of misery.

After the occurrence of this affair, our guard was doubled, and orders given to the sentinels to shoot down every prisoner who should in any manner approach the "dead-line." This action on the part of the Confederates did not, however, intimidate us in the least; for we well knew if compelled to remain there, in the condition we were then in, that death would surely overtake us; and to die in the attempt to free ourselves from the grasp of heartless tyrants would be no worse than starvation.

My plan for escape was not in the least disconcerted by this movement of the Rebels; on the contrary, my determination to be free was more fixed in my mind, and I continued the preparations for a leave-taking of Columbia and the hated Prison Pen, "Camp Sorghum."

After two days had passed, and no tidings were received from our friends, we began to feel that they must have escaped the vigilance of Rebel search. There was general rejoicing at their escape, and we worked ourselves into a state of feverish excitement over their success in passing the "dead-line." Our physical debility rendered us more intensely susceptible to excitement, and yet there is something about watching the progress of an escape from prison that will excite the most unimpassioned.

We looked upon their success as an index of what our own might be, should we make a similar attempt. And besides this, I trust we had higher motives to awaken interest. Although often reprehensibly selfish in matters that did not materially affect their lives and safety, our soldiers could still rejoice as thoroughly at the successful escape of a fellow-prisoner as though the good fortune had been their own. Many prayers were offered that a kind Providence would guide them safely through darkness and doubt to the Federal lines, and the most enthusiastic expressions of joy were manifested by all who had strength to rejoice.

The jubilation was somewhat quickened, I mistrust, by the satisfaction it afforded us to know that the Rebel guards had been outwitted, and that Yankees could make their way through the heart of the Confederacy without being recaptured.

But our gratulations were brought to a melancholy sequel. It seems, that for every prisoner who escapes to safety, some comrade must be sacrificed of those who remained. There came, in the midst of our rejoicings, the sad and whispered intelligence.—

A Prisoner Shot

Lieutenant Young of the Fourth Pennsylvania Cavalry, was shot down in cold blood, by one of the sentinels, while conversing with some fellow-officers, near a small fire. He only survived the shot a few moments. This occurred about ten o'clock on the evening of October 20th.

No reason for this atrocity was apparent, and none was offered by our guards. It was another added to the already long list of cruel, heartless murders perpetrated in southern prisons. We were overcome with grief at the report, for Lieutenant Young was a brave man, a fine officer, a pleasant companion, and withal, had for a long time been a suffering friend.

Thus another noble spirit was ushered into the presence of its Maker, sent thither by the brutal hand of a murderer.

Were they men, and suffer such conduct? had they been taught the principles of love and justice, which are given to all in the great Book of Books? had they any sense of humanity in their bosoms? No, the foul fiend of darkness possessed and influenced their thoughts. Not satisfied with depriving men of the necessary food to sustain life, they shot down our defenceless comrades like dogs, without a shudder at the heinousness of the crime.

How long, oh God! how long will such fearful atrocities be allowed?

Long Live the Dutchman

A German captain was sent by the authorities, not long since, to take command of the prison. He was a pompous individual, and did things generally on the "spread-eagle" style.

As soon as he arrived, we were ordered into line to listen to a speech from the new commandant. Everything was conducted with accurate regard to military precision, and just at the right moment our Teutonic orator stepped forward, and delivered the following oration:—

> *Shentlemens,—I comes to take command of you. I've been a brisoner mein self. Your peoples treats me like shentlemens,—I treats you like shentlemens. Break ranks! March!!*

There was a general burst of laughter among the prisoners, and cries of "Long live the Dutchman." A few days after he got drunk and was removed, and thus our hopes of making game of the Dutchman came to an unseemly end.

From the time we left Charleston the weather had been exceedingly cold and disagreeable, and no tongue can tell or pen describe the sufferings of the brave men confined there. The want of clothing made their bodies more susceptible to cold, and many were dying daily of diseases contracted from exposure to the sun and storm, and from a constant diet of coarse and unwholesome food.

Thoughts of Home

Under such circumstances it was our custom to lie down after taking our night's meal, not to sleep, but to talk over the incidents of our boyhood days, and the events of our lives. Thoughts of home, and the friends gathered around loved firesides, came crowding upon us; memory dwelt with clinging interest on scenes that might never be repeated; imagination feasted herself on pictures that might never prove a reality, and thus the long night was wearied through until the stars were growing dim in the light of approaching day, when we sought that rest which our exhausted systems so much needed.

There were but few persons among us who had ever been compelled to suffer such privations and hardships. Most of them, before entering the army, had been clerks behind the counter, students at school, or well-to-do mechanics. Some were soldiers by profession, and many were sons of wealthy men, who had never known anything but pleasure, and had always taken life easy. But all, through the common impulses of their natures, and the patriotism ever burning in the loyal American heart, had offered their services to their bleeding and distracted country, to assist in subduing the element of discontent at the South, and the foulest and most unwarrantable rebellion against just and proper authority, ever known within the annals of time.

As to their fate, many were thoughtless and indifferent, some were distrustful of our government, and its intentions to liberate them; but few were without hope of approaching succour, and depending upon the mercies of an all-wise and overruling Providence, we made the best of our miserable condition.

I did not intend to remain in "durance vile" a great while longer; but upon the first favourable opportunity to take my flight, with some one or two of my friends, if they chose to go with me; if not, I should risk my life alone. I did not think any of my companions would refuse an offer to accompany me, if I should propose a plan which presented any chances of success. I kept my own counsel, however, and when the time should arrive, I would cautiously make my intentions known to those I wished to have accompany me, and then set out together. As the days came and went, our sufferings increased.

The season being far advanced, the cold night air chilled us through, and the stars, from their lofty stations in the heavens, shone upon us clear and cold, while the moon reflected its pale, silvery light upon our pallid faces, making us look doubly haggard and ghost-like.

Allowed to Get Wood by Taking a Parole

The prison authorities adopted a rule of allowing a certain number each day to pass outside the prison limits, for the purpose of backing in such quantities of wood as we could carry. This privilege was granted to such as would give their paroles not to attempt an escape.

The following was the nature of the parole issued:—

> Confederate States Military Prison,
> Columbia, S. C., October , 1864.
>
> I, —— ——, prisoner of war, confined near the city of Columbia, S. C., Confederate States of America, do pledge my parole, as a military man, and a man of honour, that I will not attempt to escape from the prison authorities, nor pass beyond the prison limits more than three-quarters of a mile, and that at the expiration of the time named in the parole, I will return promptly to the adjutant's office and have the same revoked.
>
> It is understood by me that this parole is voluntary on my part, and that it is given with a view to securing privileges which cannot otherwise be obtained.
>
> (Signed)   —— ——

We were all very glad of the opportunity of doing something whereby the material could be procured for making a fire. Many accepted the offer, and went out to bring in what they could pick up in the shape of dry twigs, broken branches of trees and bark. It was a sad sight to see us filing along under guard, picking up what we could carry, and returning with our loads upon our backs.

Some of the men were so weak that they became as helpless as a child, and had to be carried back to camp in a state of utter exhaustion and insensibility. In trying to help themselves, they overtaxed their remaining strength, which, brought on fevers and delirium, from the effects of which many died.

I profited, however, by the arrangement; for not only a sufficient quantity of wood was procured to last me and my mess two days, but in carefully examining the plan of our pen, and the system by which it was guarded, I obtained and added to my small store of knowledge much valuable information concerning the surrounding country. All of which, at some future day, then not far distant, would be put to good use.

I was not by any means the only one to profit by these explorations. Others, as much on the alert as myself for adventure, conceived plans whereby they effected an escape; but unfortunately, after a few days had passed, were generally recaptured and thrown into county jails.

They had the satisfaction, during their absence, of getting some cornbread and bacon of the faithful negroes, out of which they could make at least a few good meals; and this alone was enough to compensate for the attempt.

Every soldier knows that the times when he succeeded in getting "good square meals," as they were called, were epochs in his military history,—so much are men the slaves of their wants.

My Old Shoes

Being badly worn, I took them to the "camp cobbler" to be repaired. He gave me no encouragement, but said they were past redemption, and could not be improved.

How could I travel barefoot through the hot burning sand of the highway, the stone-covered fields, or the dreary swamps? I must have some covering for my feet, and at once set about preparing something myself.

By dint of good luck, I obtained the rim of an old worn-out regulation hat, from which I cut some inner soles, and by tying the outer sole to the uppers with a piece of cord, made them appear no worse, and added largely to their worth and durability; thus my feet were protected from the heat and cold.

In making an escape it is absolutely necessary that there be suitable protection for the feet, and even under the most destitute circumstances all such contingencies had to be provided for.

During the last two weeks of my stay at Columbia, the nights had become so cold that we did not think of lying down, but would walk around the camp for the purpose of keeping the blood in circulation and to prevent chilling.

When the sun rose in the morning, and not till then, would we stretch ourselves on the ground to sleep, the heat from its rays warming us and keeping us warmed while locked in the arms of Morpheus. We literally turned night into day and day into night. Those who have lived in northern latitudes know how disagreeable it is to be so situated as to be obliged to exercise continually in order to keep from chilling. It may be endurable for a few hours, but one after a time becomes weary of it. But our lack of clothing was such that we had to be on the alert during the whole night,—and that night after night.

November 8, 1864.—This eventful day was one of intense excitement and anxiety with us, as it was to decide who should be our chief magistrate for the next four years. We felt satisfied that the election would result in placing Mr. Lincoln, our then respected president, in the chair which for the past four years he had filled with so much credit to himself and honour to the nation; and yet an almost certain election has its excitement, and the certainty cannot be an absolute certainty until the last vote is cast. We would rather have known the result than believed it.

Exchange rumours

We were also notified by the prison authorities that a general exchange of prisoners would take place on the 20th. Captain Hatch, the Rebel commissioner of exchange, was there; and it was rumoured about camp that a large portion of our number would be taken to Savannah immediately, causing great excitement. The "fresh-fish," especially, were in excellent humour over what they styled glorious good news. The old prisoners were not inclined, however, to be very jubilant over the announcement, as they had many times before been duped and deceived by the practical infamy of the Confederates. And it was very well that we put no faith in such loose reports, for at this time, as on many other occasions when such rumours were circulated, nothing official had been received.

Hope comes again to the heart, long a stranger;
Once more she sings me her flattering strain;
But hush, gentle siren! for, ah! there's less danger
In still suffering on than in hoping again.

The Rebels always took advantage of the natural despondency following so much excitement, to endeavour to persuade the prisoners to believe that our government cared nothing for our suffering, and would use every other means at their command to cause us to lose confidence in the Federal authorities and the commanding officers of our army. They miserably failed in their endeavours to extinguish the fire of patriotism burning in our bosoms, by such contemptible misrepresentations, and only added to the bitter hate in which we looked upon these vile traitors and inhuman wretches who guarded and starved us.

Caught by Hounds

Many of the recently-escaped prisoners were brought back to us about these times, most of whom were caught by hounds. Lieutenant Parker was so lacerated that he died the next day after his capture. On the 7th inst. Lieutenant J. Clement, of the Fifteenth Kentucky Cavalry, was captured by a Rebel living but a short distance from Chapel's Ferry, South Carolina. After he had surrendered the dogs were let loose on him; and thus he was so seriously injured as to be disabled for a long time.

I should have made my escape on the fourth, had not my health been so delicate that I could not have walked out of camp, even had the road been clear. I had been suffering very much from camp diseases, and was so weak as to be unable to walk without the aid of a friend.

Near the 12th of November rumours reached us that General Sherman had left Atlanta, and was moving through Georgia in three columns. It was currently reported that he would occupy Augusta. The "great general's" movements were little understood by the Rebels; they were greatly alarmed, and began concentrating their forces at Augusta.

Drawing Meat Rations at Camp Sorghum

About this time quite an amusing scene enlivened our camp. An old wild hog chanced to pass the guard line; and as soon as he came within range of the prisoners, a general advance was made and he was ours. But a few moments elapsed after his entrance among us before no traces of his carcase could be found. From four to five hundred half-starved men gave him a most hearty welcome. *He was a stranger and they took him in,* in more senses than one. One seized a leg, another an ear, and another his tail; and as many as his dusky exterior would accommodate twisted their skinny fingers into his long, arrowy bristles, and closed their hands and eyes and teeth as if for a death-struggle. There was tumbling and tripping and pushing and yelling and swearing, while the Rebel guards, at a "parade rest," were laughing heartily at the ridiculous scene.

Every man clung to the part he first seized, and that part was to be his portion. Richardson was the first to seize a hind leg, and this, leg he clung to through all the *mêlée* like grim death to his victim, and did not relinquish his hold until it was cut off and securely lodged in the mess kettle for supper.

Our guest was not "the fattest hog in Epicurus sty," but we were in no condition to make a point of quality, and thankfully struggled for steaks that "would not fry themselves."

This was the first and only ration of meat issued to us while at Columbia, and this—no thanks to the Rebels—very foolishly issued itself.

It would have been useless for the prison authorities to try to deprive us of this well-earned booty, for in less than five minutes after the first salute it would have been impossible to find enough of the grunting porker to grease a skillet, if we except the intestines.

When the black hog was seen on a run through the camp
Each soldier forgot his starvation and cramp;—
The grunts of the hog and his running were vain
His form will ne'er darken that campground again.
          The Wandering Poet of New Hampshire.

Sherman's March to the Sea

A few days confirmed the rumours that had been floating with regard to Sherman's movements. It came to be generally understood that he was marching on Augusta, Macon, and Savannah. These reports had the usual effects—of depressing the Rebels, and inspiring the prisoners with hope. Many attempts to escape were made at this time—with varying success. Several shots were fired into the pen by the sentinels, and one prisoner had his arm blown off in an attempt to run the guard.

On the 23rd, Lieutenant George R. Barse, Fifth Michigan Cavalry, of whom previous mention has been made, escaped by strategy while the prisoners were passing out on parole after wood. The officer of the guard had taken position without the guard-line, where he had a battalion of men in readiness to send to the woods with the paroled prisoners, allowing several to go at a time, and proportioning the number of guards to the size of the squad. As each party arrives near the "dead-line," one of the number manifests a desire to pass out, at the same time exhibiting a paper with signatures attached to a written parole. The officer of the guard then beckons to the sentinel to permit them to cross the lines, when he takes their paroles and hands

Drawing Meat Rations at Camp Sorghum

them to one of a certain number of armed men, who are detailed to act as their escort. Barse followed a squad that observed all this necessary formality; but the officer and guard were none too bright; and Lieutenant Barse went on, rejoicing no doubt at his good fortune, until he reached the woods, When he claimed that he was a hospital steward, and had nothing to do with the men, whom he had only chanced to walk out of camp with. Luckily, there was no one present to contradict his assertion, and, without further ceremony, he marched off at his pleasure.

Great excitement prevailed just now over Sherman's terrific march through Georgia, which was just beginning to develop itself. The Legislature removed to Macon, and Governor Brown issued a proclamation ordering to the front every man capable of bearing arms.

Thanksgiving Day

Brought us much to be thankful for, to be sure, but little heart to enter into the celebration of such a day. There was great suffering in camp on account of the severity of the weather. We had heavy frosts frequently, and many, having no blankets, were obliged to find warmth in exercise. Hampton, Richardson, and myself, possessed a small blanket each, but with even these it was almost impossible to keep from freezing. We sleep in the middle by turns, and this privilege with us is a matter of the gravest importance. So unpardonable was the offence of attempting to deprive one of his equal rights in this respect, that many quarrels originated from no other cause.

In a case involving so much interest we did not trust to memory, but, on turning out in the morning, marked upon the ground the name of the individual who was to have the choice of position at night. This method was not resorted to until we found it to be our only safe guard against disputes. The one who slept in the middle was usually quite comfortable, although his sphere of operations was rather limited, for those on the outside naturally inclined to crawl away from the chilly flanks towards the centre. In, this way we could get some sleep one night in three, if not drowned out by a rain storm.

Mud Burrows

After waiting our turn for more than three weeks, we at last succeeded in securing an old shovel, with which we dug a cave in the ground large enough to crawl into at night, and during storms.

There seemed no prospect of a general exchange, and the prisoners were determined to make the best of their miserable situation. So far as I was concerned, it was not my intention to spend a single night in this bear's den, if possible to effect an escape; and yet we always thought it worth our while to be prepared for the worst.

The greater part of the 25th was spent in digging, and we accomplished as much during the "long, weary day," as a first-class ditcher might have done in an hour. I became tired of it, and fully resolved to make my escape on the 26th. Saw friend Lemon, and proposed to him a plan by which we could relieve "Camp Sorghum" from any further care of our persons. We could not think of being longer dependent on the bounty of our enemies, and determined to strive for some advantage of situation which would enable us to return their compliments.

Plan of Escape

It was customary to extend the guard-line in the morning, for the purpose of allowing the prisoners to pick up wood on a piece of timbered land just opposite camp; and it was our intention to take a shovel, when permitted to pass to the woods, and make a hole in the ground large enough to receive our two skeletons, and then have our friends cover us with brush and leaves. Thus concealed, we hoped to be left without the camp when the guard should be withdrawn. Should we succeed in escaping the vigilance of the sentinels, it was our purpose to strike for Augusta, Georgia, feeling assured that General Sherman would soon occupy that place. Many preferred to strike for Knoxville, Tennessee, considering that the safer, though it was much the longer route to our lines. Our course would incur more risk, but the sooner bring us within the Federal camp. Indulging these expectations, we lay down to rest.

On the morning of the 26th Hampton and Richardson asked if we should continue work on our "mud burrow." I replied that I should dig no more holes in South Carolina; that they need make no arrangements in their cellar for me, as I did not propose to have any further use for subterranean caverns. They looked at each other with a knowing smile, doubtless thinking a temporary disgust had come over me, which would soon wear away, and I would again return to my quarters. Under the circumstances, I am disposed to pardon them.

Lemon and I kept a careful lookout, anxiously waiting for the guard to be extended out into the woods. But the morning was cold and rainy, and the guards not caring to leave their snug tents along the line of the encampment, we were left without fires.

Thus our hopes were again blasted, and nothing was left us but to make a bold strike, and pass the guards by a plentiful exhibition of "brass." How this was accomplished will be set forth in the next chapter.

CHAPTER 13

The Escape From Columbia[1]

FIRST DAY

Lexington C. H. Road, six Miles From Columbia, S. C.
Saturday, November 26, 1864.

While taking a stroll through "Camp Sorghum" in the morning for the purpose of discovering a weak point in the guard-line, I observed one of the guards to be a stupid-looking fellow, and proposed testing his abilities before he should be relieved by one of brighter appearance. Accordingly I hastened in pursuit of Lieutenant M. W. Lemon, of the Fourteenth New York Heavy Artillery, a man of courage and enterprise, and with whom I had decided to escape. I only told him to meet me at a certain point, and be ready to leave the pen in three minutes.

No time was lost in packing or checking our baggage to any given point; and we also deemed it unnecessary to bid our friends goodbye, or to thank the proprietors for hospitalities received.

PASSING THE DEAD-LINE

We were soon at the specified place, passed up to the "dead-line," as if that point possessed no further interest to us, and were in the act of stepping over, when the aforementioned worthy brought his gun to bear upon me with an uncomfortable precision; at the same time ordering a halt.

"Where are you going, Yanks?" he demanded; but with an air of offended dignity, I only said, "Do you halt paroled prisoners here?"

His meek "No, sir," was almost lost in the distance, as I boldly

---

1. Written during the escape, while in the swamps and cotton gins of South Carolina and Georgia, where we were secreted by the ever-faithful negroes.

crossed the dreaded line, adding, "Then let the gentleman in the rear follow me;" and so we passed, while the brilliant sentinel murmured, "All right."

And right it was; for now we were free, breathing the fresh air, untainted by the breath of hundreds of famishing, diseased, and dying men.

Outside of the pen were numbers of paroled prisoners gathering wood, and Rebel guards strolling about. We at once commenced discussing the most favourable locality for obtaining brush with which to cover our "mud-burrow," and thus conversing about our domestic affairs, it was not long before we were well into the woods,—the guards thinking, no doubt, if they thought at all, that we had a right to be out with the others. Once well beyond the sight of gray-coated sentinels, we put our untried strength to a test and placed a few miles between us and "Camp Sorghum" rather hurriedly.

There was not very much of dignity in our departure, to be sure,—not to say grace or beauty;—and it may be that there was something a little suspicious in a certain looking over the shoulder that might have been observed as we sloped through bushes and leaped over logs. Quite likely horse thieves, when thwarted in their purposes have propelled themselves from the scenes of their embarrassments in a manner not remarkably dissimilar. It may be that, not very high-toned curs, in getting away from the backdoors of butcher shops would find it convenient to imitate us rather closely;—and yet there was something in this style of locomotion that seemed peculiarly adapted to our circumstances, and we fell into it instinctively, as it were.

We have never, as yet, to any great extent, had occasion to regret our haste and want of dignity.

As soon as we had put sufficient distance between ourselves and the "Prison Pen" to make leisure compatible with safety, we proceeded more slowly.

The country, outside of cities and villages at the South, is always so sparsely settled that, once on the road, and no hounds upon the track, one can readily find places of concealment. Of course, it was our policy at the first to keep comparatively scarce for a time. We made a little progress, how over, following ravines and concealed places, and always avoiding roads and openings.

Several times we ran on to white people, but succeeded in hiding ourselves until they were past. About two o'clock we lay down to rest, and remained concealed until nearly dark sleeping little, however, on account of the excitement of our situation.

Meeting Negroes

When night began to fall we were up and doing, and soon struck the Lexington Court House road. Following this for some little time we heard voices behind us, and slackened our pace to discover whether they were negroes or white men. It is sometimes difficult to determine, as their manner of conversation is almost the same in the South.

When they were within ten or fifteen feet of us, partly turning, I said, "A pleasant evening, gentlemen."

This was intended to be equally applicable to both whites and negroes, but the answer was equally in definite. One of them merely remarked, "Indeed it is," and said no more.

We were rather led to believe they were white men, and so quickened our step and left them somewhat behind.

As the distance increased, their conversation commenced again, and we heard one of them say, "I guess deys Yankees."

Another replied, "I hope to God dey is."

This satisfied us that they were negroes, and we turned round, and met them face to face. I asked, in a low voice, "Do you know who I am?"

N. I reckon I dun no ye, Massa.

G. Have you ever seen a Yankee?

N. Lor bless ye, Massa. I've seed a heap ob 'em down to Columbia.

G. Do we look like Yankees?

N. Can't very well tell in de night-time; but I s'pect you talk like 'em.

G. Well, my good fellow, we are Yankees, just escaped from Columbia. Can't you do something for us?

N. Ob corse, I will do all I can for you. I'se no nigger if I wouldn't 'sist de Yankees.

Being satisfied that they were entirely trust worthy, we unfolded our plans to them. There were three of them. They had been at Columbia, working on a new prison stockade, which the Rebels were building for the reception of Federal prisoners. Judging that Sherman's movements might make this labour useless, they had stopped work and sent the negroes to their masters. These three fellows were the "property" of a Mr. Steadman, whose plantation is situated some twenty-five miles south west of Columbia, on the road to Augusta. Thus we were travelling in the same direction.

We stepped aside in the bushes to arrange a plan of procedure, and after a discussion of the subject, one of their number, "Ben Steadman" by name, agreed to become—

Our Guide

while the other two were to travel by themselves. This proved a wise arrangement in the end, for the fact that there were only three of us together probably saved us from recapture, and "Ben" from detection and punishment.

Our guide decided to leave the main road, and take a shorter cut to his master's plantation. It was arranged that "Ben" should walk in advance some little distance, and if he met any white men, give us warning by a peculiar kind of cough;—while we, on the other hand, were to give him notice of danger in a similar manner.

After a tramp of two or three hours we struck a "blind road," and, being assured by our guide that it was never frequented by white men after dark, disregarded our first precaution, and walked carelessly along, chatting vigorously with "Ben" upon those subjects which most interested us. We had not proceeded far, however, before we were reminded of the necessity of moving more cautiously. Our reminder was none other than—

A Rebel Picket

of eight men, a little to the left of the road. Fortunately for us but one of the number was awake. Supposing that we were negroes he allowed us to approach until we were nearly opposite the picket before the challenge, "Who comes there?" was given, and our guide answered, "Friends";—Lemon and myself could not see that anything would be gained by a recapture, and so we flew down the road at the top of our speed. This was the first test of our fleetness, and in justice to Lemon, I am compelled to confess myself badly beaten. I could not help saying, "Go in Lemon," nor avoid a suppressed laugh while straining every nerve to overtake my rival in the race.

"Ben" made a good story of it, telling the picket that the other two darkies got scared and ran away, adding,—

"I dunno what makes dem niggers run so."

His story being corroborated by those who had seen him leave the stockade with two other negroes, he was soon set at liberty, ready to do another good job when called for.

Expecting to be pursued, we soon concealed ourselves behind a log near the roadside. After a little a detachment of the picket passed by escorting "Ben" to the reserve of the picket; he, in the meantime, narrating the adventures of the night, and denouncing "dem two cowardly niggers" in good round terms.

After they had passed, we followed them cautiously in the deep sand, until they came to a squad of men sleeping and watching around a large fire. Not being able to flank them, on account of swamps, which lay on either side of the road, we halted and slept near them till morning.

While looking for a place of concealment, Lemon and myself became separated, and not daring to speak, crawled around nearly an hour before we found each other. We had eaten nothing save a small piece of cornbread since leaving Columbia, and had not dared to present ourselves before any habitation; but hoped to break our long fast after ten o'clock the next night.

Second Day

Near Barnwell Court House,
Sunday, November 27.

Soon after daylight the picket, near which we were sleeping, scattered in every direction, and went to their homes. They were not regular soldiers, but bushwhackers, who were on their plantations during the day, and met at night to patrol and picket the highways.

This left the coast clear, and, breakfastless, we began to pick our way through the swamp which lay before us; passing through it, we soon came into a rolling wooded country and pushed on, taking the road for a guide, but not daring to come nearer to it than a quarter of a mile. We found nothing to eat but a few blueberries, not the best travelling diet in the world, but thankfully received under the circumstances. About nine o'clock a. m. we crossed the road with a view to putting possible pursuers off the track. About eleven o'clock we came to a clearing, and made our way to a barn nearby; but seeing a planter standing by a fence across the field we hastily retraced our steps, and got into the woods again. Shortly after, we came to another open field, which we crossed successfully.

Near four o'clock in the afternoon we came to a large plantation, approaching within thirty or forty rods of the building, and lying in the bushes. Here we tried to attract the attention of negroes, but were unsuccessful. While snugly ensconced behind a large log, a white woman and several small children came riding down the road on a mule, and passed within a few feet of us, but we hugged the ground closely, and were not observed.

An Accidental Friend

As it began to grow dark, we crept cautiously on our way along the side of the road, and about nine o'clock came to the junction of four roads where we fortunately found a friend in an old guide-board.

Jumping on my companion's shoulders, I was enabled by the light of the moon to read the direction and decide upon the course to be pursued. We then pushed on our way at a rapid pace until about two o'clock a. m., when we laid down in the bushes near the roadside to sleep.

Third Day

Near Black Creek, S. C.,
Monday, November 28.

We were awakened just before daybreak by the villainous barking of dogs, and found ourselves but a few rods from the plantation of Alexander Taylor. The dogs had attracted the attention of the people towards our hiding-place, and as soon as a move was made, we were observed. Running I knew would be useless, as I could see the planter's wife looking at us.

My companion preferred remaining at a safe distance from his dogship, while I approached the ladies who were already assembled near, and after learning there were no white men on the plantation, I frankly stated my case, and appealed to their sympathies for something to eat. They were at first unwilling to grant me any assistance. Mrs. Taylor said that her husband was in the Confederate army, that her heart was with the Southern people, and further, that she thought it wrong for her to aid a Yankee in making his escape. I then addressed to her a brief speech, recounting in pitiful terms my misfortunes, and my disappointment, should I fail in reaching General Sherman's lines.

Kindness of Mrs. Taylor

I made no gestures, struck no attitudes, and used none of the enticements of rhetoric, but simply made a direct appeal to her benevolent feelings, and this, aided by my forlorn and destitute condition, seemed to win the day. The kind-hearted lady remarked that she "would see what could be done for us," and going into the house she returned with a generous supply of cornbread, bacon, and sweet potatoes.

After extorting a promise from the ladies that they would not betray us, I promised Mrs. Tailor that if ever her husband came in Yankee hands, and it was in my power, I would see no harm befall him; and this promise I would have kept even at the expense of my own life. The rations were soon hurried into my haversack, and after again thanking my benefactress for her kindness, I returned to my companion, when we hastened off to a thicket in the woods, built a pine-knot fire, roasted our potatoes, and made a "royal breakfast." Oh ye who sleep on beds of down in your curtained chambers, and rise at your leisure to feast upon the good things provided, smile not when I say you never knew the luxury of a night of rest, nor the sweets of a meal seasoned by hunger, and the grateful remembrance that it was provided by woman's kindly heart, which, wherever it may beat, sooner or later responds to the tale of misfortune and suffering humanity.

A bath in a stream nearby, with the washing of our stockings, completed the duties of the morning, and we were glad to rest, being weary, weak, and sore, the result of violent walking.

After resting all day, we roasted more potatoes at night, and putting our feet to the decaying embers, again lay down to sleep. It was our purpose to awaken at eleven o'clock and pursue our journey, but we were so much exhausted by walking and exposure that sleep entirely overpowered us, and the night was far spent before we again awoke. We were soon on our way, however, endeavouring to redeem the lost time.

Fourth Day

Near North Edisto River, on the Road to Aiken, S. C.,
Tuesday, November 29.

We reached Black Creek this morning just before daybreak, and while crossing the bridge over said stream, met a negro on his way to work, who turned back and conducted us to a hut for safe keeping during the day.

This hut, familiarly known throughout the neighbourhood as—

Aunt Katy's

was the general gathering place of all in want of assistance. The good old soul gladly roused from her morning slumbers when she learned that Yankees were at the door awaiting her attention. We were welcomed with a hearty "God bless ye, *Massa*," and while she made preparations for our "creature comforts," a little boy was sent to ask in her dusky neighbours that they might "rejoice with her" over the good fortune of having an opportunity to aid friends in escaping from a common enemy. In an incredibly short space of time the entire coloured population of the plantation were assembled.

To exhibit their deep religious interest in our welfare,

A Prayer-Meeting

was improvised for our especial benefit, and they conducted it in a manner both creditable to themselves and amusing to us. The burden of their petitions was, that all the prisoners held by the Rebels might make a general exodus and reach the Yankee lines in safety; that we in particular might succeed in making our escape; that our armies might speedily conquer the whole of Secessia, liberate the slaves, and take possession of the land.

Uncle Zeb,

who seemed to be a ruling spirit, by common consent, led off as follows:

O Lord God A mighty! we is your chil'en, and 'spects you to hear us widout delay,—'cause we all is in right smart ob a hurry. Des yer gemmen has rund away from de secetchers and wants to git back to de Norf. Dey hasn't got time for to wait. Ef it is kording to de destination ob great Heaven to help 'em, it'll be bout necessary for de help to come right soon.

De hounds and de Rebels is on dere track. Take de smell out ob de dog's noses, O Lord! and let Gypshun darkness come down ober de eyesights ob de Rebels. Confound 'em, O Lord! dey is cruel, and makes haste to shed blood. Dey has long 'pressed de black man, and ground him in de dust, and now I reck'n dey 'spects dat dey am agwine to serve de Yankees in de same way. 'Sist des gemmen in time ob trouble, and lift 'em fru all danger on to de udder side ob Jordan dry-shod.

And raise de radiance ob your face on all de Yankees what's shut up in de Souf. Send some Moses, O Lord! to guide 'em fru de Red Sea ob 'flicshun into de promised land.

Send Mr. Sherman's company, sweepin' down fru dese yer parts to scare de Rebels till dey flee like de Midians, and slew dereselves to sabe dere lives.

Let a little de best ob Heaven's best judgments rest on Massa Lincum,—and may de year ob Jubilee come sure.

O Lord! bless de gen'rals ob de Norf O Lord! bless de kunnels—O Lord! bless de brigerdeers O Lord! bless de capt'ins O

Lord! bless de Yankees right smart. O Lord! Eberlastin'. Amen.

This prayer, offered in a full and fervent voice, seemed to cover our case exactly, and we could join in the "Amen" with heartfelt devotion. We may never know how much negro prayers have aided the cause of the Union,—and availed in behalf of our escaping prisoners. Other prayers followed "Uncle Zeb's," and a "refreshing season" was the result.

As faith without works amounts to nothing—their next step was to make arrangements for our future.

It was now near daylight, and they advised that we remain within the hut during the day, assuring us that "no white folks nebber come near Aunt Katy's—so don't be 'fraid, massa."

Everyone offered to do something for us. One could make some hoe cakes, another could bring some bacon, another had some fresh pork, that had just been killed on the plantation and still another "reckoned he might git to find a dead chicken somewhar."

Encouraging Prospects

Uncle "Zeb" was a sort of universal genius, and learning that we needed a knife to cut our rations and dispose of any small game we might chance to meet with, volunteered to make us one. Another would bring us a bag to serve as a haversack. After these promises they dispersed to their work, assuring us that they would return in the evening.

Thus our whereabouts was known to about thirty negroes, young and old; and I venture that we were as safe from betrayal as though the number had been our own soldiers. The talent of the negro for concealment is something wonderful. Their whole history as a race has compelled them to it, and they have been apt scholars. They can often make white men believe a downright falsehood, when they cannot persuade them to believe the truth. A shrewd lawyer with his suspicions fully aroused, might have puzzled in vain to get any information with regard to our presence from a ten-year-old boy.

When "Aunt Katy" sent her little boy, about eight years of age, to notify the coloured people of our coming, we were apprehensive that it might not be safe to trust to so young a lad, but the old lady assured us that we need have no fears as the—"chile know'd what he's bout." She then told us that only a short time before, when some escaped prisoners were concealed in her hut, the planter had had suspicions of the fact, and riding by, had asked the little boy if there were not

Yankees in the house, when the young rascal, giving a start, rolled his eyes in the direction of the hut, with a woe-begone look, and asked quickly,—"Yankees in dar," and then added with a shudder of fear,—"Gor A'mighty, massa, ef dar was, you wouldn't catch dis darky yer no how. Dem Yankees got horns on, massa, and I'se fraid of 'um. Ef I seed one of 'um coming for me, I'd die shoore." The master rode on, doubtless well pleased with the manner in which his stories about Yankees had been treasured up.

It is an established fact that it would have been impossible for our men, held as prisoners of war in the South, to make an escape without the aid of negroes, and it would have been nearly as impossible had they been strictly truthful in all cases.

Evening brought them again to "Aunt Katy's." Uncle "Zeb" had manufactured the knife in good earnest. He had taken the largest file the plantation afforded, and hammered it into a blade nearly two feet long. To this he had attached a handle some eight inches in length, and two in diameter. With this young sword, he stalked into the room with an air of triumphant satisfaction. His ideas of the use to which it could be put, were somewhat different from ours, as his presentation speech will serve to show.

"Here, gemmen, is yer knife. I reckon ye'll find it bery useful in yer trabels. Ye can cut yer hoe cake wid it, and ef yer happens to be on de trail ob a pig ye can chop his head off afore he gits to give a squeal (flourishing the knife).

"And likewise, gemmen, ef ye comes in a bery tight place, dis yer might cut a Buckrey's (Rebel's) head off. I'se grounded it right sharp for ye (feeling of the edge), to have it ready for quick work."

This speech was delivered with all the dignity of a senator, and it never occurred to him that his labour had been thrown away.

Just here, another brought us the bag we had bargained for. It was an old tow-string sack, and would hold two bushels or more. We could hardly repress laughter at these generous attempts to meet our demands, but took them with us as relics of our experience.[2]

One of their number, a friend of "Ben Steadman," by the way, offered to accompany us as guide. Ben, he said, was taken prisoner, as before related; and upon examination, told the plausible story aforementioned, that Lemon and myself were two foolish darkies who were scared at the pickets. The latter part of the narrative being strictly true, it was hardly necessary for us to rectify the former.

---

2. Lemon had the knife at the time of our recapture.

The Steadman plantation was only three miles away, and "Ben" was afterwards brought to our place of concealment in the thicket by his coloured friend from Black Creek, and kindly offered his services for the occasion.

We told him we were anxious to learn of General Sherman's movements, and would like a paper. He insisted upon our going to his hut, although we much preferred the swamp; but were at last prevailed upon to accompany him. Arriving here, we were politely introduced to Mrs. Steadman and family. They viewed a live Yankee with not a little curiosity; after which, Ben instructed his daughter to go into her mistress house and snatch a paper at the earliest opportunity. She soon came running back with the *Augusta Constitutionalist*, published that morning. The celerity with which the blacks carry off a desired article, or accomplish a mission for a friend, is truly wonderful; and no watchfulness on the part of their masters can stay a project when once the heart is in it.

Crossing the North Edisto

Having possessed ourselves of the contents of the paper, we struck the road and crossed the North Edisto at ten o'clock p. m.

The water was over the bridge in many places. So we were compelled to ford the stream.

It was our intention to reach and cross the South Edisto before morning, but having become confused by the intersection of "blind roads," and having lost our way, we were obliged to halt for the night in a pine grove, we knew not where.

Fifth Day.

On the South Edisto,
Wednesday, November 30.

Had breakfast on hoe-cake and pindars, the latter being known at the North as peanuts. We were in great tribulation on account of the loss of our moorings. After following roads the previous evening for several hours, we were brought to a standstill at the edge of a swamp.

There were no stars visible, and we had not yet learned to take the moon for a guide. Besides, the heavenly bodies in southern latitudes have so different an appearance from those seen at the North that we were for some, time after the escape in constant doubt, as to the points of compass. I remember it caused me great grief to find that the north star was much nearer the horizon, and seemed to have lost that prominence which is given to it in high latitudes, where it is a guide standing far above treetop and mountain. Yet I soon came to hail it as a faithful sentinel "that guards the fixed light of the universe, and bids the north forever know its place."

After moving to the pine grove mentioned in the last chapter, which was only a short distance from the swamp that stopped our progress, we slept till about ten o'clock a. m. Thinking it necessary that we get our bearings by daylight, we were obliged to skulk along during the whole day, passing many plantations, and exciting the ire of an array of contemptible curs, whose only business and only pleasure was to howl at civil people who asked no recognition.

Good luck favoured us remarkably, for we were in sight of buildings several times during the day. These dangers and annoyances made us irritable. We could scarcely agree upon anything. Just before dark we heard wood-choppers, and Lemon went to spy them out. He soon returned and led the way to three negroes, who had just stopped work, and were about to return to the plantation. We accompanied them to a thicket within a few rods of their master's house, and after they had supplied us with rations one of their number piloted us to the Aiken road, which was distant about two and a half miles. This brought us within four miles of the South Edisto. The distance between the North and South Edisto at this point is twelve miles. The South Edisto is about fourteen miles north of Aiken, and Aiken is seventeen miles from Augusta.

As we pursued our way towards the South Edisto we could hear dogs barking far in advance of us, and judged that someone must be travelling the same road,—perhaps escaped prisoners,—perhaps a Rebel patrol. This gave us some uneasiness, as we knew they had a decided advantage by being in the advance. However, we plodded on, and when near the river heard a rustling in the bushes. We then laid low for a few moments, and two men passed us in the clear moonlight. It was impossible to tell whether they were Federals or Rebels, so we decided to watch their movements. After a time we followed, creeping along very cautiously.

Crossing the South Edisto

The South Edisto in that part of South Carolina has half a dozen channels or more, which are very narrow, and between them are long, narrow strips of marshy land. In fact it is nothing more than a vast swamp, with several parallel bayous running through it. These bayous are crossed by bridges, and while crossing one of these we again heard footsteps behind us, on a bridge we had just passed over. At this we ran lustily over the remaining bridges, then turned aside and concealed ourselves in some bushes.

The Challenge

Presently the two men, previously described, came trudging along with the same slow and weary pace. From the manner in which they had manoeuvred I felt assured that they were "escaped prisoners," and resolved to challenge them at all hazards; so, stepping boldly from the bushes, I sang out, "Who comes there?"

With a trembling start the foremost man replied, "Friends."

I then commanded, "Halt, friends,—advance one, and be recognised." The man stepped slowly forward, peering into my face, when a mutual recognition took place.

They were also escaped prisoners from Columbia, and yet we had been dodging each other for more than an hour. Lemon had known one of the officers while in prison.

We at once determined that it was not best to travel in company, yet we pursued our way together, talking over our adventures, until we saw a large fire in the road directly in our front. Stealthily approaching, we found a band of Rebels encamped there, and thought we must be on a picket post; they proved, however, to be a squad of "tax-gatherers" going about the country with quartermasters wagons, gathering supplies.

Here was an obstacle to our farther progress. There were great ponds of water on either side, and the road was blocked. No amount of reconnoitring could discover a solution of the difficulty. Then there was a resort to strategy by both our newly-found friends and ourselves, but both parties resorted to the same tactics. Each wished the other to advance, and incur the risk of a recapture. But neither seemed willing to accept the preference, so we found a safe retreat, and lay down for the night.

Sixth Day

Aiken Road, Seven Miles South of the South Edisto,
Thursday, December 1.

In the morning the Rebel band of tax-gatherers struck tents *like the Arabs, and silently stole away.* This left the road clear, and we parted company with our friends, each to try the chances by different routes. Just here we were overpowered with thirst, but there was nothing accessible save the swamp, so we pushed on hoping soon to find a spring or brook. Our course lay over a high, barren, sandy table-land, covered with stunted oaks, and entirely destitute of water. We travelled for a distance of seven miles, when we came to a small stream near whose banks was a beautiful spring. Here we were taught the value of *cold water to a thirsty soul.*

This stream ran through a ravine nearly a hundred feet in depth, while high up on the banks were pine groves. It was a wild, romantic spot, and we could not tear ourselves from it, but lay concealed in the grove, going occasionally to the spring to drink.

SEVENTH DAY

In a Swamp, Near Aiken, S. C.,
Friday, December 2.
Late in the night we reluctantly bade farewell to the beautiful spot where we had been refreshed so finely, and pursued our journey. Nothing of interest occurred. The march was unbroken until near daylight, when we turned into a by-road, and found a hiding-place in some thick underbrush, close by a fine stream of water. It was always our purpose to do this, as we knew thirst would drive us to searching for water during the day, and thus expose us to danger.

Just at the break of day we espied a coloured boy passing down the road with a basket on his arm. Lemon ran out to him, and called out, "Hold on, my boy, I want to see you;" thinking, meantime, that the basket doubtless contained what we most needed, something of an eatable character.

We inferred the boy had a chicken with him; for saying that word, in a manner which betokened the greatest fear, he set off at a wild run, and I would have defied a racehorse to catch him. As for the lieutenant, after exhausting all his rhetoric in endeavouring to bring back the boy, he returned to the spot where I lay, saying, "Now they will have us again, and we shall be prisoners before night."

"Never fear," I said, "as long as there is a swamp in the neighbourhood;" and, without further ceremony, we picked up our baggage and hastily decamped. Flora Temple would have been distanced had she attempted to overtake us; for her stakes would have been only a few dollars to her owners, while ours were life and liberty.

We made for a swamp, about a mile away, as fast as our tired limbs could carry us. This swamp lay on either side of the Aiken road, and our place of concealment was so near, that the passers-by were in plain sight. While lying here three ladies came walking down a forest path, accompanied by several hounds. The dogs followed squirrels and other game very near our hiding-place, but we were not discovered.

One of the ladies was telling the others what a fright her mother had early in the morning by the hurried advent of nigger boy John, who went to a neighbour's for a chicken. The boy was wild with terror, having been chased by Yankees, as he said. Thus we learned that our presence was known, and we began planning more caution. Towards evening several old—

Bushwhackers

Rode along towards Aiken, with shot guns on their shoulders. They were doubtless thinking that the foolish Yankees would be verdant enough to pass through town at night, and were determined to be ready for them. But we intended to flank the town, and, thinking with satisfaction of our purpose to give the bushwhackers the slip, fell asleep.

Eighth Day

In a Corn-Fodder House, Near Aiken, S. C.,
Saturday, December 3.

We did not resume our tramp until after midnight, when after walking a short distance we found ourselves in the village, much to our mortification and dismay. Being much nearer the town than we had supposed, we had not begun to exercise the caution resolved upon, when we found ourselves in the very midst of the danger.

Meeting Friends

It was the hour of deep sleep, however, and we quietly passed through without opposition until the outskirts on the further side were reached, when two men, accompanied by a boy, were seen approaching. When they saw us they quickly turned aside into a by-street. This convinced us that they were escaped prisoners, as Rebels had nothing to be afraid of in these parts. We called to them softly, "Don't be afraid, Yanks; we are friends." They proved to be Captain Bryant, of the Fifth New York Cavalry, and a companion whose name I did not learn. They had a negro guide, who was to secrete them in a hut until night again, when they were to proceed as we had done, and reach the lines of freedom by the nearest route.

Something of a discussion took place during the few minutes we remained, with regard to the most feasible course. They had become satisfied, from information obtained, that it was not General Sherman's intention to strike Augusta, hence they concluded it not worthwhile to go so far out of our way to reach that place. We had also learned that all the boats on the Savannah River had been destroyed south of Augusta, and were satisfied that it would not be possible to cross below that place. They, therefore, took their course and we took ours—meaning to cross the river at Augusta, and from thence strike across the country to Millin, some sixty miles south-east, where we felt certain of finding at least the rear guard of Sherman's army.

After leaving these friends with fervent wishes for their success, Lemon and myself started for a swamp about a mile away, and, becoming a little confused, another difference of opinion arose. Such things will occur. Our no patience rested on no sure foundation. The result was, he took one route and I another. We came together shortly afterward, however, and forgot our differences. We reached the swamp, where we secreted ourselves, and soon were gratified to see an old sow with a large litter of pigs approaching.

We greeted them otherwise than did wandering Æneas the "*alba sus*" lying under the hollow trees of ancient Italy,—for, enticing them with crumbs of hoe-cake, we both in unison struck one juvenile porker over the head with our heavy canes. He died easily, nothing more being necessary to stretch him a lifeless corpse at our feet. No relative waited to attend his funeral. Here Uncle Zeb's mammoth knife did excellent service. We dug a hole in the ground, and made a fire of pine-knots, which soon became a bed of intensely hot embers. Over this we spitted the dressed carcase of the unfortunate little fellow, and after it was done brown sat down to a feast that might have tempted an epicure. No more luscious barbecue ever moved the salivary glands of, a London alderman. This was a peace-offering, through not strictly according to Levitical law. Our asperities were lubricated for that day.

We heard the sound of an axe in the distance, and I crept cautiously along to reconnoitre. Found it to be a black boy, and, remembering Lemon's experience of the day before, I said, "Hollo, Sambo!" His hat came off suddenly, but he made no attempt to run, The grinning imp, when he learned who we were, gladly led us to a fodder-house nearby for concealment; and after dark a large number of coloured boys and girls came up to pay their respects. They entertained us with their views of the war, and proposed a prayer-meeting for our especial benefit; also told us where to look out for trouble from bushwhackers, hounds, and so forth. Our parting from these friendly people was tender and affecting, each one shaking hands, and saying, "God bless you, massa!"

Following their directions, we expected to strike the railroad running from Charleston to Augusta on the west side of Aiken, and pursue it west to Augusta; but instead of this we struck it on the east side, and pursued it east toward Charleston.

Ninth Day

On the South Carolina Railroad, East of Aiken, S. C.,
Sunday, December 4.

Late in the night we passed through a small village just as a freight train was leaving, and tried hard to find a hiding-place in one of the cars, expecting to be carried into Augusta before daylight. Had we succeeded in this, we would have been borne triumphantly into Charleston, and sent back to imprisonment. A merciful Providence directed our way.

We followed this railroad all night. A hound was on our track just before morning, but he must have barked on his own rash responsibility, for he soon ceased, and gave up the chase.

Soon after daylight a passenger train came sweeping along, loaded with Rebel soldiers. They set up an infernal shout as they passed; and, fearing the train might be stopped, we turned off into some scrub-oaks and secreted ourselves. Here we heard heavy cannonading all day. It came from a south easterly direction, and was the sweetest music we had heard for many an hour. It seemed as if we were in the neighbourhood of friends; and we took heart, being hopeful for the future.

Tenth Day

Seventeen Miles East of Aiken, S. C.,
Monday, December 5.

All night we travelled on, wondering why we had not reached Augusta, and having suspicions that all was not right. During the day we lay in a thicket. About dusk Lemon went in search of negroes, and soon found some wood-choppers. They soon informed us of our mistake. We were *en route* for Charleston, travelling east instead of west, and not having the least desire to visit the last-named city. Our distance east of Aiken was seventeen miles; a bad mistake, we concluded. But Providence still seemed to favour us, for we learned through our coloured friends that it was possible to cross the Savannah twenty miles below Augusta, at a place called Point Comfort. Our army was marching on Savannah; so we rather gained than lost by our mistake.

Getting a supply of hoe-cake and a guide for a few miles, we started for Tinker Creek—a station fifteen miles distant, and on the way to Point Comfort. We were in excellent spirits, and again undertook to follow the voluminous directions of our coloured friends.

Eleventh Day

Near Tinker Creek, S. C.,
Tuesday, December 6.

During the night we came to a fork in the road, and, after debating some time as to which we should follow, I jumped over the fence, and made for a negro hut, while several hounds from the plantation followed hard on my track. I managed, by some tall running, to come out a few feet ahead, and bolted into the shanty without warning or formality, slamming the door behind me to keep out the dogs. A great stupid buck negro was standing in front of the fire, his hands and face buried deeply in fresh pork and hoe-cake, which he was making poor work of eating. His broad, fat countenance glistened with an unguent distilled partly from within and partly from without.

Turning my eyes from the negro to the untidy hearth, they were greeted, as were also my olfactories, with a skillet of pork frying over the coals. Without troubling him to answer my questions, I opened the mouth of my haversack, and poured into it the dripping contents of the skillet. I next observed that the ashes on the hearth had a suspiciously fat appearance, and taking the tongs began raking among them. My suspicions were verified; for two plump-looking hoe-cakes came to light, which were also deposited in the haversack.

Looking around still farther, I saw what had not been observed before—

Dinah's Black Head

peering out from among the bed-clothes, rolling two of the most astonished white eyes that ever asked the question, "What's you gwine to do next?"

Not seeing any practical way in which I could answer her mute question, I said to Sambo, "Call the dogs into the house."

This he did hastily, when I asked, "Uncle, what road must this Rebel take for Tinker Creek?"

"De right han one, out dar, I reckon," he answered. Again bidding him keep the hounds in the house till morning, I rushed out to the road, and joined my companion. We made lively time for about three miles, after which we took it more leisurely, stopping to rest and refresh ourselves at every stream that crossed the road.

The weather was very cold, and we suffered much from its severity as soon as it was necessary to lie down.

About daylight we found shelter in a piece of woods near the roadside, and slept till ten o'clock in the morning, when we were awakened by some boys driving cows along the road. Some of the animals came within a few feet of us, but the boys kept a respectful distance.

Thinking our quarters too much exposed, we cautiously crossed the road and plunged into the woods on the other side.

About four o'clock p. m. we heard chopping in the distance, and came to a negro boy who had never seen a Yankee, but reckoned it would not be very wrong to render one a little assistance. Accordingly, he brought to our hiding-place, in the evening, several other negroes with cornbread, bacon, etc. One of their number, an intelligent fellow, volunteered to guide us to a place near Point Comfort, on the Savannah, intending to return before day and be ready for his labours without exciting suspicion.

Twelfth Day

Near Point Comfort, on the Savannah River,
Wednesday, December 7.

Our guide, being in somewhat of a hurry to get back to his work, urged us on more rapidly than we cared to proceed. Seeing that we began to lag behind, he soon offered to "tote" our baggage. We, of course, could not refuse so generous an offer, fearing that, perhaps, the effect of a refusal might be to chill the streams of benevolence flowing from his kindly heart. It is certain that there would be no call for kindness, if everybody should refuse to receive a kindness. Not caring to render ourselves obnoxious to the charge of banishing benevolence from the world, we magnanimously consented to his proposal.

But even this effected his purpose none the more surely, for we were still often far in the rear, and obliged to call on him to travel more slowly.

This noble-hearted fellow led us on for fifteen miles, and at last secreted us in a thicket by the roadside, not far from a large plantation. Advising us to find some negro to take us to the Savannah, which was only three miles away, he said goodbye, and was off.

Morning revealed to us the fact that we were rather too much exposed to be entirely safe, and as we were very thirsty, with no prospect of water near, it was decided to move farther into the woods. This seemed, in a measure, to secure both objects. A large ravine about half a mile away afforded an abundance of water, and we felt that it must be a more safe retreat. A negro, who came that way with an axe on his shoulder, informed us that boys were in the habit of hunting in the woods, and that we had better seek a more sheltered place.

He pointed to a round sand hill a short distance away, on the top of which was a sort of pitfall, and advised us to go there—promising to bring some more negroes to us in the evening. Accordingly, we made for the sand hill, and hid ourselves in the pit.

But even this could not escape the vigilance of boys, guided by no purpose whatever, but their own pleasure. In the afternoon, they came bounding over the hills with a troop of dogs, hunting squirrels, and came within a few feet of finding larger game. This disturbed us again, and we sought another shelter—and so, in fear and anxiety, spent the day.

At the appointed time in the evening, the negroes came, and one of them piloted us to the hut of some coloured fishermen on the Savannah River, which we reached late in the evening.

THIRTEENTH DAY

In a Cypress Swamp, on the Savannah,
Thursday, December 28.

These fishermen, who had plied their trade before the war, were acquainted with every bend in the river, and now proposed exercising their skill in our behalf. On a tributary of the Savannah, about a mile away from their huts, there lay an old cypress-tree canoe, and to this one of their number conducted us—taking with him a supply of cotton and pitch. This craft had recently come under the boat-destroyer's notice, and had been pretty roughly handled; and yet our coloured friend thought he could make it seaworthy. All night long the faithful fellow worked, caulking and pitching, while we lay concealed in an old hollow cypress log. The ring of his hammer went out through the forest as if bidding a "beautiful defiance" to those who had destined his property.

Near morning, he seemed to have satisfied himself, for throwing her into the stream, he called out, "Now she's ready, massa. I'll soon land you in Georgia."

The moon was shining brightly, and viewing the shabby dugout by her treacherous light, I confess to a want of faith in its ability to carry us safely to the other side.

We lost no time in speculations, but resolved to put the matter to the test at once. Hastily taking our seats in the boat, which at once commenced leaking fearfully, our pilot pulled for dear life, while Lemon and myself lustily bailed her out with a couple of large gourds. In spite of our utmost endeavours the water kept gaining on us, and when within a few rods of the other side, seeing that she was going down, we sprang into the stream which happened to be shallow, and dragged the swamping boat up the beach.

A Narrow Escape,

for had our craft gone down when out in the stream, the alligators would have made our chance of escape rather slim. The Savannah here is about half a mile wide. We at once plunged into the swamp, leaving the good negro wadding his boat with cotton, preparatory to his return. Our prayer was that he might reach the other side in safety, and live to send many other poor fellows on their way rejoicing.

We were in the midst of a Southern cypress swamp. These swamps extend continuously along both banks of the Savannah, and are about three miles in width. They are thickly interlarded with bayous and small streams, and abound in small lakes and ponds. The ground in the wet season is entirely overflown, and it is next to impossible to travel over it.

The cypress-tree, which is the glory of these swamps, grows to immense size. The trunk of the tree near the ground swells out somewhat like the base of a cone, terminating in huge roots that stand widely apart—making splendid hiding-places for escaped prisoners, etc. In cutting down these trees, it is customary to build a scaffolding to a considerable height in order to get above the bulge.

All who have visited these swamps have been struck with the number and appearance of the *natural stumps* with which they abound. I can call them by no other name. They are all heights from one foot to ten, look like stumps at a distance, are cone-shaped and rounded at the top, and the most of them are alive. The impression conveyed is, that trees of full size had commenced to grow from the ground, and after reaching the height of a few feet had changed their minds, and concluded that they had grown into a stump. Add to all this, the long, trailing Spanish moss that burdens every tree, from the sapling to the king of the forest, and you have some idea of a Southern swamp.

In such a place were we—and we wandered about nearly the whole day in our attempts to get out. Great winking

Alligators

lay along the bayous, and on every cool, damp log, watching our motions, apparently pleased at our misfortunes, and sending towards us loving, hungry glances. As soon as we approached, they would hobble to the water's edge, and apparently fall in. They, too, might have belonged to some detachment of Southern chivalry, doing duty on their own grounds.

Towards night we came to a cornfield skirting the swamp and rising towards the highlands. Here was a most delightful spring of water, and near it a kettle of clothes boiling. Expecting to see the owners soon, we lay down in the bushes and waited. Soon a coloured man came, found us a hiding-place, and promised to meet us again at eight o'clock in the evening.

While we were waiting the washerwoman returned, accompanied by several white children. Their contemptible little dog came yelping to within a few feet of our place of concealment, while the children stood back urging him on. His discretion proved the better courage, however, and he became tired eventually, and went away. In the evening our negro returned and conducted us to some friends of his a few miles away. On the way we met a planter, who was a sort of independent scout. The negro was somewhat in advance, and when the planter stopped him, we skulked behind some logs and were not observed.

The whites were on the alert at this time, as it was only a short time since "Mr. Kilpatrick's company had flogged Mr. Wheeler's company right bad," down at Waynesboro', only a few miles distant, as our coloured friends informed us. Cavalry men were patrolling the roads during the whole night, and we began to feel the necessity of the greatest caution.

Our guide led us to a field a short distance from some negro huts, and made our whereabouts known to the occupants. Soon some negroes came out with a generous supply of hot griddle-cakes. We left this place after a brief halt, with a guide who knew where the pickets were stationed, and travelled cautiously on towards Brier Creek, a stream about eighteen miles distant in the direction of Millin.

Fourteenth Day

Near Brier Creek, Ga.,
Friday, December 9.

Our guide left us before morning secreted in a thicket at a fork of the road, about four miles from Brier Creek. Being weary, we soon fell asleep. Nothing occurred to disturb our slumbers, but when we awoke sentinels were guarding us.

Four large hounds stood looking down on us with an air of calmness and responsibility, snuffing occasionally to know whether we had the scent of game. After we awoke they seemed to consider their guardianship at an end, and, walking around us a little in the most natural manner imaginable, they quietly, and with much show of dignity, swaggered away without deeming it worthwhile to salute us. We were not deeply offended by their silence.

A large cavalry patrol passed near us, and judging it not safe to be very demonstrative, we ate our sweet potatoes raw—they composing our only rations. A fire was out of the question.

We had, up to that time, no information with regard to General Sherman's army. The bridges across all the principal streams were either broken down, or heavily guarded, to check the advance of raiding parties. The planters drove their stock far into the swamps, and remained with it during the day, returning at night to their plantations.

An old woman came down into the swamp in plain sight of us, and called her "critters" together to feed them. We would gladly have answered the call for ration's sake, had it been prudent.

Found an old darkey near our hiding-place splitting rails, and warmed ourselves a few moments at his fire, as it was very cold and raining fiercely, after which we sought our shelter again, and made a roof of our blankets to keep off the rain. This old friend promised to find us in the evening, and bring some hoe-cake. What was best of all, he could repair my shoes. These old shoes, like many other unimportant looking things, have a history. Shortly after my capture I was relieved of my cavalry boots, and a pair of pasted shoes given me, which yielded to the first moisture and left me worse than barefoot. A fellow-prisoner having received a remittance of good things from home, among them a pair of boots, kindly presented me with his shoes.

Smile not, gentle reader, at the gift, for to me they were invaluable; and with these I marched many weary miles, although they were patched and wired together until little remained of their former sub-

THE ESCAPE—FED BY NEGROES IN A SWAMP

stance, and now they were well-nigh gone. Cuffee took them home, and spent the greater part of the night in making them answer their appointed end. A piece of 'possum skin formed the uppers, which was nicely tucked under. The whole shoe was covered with the skin, and a slit cut in the top, in the right place, or somewhere near it, to admit the foot. I was disposed to find fault at first with their generous dimensions, but soon learned, partly from the good darkey and partly from experience, that the cobbler knew best, for the 'possum skin, though soft and pliable when moist, is hard and wrinkled as a horn when dry.

This man took us in the evening to the negro quarters, and the warm-hearted black insisted on our staying with them all night, as it was cold and rainy.

Fifteenth Day

Near Godbey's Bridge, Five Miles From Alexander, Ga.,
Saturday, December 10.

Before morning our negro friends conducted us back to the swamp, where we passed another gloomy, disagreeable day. The rain kept drizzling from morning till night. We had nothing to eat but an ear of dry corn picked up on an old camping ground, and refused by some aristocratic horse.

Our black cobbler came at night and accompanied us to Brier Creek, which we crossed at Godbey's Bridge, and thence proceeded wearily to Alexander. Lemon knocked at a poor white woman's shanty to inquire the road to Millin; but she knew nothing about it.

Near Alexander was a shanty about one hundred feet in length, used as the quarters of negroes employed in the Confederate ironworks which were near. This building we reconnoitred for half an hour, and then entered. Fortune favoured us—they were all negroes, and taking directions as to our route, we pushed on.

CHAPTER 14

The Escape—Following the Rebel Army in Georgia

SIXTEENTH DAY

Between Station No. 1 and Millin, Ga.,
Sunday, December 11.

About midnight, a large creek stopped our further progress. Here was a dilemma. A faithful search could discover no bridge, nor fallen logs from opposite sides, as sometimes happens, nor any other means of crossing. The night was bitterly cold, so that ice formed plentifully on still water. There seemed to be no other way but to wade.

Sitting on a log and ruminating over our chances, a very selfish piece of strategy suggested itself. Accordingly I said to Lemon, "There is no use of both getting wet; we can carry each other over these streams. If you will carry me over this, I will carry you over the next." I said "these streams," although only one was before us, and the most prominent thought in my mind was, that in all probability there would be no more.

Lemon somehow failed to see the point, and consented. Accordingly, taking off our shoes, I mounted on the lieutenant's shoulders, as schoolboys sometimes carry each other, and he staggered through the stream with me, doing no worse than wetting my feet. This worked well. I congratulated myself, and gave a generous sympathy to Lemon in his shiverings. The chances were ten to one, I thought, that the carrying business was at an end, when suddenly another stream, wider than the first, rose up in the darkness before us. There was no use in wincing, and I stripped for the task. The lieutenant "ascended to the position he had fairly earned." I plunged into the water.

The middle of the stream was reached in safety, when, through no fault of mine, either the water became too deep, or my back became too weak for the burden, and the consequence was, the worthy gentleman was nearly as well soaked as myself when we reached the opposite shore. Selfishness, as well as virtue, sometimes brings its own reward.

We crossed three other streams that night, and as a result of our past experience chose unanimously to do our own wading. Thus another grand scheme for human elevation fell to the ground.

Wet and weary we continued our tramp until near daylight, when quarters for the day were chosen in a cypress swamp close by a road over which General Kilpatrick's cavalry and the Fourteenth Army Corps had marched, but a week before.

There were evident traces of their presence. The fences were gone, or lay half-consumed by the road side. Buildings were still smoking in the distance or standing charred and blackened. The ground was covered with ears of corn, torn haversacks and blankets, "hard-tack" boxes, broken muskets, dead horses, etc.

Being exhausted with fatigue, we slept the whole day without disturbance, as we did also the next night, not awaking until nearly day.

Seventeenth Day

In a Swamp on the Savannah River Road,
Monday, December 12.

Having wasted the greater part of the night, we determined, at all hazards, to make it good by travelling during the day. And yet the streams were so high that little progress could be made.

We were evidently on General Sherman's trail, though he was six days in advance of us. In our physical and mental weakness, we wondered whether the good man would halt if he knew we were in pursuit of him. We thought he would at least send a detachment to bring us to his lines. Suffering soldiers can scarcely be induced to think anything of more importance than their preservation. We determined to turn from the road to Millin, and follow the trail of the army.

Hounds were on our track at one time during the day. Had the wretches known how little there was left of us, they would have given up the pursuit as fruitless, or meatless at least. It may be that they suspected this, for we were not pursued far. It was much safer travelling just here than it had been previously; for as a general thing, Sherman's boys had killed all the hounds in their march, as they had heard of their being used to overtake, escaped prisoners. Most of the Rebels, also, had been either carried or frightened out of the country.

One old sinner had unfortunately escaped, and we heard of him as hunting Yankees on his own responsibility, and gave him a wide berth. It may have been his hounds that followed us. Nothing could be more desirable in escaping under such circumstances than to have a small quantity of strychnine along. There would generally be means of making it an acceptable offering to the dogs.

We turned from the road into a piece of woods about four o'clock, and as the country was smoking in all directions, did not hesitate to make a fire and lie down on the grass beside it. During our sleep the fire had crept along the grass and laid hold of my pantaloons; and when I awoke the outside seam of the leg next the fire was burned completely out. The fire had formed appropriate food in the dry furze accumulated there, and so ran along it as it would run along a fence. Some strings from our large tow haversack served to sew the burnt edges together, and by nine in the evening we were again ready to take up our march.

Eighteenth Day

Sixty Miles North of Savannah,
Tuesday, December 13.

Continued to follow on in the trail of our army. We were without food, and sorely pressed with hunger. Now and then we could find an ear of corn, left by a Rebel cavalryman. In the latter part of the night we stopped at a plantation, and, seeing no plantation house, concluded they were all negro huts. Approaching the most respectable looking one, I rapped at the door, when someone sang out, "Whose thar?"

From the answer, I was unable to guess whether the occupants were black or white, and accordingly said, "Are you black or white in there?"

The answer, "There ain't no niggers here;" and the very indignant tone satisfied me that I had fallen upon some "poor white trash," as they are familiarly called.

Determined to have something to eat, at all events, besides being anxious to learn something of our course, I assumed a tone of offended dignity, and summoned the speaker to the door, I demanded, in the name of an injured Rebel officer why he was not forthcoming at once.

Upon meeting "mine host," I soon found he had seen his best

days; and feeling quite at home, asked how long since our army had passed.

"What army?" he inquired, as if to make sure of no mistake.

"The Rebel army, of course," I replied. He then told me Wheeler's cavalry had passed a week since, in pursuit of Sherman's rear-guard.

"Can you tell me how far it is to Wheeler's headquarters?" I asked.

"Indeed, I cannot," he answered; "but I reckon it's a right smart distance, sir."

"Are there any horses or mules in the neighbourhood?" I asked.

"Not one," he replied, "the cursed Yankees have cleaned us out, and done gone with our last piece of bread."

"Well, come now, uncle, can't you give this Rebel something to eat?"

"No," he returned; "there is not a mouthful in the pantry, we are whipped clean out."

"I know better, sir," I said; "you have bacon and sweet potatoes; you must shell out or I shall have to help myself."

Rebel wishing to shirk the responsibility of a falsehood from his own shoulders, called to Mrs. Rebel to know if there was anything eatable on the premises; to which she replied, "I reckon you will find something in the pantry;" and in a moment more my rebellious friend returned with a small bit of bread and two sweet potatoes. After receiving which, I delivered him a lecture upon his treatment of a soldier who had ventured all upon the defence of his country; telling him he was unworthy the cause he had espoused, and that his patriotism did not reach to his pockets, to say nothing of his falsehood and mean attempts to defraud me of a breakfast.

Expressing the hope that I should find him a better Rebel when we again met, I hurried off to Lemon, who was still waiting by the road, and shared our hard-earned meal with an appetite well whetted by hunger.

Pushing on at a rapid pace in the direction of our army, we spied a person crossing the road a short distance before us, and as the whites seldom stir before daylight, our first conclusion was that we had found a coloured friend, but were soon undeceived by discovering a burly-looking white man. After passing the compliments of the morning, we inquired how long since our cavalry passed. "Last Tuesday," he replied; and not wishing to detain him, we proceeded on our way, grateful that our uniforms were hidden under our blankets, which answered at once as overcoats and a good disguise.

Leaving planter No. 2, to his own reflections, we reached a swamp at daybreak. Here met two negroes going to their work, and after a "Good-morning, boys," inquired the distance to the next plantation.

"Just a mile from this swamp, massa."

"Are there any white people there?" we asked.

"Not one, massa."

DE PLANTER WAS A BUSHWHACKER,

and Mr. Sherman's company took 'em all off."

Wishing to have my stories of the morning agree, and not knowing how soon they would be tested, I did not think it necessary to make myself known to my coloured friends, but asked whether they had seen any of Wheeler's cavalry of late.

"There's a right smart of 'em down at Massa Brown's three miles from de swamp, and dey's hazin' about de country in ebery direction."

Feeling a little uneasy after the above information, we started for the plantation described. As we hove in sight, I saw the house was closed, but that smoke was rising from a hut in the grounds—so made for it in double-quick time; walked up to and opened the door without hesitation, when to my surprise and horror, I beheld—

A REBEL OFFICER,

standing before the fire. Without the least hesitancy I advanced, gave him the military salute and said, "I see you, too, are in the service, sir; but hope, like myself, you have not been unfortunate."

"How unfortunate may you have been, sir?" he asked.

Now I might have stated all the mishaps of my life; but only quietly said, "I was in the cavalry fight at Waynesboro' the other day, had my horse shot from under me, failed to get remounted, and have walked the entire distance to this place."

"I reckon our cases are not unlike, after all," he rejoined; "I had my horse shot there, too, but luckily got a mule;" and, stepping to the door, he pointed out his long-eared animal, eating hay at the gate.

Fearing he might get the start of me, I asked to what command he belonged.

"The Fifty-third Alabama Mounted Infantry," he returned; and then inquired my regiment.

"The Third South-Carolina Cavalry," I said; and true it was, that my last service was in that State.

I was careful to name some other State than Alabama, as he would be better posted with regard to the regiments of his own State than those of any other. Lemon, during this time was walking uneasily backwards and forwards in front of the gate. He once carelessly remarked that we had better be going, but I thought haste would be the ruination of us, and so occupied a few minutes more in recounting the barbarities of General Sherman's army, remarking, "Now we have him just where we want him—between two swamps; and when he is thoroughly starved out we shall catch him easy enough."

The lieutenant seemed to indorse my remarks, notwithstanding my blue clothes; and just as I thought his suspicions fully allayed he remarked that it was strange for a gentleman of my professions to be dressed in Federal colours.

I returned, "It is not strange at all, sir. A poor fellow must wear what he can get in these times. I have not had a full equipment since I came into the service, and I never expect one. You know, in the fight at Waynesboro' we captured a few Yanks; and I just stripped a dead one, and appropriated his attire to myself."

"A good idea," he said, pointing to his tattered pants; "I wish I had been as sensible."

My poor stomach had gained nothing during this interview, so I asked, "Do you suppose aunty could give me some breakfast?"

"I reckon not, stranger," he returned; "the Yanks have done gone with all the corn on this plantation; but if you will go down to Mr. Brown's, you can get all you ask for. He was a good Union man when General Sherman passed through, and on that account had a guard set over his property; then, when our army came along he was all Secesh."

"Well, sir, I shall be at Mr. Brown's without delay, and shall be happy to breakfast with you there. How far do you call it to his plantation?"

"About two sights and a *jambye*," he returned, in true Rebel parlance.

A "sight" was as far as one could see in that broken country, while a "*jambye*" was nothing more than a swamp—neither of the terms being a very accurate measure of distance.

The good officer also informed me it was fifty-two miles to Savannah, twenty-five to Wheeler's head quarters, and about thirty-five to the rear of Sherman's army; adding, "It's a smart walk you'll have, I reckon."

With a hearty, "Thank you, sir, and a good-morning; we shall meet you at Mr. Brown's," we left him, and kept the road until entirely out of his range, when we suddenly struck into a swamp. Messrs. Brown & Co. may be still waiting that breakfast for us, for aught I know; may they wait and watch with due patience.

We made rapid strides for a mile or more, and finally concealed ourselves in some bushes. Seeing a smoke in the woods, we crept towards it, and found a black man and his wife lying by the fire. After arousing them, we learned their history.

They had followed General Sherman's army from Burke County, Ga., and being encamped on an island in Big Ebenezer Creek, with four or five hundred others, were shelled out by the Rebels, and compelled to seek safety by flight into the swamps.

In this way they lost his trail, and reasoning that if the slaves were all emancipated they should be free when the war ended, without any trouble of their own, they were going back to their masters.

We were at this time without food and very hungry, and as our coloured friends had nothing but a little shelled corn, we lent Sambo our haversack and sent him to find some negroes, detaining Dinah as a hostage for his safe return. He rather objected to the risk of such an expedition, but as we were very urgent, at last complied, while we sat roasting and eating corn during his absence. He brought back some sweet potatoes, which were in no way objectionable.

Very soon the worthy couple decided, after a little persuasion on our part, that they were not in very safe quarters, and consequently left us in full possession of the fire and potatoes, the latter of which we roasted in the former. Here we spent the remainder of the day and the early part of the following night.

NINETEENTH DAY

On the Savannah River Road,
Wednesday, December 14.

We did not travel much till after midnight, when we pursued our way without interruption till daylight; then turned into a swamp. We heard the sound of an axe. Early in the afternoon Lemon went to reconnoitre, while I sat down to write in my journal. I had no pencil of my own, but Lemon had a short piece which he kindly lent me. Having no knife, I was obliged to sharpen it by picking the wood away from the lead with my finger nails.

Soon Lemon returned in extreme consternation. Seeing a negro, he had walked boldly up to him, when, to his utter dismay, he saw a great burly, white man sitting on a log. Springing from the log, the planter demanded almost in a fury, "What are you doing here, in a blue uniform?"

The lieutenant replied, "I am serving my country, as every loyal man should be."

The planter then said, "I believe you're a damned Yankee."

Lemon returned the gallant answer, "You are welcome to your opinion, old Blowhard,—this is a free country. I *am* a Yankee—all but the damned—and what do you propose to do about it?"

"We'll see, we'll see," said the planter, and at the same time started hurriedly toward the house. Lemon came back double-quick, and we suddenly decamped, supposing of course, that the planter had gone for his gun and hounds.

Taking the sun for a guide, we set off in a south easterly direction, and did not venture to halt before dark.

We were pursued by hounds for more than two miles, but struck a stream of water, and waded up a half mile to evade our pertinacious followers. This put them off the scent, as it usually did. The cowardly old stay-at-home had been true to his instincts. Nature had printed no lie on his face. He might have taken Lemon by the collar, and walked him off to his home as he would a negro boy; but his big fists had no manly courage to back them, and he lost his prey.

During our run we found some ears, of corn and a piece of pork, left by the army. The meat was badly tainted,—but no matter it was no time to be fastidious. Making a small fire, we roasted it and made a good meal. There was no prospect of better, for the country was thoroughly stripped, and there were very few negroes to befriend us.

Several planters galloped along to take possession of Sherman's corduroy road through the swamp just ahead, thinking, no doubt, that we could not possibly find another passage through it. This put us on our guard, and lying low till late in the night, we determined to flank their position.

TWENTIETH DAY

In a Swamp Near Big Ebenezer Creek,
Thursday, December 15.

Began about ten o'clock to creep cautiously up to the edge of the swamp. Soon discovered a large fire. This gave us their locality, and in the darkness we began to wade through the mud and water on their

Rebel mode of capturing escaped prisoners

left flank. It was a terrible undertaking, but there was no alternative. Sometimes in to our armpits, we continued to push our way through. We were never further from the picket than fifteen rods, and on account of stopping to rest, and the obstacles in the way, were about two hours in going two hundred yards. Several other pickets were passed during the night; in fact, we approached so near as to hear their conversation; but as the ground was firmer, had no difficulty in turning their flank. The last was passed at the edge of the swamp skirting the Big Ebenezer Creek. This swamp was corduroyed, and had been passed through by a portion of General Sherman's army.

On either side of the road the land was entirely submerged, and it was not among things possible to travel through it. Three miles or more brought us to the stream, which was very wide.

The bridge had been burned, and we stood on the charred abutment, surrounded by water, with no visible means of making a crossing. Although inspection did not bring to light anything satisfactory, daylight war just coming, and through the rising mists we could see the opposite shore. Were there friends there, or foes? We did not know. A sense of desolation came over us. A broad river lay before us and an impenetrable swamp all around, and we possessing not even a pocket-knife to aid us. We thought of secreting ourselves, and stealing back past the pickets at night, to get boards with which to construct a raft. Just how this was to be done we did not know; but it was a plan, and better than no plan at all.

Accordingly, we began searching for a place of concealment. In walking back along the road toward the picket we saw what had the appearance of being a walk of logs leading out into the swamp. Following along this, and jumping from log to log, we soon came to an island, or elevated bit of ground, in the midst of the swamp. No discussion was needed to determine that this was the place we were looking for. Men had evidently rested there before. There were pieces of garments, and ashes of fires. Weary with our tramp of more than twenty miles, we soon fell asleep. Our nap was short, however. Lemon soon shook me, saying that he had heard a noise like the sound of oars falling into a boat. Most are familiar with this peculiar ringing sound. Wide awake then, we watched the road, and soon saw two Rebel couriers pass along with papers in their hands. Waiting till they were well past, we crept out, and watched them till they were out of sight, when we went down to the river's edge.

Here we found a boat with two broken paddles pushed up among the trees in the swamp.

Seeing the coast apparently clear on the opposite side, it was only the work of a moment to get it back into the stream. There was no quarrelling for the post of honour; each took what his hand first reached, and we were soon standing "on the other shore." A hurried pull of the boat up the beach and we were away. Following the corduroy we soon came to two horses tied under the trees. These evidently belonged to the couriers. It was a hazardous affair throughout, and thinking the danger would be no greater on horseback than on foot, we borrowed the gentlemen's horses.

It was a splendid ride. Two miles or more we sailed along, when, the country becoming more open, we reluctantly slipped bridles, and let the noble animals loose to grass.

Turning into the woods we soon heard voices in the distance. They proved to be Rebel pickets. Fearing to venture any more that day, we found a close retreat, and lay down for the day, employing our waking hours in eating corn from the cob—our only diet for several days. Slept till nearly midnight, and then, flanking the picket, pursued our way.

CHAPTER 15

Recaptured by a Rebel Picket

TWENTY-FIRST DAY

Twenty Miles From Savannah, Ga.
Friday, December 6.

While lying in our hiding-place near Big Ebenezer Creek, we congratulated ourselves on our escapes thus far, and felt as though our toils and marches were nearly over. Our hearts beat high with delight at the thought that we were near the Federal lines, for we knew that at the utmost it could be but a few hours walk to Sherman.

Feeling thus elated, we left our place of concealment with joyous hearts, although we had been without rations for more than thirty-six hours, and were unable to obtain either guides or information with regard to the situation of our armies. In fact, we were groping about like blind men—driven from point to point by the yelping of hounds or the movements of troops.

The Little Ebenezer was reached about midnight, and to our chagrin we found the bridge destroyed. After reconnoitring a few moments, to ascertain, if possible, whether there was a picket on the opposite bank, we became satisfied that the coast was clear, find, constructing a raft out of such boards as we could find, made our way across the stream.

We then proceeded very cautiously, examining closely all the old camping grounds for crumbs of hard bread, and any other rations that we thought might have been left by our army; for we were now on the Savannah River road, over which Kilpatrick's cavalry and the Fourteenth Army Corps had passed but a week before.

It was just as we were about turning from the road for the above mentioned purpose, that we were challenged in a very gruff tone of voice,—

"Who Comes There?"

I had long ere this decided upon the course to be pursued in case that we should be so unfortunate as to run upon a picket; and being too near the challenger to make running a safe expedient, I answered without hesitation, "Friends."

Upon which the picket commanded, "Advance one."

I advanced promptly, and, arriving near my captors, found them to be mounted infantrymen. They were sitting upon their horses, in the shade of some cypress-trees.

One asked, "Who are you?" to which I replied, "I am a scout to General Hardie, and must not be detained, as I have important information for the general."

Sentinel. "I am instructed to take every person to the officer of the picket that approaches this post after dark."

"I can't help it, sir. It is not customary to arrest scouts, and I must pass on."

"You cannot; I must obey orders. I do not doubt the truth of your assertion; but until you have seen the lieutenant, you will not be allowed to pass this post."

Finding that I had met a good soldier, I saw that it was useless to trifle with him, and tried to console myself with the thought that I should be able to dupe the lieutenant; and as we were hurried on toward the reserve of the picket, my mind was occupied in arranging a plan for our defence as spies to the great "Rebel Chief." Reaching the reserve, we found nearly all asleep, in close proximity to a large rail fire, including my antagonist the lieutenant. He, being roughly shook by one of the men, soon became sensible of his unconscious state, and, rubbing his eyes for a moment, he asked, "What is wanted?"

I answered, "I am surprised, sir, that scouts to our generals should be arrested by your picket."

He said, "My instructions are positive, and no man can pass this post without examination."

"Very well, then," said I, "be good enough to examine us at once."

"Have you passes?"

"No, sir; not at present. We had papers when I've left the general's headquarters; but having been scouting in Northern Georgia for the past two weeks, our papers are worn out and lost."

"You have some papers about you, I suppose?"

Thinking that by answering in the affirmative, and producing quickly an old package of letters which had been received while in Libby Prison, that none of them would be criticised, I hastily drew them from the side-pocket of my jacket and held them before me, saying, "I hope here are enough, sir." The lieutenant's curiosity led him to take one which had been received from Colonel C. Buel, of Troy.

Regarded as a Spy

He held it near the fire, and noticing the date, turned his eyes towards me and again to the letter; the second glance seemed to satisfy him that I was not a Rebel, and he remarked very indignantly, "Then you are scouting for General Hardie, are you? I believe you are a damned Yankee spy, and if you were to get your just deserts I should hang you to the first tree I come to."

Said I, "Lieutenant, do not be too hasty, I can convince you that I have been a prisoner of war, and if you are a true soldier, I shall be treated as such."

The lieutenant, becoming a little more mild, gave us to understand that we should start at ten o'clock the next morning, for Springfield, the headquarters of General Wheeler.

After detailing a special guard for the prisoners, and instructing them to be on the alert, the lieutenant laid himself down by the fire, leaving us to reflect upon the hardness of fate, and the uncertainties attending an effort to escape the clutches of a barbarous enemy.

I soon found an opportunity of speaking to Lemon, and communicated to him my intention of making another attempt to reach the Federal lines. I told him that I did not know what he had determined to do, but us for myself, I should never return to South Carolina a prisoner. I recounted to him the horrors and frightful consequences of prison life, and the privations and long suffering attending our attempt to escape from the hands of our merciless enemies. I told him that in my estimation it was quite as well to be hung by bushwhackers or torn to pieces by hounds in Georgia, as to return to South Carolina and meet a miserable death from starvation and exposure. I was terribly exasperated, and could hardly contain myself.

The lieutenant seemed to agree with me in every particular, and although he made no decisive answer, I concluded that I could count upon his co-operation. While with the picket, we learned that we had been arrested at the outpost, and that if we had been so fortunate as to pass this post, we might have reached General Sherman's lines in less than an hour. This intelligence was very disheartening indeed, when we saw that but a step intervened between suffering and happiness. Still, I endeavoured to look upon the bright side of the picture, thinking that if I could but have another chance in the "swamps," I should be more successful.

A Kind Act

I shall never forget the kindness of James Brooks, one of the pickets, who came to us a little after daybreak, and asked if we would like some hoe-cake and bacon (he said he had been out "prowling," and would share his rations with the prisoners); we answered in the affirmative, as a matter of course, having been without food for more than forty-eight hours, save a few ears of corn which we had been so fortunate as to find by the roadside, where the cavalrymen had fed their horses. In a moment more the hoe-cake was forthcoming, much to the disgust of our friend's comrades, who called him "blue belly," and said he must be a fool to give his bread to the damned "Yanks." He made no reply to their insults, but set before us a most excellent breakfast.

An Attempt to Bribe the Guard

After we had finished the hoe-cake and bacon, we asked permission to pass under guard to a little stream of water which was in sight of, and but a few rods, from the reserve.

The favour was granted, and after we had taken a bath, I endeavoured to bribe the guard by offering them one hundred dollars in "Confederate scrip" (which had been given to me by the negroes), if they would give us an opportunity to make our escape.

They said that they would be right glad to have the money, but feared the consequences, as they were held responsible for our return. I told them that if they would listen to me, I would show them how they could make a good pile of Confed., and have no fears of punishment.

As we could be easily seen by the picket, my plan was to apparently take advantage of the guard by setting off at a run for the swamps, when they were to turn in pursuit, and without taking aim, fire in our direction.

I was confident that the scheme would work admirably, but the guards seemed to distrust each other, and instead of acceding to my proposition, they marched us back to the picket, and reported that we had attempted to bribe them. The lieutenant ordered a search at once, and what little scrip had been given us by our coloured friends was soon in the hands of the "gray jackets." We were also threatened with severe punishment; one said, "Shoot the damned Yankees;" another,

"LET 'EM STEETCH HEMP."

Several reckoned that they had better take us into the swamp, and send us after Sherman's raiders; referring, I suppose, to the manner in which they had disposed of some of our sick that had necessarily been left in rear of the army; for, before our recapture, we were told by the negroes that fifteen of our sick that fell into the hands of the Rebels but a few days since were taken to a swamp where their throats were cut, and their bodies thrown into a slough hole.

I cannot vouch for the truth of this statement; but it came to me from many whose veracity I had no reason to doubt.

Our guard was universally applauded for their fidelity; but I am thoroughly convinced that if either had been alone, he would have thanked me for the suggestion and pocketed the money.

We remained with the picket until ten o'clock a. m., when a guard, consisting of a corporal and two men, were detailed for the purpose of taking us to General Wheeler's headquarters.

We had not proceeded far, however, when very suddenly I became so footsore as to render it seemingly impossible for me to walk, which I claimed was the result of my long tramp since my escape from Columbia.

ONCE MORE IN THE SADDLE

I affected to be too weak to mount without assistance, and allowed "Johnny Reb." to help me into the saddle. It was not long before we came to some little trees by the roadside, and, riding under one, I broke off a small limb which I thought might be of some service in the future; for I was no sooner in the saddle than I had decided to effect my escape by flight, and determined to watch my opportunity.

I had ridden the Rebel charger but a short distance, when my guard espied a black squirrel a few rods from the road. Forgetting the responsibility of his detail, he set out at a wild pace after the squirrel, which, after darting off a short distance, ran up a tree, and then, as if to show his superiority over Blondin, leaped from limb to limb with an expertness creditable, to his species. His follower was upon the point of giving up the chase as a poor investment, when, suddenly, the little fellow halted, and perching himself upon a limb, seemingly bade defiance to pursuit. I could not help regarding this little animal with some favour; for it appeared that he was about to sacrifice his life to my interests.

The Escape and Pursuit

The carbine was instantly brought to the shoulder, and its report told me then was my time, while the piece was unloaded; and, without waiting to mark the result of the shot, I whipped up and dashed off at a fearful rate, urging my charger to the top of his speed.

I was noticed immediately by the corporal, who left the other guard with Lemon, and came after me in a manner that was not the most flattering to my prospects. He was armed with a Colt's revolver, and while in pursuit discharged its contents at my unfortunate self, ordering me to halt at every shot. I paid no attention to the summons, but continued to urge my pony to his utmost.

His time, however, at the best, was quite unsatisfactory to my wishes; for had he been more fleet, I could have distanced the corporal, dismounted, and got into the swamps unobserved; but in this respect I was unfortunate, and was soon surprised to find myself approaching a camp, which was situated on both sides of the road. I turned my horse, leaped a fence, and endeavoured to make my way across an open field; but the corporal's demand, to halt the damned Yankee, was responded to by not less than fifty Texan rangers, from the Rebel General Iverson's Cavalry Division. They came hooting and yelping, mounted and dismounted, armed and unarmed. Several blazed away at me with carbines and revolvers, but without effect.

I was, however, soon overtaken by fresh horses, and compelled to surrender myself once more a prisoner of war into the hands of the Texans.

The guard, whom I thought so kind, and whose horse I had thus unmercifully ridden, came up in time to heap a most fearful tirade of curses upon me before we again resumed march.

The Texans seemed to enjoy the sport hugely. One of them said to the squirrel-hunter, "You are a damned smart soldier, you are, to let a blue-belly get away from you—and on your own horse, too!"

Another put in, "I say, corporal, which of them nags can run fastest?"

The corporal had little to say, and as soon as Lemon and the other guard came up he started us on. We were then forced to walk the entire distance—my lameness exciting no more sympathy from the mortified guards.

Arrival at Wheeler's Headquarters

We reached General Wheeler's headquarters late in the afternoon, and the corporal reported to the general that he was in charge of two prisoners that had attempted to pass the outposts as scouts to General Hardie. Wheeler ordered us into his presence, questioned us closely, and ordered our clothing searched. This investigation over, we were sent to the county jail and locked up in a cell, ten by fifteen feet, to await our trial as "Yankee spies."

We considered it an easy matter to prove our identity as escaped prisoners, and the only facts that could tell against us were, that I wore a gray jacket, and that we had represented ourselves to be scouts to a Confederate general.

I shall ever remember our interview with General Wheeler; for it was quite an amusing scene, and illustrates, to some extent, the character of that Rebel cavalry chief, whose career in the South and West had made his name so famous in the history of the Rebellion. He first said to us,—

"Then you are scouting for Confederate generals, are you?"

I replied, "We would have rejoiced could we but have convinced your outpost that we were—"

W. Enough of your impudence, sir. Remember that you are a prisoner.

G. Very true; but when you ask questions, you may anticipate answers.

W. What are you doing with that gray jacket?

G. I wear it, sir, to protect myself from the sun and storm.

W. Where did you get it?

G. One of the guard at Columbia was kind enough to give it to me, when he saw that I was suffering for the want of clothing with which to cover my nakedness.

W. He could not have been a true Rebel, thus to assist a Yankee in making his escape.

G. He knew nothing of my intention to escape; and I believe he was, at least, a sympathizing, kind-hearted man.

W. Why don't you wear the Federal uniform? Is it possible that the Yankees are ashamed of the blue?

G. By no means, sir. What few garments were spared me at the time of my capture were worn out during a long imprisonment, and the clothing which was sent on to Richmond by our government during the winter of '63 for distribution among the prisoners, was, for the most part, appropriated by your authorities.

W. Like many others of the contemptible Yankee crew, I believe you to be a lying scoundrel, and you shall answer to the charge of spy.

G. Very well, sir, I am compelled to await your pleasure; but you have heard nothing but the truth.

W. Guard, take the prisoners to the jail, place them in a cell, and keep them in close confinement until further orders.

Twenty-Second Day

County Jail, Springfield, Ga.,
Saturday, December 17.

Springfield is a very pleasant little village on the Middle Ground Road. It is the county seat of Effingham County, and before the war contained several fine public buildings, which have recently been laid in ruins by the hostile armies.

We were the only military prisoners confined in the jail, which was then in the hands of the military authorities. We were kindly allowed to leave our cell and go into the yard to take the fresh air. The news spread rapidly that there were—

Two Live Yanks in the Jail Yard.

The citizens became alarmed and enraged to think that we should be permitted to leave the cell, and threatened to take the keys into their own hands, if we were not taken back.

The officer in charge told them that he was personally responsible for our safe keeping, and that they need not give themselves any uneasiness.

A large crowd gathered around and looked upon us with seeming wonder. Seeing that we appeared quite harmless, several ventured up to us and asked many curious questions. I found them to be the most ignorant class of people that I have ever met in the South. Many of them have supposed, until very recently, that the Yankees actually wore horns.

Their ideas of the war were laughable in the extreme.

Twenty-Third Day

Middle Ground Road, Near Springfield, Ga.,
Sunday, December 18.

In the afternoon, we were brought up before a Military Commission, composed of officers from General Wheeler's staff.

The officials had already become pretty well satisfied that we were only prisoners of war, and all the Commission did, was to ask us where we were captured, where we had been imprisoned, when we made our escape, etc. This farce of a trial being over, a heavy guard was detailed from the Second Georgia Cavalry, with instructions to proceed with us to Waynesboro', together with fifteen prisoners from our Fourteenth Army Corps, who were captured while out on a foraging expedition a few days before.

From them I gained much valuable information concerning the situation of our army.

I also learned where the Rebel troops were stationed in General Sherman's rear. Such information was absolutely necessary in the event of another attempt to escape. No rations were issued to us. The Rebel troops depended entirely on foraging for their supplies, and seemed to care very little for the wants of the prisoners. A few ears of corn were all we had to keep soul and body together. As night drew on, we were in very low spirits—owing to the fact that all attempts to elude the vigilance of the guards during the day had failed.

I first urged the prisoners to straggle, so as to lengthen the column as much as possible, thinking that if we were permitted so to do, I might succeed in dodging into a swamp unobserved; but the vigilant sergeant was too shrewd to be duped in this manner, and instructed his men to keep us closed up.

Failing in this scheme, I hoped that the sergeant would continue to march us during the night, in which case I could take advantage of the darkness and make off at my pleasure; but in this plan also I was destined to be disappointed; for much against my wishes we came to a halt but a few moments after dark, and were hurried into an old building for the night.

Just before halting we had passed through a large swamp, where the water was so deep in the road as to compel each man to use his own discretion in making his way through.

The guard did its best to keep us together and prevent escapes; but in spite of their exertions one of our enlisted men fell out, whose absence was soon noticed by the sergeant.

Verifying Rebel Details

We succeeded in convincing him that all the prisoners were present with whom he had started from Springfield. Our programme was this: I found out the absent man's name: and then as the sergeant had a list of the prisoners, I volunteered to call the roll for him. Getting us into a safe position, and lighting a piece of fat pine, he handed me the list, and I proceeded to call the names; as a matter of course, all who were present answered promptly, and then (according to previous instruction), as no one had heard such a name as the absent man bore, the sergeant concluded that it must have found its way upon the roll through mistake.

Under ordinary circumstances, I should be far from volunteering to aid a Rebel in verifying his details; but, in this case, I thought that by a little ingenuity, a fellow-sufferer might return to liberty; for had not this scheme been devised, strenuous efforts would have been made by the guards to insure his capture. Picked men would have been detailed, hounds called out, and a few hours, at the furthest, would doubtless have convinced the unfortunate victim how little hope there is for him who seeks to shun the horrors of prison life by an escape.

We were entertained during the evening by the good humour of one of the guards, who, having seen something of the world, was inclined to make light of the verdant and somewhat peculiar speeches of his more unfortunate fellow-Georgians, who had never passed the limits of the swamps that surround their dreary homesteads. A story was told by this jovial cavalier of an old lady to whom he had applied for bread during the day. It was designed to show her appreciation of General Wheeler. She struck out as follows

> Mr. Wheeler and his critter-company drove into my back yard t'other day, tipped my ash hopper over, and drawed out ten streaks of fight half a mile long, with his wagon-guns on the ends of 'em—and when he went away he never paid me nary cent. I allers thought you'uns was a decenter set of men, but the Yanks theirselves is no wusser. Now, ef you'uns don't go long and leave us what little we've got, we'll surely perish.

Twenty-Fourth Day

Near Sylvania, Ga.,
Monday, December 19.
Commenced our march at daybreak, and made about twenty-five

miles during the day.

Sylvania is a small town, and to all appearances of but little importance. It is situated on the Middle Ground Road, midway between Springfield and Waynesboro'. The armies did not halt here; and, consequently, the people knew but little of the sad realities resulting from the devastating tread of armed hosts.

They were generally disposed to be talkative and friendly. Many of them besieged the guard and prisoners with questions and observations. This was just what we wanted—for the guard could not be vigilant when entertaining citizens.

Early in the evening our station was on the porch of a large unoccupied building, while the sentinels were posted in front in the form of a semicircle.

Soon after halting, the sergeant came to me and said, "My foragers have found some cornbread and sweet potatoes, which you see at the other end of the porch. I will give you all some potatoes, and keep the bread for the guard."

"Very well—very well," I said, and continued to myself, "If we are permitted to remain outside the building till dark, your guard will get very little of that bread, unless it is issued soon."

As he was walking away, I called to him, "Sergeant, have you any objection to our remaining outside till after supper, as we shall want to use the fire?"

After looking carefully around and hesitating a moment, he answered, "Ye-es, I reckon you can."

"Thank you—thank you," I replied; "We will consider it a privilege." This favour granted, I at once set myself at work on a plan of escape.

CHAPTER 16

The Escape From Sylvania, Georgia

TWENTY-FIFTH DAY

In a Swamp Near Sylyania, Ga.,
Tuesday, December 20, 1864.

Having been told by the sergeant that we would be allowed to remain without the building until after supper, I called the attention of Lieutenant J. W. Wright, Tenth Iowa Volunteers, who was conversing with a citizen, and asked him if he had not better get his potatoes. I at the same time gave him a look, which he understood to mean a change of base. Hastily withdrawing from the citizen he met me on the porch, where I communicated to him my plan for escape, and inquired if he would join me in its execution. He replied without hesitation that he was up to anything but going back to South Carolina, and would not shrink from bearing a hand in any move which I might make.

Lemon, my former companion, was prevented by circumstances from participating in this plan, and was taken back to Columbia. I will here say that Lieutenant Wright was also an escaped prisoner from Columbia, whom I had often met during my imprisonment; he left Columbia a few days after Lieutenant Lemon and myself, but unfortunately, like us, was recaptured at a time when he felt that he was about to say *adieu* to the scenes of his suffering. Finding that Wright had—

"ESCAPE ON THE BRAIN,"

I lost no time in making what I considered the necessary preliminaries.

I first saw one of the prisoners, whom I had been told by the sergeant would be allowed to issue the potatoes. I requested him to make the issue upon receiving a certain signal from me, which I made him understand perfectly.

I then asked Lieutenant Wright to step to the end of the porch, near where the cornbread lay that was intended for the Rebel guard. I followed immediately after, but was observed by the sergeant, who seemed to wonder at this singular flank movement; he said nothing, however, as we allayed his suspicious of our intentions, by sitting down and entering into conversation. In a moment more a citizen came up, and called the attention of the sergeant.

A Valuable Capture

The signal was made, and the half-starved men, closed up for their potatoes. It was now getting dark; I hastily took possession of the cornbread, and taking advantage of the crowd, which screened us from the guard, we sloped for a small clump of bushes that were but a few rods distant. The potatoes were no sooner distributed than our absence was noticed.

The sergeant suddenly aroused himself, and exclaimed, "By dog on't, the damned Yankee officers have done gone, and taken all of our cornbread. I will have them, if it costs me a horse."

Calling out a corporal and four men, he instructed them to proceed to a plantation for hounds, and to bring back the Yanks either dead or alive. He thought it probable that we would take the Springfield Road, as that was the nearest route to our lines.

We were all this time so near the guard that we could hear distinctly every word that was spoken, and, as a matter of course, understood the programme perfectly.

We decided with the sergeant, that the route by way of Springfield was unquestionably the one to be preferred; but we did not consider it policy to strike the road when we knew it was being patrolled with hounds, and concluded not to be in any hurry until the excitement was over.

As soon as it was sufficiently dark to warrant a movement, we hurriedly decamped from our place of concealment, and made our way around to the Middle Ground Road, over which we had passed but a few hours before under guard. We leaped across it, so as to avoid the suspicion which tracks would very naturally excite, and hastened into a large swamp but a short distance from town. While there, we decided upon the course to be pursued, which was recommended by Wright.

The lieutenant had been over the Middle Ground Road before, to within a few miles of Springfield, when he was recaptured; and his experience we considered a valuable possession, as we intended to get back to Springfield as quickly as possible, and then strike for some point on the Savannah, near which Lemon and I were recaptured.

We remained in the swamp until after ten o'clock, when Wright started up and told me to follow. He then went in quest of an old negro hut, where he had before obtained succour. It was within a stone's throw of the plantation house, and therefore not safely approached without a thorough reconnoissance.

Secreting me in a corner of the fence which surrounds the plantation, Wright proceeded forthwith to the hut, in which he was confident that—

OLD RICHARD

slept; for this was the name of the kind-hearted negro who had supplied him with hoe-cake and bacon before he was retaken at Springfield.

It required but a moment to convince Richard that his guest was none other than Massa Wright, whom he had befriended during his escape, and whom he had the mortification to see pass back toward Sylvania a prisoner in the afternoon.

I was soon introduced, with all due formality, to this swarthy descendant of Ham, whose warm and hearty shake of the hand convinced me, beyond a doubt, that he was an earnest friend to the Yankee, who would not hesitate to stake his life, if necessary, in an endeavour to further our wishes.

Wright said that he had found a friend, and that I must make arrangements for the "grub." I said to Richard, "We want to leave this place tomorrow night at twelve o'clock, and would like to take four days rations with us. Can you let us have some bacon and sweet potatoes to put with our cornbread?"

He replied, "It is a pretty hard case, massa; but dis yer darkey will do de best he can. Can't get nuffin on dis plantation, but reckon I can buy some potatoes down at Massa Smith's three miles from yer, and will go down there after I finish my task tomorrow. As to meat," he said, "you know, massa, dat in the Souf de slave takes what de white folks frows away; and I reckon you all couldn't eat a tainted ham dat old massa gib me tother day; but if you can, God knows dis chile gibs it to you wid all his heart."

I gave him to understand that we should be greatly obliged for the described ham; as we had become so entirely oblivious to the sense of taste that we do not stop to question the quality of anything which could be eaten by man.

The ration question being settled, we asked Richard if he could not take us to some safe spot where no Rebel would ever think of coming. Leading the way, our coloured friend conducted us to a swamp, and found a secure place of concealment in the top of an old pine tree.

Here we spent the day unmolested and unobserved by anyone. The whippoorwill and turtle dove enlivened us with their inspiring notes during the day, and as night began to approach the gloomy owl from the tree-tops uttered his solemn warning cry. The pine and cypress-trees, swayed by the breeze, moaned a perpetual chorus, and under their tuition we learned, during the long, dreary hours, how much we were indebted to these dismal wilds that have concealed alike both friend and foe.

Here the Rebel deserter concealed himself from his pursuers. Here the loyalist found a hiding-place from the Rebel conscripting officer. Here the trembling negro had his first taste of freedom. Here the escaped prisoner was enabled to baffle bloodhounds and human hounds, and make his way to the Federal lines.

I always considered that a prisoner of war was justified in making his escape, and might claim the consideration due to a human being, even though he were depriving his enemies of the fruits of victory; and it hardly seems possible that in our own free country such a one should be tracked with bloodhounds, like a wild beast, and shot down without mercy, like an outlaw.

I cannot help asking, with the poet Whittier,—

Is this the land our fathers loved,
The freedom which they toiled to win?
Is this the earth whereon they moved?
Are those the graves they slumber in?

How wonderfully degenerated have become these unworthy descendants of the mighty fathers of the revolution. Could their spirits but speak from the heavens, they would warn these fiends of earth not to stain the pages of history by acts so foul and barbarous that the most unfeeling savage would shrink with horror from their contemplation.

Twenty-Sixth Day

Between Sylvania And Springfield, Georgia,
Wednesday, December 21.

We met Old Richard in the evening at the spot agreed upon, near a spring on his master's plantation. He gave us the tainted meat which had been spoken of the previous night, and a few sweet potatoes. This was the best that he could do for us; and after we had asked God to bless him for his kindness, and told him that we believed the day was not far distant when he would be a free man, started on our way rejoicing, hoping that we might reach our lines before we should need another supply. We walked about twenty-five miles after leaving Richard, for the most part keeping the road over which we had marched while prisoners on our way to Sylvania.

Our progress was necessarily very slow, for, to use an army phrase, I was about *played out*, from starvation and long exposure. My weight could not have been more than ninety pounds. Wright is a hardy Western man, much larger than myself, and, besides, he had a good pair of shoes, which are almost indispensable to the success of an escaped prisoner. They were given him by a negro, soon after his escape from Columbia. During the night's tramp he carried me through several swamps on his back, as I was entirely too weak to make my way alone without falling into slough-holes. Nothing occurred during the night to lessen our chances of reaching Sherman's lines, although at one time we came so near being seen by two

Rebel Deserters,

that we had barely time to turn from the road and secrete ourselves behind a log, when they passed the spot where we had stood but a moment before. It was a bright moonlight night; and had they been looking for Yanks, they could have found us very readily; but it appeared from their conversation that they were conscripts, and that not feeling disposed to fight against the defenders of the "old flag," they had deserted from General Wheeler's command, and were making their way back to their homes in Tennessee. We did not venture to hail them, but thinking that for the alleged reasons they were justified in deserting the Rebel ranks, we silently wished them success, and pushed on.

At daybreak we came to a halt, thinking we had secured a hiding-place entirely removed from the haunts of men, but soon discovered a plantation house nearby. Finding that it was occupied, we deemed it wisdom to change our base of concealment, and accordingly "got up and dusted."

Half a mile brought us to a swamp, where we found a lodgement between the roots of a large cypress-tree. As the moon did not rise till midnight, we determined to get an early start and improve the darkness. Heavy cannonading was heard all day in the direction of Savannah.

Twenty-Seventh Day

On Our Way, With Renewed Obstacles,
Thursday, December 22.

In accordance with our intentions, we set out at an early hour. Had not proceeded far when a plantation became visible.

A Proposition

Wright said, "Glazier, if you would like a good supper and something to put in the haversack, I will tell you where you can make a raise on a safe scale, by just representing yourself to be a Rebel, and trusting to your face."

We always considered it advisable to replenish the commissary department as often as possible; and I asked him to mention the particulars. He replied that the plantation house, toward which we were directing our eyes, was occupied by a planter's wife and some small children, whose husband and father was in the Rebel army. He had also been informed that there were no hounds upon the plantation.

The Interview With Mrs. Keyton.—Turning the Tables

After listening to the details, we agreed upon a signal which should warn him of my approach upon returning from the designed foraging expedition, and then I went in quest of the house. Stepping up to the door, I rapped, and a very intelligent lady soon made her appearance. I asked, "Can you give this Rebel a supper?"

She replied, "You shall have the best the house affords," and invited me to step in and take a seat by the fire.

I did so, saying, as I took my seat, "Madam, I am shocked at the dastardly conduct of General Sherman in his march through Georgia. It has been characterized by nothing but what should excite the revenge, and move to action, every man possessing a true Southern spirit. Our aged citizens, who have banded together for mutual protection, have been treated as bushwhackers—have been driven from their homes, and their property confiscated. Our hounds, always true to the interests of the South, have been shot down by the roadside for no other reason than because they have been used in tracking escaped prisoners—"

Here I was interrupted by the lady, who remarked, to my great surprise, that she could not see that the Yankees were much worse than the Confederates, after all. She said,—

"When the Federal army passed through the State, it took from the rich the supplies necessary for its sustenance; and when our cavalry followed on in the rear, it took nearly, all that was left, seeming to care but little for our wants; often stripping defenceless women and children of their last morsel of bread."

G. I regret that the conduct of our troops has been such as to give you reasons for complaint.

Lady. I, too, regret that our men have not proved themselves worthy of a cause which they appear so willing to defend.

G. Remember that our commissary department has been broken up, and that we are entirely dependent upon the people for the subsistence of a large army.

L. And what do you think of present prospects?

G. Our future seems dark—our cause appears almost hopeless; but the sacrifices of our gallant dead remain unavenged. We must fight while there is a man left, and die in the last ditch."

L. If there is no longer any hope of success, I should say that it would be better to lay down our arms at once, and go back under the "old flag."

G. We must fight.

L. It is wickedness to continue this awful massacre of human beings, without some prospect of ultimate success,

G. Very true; but we have lost all in this struggle, and must sell our lives as dearly as possible.

L. My husband is a captain in the Twenty-fifth Georgia Infantry. He is the father of these children, and is very dear to both them and me. Long have I prayed that he might be spared to return to his family, but fear that we shall never be permitted to see him again. When he entered the army I admired his patriotism, and was glad to see him go in defence of what I supposed to be the true policy of the Southern people; but we have been deceived from the beginning by our military and political leaders. It is time to open our eyes, and see what obstinacy has brought us. We are conquered. Let us adhere to the administration of the Federal government, ere we are ruined.

G. Madam, your sympathies appear to be with the Federals.

L. It is not strange; I was born and educated in New England;- and your speech would indicate that you, too, are not a native of the South.

G. You are right; I am a New Yorker by birth, but have been for a long time in South Carolina.

After partaking of the frugal meal set before me, which consisted of cornbread and sweet potatoes, I thanked the lady for her kindness, and told her that I regretted very deeply that I was not in a situation to remunerate her for so much trouble. Noticing my blue pants as I arose from the table, she observed: "It is impossible for me to know our men from the Federals by the uniform; but a few days since, two soldiers asked me to get them some supper, claiming to be scouts to General Wheeler; they told many very plausible stories, and the next day, to my astonishment, I was charged with harbouring Yankee spies."

G. I do not wonder that you find it difficult to distinguish the Confederate from the Yankee soldier, for in these trying times a poor Rebel is compelled to wear anything he can get. The dead are always stripped, and at this season of the year, we find the Federal uniform far more comfortable than our own.

L. It must be an awful extremity that could tempt men to strip the dying and the dead.

G. We have become so much accustomed to such practices, that we are unmoved by scenes which might appal and sicken those who have never served in our ranks.

L. I sincerely hope that these murderous practices will soon be at an end.

G. I must go, madam; may I know to whom I am so much indebted for my supper and kind entertainment this evening?

L. Mrs. James Keyton. And what may I call your name?

G. Willard Glazier, Fifty-third Alabama Mounted Infantry.

L. Should you chance to meet the Twenty-fifth Georgia, please inquire for Captain Keyton, and say to him that his wife and children are well, and send their love.

G. He shall certainly have your message if it is my good fortune to find him out. Goodnight.

The interview with Mrs. Keyton ended, which seemed to convince her that I was a bitter Rebel, I hastened out to receive the congratulations of Wright upon my success, but found him in very bad humour, as he was entirely out of patience with waiting for my return.

I explained to him the reason of the delay, but all to no purpose, for he was so provoked that he would not listen; and thus feeling a little angry at each other, we moved toward Springfield. Being determined to gain as much information as possible concerning the strength and movements of the enemy in General Sherman's rear, we made a thorough reconnoissauce before leaving Springfield.

We found General Iverson's headquarters to be at that place, and were at one time within fifteen paces of the house which he occupied.

We were so near his provost guard, as to hear distinctly every word that was spoken. They were discussing present prospects, and the news which they had received the day before of the fall of Savannah. It seemed to be the prevailing opinion that the Confederate army was about played out, and that sooner or later

Ill-Fated Dixie

would be compelled to submit to the tyrannical rule of the invader. One long, gaunt-looking fellow, who appeared to be the mouth-piece for a large number, straightened himself up in front of a fire, around which a group had gathered, and burst forth as follows: "By dog on't, the damned blue-bellies have got ahead of we'uns on this tramp." I could not help thinking what a change had taken place in their views since the 17th, when we were prisoners at Wheeler's headquarters, for at that time they asserted that they had—

General Sherman just where they wanted him

Now their victim is evidently in the ascendant, and the army that was to sacrifice its chivalrous blood in the defences of Savannah, seeks safety in flight, having abandoned its artillery and supplies. Leaving Springfield, it was the intention to strike the Savannah River road at Helmy, where we supposed the enemy's outpost to be. My companion knew nothing about this route, and left all to me, as I had been recaptured near that point.

It was by no means an easy task to pursue any direct course in this swampy country, intersected as it is by blind roads. The sun, moon, and stars, were our only guides; and it was to them that we were chiefly indebted for our success thus far.

While in South Carolina and Northern Georgia, we depended entirely upon the negroes for guidance; but the passage of our army through this section of the State opened the way to freedom, and invited the bondman to cast off his shackles, and enjoy the blessings of liberty.

Strange as it may seem, nearly every slave had embraced the opportunity presented him, and very quietly taken leave of his kind old master without waiting for ceremony. I say strange, for the simple reason, that it has been the boast of the Southerner that the slave would not exchange his chains for freedom; that he was happy when governed by a kind master, and would not seek to better his condition by a change:

Having passed Springfield about six miles, we found daylight approaching, and hurriedly turned from the road which we had been following for more than an hour, and secreted ourselves in some tall swamp grass. Here we laid little more than an hour, when we were suddenly—

Startled by Hounds

Wright turned to me and said, "We are followed."

I asked, "What do you propose to do?"

"I am undecided," was his reply.

"It is my opinion," I said, "that there is no time for reflection. If we are not off at once, we will be prisoners before leaving this swamp."

"Well, off it is, then," said Wright; and jumping into our shoes, which we had taken off in order to dry our feet, we got out of the swamp in double-quick time, crossed the road, and, taking the sun for a guide, struck a south-easterly course, leaping fences and ditches, fording streams, and passing through thickets, that would greatly retard the progress of the bushwhackers in pursuit.

The chase continued until about one o'clock. The hounds, for the most part, being so near that we could hear their yelping distinctly, when, fortunately, we came to a large creek , jumping into the stream, we followed the current fifty or sixty rods, and then, turning to the sun for our point of compass, pushed on.

The precaution taken upon our arrival at the creek must have foiled the hounds; for we had not proceeded far when we became fully satisfied that we had outgeneralled the bushwhackers. We did not halt, however, but continued on towards the promised land. Greatly encouraged by our success since morning, we became so indiscreet and reckless as to venture into open fields whenever they happened to be in our line of escape.

A Narrow Escape

At about two o'clock p. m., just as we were clearing the outskirts of a swamp, I was surprised to see my companion drop suddenly behind a large cypress-tree without uttering a word. I followed his example, not deeming it prudent to ask a question.

I fixed my attention upon Wright, who, after remaining motionless a few moments, raised his head and looked to the front. Falling back behind the aged cypress, he whispered, "Did you see the picket?"

I answered, "No;" but looking up, saw that we were within twenty rods of armed men.

No farther observations were necessary to convince us that the sooner out of such quarters the better. We had not time to move, however, before a cavalry patrol came up to visit the post, and to give new instructions. As soon as the patrol had passed, we crawled back upon our hands and knees into the swamp, keeping behind a clump of large trees that screened us from the picket. Coming to a dry spot, we halted to consider the propriety of proceeding farther, as there was great danger of being seen in an attempt to leave the place.

Wright decided that it would be policy to remain where we were, and here a difference of opinion arose again; as I was so wet and cold that the thought of confining myself to such limited quarters, I confess, made me not a little uneasy; for we could neither stand up nor lie down. Our clothes, too, were wet, the weather extremely cold, and we had not slept in forty-eight hours; and then, too, the idea of sitting up like a pair of mummies five hours.

I told my companion the thing was not to be thought of, and that I would strike for dry land if it cost me a recapture.

Wright said he preferred to remain, and I set off without him. The doubtful point was passed by watching the picket and making good time when their backs were turned.

Getting out of the swamp, I went in quest of a favourable haunt where I might lay my weary limbs and dry my clothes.

I was delighted as well as amused to find W. close upon my heels, glad enough to abandon the sitting posture for something more agreeable. I welcomed him to my new place of concealment; and here we have spent the afternoon unmolested by anyone. Our distance from the picket is not more than eighty rods. We are inclined to think it the outpost.

An Amusing Incident

occurred this evening a few moments after sunset. The weather being extremely cold, and our clothes still damp, we agreed that a small fire would be very pleasant; and, suiting the action to the thought, dug a hole in the ground, gathered some pine knots and started a blaze, which in my judgement could not have been seen by anyone at a distance of fifty feet, but, to my companion, it appeared to be of gigantic proportions; and his imagination became so much excited, that he set one of his feet over it, and thus put an end both to my enjoyment and the fire.

I was disposed to be angry, but thinking it not best to challenge a recapture by loud words, *Nursed my wrath to keep it warm.*

These little differences of opinion are things to laugh at after the danger is over,—but then they might have proved serious. It is next to impossible for two men to travel under such circumstances without more or less of disagreement, and when a man considers that his life may depend upon some thoughtless act of his companion, he is disposed to adopt energetic measures.

We congratulated ourselves very much on having escaped the pursuit of the hounds. It is a difficult matter to elude them, as their scent is very accurate. There are two kinds of hounds,—bloodhounds and baying hounds. The baying or yelping hounds take the lead, and are followed by the bloodhounds, which make little noise.

These yelping curs will not come nearer to a person than four or five rods, but will cut circles, and thus mark their locality until the bloodhounds or planters come up.

Twenty-Eighth Day

Savannah Ga.,
Friday, December 23.

December 23rd was the happiest day of my life. and one that will ever remain a bright landmark in the recollection of the past.

We succeeded in flanking the picket the previous evening just after dark, and were not long in finding a coloured friend, familiarly known as—

"Uncle Philip"

among his acquaintances. From him we learned that we had passed the Rebel outposts. Our joy was inexpressible and emotions beyond control for more glorious news never fell upon the ear.

Uncle Philip also informed us that our friends were at Cherokee Hill, on the Savannah River road, only eight miles distant. We asked him if he could not guide us to the lines. He replied, "Ize neber been down dah, massa, since Mr. Sherman's company went to Savannah; but I reckon you can get Mr. Jones, a free culerd man, to take you ober. He is a mighty bright pusson, and understands de swamps jest like a book."

Calling at Mr. Jones' hut, we learned from his wife that he was out on a scout, but would be in by eleven o'clock. She assured us that he was ever glad to do all in his power for the Yankees, and asked us to come into the hut and await his return. We very reluctantly complied with her invitation, fearing that—

Rebel Scouts

might venture down between the lines, and thus blast our brilliant prospects.

Mrs. Jones, however, was by no means a dull tactician, and offered her two sons, one a lad of eight, and the other six years, for outpost duty.

I divided the command and posted the pickets, stationing the oldest boy in the road, at a distance of twenty rods from the hut, and used the other for patrol, who was to keep a sharp lookout; and, in case anyone might be seen approaching the post, was to notify his mother, thereby giving her an opportunity to conceal us.

This matter attended to, a generous supply of hoe-cake and parched corn delighted our eyes; for Auntie was not long in appeasing our hunger with the best her humble cot afforded. Jones came in at the mentioned hour, but did not think himself sufficiently well acquainted with the safest route to warrant his acting in the capacity of guide; but, like all other negroes that I have met in the South, he very readily called to mind one whom he thought would accompany us, and whom he could recommend very highly as an active and intelligent fellow. Securing a small piece of fat pine for a torch to light our way through an intervening swamp, we started for the Savannah River road, beyond which the negro could be found whose many good qualities had been pointed out to myself and companion. Much to our astonishment, —

Coloured Man No. 2

was not so well posted as the man who recommended him; but luckily, and much to our delight, he very promptly referred to another negro, who had come up from our lines the same morning, and who, he thought, would be glad to return with us. The negro last recommended bore the name of—

March Dasher

We found him to be a genuine Ethiopian, as black as any coloured individual I have ever met; and as dignified and devout as he was active and swarthy. Upon being asked if he could show us the way to Cherokee Hill, he replied,—

"I'll do it, Massa, if God be My Helper."

We desired to start at once, but could not persuade him to move before daylight. He said, "Dis chile knows where de pickets is in de day time, but knows nuffin bout 'em after dark." Several attempts were made to induce us to remain in the hut till morning; but no amount of safety insurances could persuade us to take such an apparently inconsiderate step.

The idea that it would not be policy to move on before morning inclined us to think that our land lord might be treacherous, and we were not a little uneasy until prayer was offered for our benefit, when we became fully satisfied that we could at least repose confidence in his fidelity. As soon as prayers were concluded, we betook ourselves to a pine thicket, determined to give March no peace until he should set off with us.

The Negro's Clock Needs No Repairing

At about one o'clock in the morning, Wright turned out and told him that day had just began to break. He got up, came to the door, looked for the seven stars, and then remarked, in a very good humoured way, "I reckon it's good many hours yet till break ob day, massa. Yer can't fool March on de time; his clock neber breaks down. It's jest right ebery time."

Feeling somewhat chagrined at his ill success, Wright returned to the thicket saying, "Glazier, there is no use of being in a sweat; for you might as well undertake to move a mountain as to get the start of that coloured individual."

We made no further attempt to dupe our guide, but very impatiently awaited his call. He came to our place of concealment at the first peep of day, and said, "Gemmen, now I'ze ready to take you right plum into Mr. Sherman's company by sun up."

We followed him without ceremony; and just as old Sol began to tint the hillsides with his first rays, we saw, with unbounded joy,—

A Group of Blue Coats

watching very eagerly our approach; for it was the Federal outpost.

At first, we were evidently regarded as an enemy; but by taking off our hats and making friendly signs, their suspicions were allayed, and they beckoned us to come on. A most cordial reception was given us by the picket, which proved to be a detail from the One Hundred and First Illinois Volunteers, Twentieth Army Corps.

We took each man by the hand, congratulating him upon his good fortune in surviving the death blow to Rebellion in Georgia; and they, in return, rejoiced at our successful escape. Haversacks were opened, and placed at our disposal. There was a great demand for hard tack and coffee; but the beauty of it all was,—

Major Turner was not there

to say what he has often repeated, "Reduce their rations; I'll teach the damned scoundrels not to attempt an escape." I shall ever remember my feelings when I began to realize the fact that I was no longer a prisoner, and when I beheld the "old flag" floating triumphantly over the invincible veterans, who followed the "Great General" down to the sea,

CHAPTER 17

Homeward Bound

Savannah, Ga., *December 24,* 1864.

After breakfast at the picket post, we came into the city with a brigade of the Twentieth Army Corps, which formed a part of the rear-guard of General Sherman's army. It would have been a difficult matter, even for intimate friends, to have identified us in our motley uniforms. For myself, I was clad in a coat of Southern gray, blue pants, my shoes,—before described,—a bewitched looking hat, and gray blanket, which for months had answered the purpose of bed and bedding.

My haversack was a curiosity in its way, being composed of an old towel, which was sewed up by Lemon many weeks before. Said haversack had borne its journey well, but now showed unmistakable signs of dissolution. Sweet potatoes, unless of a fabulous size, slipped through as readily as money through a soldier's fingers; and large must have been the loaf which could retain quarters within its awful depths. I would give Wright the preference of a description, but having had the impudence to look better than I did, he does not deserve it.

Many pleasant incidents occurred during our ride into the city. A major and a surgeon, whose names I have been so ungrateful as to forget, kindly offered us their horses, and dismounted for our convenience. The offer was gratefully accepted, for we were both weak and weary, and Lieutenant Wright had assisted me for some time on our way.

On reaching the city, Wright's first inquiry was for his old regiment; but it was like a search in the dark. The unsettled state of the army rendered it difficult to learn the location of any particular regiment or brigade; but we found the corps to which his regiment belonged, and were sent under guard from corps to regimental headquarters with a demand for recognition, and a receipt therefore.

Such treatment seemed hard at first; but when we reflected upon our checkered costume and suspicious appearance, we readily fell into their way of thinking; for, until we were identified, it would have been no wonder that we were looked upon as spies or *desperadoes*.

Having played the Rebel so long, we ourselves had our allegiance slightly mixed, but by a deal of recollecting and protesting, we came at length to convince ourselves, and the authorities also, that some time, away back in the past, we had been Union men, and belonged to the Federal army. In accordance with which conclusion we were pronounced genuine Union soldiers, and received certificates of the sane to jog our memories in the future. At night we stopped with Captain A. L. Swallow, of Lieutenant Wright's company. He is a noble man, and ministered to our wants like a father. Our circumstances becoming known, no pains were spared to make us comfortable and happy. Comfortable clothing was soon distributed to us, and we began to look like civilized persons.

Christmas Day

The greater part of the day was spent in the city. Took dinner with Mr. H. Brown. His residence was on Congress Street opposite the Pulaski House. Mr. Brown was known as a firm Union man, and although he had suffered much from adherence to his principles, and frequently been stripped of his goods, he still remained true to the old flag and the government of his fathers. Lieutenant E. H. Fales, who was a fellow-prisoner at Charleston, was found secreted at Mr. Brown's house when our army entered Savannah. The lieutenant was in the city for more than a month, representing himself as a very innocent foreigner, but was at one time conscripted and ordered on the defences.

At Kilpatrick's Headquarters, *December 26.*

Lieutenant Fales and myself procured horses from the quartermaster of the Twentieth Corps and rode out to Kilpatrick's headquarters in the afternoon, my object being to secure identification by General Kilpatrick, in order to obtain transportation North, as he was the only officer in the department who knew me to have been in the United States service previous to my capture. The general had the kindness to furnish me with the necessary papers, which were all that detained me from going by the first boat.

We took supper with the general and Captain Estes of his staff, who were much interested in my account of prison life and escape. One hardly likes to be the hero of his own tales, but modesty was no plea for silence under the circumstances.

My term of service having expired, I was very anxious to get home to the North. The unsettled state of the army made delays unavoidable, and I was forced to bide my time.

Steamship *Planter, December 29.*

Took passage on the steamship *Planter* early in the evening. This is the boat which was run out of Charleston harbour by a negro pilot then in command of her as captain. The craft had seen hard service, and was badly peppered on her retirement from Rebel service. She was then running in government employ, as far as the obstructions at the mouth of the Savannah River, where she transferred her cargo and returned again. There was a channel through these obstructions, but few pilots could take a vessel through them.

Only a few days after the capture of the city, a blockade-runner, fresh from Manchester, England, in happy ignorance of the result, carefully dodged our vessels, which, just as carefully kept out of the way, and made her way into the harbour. She was fast to the dock before the mistake was discovered, when her commander was arrested, and her cargo confiscated.

The commander of the *Planter* was a "coloured person" of some consequence. One of our officers going on board mistook him for the boot-black, and sang out, "Hello, cuffee, black my boots?"

The dusky captain turned, with a look of disdain and answered, "I dunno nuffin bout boot blackin'. I commands dis craft, I is."

Lieutenant Fales took passage with me for New York. Wright's term of service having expired, he remained at Savannah to be mustered out, and I bade him an earnest farewell.

Steamship *Ashland*, Hilton Head, *December 30.*

We were transferred from the *Planter* to the *Delaware* during the night, and reached Hilton Head, S. C., in the afternoon where we were ticketed by the steamer *Ashland* for the Empire State—bless her dear old name! Many a poor fellow who started out with us will never again press her soil, nor be welcomed home by those who are anxiously awaiting their coming.

The *Ashland* is a small ocean steamer, and was commanded by Thomas Cowdry, an old sea captain, weather-beaten and brave.

In a Gale off Cape Hatteras, *January 2,* 1865.

New Year's day we were in an awful gale, which threatened us with a speedy and watery grave. All the passengers were sea-sick, and all of the crew, save those directly connected with the management of the vessel. This being my first experience with old Neptune, my case was none of the mildest. The captain comforted us by expatiating on the strong points of his vessel, and pointing out her beauties in a manner quite mystifying to a landsman.

New York, *January 4.*

Our vessel grated along the wharf about twelve o'clock at night, and I awoke to the glorious realisation that I was again breathing the air of my native State. There was an exhilarating rapture in the thought, that has fixed its memory firmly in my mind. I hope never to become so hardened that that patriotic and Christian exultation will be an unpleasant recollection.

With many a brave and fondly cherished comrade,—and with thousands whose faces I never knew, but whose sufferings I shared,—I can sing,—

> *Now our prison life is over! Ah! it is a pleasant thought,*
> *And we here await our furloughs, ere again our homes are sought.*
> *Farewell South, and all thy dead lines! Farewell traitors, robbers too!*
> *Cherished friends of youth and childhood, we are coming home to you!*
> *And will not your smiles of welcome half repay our griefs and cares,*
> *When once more you see us sitting in the old familiar chairs?*
> *But there's One who reigns above us—we should give our thanks to him,*
> *For the bright hopes in the bosoms, where sweet hope alas was dim.*
> *For his kind and loving presence, that at last we lived to stand*
> *Free from prison life in Dixie, in our own beloved and loyal land.*
> *Let us pray for peace forever, for the Union glad and free,*
> *With a tear for comrades faithful, whom we never more shall see.*
> *Ever trusting One above us, though the clouds may gather fast,*
> *Knowing well our Father's mansion will receive us at the last.*

CHAPTER 18

At Millin—"Camp Lawton"

(*The succeeding pages are devoted principally to the testimony of individuals who have been confined in other prisons.*)

Conspicuous upon the list of Rebel prisons stands the pen known South as Camp Lawton, near Millin, Georgia.

The following is the testimony of Sergeant W. Goodyear, Seventh Regiment, C.V., who was removed to that place from Andersonville on the 1st of November, 1864.

It was pleasantly situated, about eighty miles north of Savannah, in a country where pine forests abound. Indeed, these were a prominent feature in the external surroundings of many of the Southern prisons. Trees would be felled, a clearing made, and here located the rude structure that was to be the cheerless home of thousands for long, weary months. Could a voice be given to these silent groves, and they become witnesses of what they have seen and heard, what revelations would be made of things that can never be known now!

The medium of human language fails to convey all the meaning involved in prison life in the South. It is true that a great part of the suffering in this present war, as in all wars, must forever remain with the secrets of unwritten history. A few, who were themselves actors in the tragic scenes, may rehearse the story of their individual experience, and thus furnish, as it were, a key to unlock the gates through which others may enter and take a look. This is the only way in which the people at large can become acquainted with this thrilling portion of the war; and authentic and reliable statements are therefore of deep interest and importance.

The Inclosure

Forty-four acres of ground were inclosed by the stockade at Millin. The large pine timber, which was cut down at the commencement of operations for building the prison, was left upon the ground; and when the first prisoners went into their confine ent there, they found these to be greatly to their advantage; for they were able to construct for themselves comfortable huts of logs and branches lying about them. In this respect they were more fortunate than many, or most others. The last division that entered had no shelter at all, or at least of any account. A small stream of good water ran through the centre, which the men highly prized, particularly as it afforded the much needed privilege of bathing. At the time of my arrival there, the list of prisoners numbered nine thousand. The weather was very cold and stormy; and as the majority of the men were very poorly clad, many of them being without shoes, blankets, or coats, and also without shelter, the suffering was very great; No medicine was issued to the men within the stockade, and but very few were taken outside to the hospital; consequently the mortality was fearful.

Average Number of Deaths Per Day

The number of deaths averaged from twenty-five to thirty-five per day. The prevailing diseases were such as are common to almost all prisons—the scurvy, diarrhoea, and rheumatism. It was no uncommon occurrence for the morning light to reveal the pallid faces of three or four prisoners who had laid down side by side, showing that death had claimed them all during the night. Such sights were heart-rending to the most unfeeling- the most stoical.

The prisoner is condemned to these things, and there is no alternative but for him to gaze upon them, however sad and revolting they may be. He must steel himself against that which once would have sent sympathy through his whole being—a gushing tide. It could not be that the fountain of pity be stirred to its depths so often. Nature could not sustain the pressure; therefore it seems that the whole is something like a martyr process, in which the very juices of life are crushed out by an uncontrollable force.

At the beginning of my stay at Millin, the rations which were issued were double the amount we had at Andersonville. We drew one pint of meal, six ounces of uncooked beef, six spoonfuls of rice, one teaspoonful of salt, as our allowance for twenty-four hours. Beans were sometimes substituted for rice; but these were so much eaten by insects that they were often thrown away without being tasted. After a little while, however, the quantity decreased every day, so that it became nearly as small and poor as those issued in other prisons.

Inducements to Enter the Rebel Service

The prospect of being exchanged or paroled was so small that some availed themselves of the opportunity to take the oath of allegiance to the Confederate government, and entered the Rebel service. The inducements which were offered them to do this, were three bushels of sweet potatoes, a suit of clothes, and one hundred dollars in Confederate scrip. I was myself acquainted with quite a number who did this; and although I would make no excuse for them, I know the motive by which they were actuated. They knew no chance of getting out of prison alive. They had barely clothes to cover their nakedness, and they thought to prolong their existence in this way; and coupled with this was the idea of escaping and fleeing to the Union lines at the very first opportunity. But the whole thing was considered a mean, disgraceful act by every true patriot I would have died a dozen deaths rather than to have been guilty of such a thing, and there were thousands of others of the same mind.

Voting at Millin Prison

As the time of the presidential election drew near, the Rebels expressed a desire that we should vote upon the question ourselves. Accordingly ballot-boxes were procured, and on the day when the people of the North were deciding the momentous issue, we gathered together in Millin Prison, and in the midst of great excitement, gave expression to our political preferences. We knew that it was war or peace. As we deposited our votes, so did we speak for one or the other, and show forth our position in the country's cause. At sunset the votes were counted, and the result was three thousand and fourteen votes for Lincoln, and ten hundred and fifty for McClellan.

CAMP TOO NEAR THE DEAD-LINE

Came too Near the Dead Line

I am indebted to O. E. Dahl, late lieutenant, Fifteenth Wisconsin Infantry, for the following particulars relative to the murder of Lieutenant Turbayne, which occurred after my escape from Columbia.

About ten o'clock on the morning of the 1st of December, 1864, Camp Sorghum was startled with the report of a musket, and soon the news spread through camp that Lieutenant Turbayne, Sixty-eighth New-York Infantry, had been shot-murdered by one of the guard, a Mr. Williams of Newbury Court House, South Carolina.

Turbayne was walking along a path that ran by the corner of a hut, near the "dead-line," but inside of it. Along this path the prisoners had walked hundreds of times without fear, for it was on our own ground. As Turbayne came along, the guard brought his piece to the shoulder, halted, and ordered him back. He turned to go, walked a step or two, when the villain shot him through the back, the ball passing through his lungs. He staggered a few steps, fell, and died within a few minutes.

Not only did Major Griswold refuse to investigate the matter, but after the murderer had been relieved by the officer of the day, he sent him back on duty that afternoon on the front line, and also into camp next morning, surrounded by a bodyguard, for fear the officers would do violence to him—an insult of the blackest dye.

Chapter 19

Salisbury Prison

The prison at Salisbury, North Carolina, which became so, notorious during the war as one of the most loathsome dungeons in Rebeldom, was at first intended as a place of punishment for Southern soldiers guilty of military offences, and as a place of committal for hostages, who where usually sentenced to hard labour. It more recently came into general use, and hundreds of unfortunate victims said their last farewell in that miserable den. In order that we may obtain a better view of this horrible abode, I will transcribe the testimony of Messrs. Richard son and Brown, both widely known as correspondents for the public press.

The following statement was made by the former, before the Committee on the Conduct of the War:

> I was captured on a hay-bale in the Mississippi River, opposite Vicksburg, on the 3rd of May, 1863, at midnight. After a varied experience in six different prisons, I was sent to Salisbury on the 3rd of February, 1864, from which place I escaped on the 18th of December following.
>
> For months, Salisbury was the most endurable prison I had seen; there were six hundred inmates. They were exercised in the open air, comparatively well fed, and kindly treated. Early in October ten thousand regular prisoners of war arrived. It immediately changed into a scene of cruelty and horror; it was densely crowded, rations were cut down and issued very irregularly; friends outside could not even send in a plate of food.
>
> RATIONS.
>
> The prisoners suffered considerably, and often intensely, for the want of bread and shelter; those who had to live or die on pris-

on rations, always suffered from hunger; very frequently, one or more divisions of one thousand men would receive no rations for twenty-four hours; sometimes they were without food for forty-eight hours. A few, who had money, would pay from five to twenty dollars in Rebel currency for a little loaf of bread. Many, though the weather was inclement and snow frequent, sold the coats from their backs and shoes from their feet. I was assured, on authority entirely trustworthy, that a great commissary warehouse near the prison was filled with provisions. The commissary found it difficult to find storage for his corn and meal; and when a subordinate asked the post commandant, Major John H. Gee, "Shall I give the prisoners full rations?" he replied with an oath, "No! give them quarter rations."

I know from personal observation, that corn and pork, are very abundant in the region about Salisbury.

Prisoners Without Shelter

For weeks the prisoners had no shelter whatever; they were all thinly clad, thousands were barefooted, not one in twenty had an overcoat or blanket, many hundreds were without shirts, and hundreds were without blouses. One Sibley tent and one A tent were furnished to each squad of one hundred; with the closest crowding, these sheltered about half the prisoners. The rest burrowed in the ground, crept under the buildings, or shivered through the night in the open air upon the frozen ground.

If the Rebels, at the time of our capture had not stolen our shelter-tents, blankets, clothing, and money, they would have suffered little from cold. If the prison authorities had permitted them, either on parole or under guard, to cut logs within two miles of the prison, the men would have built comfortable and ample barracks in one week; but the commandant would not consent,—he did not even furnish one-half the fuel needed.

Horrible Condition of the Hospitals

The hospitals were in a horrible condition. More than half who entered them died in a few days. The deceased, always without coffins, were loaded into the dead carts, piled on each other like logs of wood, and so driven out to be thrown in a trench and covered with earth.

The Rebel surgeons were generally humane and attentive, and endeavoured to improve the shocking condition of the hospitals; but the Salisbury and Richmond authorities disregarded their protests.

THE ATTEMPTED OUTBREAK

On the 25th of November, many of the prisoners had been without food for forty-eight hours, and were desperate, without any matured plan. A few of them said, 'We may as well die in one way as another; let us break out of this horrible place.' Some of them wrested the guns from a relief of fifteen Rebel soldiers, just entering the yard, killing two who resisted, and wounding five or six others, and attempted to open the fence; but they had neither adequate tools nor concert of action. Before they could effect a breach, every gun of the garrison was turned on them.

The field pieces opened with grape and canister, and they dispersed to their quarters. In five minutes from its beginning the attempt was quelled, and hardly a prisoner was to be seen in the yard. The Rebels killed sixteen in all, and wounded sixty. Not one-tenth of the prisoners had taken part in the attempt; and many of them were ignorant of it until they heard the guns. Deliberate, cold-blooded murders of peaceable men, where there was no pretence that they were breaking any prison regulation, were very frequent.

Our lives were never safe for one moment. Any sentinel, at any hour of the day or night, could deliberately shoot down any prisoner, or fire into a group of them, black or white, and never be taken off his post for it.

I left about six thousand and five hundred remaining in garrison on the day of my escape, and they were then dying at the average rate of twenty-eight per day, or thirteen *per cent*, a month. The simple truth is, that the Rebel authorities are murdering our soldiers at Salisbury by cold and hunger, while they might easily supply them with ample food and fuel. They are doing this systematically, and I believe are killing them intentionally, for the purpose either of forcing our government to an exchange, or forcing our men into their own army.

The testimony of Mr. Brown, also a correspondent of the *Tribune*, corroborates the above statements of Mr. Richardson. He says:

> I have often wished that I could obtain a photograph of that room in Salisbury Prison; for I can give no idea of its repulsive-

ness and superlative squalor.

ORIGINAL DESIGN OF SALISBURY PRISON.

The prison was formerly a cotton factory, about ninety by thirty feet; and when we were there, they had only six or seven hundred confined within its walls. A dirtier, smokier, drearier, and more unwholesome place I had never seen than the room in which we were placed. It reminded me of some old junk-shop in South Street of the city I had left, and was hung round with filthy rags, tattered quilts and blankets, reeking with vermin, which the wretched inmates used as clothes and bed covering, and thronged mostly with Northern and Southern citizens, most of whom were in garments long worn out, and as far removed from cleanliness as the wearers from happiness. In that abhorred abode we were compelled to eat and sleep as best we might.

There were but two stoves, both old and broken, in the room; and they gave out no heat, but any quantity of smoke, which filled the apartment with bitter blueness. Vermin swarmed everywhere; they tortured us while we tried to sleep on our coarse blankets, and kept us in torment when awake. No light of any kind was furnished us; and there we sat night after night in the thick darkness, inhaling the foul vapours and the acrid smoke, longing for the morning, when we could again catch a glimpse of the overarching sky.

PRISON LIFE

Think of this death-life month after month! Think of men of delicate organisation, accustomed to ease and luxury, of fine taste, and a passionate love for the beautiful, without a word of sympathy, or a whisper of hope, wearing their days out amid such scenes. Not a pleasant sound, nor a sweet odour, nor a vision of fairness, ever reached them. They were buried as completely as if they lay beneath the ruins of Pompeii or Herculaneum. They breathed mechanically, but were shut out from all that renders existence endurable. Every sense was shocked perpetually, and yet the heart, by a strange inconsistency, kept up its throbs, and preserved the physical being of a hundred and fifty wretched captives, who, no doubt, often prayed to die.

Few persons can have any idea of a long imprisonment in the South. They usually regard it as an absence of freedom, a deprivation of the pleasures and excitements of ordinary life. They do not take into consideration the scant and miserable rations that no one, unless he be half-famished, can eat; the necessity of going cold and hungry in the wet and wintry season; the constant torture from vermin, of which no care or caution can free one; the total isolation; the supreme dreariness, the dreadful monotony, the perpetual turning inward of the mind upon itself, the self-devouring of the heart, week after week, month after month, and year after year.

CHAPTER 20

At Andersonville—"Camp Sumter"

It is from no unfair motives that I am induced to make the following statement of what I saw and experienced while a prisoner in the hands of the Rebels during the spring, summer, and autumn of 1864. I have tried to give a truthful account of some of the cruelties and sufferings which our poor boys were called to endure in filthy, loathsome Southern prisons and hospitals. It seems to me there can be no reason for anyone to make a false report of the miseries we received at the hands of our heartless captors and brutal prison-keepers. To tell the truth of them is all that is needed to convince any reasonable man of their barbarities and fiendish attempt to deprive our soldiers, whom the fortune of war had thrown into their power, of every comfort and enjoyment of life.

CAPTURE OF PLYMOUTH

But to my narrative. I was captured April 2nd, 1864, at Plymouth, North Carolina. It is to the credit of the Rebel soldiers whose good fortune it was to capture our command, stationed there to hold and defend the place, that we were treated with considerable courtesy and kindness while in their power. To my knowledge, no outrages were committed upon any of our white troops, though I believe the small negro force with us fared very hard. Our men were allowed to retain their blankets and overcoats, and all little articles of value which they might have upon their persons. Many of the men had about them large sums of money, which they were allowed to keep.

MARCH FROM PLYMOUTH TO TARBORO'

From Plymouth a long and wearisome march was made to Tarboro', a very pretty town, situated on the Neuse, a few miles from Goldsboro. By the time we arrived there the men were much fagged and worn out. The last day of the march we were without rations, and suffered a great deal from hunger and weariness. Soon after reaching our camping-ground, near the town, rations were issued to us. There were a few cow peas, or beans, more properly, some cornmeal, a small piece of bacon, and a very meagre allowance of salt, for each man. Some old iron kettles, tins, etc., were provided for us to cook our food in, and a small quantity of wood furnished; and we managed to prepare a repast which was very palatable to our well-whetted appetites. A system of trading was immediately commenced, which was carried on for a while very briskly, but was finally prohibited by the Rebel authorities. Our men would barter away their watches, rings, gold pen-holders, pocket-knives, coat-buttons, etc., for Confederate pone cakes, Hard bread, and bacon, from the Rebels. The most exorbitant prices were demanded by both parties; our men, however, generally getting the best bargain. We had remained at Tarboro' but a few days when orders were received to remove all the Union prisoners who could travel to Andersonville, Ga., immediately. We had already suffered much, both from hunger and exposure. Many were sick and feeble. All were anxious to leave, and we felt much relief at hearing that preparations had been made to remove us to a pleasanter and more fruitful portion of the Confederacy.

Andersonville in the Distance

We were informed that Camp Sumter, the prison to which we were going, occupied a delightful locality, and also that our food there would be more wholesome and plenteous than that which we had yet received. Their fair accounts and pleasing stories but increased our anxiety to be off; and it was with no little pleasure that, on the morning of April 29th, we bade *adieu* to the gloomy field into which we had been turned as so many brutes, and marched with quite joyous hearts to the depot in town. Here we were confined, crowded by forties into small and loathsome box-cars.

Besides our own enormous numbers, six Rebel guards were stationed in each carriage; a name which I heard applied by a foppish young officer to the miserable concern aboard which we were literally packed. Of course, the Rebels occupied the doors, and we nearly suffocated. Under such circumstances, many of the boys, less sanguine and hopeful than others, began to express doubts concerning the stories which we had heard; and intimated that they were all mere fabrications to deceive us, and make it an easier matter to convey us to Camp Sumter. Without doubt, such was the case. It is certain that they made the utmost efforts to get us through to the stockade at Andersonville under as small a guard as possible.

Arrival at Charleston

We arrived in Charleston on Sunday morning, May 1st. To our great surprise, we found that some of the inhabitants of the city were friendly to us. They distributed tobacco and cigars among the men, and some secretly brought them food. Months afterwards, some of our suffering, dying boys found inestimable friends in the Sisters of Charity, who abode in the city.

Leaving Charleston at an early hour in the afternoon, we were hurried on at quite a rapid rate toward Savannah, Georgia. About six o'clock in the evening it commenced storming very hard, and, being on platform cars, we were thoroughly drenched with rain.

At about nine o'clock we changed cars a short distance from Savannah for Macon, at which place we arrived the following day a little past noon.

I was much pleased with Macon. It is a handsome city, and pleasantly situated on the Ocmulgee River—a stream of some importance. It contained a number of fine residences, several churches, two or three large iron foundries, and a car-factory, I believe. Trees, flowers, and gardens, presented an appearance not unlike that of early summer at home. Almost everything there was looking pleasant and beautiful, and I felt very sad at leaving, knowing, as I then did, something of the true character of our future abode.

Arrival at Andersonville

Late in the afternoon of May 2nd we left Macon on our way to Andersonville, at which place we arrived sometime in the evening. Soon after our arrival there, we were marched into an open field nearby, where we remained during the night. It being very cold, large fires had been made by the Rebel soldiers for our comfort. For this little act of kindness we indeed felt very grateful to them. The next morning, May 3rd, a sinister-looking little foreigner came down to us, and, with considerable bluster and many oaths, began to form us into detachments, containing two hundred and seventy men each. These detachments were subdivided into messes of ninety each, and placed under the control of a sergeant, whose duty it was to attend roll-call, drawing rations, etc. At length, everything being ready, we were escorted into the prison under a strong guard.

It is impossible to describe our feelings at this time. Everywhere around us were men in the most abject wretchedness and misery. Immediately on our arrival among them they began to gather around us, and, in a very touching manner, related the sad story of their sufferings and wrongs. We could only sympathize with them. Beyond that, we could do nothing. We knew full well that the same cruelties which they had experienced were in store for us. The prospect before us was dark indeed. In the afternoon of the day on which I entered the prison, I ventured out some distance into the camp. Everywhere was the most unmistakable evidence of intense suffering and destitution. Hundreds of the men were without shelter, and but very few had any comfortable clothing.

The supply of wood was very small—scarcely enough to cook with; and the poor fellows were obliged to lie, night after night, week after week, on the cold, damp ground, without even a fire to warm themselves by.

The Rebels may claim that there was some cause for not issuing a sufficient quantity of food to our prisoners at Andersonville; but for not granting us wood enough to keep us warm, and to cook with, there can be no apology. On three sides of the prison there was an immense woodland, from which all the wood that we needed could have been provided with very little difficulty. The same holds true in regard to shelter. I am persuaded that it was an act of premeditated inhumanity on the part of our enemies not to give us shelter.

It would have required but a few weeks time, and a few scores of hands, to have built barracks for our comfortless boys there, which would have been the means of saving hundreds of precious lives. If the Rebels would have granted us even the rough, unhewn logs, and axes to work with, we would have built them ourselves.

The camp at this time was in a most loathsome condition. It then covered an area of about fifteen acres, and was inclosed by a high stockade, built of pine logs, hewn and closely joined together.

Upward of twenty feet from the stockade was—

The Fatal Dead-Line,

Beyond which any poor fellow passing was almost certain to be fired upon by some of the ever watchful sentries. In the centre of the camp, and extending entirely around it, was a broad ravine, which, toward the beginning of summer, became one of the filthiest places imaginable, and was one of the chief causes of the vast amount of sickness which existed during the months of July and August following. About this time, May 10th, the average rate of mortality daily, was upward of fifteen. It afterward rose as high as seventy-five and one hundred.

Sunday, May 15th, a wretched cripple, who had the reputation about camp of being a very dangerous fellow, willing, for a double ration, to inform the Rebels of all plans made for escape which he might discover or accidentally hear of, was mortally wounded by a Rebel sentinel while on duty. For some unknown reason, the miserable man purposely passed beyond the dead-line. The guard ordered him to go back; he refused to do so, and used some insulting language in reply. The sentry then fired upon him. He fell, horribly wounded, and lived only about two hours.

Sunday, May 22nd, a little incident of some note occurred in camp, to the great satisfaction of the well-disposed. It must be confessed that great demoralisation prevailed among the prisoners. Quarrels and fights were of frequent occurrence.

A Band of *Desperadoes*

But the worst of all were the murderous deeds perpetrated by a desperate set of fellows, who had banded themselves together for the purpose of robbing the defenceless among them. From the sick and powerless they would steal blankets and pails for cooking in; and if a man was known to possess money, he was in danger of being deprived of it all, and possibly of his life besides. This morning one of the heartless scoundrels had been caught in the act of stealing from some one of his companions, and

Interior view of Anderson Prison

met with summary punishment. A part of his head and beard were shaven, and he was then exposed to the view of any who might wish to see him.

After this he was turned over to the commandant of the prison, who immediately released him, but promised the men that in the future they might inflict what punishment they should deem proper on all whom they should catch engaged in robbing their comrades. The prime cause of all this demoralisation among the men was the treatment they received at the hands of the Rebels. Had the Confederate authorities provided food in sufficient quantities for our men, and furnished other necessary comforts, it is altogether possible that no such deeds would have been committed in the camp; certainly, they would have been very rare.

Rations

Toward the close of May our rations were cut down fearfully. Starvation really began to stare us in the face. There were but few who were not suffering the pangs of hunger continually. Our daily allowance was only about half of a small loaf of corn bread, about four ounces of bacon, and a little mush made of Indian meal partially cooked in water.

A portion of the camp drew raw rations, and fared somewhat better than those whose food was prepared before issued to them. Our food, when cooked outside, was always prepared in the most careless and indifferent manner. It not unfrequently occurred that even the meagre supply of bread which we did receive was sent into us half cooked, and, when in this condition, it would become during the night totally unfit to eat.

About the close of summer, cooked beans were issued to us. These were always in a most disgusting state, and could have been eaten only by starving men. There was always a copious supply of gravel, pods, and, what was still worse, bugs, in each man's allowance of this miserable farce.

June 3rd, a large number of wounded men were received at the camp, many of them in very destitute circumstances.

But few, if any of them, were admitted to the hospital, though a large number had severe and painful wounds. Their sufferings became intense, almost unendurable. Without shelter during the day, they suffered indescribably from scorching, burning heat, and at night perhaps not less so from the cold. Many died. It could not be otherwise. Who but the merciless enemies of our country can be held accountable for this fiendish sacrifice of valuable lives?

An Unjust Order

The morning of June 9th, a very unjust order was promulgated throughout camp. We had been permitted to send, nearly every day, a small squad of men from some of the detachments, under Rebel guards, into the woods nearby, to procure some fuel for the camp, but it was now decided that no more should be allowed to go forward until they would solemnly pledge themselves not to attempt to escape while outside the stockade for that purpose; and if, after having given their pledge, they should violate it, the detachment to which they belonged should receive rations only every alternate day until the time that those who had escaped should be recaptured. To go without wood was impossible; to submit was the only way by which we could obtain it, and consequently we were under the necessity of yielding to the base demand.

Sunday morning, June 19th, one of our men, unfortunately getting beyond the dead-line, was fired upon by the guard. He was missed, but the ball wounded two others, one severely.

On the 21st, another man was shot while merely reaching beyond the dead-line for a small piece of wood which he needed.

Barbarous Treatment of the Sick

Toward the close of June, sickness and death began to prevail in camp to an alarming extent. The men died by scores daily. But few were admitted to the hospital, and even when received there, it was not until life was nearly extinct. The old prisoners who had been incarcerated for months at Belle Island, were falling away with fearful rapidity. Nearly all those still living, could see nothing before them but a slow, torturing death, from a most painful disease, which had been caused by a want of proper food, and constant exposure. None can fully realize the intense agony, the horrid suspense and wretchedness, felt by these unfortunate men, but those who have had a like experience.

Indeed, their sufferings were beyond description. Only a few could receive medical treatment, and that scarcely worth mentioning, while in every part of camp were as brave and loyal soldiers as any that had ever taken up arms in defence of freedom, suffering and dying in a manner that might have shocked even the rude sensibilities of an American savage. It seemed that the more bitter our anguish became, the more delighted were our fiendish keepers. Not satisfied with the cruel ties inflicted upon us, they even carried their animosities beyond this life, and declined to give a Christian burial to our dead. I will not now longer dwell upon this subject. It is too painful to contemplate.

July 13th, one of the men in attempting to procure some clean water to drink, passed a little beyond the dead-line, and was fired upon by two of the guards almost simultaneously. Both balls missed him, but took effect upon two other men, killing one of them immediately.

About the middle of July I was fortunate enough to make the acquaintance of a most excellent young man from Philadelphia, a member of the Seventh Pennsylvania Reserve Corps Volunteers—

Joseph Egalf,

by name, who was actively engaged in caring for our neglected wounded men. From morning to night, he went about dressing their wounds, and ministering to their wants, and was unremitting in his efforts to benefit and comfort them. All in suffering had his sympathy and compassion, and his aid, so far as it was in his power to render assistance. What finally became of him I do not know, but, should he be living, it is hoped something may be done to reward him handsomely for his many acts of love and kindness toward our poor boys who were with him at Andersonville.

I find the following written in my diary under date of July 25th: While walking in camp this morning, I observed several poor fellows lying upon the ground, without shelter, blanket, coat, or even blouse—merely shirt and pants to protect them from the bitter cold of the past night. There are a great many in camp in the same condition, and hundreds who are without shelter, blanket, and overcoat.

To some it may seem incredible that it should be very cold

during the night at this season of the year, but such was indeed the case.

It may be asked, what became of the prisoners clothing? I answer that, except in a few instances, it was stolen by the Rebels. Many a poor fellow can remember how unceremoniously he was stripped of almost everything of value in his possession in an hour after his capture. Resistance was useless. To resist was to expose one's self to certain death. If a bare command would not bring a man out of his new boots, or induce him to give up his coat, a loaded pistol pointed at his head would.

July 27th, another of our men was shot. He received a horrible wound in the head, and was carried out of camp in a dying condition.

August 4th, still another was shot, receiving a severe wound through the body. August 6th, another cold-blooded murder was committed.

One of the men, passing a little too near the stockade, was shot dead by a guard on duty. It had become dangerous to pass at the regular crossing. The sentinels seemed to be more vigilant than ever before in watching for opportunities to shoot down our poor unarmed men. No one was safe. No warning was given to a thoughtless intruder. The first thing one would know of his terrible condition after passing the fatal line, was a quick, sharp report, a groan, and all was over—another murder was committed.

About the middle of August, the rate of mortality was about eight per day. Diarrhoea and scurvy were the chief scourges of the camp. The fearful work of death was visible everywhere around us. I have frequently seen as many as thirty dead men lying in a row at the prison gate to be carried out for burial. It was sad, indescribably so, to see these brave men dying so far from home and its hallowed associations. No fond parents near to speak words of comfort and tenderness. None able to minister to their temporal necessities—none who could alleviate their sufferings. Alone they must writhe in the agonies of death, alone to die.

It was under such circumstances of darkness and misery, that the shining truths of Christianity shone out before men in their unsurpassed glory and heavenly beauty. Many a freed, joyous spirit, went from that foul, loathsome prison, to immortal life and happiness.

Thus far, only some of the physical sufferings consequent to our imprisonment have been briefly mentioned; it is now time to refer, for a few moments, to the—

Intense Mental Trials

and afflictions which we prisoners experienced.

In my diary, under date of August 24th, I find the following:—

> 'I believe the loss of health, exposure to privations, and physical sufferings consequent upon the manner of life in which we are now compelled to live, are not the saddest effects of our present captivity. But that which is the most lamentable is the mental debility, which, under the present state of things, we must necessarily experience.'

Again,

> 'The finer feelings—that which makes more lovely—as social being, love, affection, friendship, kindness, and courtesy, are being constantly deadened—rooted out from the heart, leaving it in a most woeful condition.'

Scarcely an hour in which anxiety about distant friends, suspense in regard to the future, and frequent despair, were not felt. It seems to me that the mind must have been in a state of trouble and anxiety nearly all of the time its frail tenement was suffering from confinement and disease. It was almost impossible to procure reading matter. Some of the soldiers had Bibles and Testaments, which were eagerly sought after, and read by many of the men.

It was with great difficulty one could think very attentively about other subjects than home and release from imprisonment. A topic for conversation might be introduced among a squad of men; perhaps they might talk about it for a few moments, but it would soon be dropped, and home, friends, and possibility's or probability of exchange would come up for discussion.

Men—brave men, indeed—became gloomy and despondent. Light faded from the once brilliant, fiery eye; the colour disappeared from the manly countenance; manhood seemed to forget itself; the entire man was speedily drifting toward a fearful ruin. Hope had nearly vanished. The mind was labouring under intense agony. To some the burden was too much, and they have never recovered from its baneful effects. Others have nearly recovered, but the scars remain.

REMOVAL OF PRISONERS FROM ANDERSONVILLE

September 7th, the removal of the prisoners from Camp Sumter to other parts of the Confederacy was commenced. We were induced by the Rebel authorities to believe that this unexpected movement was for a general exchange. With this belief our men could be sent away with only a small force guarding them, which was a consideration of no little importance with the Rebels just at that time.

Suddenly stricken down with a violent attack of the scurvy, I was unable to leave with my detachment, and was left with the sick in camp. After suffering several days, I managed to get out with the first squad of sick which left for Florence, South Carolina. I was quite weak and feeble when I arrived at Florence, but a change of climate and diet rapidly improved my condition, and in a few days I was able to walk about without crutches. Soon afterward I was detailed as hospital steward, and paroled. From that time till my release, Nov. 30th, my treatment was much better than it had been while I was at Camp Sumter. But in regard to that received by the thousands of poor fellows in the prison, there was but little apparent change. They suffered from cold and hunger perhaps more than while at Andersonville.

I will here close my accounts of the sufferings of our friends. So far as I am concerned personally, I can forgive our bitter foes the cruelties which they have inflicted upon me. I do not desire revenge. That is farthest from my heart. God will punish them for their evil deeds. They have already suffered terribly. I feel that all should now try to do whatever they can to narrow the breach which exists between them and ourselves. I have always been glad our government so nobly declined to resort to retaliation. We cannot afford to be cruel. It is, our highest honour to award good for evil.

The magnanimity of our people is beyond question, and our enemies must acknowledge it. Our arms have conquered their proud hosts; our kindness must now subdue the enmity of their hearts. We must be neither too lenient nor too severe. To the leaders who precipitated us into four years of bloodshed and war, the severest punishment which the law can give; but to the poor misguided masses, that clemency which only a noble people are capable of exercising.

(The following poetical description of prison life in the South is from the genial pen of an Andersonville prisoner, whose name I have not been able to learn.)

Union Prisoners, From Dixie's Sunny Land
Air—*Twenty Years Ago.*

1.

Dear friends and fellow-soldiers brave, come listen to our song,
About the Rebel prisons, and our sojourn there so long;
Yet our wretched state and hardships great no one can understand,
But those who have endured this fate in Dixie's sunny land.

2

When captured by the chivalry, they strip't us to the skin,
But failed to give us back again the value of a pin—
Except some lousy rags of gray, discarded by their band—
And thus commenced our prison life in Dixie's sunny land.

3.

With a host of guards surrounding us, each with a loaded gun,
We were stationed in an open plain, exposed to rain and sun;
No tent or tree to shelter us, we lay upon the sand—
Thus, side by side, great numbers died in Dixie's sunny land.

4.

This was the daily "bill of fare" in that Secesh saloon—
No sugar, tea or coffee there, at morning, night or noon;
But a pint of meal, ground cob and all, was served to every man,
And for want of fire we ate it raw in Dixie's sunny land.

5.

We were by these poor rations soon reduced to skin and bone,
A lingering starvation—worse than death! you can but own,
There hundreds lay, both night and day, by far too weak to stand,
Till death relieved their sufferings in Dixie's sunny land.

6

We poor survivors oft were tried by many a threat and bribe,
To desert our glorious Union cause, and join the Rebel tribe,
Though fain were we to leave the place, we. let them understand,
We had rather die than thus disgrace our flag! in Dixie's land.

7.

Thus dreary days and nights roll'd by—yes, weeks and months untold,
Until that happy time arrived when we were all paroled.
We landed at Annapolis, a wretched looking band,
But glad to be alive and free from Dixie's sunny land.

8

How like a dream those days now seem in retrospective view,
As we regain our wasted strength, all dressed in "Union Blue."
The debt we owe our bitter foe shall not have long to stand;
We shall pay it with a vengeance soon in Dixie's sunny land.

RATIONS ISSUED BY THE UNITED STATES GOVERNMENT TO REBEL PRISONERS OF WAR. (NOTE THE DIFFERENCE.)

Hard bread,	14 oz. per one ration, or 18 oz. soft bread, one ration.
Corn meal,	18 oz. per one ration.
Beef,	14 " " " "
Bacon or pork,	10 " " " "
Beans,	6 qts. per 100 men.
Hominy or rice,	8 lbs. " " "
Sugar,	44 " " " "
R. Coffee,	5 " ground, or 7 lbs. raw, per 100 men.
Tea,	18 oz. per 100 men.
Soap,	4 " " " "
Adamantine candles,	5 candles per 100 men.
Tallow candles,	6 " " " "
Salt,	2 qts. " " " "
Molasses,	1 qt. " " " "
Potatoes	30 lbs. " " " "

STATEMENT OF CLOTHING ISSUED TO PRISONERS OF WAR AT FORT DELAWARE,

From Sept. 1st, 1863, to May 1st, 1864.

7,175 pairs Drawers (Canton flannel).
6,260 Shirts (flannel).
8,807 pairs woollen Stockings.
1,094 Jackets and Coats.
3,480 pairs Bootees.
1,310 pairs Trousers.
4,378 woollen Blankets.

2,680 Great Coats.
Average number of prisoners. 4,489.

Appendix

The following Appendix is not as perfect as I could wish, it being very difficult to avoid errors in lists of this kind. The principal portion of the names were taken from the Rebel adjutant's book at Libby Prison, during the winter and spring of 1864, by Captain Fisher, to whom I have alluded in my preface. I compiled the remainder while imprisoned at Columbia. The post-office address of the officers has been given, as far as they could be obtained.

Those marked thus (★) died during their imprisonment.

OFFICERS

OF THE

UNITED STATES ARMY AND NAVY,

Prisoners of War, Libby Prison, Richmond, Va.

[This list comprises those officers who were imprisoned at Libby Prison during the winter and spring of 1864. They were removed from Richmond to Danville in the early part of May, and from thence to Macon, Savannah, Charleston, Columbia, Charlotte, Raleigh, and Goldsboro'.★ The succeeding list furnishes the additional captures of the summer and fall campaigns:]

BRIGADIER GENERALS.

Names.	Regiment, or Command.	Residence.
Neal Dow,	1st Brig. 2d Div. 19 A. C.,	Portland, Me.
E. P. Scammon,	3d Dept. W. Va.	
H. W. Wessells,	Plymouth, N. C.,	Washington, D. C.

COLONELS.

F. A. Bartleson,	100th Ill. Vols.	
C. H. Carlton,	80th O. Vols.,	Oswego, N. Y.
P. De Cesnola,	4th N. Y. Cav.,	New York City.
Wm. G. Ely,	18th Conn. Vols.,	New Haven, Conn.
W. P. Kindrick,	3d W. T. Cav.	
O. A. Lawson,	3d O. Vols.	
H. Le Favour,	22d Mich. Vols.,	Detroit, Mich.
R. W. McClain,	51st O. Vols.	
W. H. Powell,	2d Va. Cav.	
Thos. E. Rose,	77th Pa. Vols.	
A. D. Streight,	51st Ind. Vols.,	Indianapolis, Ind.

* A small portion of the Libby prisoners were sent North for special exchange during the month of March, and a few succeeded in escaping before we reached Georgia.

Chas. W. Tilden,	16th Me. Vols.	
A. H. Tippin,	68th Pa. Vols.,	Philadelphia, Pa.
W. T. Wilson,	123d O. Vols.	

LIEUTENANT COLONELS.

S. M. Archer,	17th Ia. Vols.,	Indianapolis, Ind.
I. F. Boyd,	20th A. C.	
T. F. Cavada,	114th Pa. Vols.	
C. Farnsworth,	1st Conn. Cav.,	Hartford, Conn.
W. A. Glenn,	89th O. Vols.	
H. B. Hunter,	123d O. Vols.	
A. P. Henry,	15th Ky. Cav.	
E. L. Hays,	100th O. Vols.,	Columbus, O.
H. C. Robart,	21st Wis. Vols.	
Wm. Irvine,	10th N. Y. Cav.,	Albany, N. Y.
O. C. Johnson,	15th Wis. Vols.	
G. C. Joslin,	15th Mass. Vols.,	Boston, Mass.
W. P. Lasselle,	9th Md. Vols.	
A. C. Lichfield,	7th Mich. Cav.,	Grand Rapids, Mich.
W. O. McMackin,	21st Ill. Vols.	
D. A. McHolland,	51st Ind. Vols.	
C. H. Martin,	84th Ill. Vols.	
J. D. Mayhew,	8th Ky. Vols.	
D. Miles,	79th Pa. Vols.	
W. B. McCreary,	21st Mich. Vols.,	Flint, Mich.
R. S. Northcott,	12th Va. Vols.	
M. Nichols,	18th Conn. Vols.,	Hartford, Conn.
Wm. Price,	139th Va. M.	
P. S. Piper,	77th Pa. Vols.	
I. J. Polsley,	8th Va. Vols.	
A. F. Rogers,	80th Ill. Vols.	
J. T. Spofford,	79th N. Y. Vols.,	Little Falls, N. Y.
J. M. Sanderson,		Brooklyn, N. Y.
G. Von Helmrich,	4th Mo. Cav.,	St. Louis, Mo.
A. Von Schrader,	A. I. Gen.	
I. H. Wing,	3d O. Vols.	
J. N. Walker,	73d Ind. Vols.	
J. Williams,	25th O. Vols.	
T. S. West,	24th Wis. Vols.,	Racine, Wis.

MAJORS.

A. Bogle,	35th U. S. C. T.,	Boston, Mass.
E. N. Bates,	80th Ill. Vols.	
W. T. Beatley,	2d O. Vols.	
C. H. Beers,	16th Ill. Cav.	
J. P. Collins,	29th Ind. Vols.	
M. E. Clarke,	5th Mich. Cav.,	Ann Arbor, Mich.
D. A. Carpenter,	2d Tenn. Cav.	
E. F. Cooke,	2d N. Y. Cav.,	Deckartown, N. J.
J. J. Edwards,	32d Mass. Vols.	
G. W. Fitzsimmons,	30th Ind. Vols.	
N. Goff, Jr.,	4th W. Va. Cav.	
J. H. Hooper,	15th Mass. Vols.,	Boston, Mass.
J. Hall,	1st Va. Cav.	
J. Henry,	5th O. Cav.	
J. B. Hill,	17th Mass. Vols.,	Chelsea, Mass.
I. H. Johnson,	11th Tenn. Vols.	
S. Kovax,	54th N. Y. Vols.	
D. M. Kercher,	10th Wis. Vols.	
W. D. Morton,	14th N. Y. Cav.,	Brooklyn, N. Y.
S. McIrvin,	2d N. Y. Cav.,	Lafayette, Ind.
B. B. McDonald,	101st O. Vols.	
A. McMahan,	21st O. Vols.	
M. Moore,	29th Ind. Vols.	
W. S. Marshall,	5th Iowa Vols.	
S. Marsh,	5th Md. Vols.	
J. R. Muhlman,	A. A. Gen.,	Woodburn, Ill.
W. P. Nieper,	57th Pa. Vols.	
W. N. Owens,	1st Ky. Cav.,	Somerset, Ky.
E. M. Pope,	8th N. Y. Cav.,	Rochester, N. Y.
L. N. Phelps,	5th Va. Vols.	
A. Phillips,	77th Pa. Vols.	
H. L. Pasco,	16th Conn. Vols.,	Hartford, Conn.
T. B. Rodgers,	140th Pa. Vols.	
W. I. Russell,	A. A. Gen.,	Albany, N. Y.
I. C. Vananda,	3d O. Vols.	
A. Von Witzel,	74th Pa. Vols.	
H. A. White,	13th Pa. Cav.	
J. B. Wade,	73d Ind. Vols.	
Harry White,	67th Pa. Vols.,	Indiana, Pa.

CAPTAINS.

W. F. Armstrong,	74th O. Vols.	
S. C. Arthurs,	67th Pa. Vols.,	Brookville, Pa.
W. Airey,	15th Pa. Cav.,	Philadelphia, Pa.
E. C. Alexander,	1st Del. Vols.	
W. B. Avery,	132d N. Y. Vols.	
J. A. Arthur,	8th Ky. Cav.	
H. H. Alban,	21st O. Vols.	
W. R. Adams,	89th O. Vols.	
C. A. Adams,	1st Vt. Cav.,	Wallingford, Vt.
J. Albright,	87th Pa. Cav.	
E. W. Atwood,	16th Me. Vols.	
C. S. Aldrich,	85th N. Y. Vols.,	Canandaigua, N. Y.
S. Allen,	85th N. Y. Vets.,	Black Creek, N. Y.

S. B. Adams,	85th N. Y. Vets.	
M. Boyd,	73d Ind. Vols.,	
Chas. Byron,	3d O. Vols.	Lenox, O.
E. Baas,	20th Ill. Vols.	
L. T. Borgess,	67th Pa. Vols.	Dyberry, Pa.
W. K. Boltz,	181st Pa. Vols.	
H. R. Bending,	61st O. Vols.,	Circleville, O
M. R. Baldwin,	2d Wis. Vols.	
C. D. Brown,	18th Conn. Vols.	
W. P. Bender,	123d O. Vols.	
John Bird,	14th Pa. Cav.	
L. D. Blinn,	100th O. Vols.	
D. E. Bohannan,*	3d Tenn. Cav.	
D. I. Bailey,	99th N. Y. Vols.	
A. J. Bigelow,	79th Ill. Vols.	
J. Birch,	42d Ind. Vols.	
D. M. Barritt,	89th O. Vols.	
W. M. Beeman,	1st Va. Cav.	
F. Barton,	10th Mass. Vols.,	Boston, Mass.
J. H. Barton,	1st Ky. Cav.	
E. B. Bascom,	5th Iowa Vols.	
B. V. Banks,	13th Ky. Vols.	
J. G. Bush,	16th Ill. Cav.	
W. J. Barnes,	83d N. Y. Vols.	
J. A. Brown,	85th N. Y. Vets.,	Wellsville, N. Y.
G. W. Bowers,	101st Pa. Vols.,	Pittsburg, Pa.
H. S. Benner,	101st Pa. Vols.,	Gettysburg, Pa.
A. Berry,	3d Md. Cav.,	Baltimore, Md.
E. Beale,	8th Tenn. Vols.	
T. F. Burke,	16th Conn. Vols.,	Hartford, Conn.
A. Carley,	73d Ind. Vols.	
H. Casker,	1st N. Y. Cav.	
W. F. Conrad,	25th Iowa Vols.	
J. W. Chamberlin,	123d O. Vols.	
J. Carroll,	5th Md. Vols.	
J. C. Carpenter,	67th Pa. Vols.	
B. G. Casler,	154th N. Y. Vols.,	East Randolph, N. Y.
C. C. Comee,	94th N. Y. Vols.	
E. Charlier,	157th N. Y. Vols.,	New York City.
Jno. Cutler,	34th O. Vols.	
R. T. Cornwall,	67th Pa. Vols.	
Jno. Craig,	1st Va. Cav.,	Wheeling, W. Va.
Jno. Christopher,	16th U. S. Infty.	
J. P. Cummins,	9th Md. Vols.	
M. A. Cochran,	16th U. S. Infty.	
T. Clarke,	79th Ill. Vols	
J. Cusac,	21st O. Vols.	
W. A. Collins,	10th Wis. Vols.,	Milwaukee, Wis.
B. F. Campbell,	36th Ill. Vols.	
S. S. Canfield,	21st O. Vols.	
T. Cummins,	19th U. S. Infty.	
Miles Canton,	21st O. Vols.	
S. D. Connover,	121st Ill. Vols.,	Squaw Village, N. J.
G. A. Crocker,	5th N. Y. Cav.	
W. N. Cochran,	42d Ill. Vols.	

Name	Unit	Location
M. Callahan,	9th Md. Vols.	
W. E. Conway,	9th Md. Vols.	
J. P. Cummins,	9th Md. Vols.	
M. C. Carns,	3d Tenn. Vols.	
J. R. Copeland,	7th O. Cav.	
A. R. Calhoun,	1st Ky. Cav.,	Louisville, Ky.
R. S. Curd,	11th Ky. Cav.	
J. A. Clark,	7th Mich. Cav.	
A. G. Cartwright,	85th N. Y. Vets.,	Philips Creek, N. Y.
M. L. Clark,	101st Pa. Vols.,	Mansfield, Pa.
A. Compher,	101st Pa. Vols.,	Ramsburg, Pa.
J. B. Clapp,	16th Conn. Vols.,	Wethersfield, Conn.
E. G. Cratty,	103d Pa. Vols.,	Butler, Pa.
H. A. Coats,	85th N. Y. Vets.,	Wellsville, N. Y.
J. Donaghy,	103d Pa. Vols.,	Alleghany City, Pa.
E. M. Driscoll,	3d O. Vols.,	
W. N. Deung,	51st Ind. Vols.	
B. Domschke,	26th Wis. Vols.	
F. B. Doten,	14th Conn. Vols.	
F. W. Dillion,	1st Ky. Cav.	
H. C. Davis,	18th Conn. Vols.,	Canterbury, Conn.
Jno. Dunce,	A. D. C.	
W. H. Douglass,	C. S.	
K. S. Dygert,	16th Mich. Vols.	
H. Dietz,	45th N. Y. Vols.,	New York City.
J. M. Dushane,	142d N. Y. Vols.	
G. C. Davis,	4th Me. Vols.	
R. H. Day,	56th Pa. Vols.	
E. Day, Jr.,	89th O. Vols.,	Bainbridge, O.
R. Dinsmore,	5th Pa. Vols.	
E. J. Dunn,	1st Tenn. Cav.	
E. Dillingham,	10th Va. Vols.	
F. C. Dirks,	1st Tenn. Vols.	
O. Eastmond,	1st N. C. U. Vols.,	New York City.
H. H. Eberheart,	120th O. Vols.,	Wooster, O.
B. F. Evers,	100th O. Vols.	
S. H. Ewing,	26th O. Vols.	
M. Ewen,	21st Wis. Vols.,	Fond Du Lac, W.
A. Eglin,	45th O. Vols.	
Jno. M. Flinn,	51st Ind. Vols.	
E. A. Fobes,	C. S. U. S. Vols.	
B. F. Fischer,	S. O.	
A. Field,	94th N. Y. Vols.	Weedsport, N. Y.
J. B. Fay,	154th N. Y. Vols.	
E. Frey,	82d Ill. Vols.	
W. Forrester,	24th O. Vols.	
J. W. Foster,	42d Ill. Vols.,	Belvidere, Ill.
D. W. D. Freeman,	101st Pa. Vols.,	Irish Ripple, Pa.
J. E. Fisk,	2d Mass. Arty.,	Grantville, Mass.
Dl. Getman,	10th N. Y. Cav.,	Mayfield, N. Y.
G. C. Gordon,	24th Mich. Vols.,	Detroit, Mich.
G. W. Green,	19th Ind. Vols.,	Muncie, Ind.
H. W. Gimber,	150th Pa. Vols.,	Philadelphia, Pa.
W. L. Gray,	151st Pa. Vols.	
J. H. Green,	100th O. Vols.,	Fremont, O.

Name	Regiment	Residence
Chas. Gustaveson,	15th Wis. Vols.	
J. F. Gallaher,	2d O. Vols.	
J. Goetz,	22d Mich. Vols.,	Mt. Clemens, Mich.
A. G. Galbraith,	22d Mich. Vols.,	Lexington, Mich.
J. Gates,	33d O. Vols.	
O. C. Gatch,	89th O. Vols.,	Millford, O.
S. A. Glenn,	89th O. Vols.,	Hillsboro', O.
J. W. Grose,	18th Ky. Vols.	
B. Grafton,	64th O. Vols.,	Marion, O.
H. H. Gregg,	13th Penn. Cav.,	Philadelphia, Pa.
Jas. Galt,	A. Q. M.	
M. Gallagher,	2d N. J. Cav.	
Daniel Hay,	80th Ill. Vols.	
A. Hodge,	80th Ill. Vols.,	Fosterbury, Ill.
J. G. Hagler,	5th Tenn. Vols.	
A. M. Heyer,[a]	10th Va. Cav.	
J. Hendricks,	1st N. Y. Cav.	
J. Heil,	45th N. Y., Vols.,	New York City.
A. Haack,	18th N. Y. Vols.	
S. G. Hamlin,	134th N. Y. Vols.,	Schenectady, N. Y.
W. L. Hubbell,	17th Conn. Vols.	
P. H. Hart,	19th Ind. Vols.,	Edensburg, Ind.
A. Heffley,	142d Pa. Vols.,	Berlin, Pa.
W. W. Hant,	100th O. Vols.	
Chas. Hasty,	2d N. Y. Cav.,	Lafayette, Ind.
A. G. Hamilton,	12th Ky. Vols.	
T. Handy,	79th Ill. Vols.	
V. K. Hart,	19th U. S.	
H. Hescock,	1st Mo. Art'y,	St. Louis, Mo.
R. Harkness,	10th Wis. Vols.	
H. E. Hawkins,	78th Ill. Vols.,	Coastbury, Ill.
C. C. Huntley,	16th Ill. Vols.,	Springfield, Ill.
J. B. Herold,	9th Md. Vols.	
S. C. Honeycutt,	2d E. Tenn. Vols.	
J. W. Hetsler,	9th O. Cav.,	Calvina, O.
A. H. Hays,	7th Tenn. Cav.,	Lovington, Tenn.
W. Harris,	24th Mo. Cav.,	Mount Vernon, Mo.
R. H. O. Hertzog,	1st N. Y. Cav.,	New York City.
H. Hintz,	16th Conn. Vols.,	Hartford, Conn.
R. B. Hock,	12th N. Y. Cav.,	New York City.
W. C. Holt,	6th Tenn. Vols.,	Trenton, Tenn.
S. Irwin,	3d Iowa Vols.	
J. M. Imbric,	3d O. Vols.,	Wellsville, O.
F. Irsch,	45th N. Y. Vols.,	New York City.
R. O. Ives,	10th Mass. Vols.,	Rochester, N. Y.
S. F. Jones,	80th Ill. Vols.,	Jones' Creek, Ill.
R. Johnson,	6th N. Y. Cav.,	Ogdensburgh.
J. C. Johnson,	140th Pa. Vols.,	Couder's Port, Pa.
F. R. Joselyn,	11th Mass. Vols.,	Boston, Mass.
D. I. Jones,	1st Ky. Cav.	
J. S. Jackson,	22d Ill. Vols.	Salem, Ill.
J. M. Johnson,	6th Ky. Vols.	
J. A. Johnson,	11th Ky. Cav.	
J. T. Jennings,	45th O. Vols.,	Kenton, O.
W. M. Kendall,	73d Ind. Vols.,	Plymouth, Ind.
E. M. Koch.	5th Md. Vols.	

Name	Regiment	Location
S. B. King,	12th Pa. Cav.,	New Haven, Conn.
A. M. Keeler,	22d Mich. Vols.,	Disco, Mich.
D. A. Kelly,	1st Ky. Cav.	
J. Kelly,	73d Pa. Vols.	
D. F. Kelly,	73d Pa. Vols.	
J. Kennedy,	73d Pa. Vols.	
T Krause,	3d Pa. Art'y.	
W D. Lucas,	5th N. Y. Cav.,	East Gainsville, N. Y.
R. F. Lounsberry,	10th N. Y. Cav.	
L. P. Lovett,	5th Ky. Vols.	
John Lucas,	5th Ky. Vols.	
J. W. Lewis,	4th Ky. Cav.	
E. M. Lee,	5th Mich. Cav.	
J. E. Love,	8th Ky. Vols.,	St. Louis, Mo.
J. R. Laud,	66th Ind. Vols.,	Leavenworth, Ind.
J. K. Loyd,	17th Mass. Vol.,	Boston, Mass.
S. McKee,*	14th Ky. Cav.	
D. H. Mull,	73d Ind. Vols.	
D. A. McHolland,	51st Ind. Vols.,	Adriance, Ind.
J. B. McRoberts,	3d O. Vols.	
McMoor,	29th Ind. Vols.	
W. M. Morris,	93d Ill. Vols.	
H. C. McGuiddy,	1st Ten. Cav.	
F. Mennert,	5th Md. Vols.	
E. J. Mattherson,*	18th Conn. Vols.,	Dixon, Conn.
W. F. Martins,	14th Mass. Arty.	
P. Marsh,	67th Pa. Vols.	
D B. Meany,	13th Pa. Cav.	Philadelphia, Pa.
C. C. Moses,	58th Pa. Vols.	
C. A. Mann,	5th Ill. Cav.	
S. Marsh,	5th Md. Vols.	
J. McMahon,	94th N. Y. Vols.,	Titusville, Pa.
E. A. Mass,	88th Pa. Vols.	
A. J. Makepeace,	19th Ind. Vols.,	Anderson, Ind.
H. H. Mason,	2d N. Y. Cav.,	Lafayette, Ind.
C. W. Metcalf,	42d Ind. Vols.,	Dale, Ind.
J. S. McDowell,	77th Pa. Vols.	
J. G. Williams,	51st Ill. Vols.	
J. Meagher,	40th O. Vols.	
W. McGinnis,*	74th Ill. Vols.	
J. M. McComas,	9th Md. Vols.	
A. W. Metcalf,	14th N. Y. Cav.	
M. R. Milsaps,	2d E. Tenn. Vols.	
A. Marney,	2d E. Tenn. Vols.	
W. M. Murray,	2d E. Tenn. Vols.	
J. C. Martin,	1st Tenn. Arty.	
S. Meade,	111th N. Y. Vols.,	Moravia, N. Y.
G. W. Moore,	7th Tenn. Vols.,	Lovington, Tenn.
A. H. Mooney,	16th N. Y. Cav.,	Plattsburg, N. Y.
D. W. Mullin,	101st Pa. Vols.,	Bedford, Pa.
J. F. Mackey,	103d Pa. Vols.,	Clarion, Pa.
G. A. Manning,	2d Mass. Cav.,	Oldtown, Mass.
W. A. Noel,	5th Md. Vols.	
H. Noble,	9th Md. Vols.	
T. W. Olcott,	134th N. Y. Vols.	Cherry Valley, N. Y.

Name	Unit	Location
E. O'Brien,	29th Mo. Vols.,	Cape Girardeau, Mo.
W. Ottinger,	8th Tenn. Vols.	
N. C. Pace,	80th Ill. Vols.	
J. D. Phelps,	73d Ind. Vols.	
F. A. Patterson,	3d Va. Cav.	
J. F. Porter,	154th N. Y. Vols.	
J. A. Pennfield,	5th N. Y. Cav.,	Crown Point, N. Y.
E. Porter.	154th N. Y. Cav.,	Olean, N. Y.
S. V. Poole,	154th N. Y. Vols.,	Springfield, N. Y.
F. Place,	157th N. Y. Vols.	
S. H. Pillsbury,	5th Me. Vols.,	Biddeford, Me.
R. Pollock,	14th Pa. Vols.,	
G. S. Pierce,	19th U. S.,	Dubuque, Iowa.
F. W. Perry,	10th Wis. Vols.,	Menasha, Wis.
E. J. Pennypacker,	18th Pa. Cav.,	Philadelphia, Pa.
W. F. Pickerill,	5th Iowa Vols.	
J. E. Page,	5th Iowa Vols.,	Iowa City, Iowa.
J. A. Parmalee,	7th Ind. Vols.,	Valparaiso, Ind.
J. L. Poston,	13th Tenn. Vols.,	Cageville, Tenn.
J. A. Richley,	73d Ind. Vols.	
M. Russell,	51st Ind. Vols.	
P. C. Reed,	3d O. Vols.,	Hamilton, O.
W. C. Rossman,	3d O. Vols.,	Hamilton, O.
J. F. Randolph,	123d O. Vols.	
A. Robbins,	123d O. Vols.	
C. H. Riggs,	123d O. Vols.	
O. H. Rosenbaum,	123d O. Vols.,	Sandusky City, O.
W. Rowan,	Indp. Cav.	
M. Rollins,	2d Wis. Vols.	
J. C. Rose,	4th Mo. Cav.	
Thos. Reed,	1st Va. Vols.	
W. A. Robinson,	77th Iowa Vols.	
B. F. Riggs,	18th Ky. Vols.	
N. S. Randall,	2d Mo. Vols.	
J. A. Rice,	73d Ill. Vols.,	Harrisburg, Ill.
W. J. Robb,	1st Va. Vols.,	Wheeling, W. Va.
A. Rodgers,	4th Ky. Cav.,	Louisville, Ky.
C. Rowan,	96th Ill. Vols.	
S. B. Ryder,	5th N. Y. Cav.,	Arbane, N. Y.
C. Reynolds,	8th Tenn. Vols.	
W. H. Robins,	2d E. Tenn. Vols.	
J. A. Russell,	93d Ill. Vols.	Neponset, Ill.
W. J. Robb,	1st W. Va. Vols.,	Wheeling, W. Va.
T. B. Robinson,	10th Conn. Vols.,	Bristol, Conn.
W. L. Starkweather,	85th N. Y. Vols.,	Olean, N. Y.
Jas. Shaefer,	101st Pa. Vols.,	Carlisle, Pa.
F. Smullin,	103d Pa. Vols.,	Oakland, Pa.
I. B. Sampson,	2d Mass. H. Artillery,	Springfield, Mass.
A. Stewart,	—— ——,	Uniontown, Pa.
J. C. Stover,	3d Tenn. Vols.	
W. W. Searce,	51st Ind Vols.	
W. A. Swayzie,	3d O. Vols.,	Columbus, O.
D. D. Smith,	1st Tenn. Cav.	
E. Szabad,	A. D. C.,	Washington, D. C.
H. W. Sawyer,	1st N. J. Cav.	
E. A. Shepherd.	110th O. Vols.	

Name	Regiment	Location
D. Schirtz,	12th Pa. Cav.	
Geo. L. Schell,	88th Pa. Vols.,	Philadelphia, Pa.
G. H. Starr,	104th N. Y. Vols.	Rochester, N. Y.
J. R. Stone,	157th N. Y. Vols.	
Wm. Syring,	45th N. Y. Vols.	
R. Scofield,	1st Vt. Cav.,	Brattleboro', Vt.
F. M. Shoemaker,	100th O. Vols.,	Waterville, O.
J. A. Schemmerhorn,	112th Ind. Vols.	
J. C. Schroade,	77th Pa. Vols.,	Lancaster, Pa.
A. H. Stanton,	16th U. S. Inf.	
R. H. Spencer,	10th Wis. Vols.	
J. C. Stover,	3d E. Tenn. Vols.	
S. A. Spencer,	82d O. Vols.	
E. L. Smith,	19th U. S. Inf.	
J P. Singer,	33d O. Vols.	
A. P. Seuter,	2d E. Tenn. Vols.	
P. S. Scott,	85th Ill. Vols.	
M. C. Turner,	16th Conn. Vols.,	Hartford, Conn.
T. Thornton,	161st N. Y. Vols.	
John Téed,	116th Pa. Vols.	
O. Templeton,	107th Pa. Vols.	
H. D. Taylor,	100th O. Vols.	
B. E. Thomson,	A. D. C.	
T. Ten Eyck,	18th U. S. Inf.	
A. Tubbs,	9th Ky. Cav.	
T. Thornton,	5th U. S. Inf.	
G. C. Urwiler,	67th Pa. Vols.	
S. A. Urquhard,	C. S. U. S. Vols.	
J. D. Underdown,	2d E. Tenn. Vols.	
J. W. Vanderhoef,	45th N. Y. Vols.	
G. M. Van Buren,	6th N. Y. Cav.,	Washington, D. C.
J. D. Wheeler,	15th Conn. Vols.,	New Haven, Conn.
A. Wilson,	80th Ill. Vols.	
W. R. Wright,	80th Ill. Vols.	
J. A. Wistlake,	73d Ind. Vols.	
Wm. Walleck,	51st Ind. Vols.	
G. W. Warner,	18th Conn. Vols.	
C. W. White,	3d Va. Cav.,	Baltimore, Md.
W. Willets,	7th Mich. Vols.,	Birmingham, Mich.
J. C. Whiteside,	94th N. Y. Vols.,	Wyoming, N. Y.
T. E. Wentworth,	16th Me. Vols.	
W. C. Wilson,	104th N. Y. Vols.,	Spencer, Mass.
H. C. White,	94th N. Y. Vols.,	Lysander, N. Y.
C. C. Widdis,	150th Pa. Vols.,	Germantown, Pa.
Geo. M. White,	1st Va. Vols.,	Wellsburg, W. Va.
W. H. Williams,	4th N. Y. Cav.,	Albany, N. Y.
P. Wellsheimer,	21st Ill. Vols.,	Neoga, Ill.
H. P. Wands,	22d Mich. Cav.,	St. Clair, Mich.
W. B. Wicker,	21st O. Vols.	
J. E. Wilkens,	112th Ill. Vols.	
J. G. Wild,	9th N. Y. Cav.	
J. H. Wheelan,	A. Q. M.	
E. A. Wolcott,	10th Ill. Vols.	
M. G. Whitney,	29th Mo. Vols.	
H. Zeis,	80th Ill. Vols.	

LIEUTENANTS.

M. Ahern,	10th Va. Vols.	
C. L. Alstaed,	54th N. Y. Vols.,	Newark, N. J.
S. A. Albro,	80th Ill. Vols.,	Upper Alton, Ill.
Jas. Adams,	80th Ill. Vols.,	Nashville, Ill.
W. A. Adair,	51st Ind. Vols.,	North Salem, Ind.
H. Appel,	1st Md. Cav.,	Washington, D. C.
R. W. Anderson,	122d O. Vols.,	Columbus, O.
H. F. Anshutz,	12th Va. Vols.,	Moundville, W. Va.
P. S. Armstrong,	122d O. Vols.,	Gratiot, O.
H. M. Anderson,	3d Me. Vols.	
J. H. Ahlert,	45th N. Y. Vols.,	New York City.
C. L. Anderson,	3d Iowa Vols.	
G. D. Acker,	123d O. Vols.,	Fostoria, O.
H. W. Adams,	37th Ill. Vols.,	Frankfort, Ill.
E. E. Andrews,	22d Mich. Vols.,	Millford, Mich.
A. Allee,	16th Ill. Cav.,	Lincoln, Ill.
H. S. Albin,	79th Ill. Vols.,	Tuscola, Ill.
R. J. Allen,	2d E. Tenn. Vols.	
P. Atkin,	2d E. Tenn. Vols.	
A. B. Alger,	22d O. Bat.,	Mansfield, O.
J. W. Austin,	5th Iowa Vols.,	Lansing, Iowa.
H. C. Abernathy,	16th Ill. Cav.,	Paris, Mo.
W. F. Allender,	7th Tenn. Cav.	
W. R. Andrus,	16th Conn. Vols.,	East Lynn, Conn.
S. T. Andrews,	85th N. Y. Vets.,	Black Creek, N. Y.
T. I. Brownell,	51st Ind. Vols.	
J. W. Barlow,	51st Ind. Vols.,	London, Ind.
J. G. Blue,	3d O. Vols.,	Gardington, O.
O. P. Barnes,	3d O. Vols.,	Barnesville, O.
G. W. Bailey,	3d O. Vols.	
J. L. Brown,	73d Ind. Vols.	
A. H. Booher,	73d Ind. Vols.,	Westville, Ill.
J. F. Bedwell,	80th O. Vols.	
W. Blancherd,	2d U. S. Cav.	
B. F. Blair,	123d O. Vols.,	Norwalk, O.
H. S. Bevington,	123d O. Vols.	
F. W. Boyd,	123d O. Vols.,	
F. A. Breckenridge,	123d O. Vols.	Monroeville, O.
Jno. D. Babb,	5th Md. Vols.	
J. G. W. Brueting,	5th Md Vols.,	Baltimore, Md.
T. J. Borchess,	67th Pa. Vols.,	Dyberry, Pa.
W. Bierbower,	87th Pa. Vols.,	York, Pa.
G. C. Bleak,	3d Me. Vols.	
W. H. Berry,	5th Ill. Cav.	
H. Bath,	45th N. Y. Vols.,	New York City.
L. C. Bisby,	16th Me. Vols.,	Canton Mills, Me.
M. Beadle,	123d N. Y. Vols.,	South Easton, N. Y.
C. T. Barclay,	149th Pa. Vols.	
J. D. Bisby,	16th Me. Vols.,	Canton Mills, Me.
S. G. Boone,	88th Pa. Vols.,	Reading, Pa.
D. S. Bartram,	17th Conn. Vols.,	Redding, Conn.
Jas. Burns,	57th Pa. Vols.,	Clark's Post, Pa.
S. H. Ballard,	6th Mich. Cav.,	Battle Creek, Mich.

S. T. Boughton,	71st Pa. Vols.	
M. M. Bassett,	53d Ill. Vols.	
R. Y. Bradford,	2d W. Tenn. Vols.	
W. H. Bricker,	3d Pa. Cav.,	Newville, Pa.
J. T. Brush,	100th O. Vols.	
U. G. Ballow,	100th O. Vols.	
J. F. Baird,	1st Va. Vols.,	Wheeling, Va.
E. G. Birun,	3d Mass. Vols.	
G. E. Blair,	17th O. Vols.	
Jas. Biggs,	123d Ill. Vols.	
T. Bickham,	19th U. S. Inf.	
J. P. Brown,	15th U. S.,	Dayton, O.
M. C. Bryant,	42d Ill. Vols.,	Kankakee, Ill.
O. B. Brandt,	17th O. Vols.,	Lancaster, O.
G. W. Button,	22d Mich. Vols.,	Farmington, Mich
C. A. Burdick,	10th Wis. Vols.	
J. L. Brown,	73d Ind. Vols.	
F. T. Bennett,	18th U. S. Inf.	
Jno. Baird,	89th O. Vols.	
W. O. Butler,	10th Wis. Vols.	
D. A. Bannister,	59th O. Vols.	
Jno. Bradford,	C. S., U. S. Vols.,	Hoboken, N. J.
G. R. Barse,	5th Mich. Cav.	
C. P. Butler,	29th Ind. Vols.,	Peru, Ill.
E. P. Brooks,	6th Wis. Vols.	
W. L. Brown,	17th Tenn. Vols.	
G. W. Buffum,	1st Wis. Vols.	
Guy Bryan,	18th Pa. Cav.,	Vincenttown, N. Y.
S. S. Baker,	6th Mo. Vols.	
H. Bader,	29th Mo. Vols.,	Cape Girardeau, Mo.
S. H. Byers,	5th Iowa Vols.,	Newton, Iowa.
W. L. Bath,	132d N. Y. Vols.	
Geo. M. Bush.		
A. H. Bassett,	79th Ill. Vols.	
A. B. Bradley,	85th N. Y. Vets.,	Friendship, N. Y.
L. A. Butts,	85th N. Y. Vets.,	Cuba, N. Y.
G. A. Bowers,	16th Conn. Vols.	Hartford, Conn.
B. F. Blakeslee,	16th Conn. Vols.,	New Britain, Conn.
H. Bruns,	16th Conn. Vols.,	Bridgeport, Conn.
R. R. Bryson,	103d Pa. Vols.,	Butler, Pa.
S. D. Burns,	103d Pa. Vols.,	Circlesville, Pa.
D. F. Beegle,	101st Pa. Vols.,	Rainsburg, Pa.
J. H. Bryan,	184th Pa. Vols.,	Harrisburg, Pa.
R. Bascomb,	50th N. Y. Vols.,	Rome, N. Y.
W. H. Brown,	93d O. Vols.,	Dayton, O.
W. Bath,	132d N. Y. Vols.	
P. Bischoff,	6th U. S. Artillery,	St. Louis, Mo.
G. L. Brown,	101st Pa. Vols.,	Milton, Pa.
C. L. Brandt,	1st N. Y. Vets.,	Belmont, N. Y.
S. Byron,	2d U. S. Infantry.	
H. Caswell,	95th Ill. Vols.	
E. Barroll,	11th Tenn. Vols.	
P. Cameron,	10th N Y. Cav.	
C. Caldwell,	1st Wis. Cav.,	Lind, Wis.
A. Cooper,	12th N. Y. Cav.,	Oswego. N. Y.
A. G. Chase,	16th Conn. Vols.,	Simsbury, Conn.

Name	Regiment	Location
J. C. Cubbinson,	101st Pa. Vols.,	Irish Ripple, Pa.
H. L. Clark,	2d Mass. Artillery,	Springfield, Mass.
J. C. Colwell,	16th Ill. Cav.,	Chicago, Ill.
Jno. H. Conn,	1st Va. Cav.	
S. D. Carpenter,	3d O. Vols.,	Springfield, O.
W. A. Curry,	3d O. Vols.	
R. J. Connelly,	73d Ind. Vols.	
A. M. Callahan,	73d Ind. Vols.	
J. W. Custed,	23d Ind. Vols.	
J. D. Cook,	6th Iowa Vols.,	St. Louis, Mo.
J. Carothers,	78th O. Vols.	
S. R. Colloday,	6th Pa. Cav.	
T. B. Calver,	123d O. Vols.	
L. B. Cumins,	17th Mass. Vols.	
J. H. Cook,	5th Md. Vols.	
J. H. Chandler,	5th Md. Vols.	
E. D. Carpenter,	18th Conn. Vols.,	Putnam, Conn.
H. F. Cowles,	18th Conn. Vols.	
W. Cristopher,	2d Va. Cav.	
J. Q. Carpenter,	150th Pa. Vols.,	Germantown, Pa.
H. B. Chamberlain,	97th N. Y. Vols.	
T. J. Crossley,	157th Pa. Vols.,	Titusville, Pa.
J. A. Carman,	107th Pa. Vols.	
J. A. Coffin,	157th N. Y. Vols.,	Oswego, N. Y.
D. J. Conelly,	63d N. Y. Vols.,	New York City.
J. U. Childs,	16th Me. Vols.,	Farmington, Me.
D. B. Caldwell,	75th O. Vols.	
W. B. Cook,	140th Pa. Vols.,	Candor, Pa.
G. W. Chandler,	1st Va. Cav.,	Birmingham, O.
H. A. Curtice,	157th N. G. Vols.,	Courtlandt, N. Y.
J. Chatburn,	150th Pa. Vols.,	Germantown, Pa.
S. E. Cary,	13th Mass. Vols.	
A. Cloadt,	119th N. Y. Vols.,	Washington, D. C.
J. Clement,	15th Ky. Cav.,	Hewalton, Ind.
G. A. Chandler,	15th Mo. Vols.	
J. H. Cain,	104th N. Y. Vols,	Albany, N. Y.
B. Coles,	2d N. Y. Cav.,	New York City.
J. B. Carlisle,	2d Va. Vols.,	Ironton, O.
G. B. Coleman,	1st Mass. Cav.	
Hyde Crocker,	1st N. J. Cav.,	Port Jervis, N. J.
G. A. Coffin,	29th Ind. Vols.	
J. L. Cox,	21st Ill. Vols.	
W. M. Cubbetson,	30th Ind. Vols.	
T. G. Cochran,	77th Pa. Vols.,	Chambersburg, Pa.
Geo. Cleghorn,	21st O. Vols.	
W. W. Calkins,	104th Ill. Vols.,	Ottawa, Ill.
G. Celly,	4th O. Cav.	
H. B. Crawford,	2d Ill. Cav.	
T. S. Coleman,	12th Ky. Cav.	
O. L. Cole,	51st Ill. Vols.,	Elgin, Ill.
Rudolph Curtis,	4th Ky. Cav.,	Louisville, Ky.
M. C. Causton,	19th U. S. Inf.	
E. Cottingham,	35th O. Vols.	
W. Clifford,	16th U. S. Inf.	
M. Cohen,	4th Ky. Cav.,	Louisville, Ky.
A. S. Cooper,	9th Md. Vols.	

J. F. Carter,	9th Md. Vols.,	Baltimore, Md.
C. W. Catlett,	2d E. Tenn. Vo's.	
W. H. Crawford,	2d E. Tenn. Vols.	
C. J. Carlin,	151st N. Y. Vols.	
H. Cuniffe,	13th Ill. Vols.	
C. H. Casdorph,	8th Va. Cav.,	Kanawha, W. Va.
G. W. Carey,	65th Ind. Vols.	
J. G. Doughty,	51st Ind. Vols.	
J. A. Dilan,	51st Ind. Vols.	
T. A. Dooley,	51st Ind. Vols.,	Winchester, Ind.
T. B. Dewies,	2d U. S. Inf.	
M. Dienner,	10th Mo. Vols.	
V. R. Davis,	123d O. Vols.	
C. G. Davis,	1st Mass. Cav.,	Worcester, Mass.
L. N. Ducherney,	1st Mass. Cav.	
J. R. Day,	3d Me. Vols.,	Waterville, Me.
J. S. Devine,	71st Pa. Vols.,	Philadelphia, Pa.
Geo. A. Deering,	16th Me. Vols.	
A. Dixon,	104th N. Y. Vols.	Le Roy, N. Y.
Jno. Daily,	104th N. Y. Vols.,	Troy, N. Y.
C. H. Drake,	142d Pa. Vols.	Stroudsburg, Pa.
B. Davis,	71st Pa. Vols.	
A. W. Dukel,	114th Pa. Vols.	
F. Donyley,	27th R. I. Vols.	
J. W. Drake,	136th N. Y. Vols.,	Dansville, N. Y.
C. D. Dillard,	7th Iowa Vols.	
J. W. Day,	17th Mass. Vols.	Averill, Mass.
J. M. Dushane,	142d Pa. Vols.,	Connelsville, Pa.
O. G. Doughton,	100th O. Vols.,	Stryker, O.
T. G. Darnin,	16th U. S. Inf.	
H. C. Dunn,	10th Ky. Vols.	
W. G. Dutton,	67th Pa. Vols.,	Philadelphia, Pa.
L. Drake,	22d Mich. Vols.,	Pontiac, Mich.
E. J. Davis,	44th Ill. Vols.,	Rocktown, Ill.
M. V. Dickey,	94th O. Vols.,	Franklin, O.
Jno. Dugan,	35th Ind. Vols.,	Richmond, Ind.
Thos. J. Dean,	5th Mich. Vols.,	Wayne, Mich.
John Davidson,	6th N. Y. Artillery,	Haverstraw, N. Y.
W. A. Daily,	8th Pa. Cav.,	Philadelphia, Pa.
E. H. Duncan,	2d E. Tenn. Vols.	
A. C. Driffenbach,	73d Pa. Vols.,	Philadelphia, Pa.
J. W. Day,	17th Mass. Vols.,	Averill, Mass.
A. A. Dickerson,	16th Conn. Vols.,	Hartford, Conn.
A. P. Day,	15th Conn. Vols.,	New Haven, Conn.
J. W. Davis,	115th N. Y. Vols.	
T. D. Edwards,	U. S. Navy.	
C. L. Edmunds,	67th Pa. Vols.	
D. C. Edwards,	2d Md. Vols.,	Baltimore, Md.
J. Egan,	69th Pa. Vols.	
S. Edmiston,	89th O. Vols.	
W. H. Ellenwood,	10th Wis. Vols.	
C. W. Earle,	96th Ill. Vols.	
G. H. Errickson,	57th N. Y. Vols.,	Brooklyn, N. Y.
Geo. W. Fish,	3d O. Vols.,	Hamilton, O.
A. Fry,	73d Ind. Vols.,	Crown Point, Ind.
J. A. Francis.	18th Conn. Vols.	

W. Flick,	67th Pa. Vols.	
J. M. Fales,	1st R. I. Cav.,	Providence, R. I.
L. P. Fortescue,	20th Pa. Vols.	
M. Fellows,	140th Pa. Vols.	
W. Fenner,	2d R. I. Cav.	
G. D. Forsyth,†	100th O. Vols.	

† Captain Forsyth was shot dead by a sentinel at Libby Prison in the spring of 1864, while standing near one of the prison windows.

G. H. Fowler,	100th O. Vols.	
J. C. Fisher,	7th Ind. Battery.	
T. C. Freeman,	18th U. S. Infty.	
R. J. Fisher,	17th Mo. Vols.	
Chas. Fritze,	24th Ill. Vols.,	Chicago, Ill.
J. A. Flemming,	90th N. Y. Vols.	
E. F. Foster,	30th Ind. Vols.	
H. Fairchild,	89th O. Vols.,	Plattville, Wis.
W. H. Follette,	Mass. Artillery,	Quincy, Mass.
A. W. Fritchie,	26th Mo. Vols.,	St. Louis, Mo.
J. Fontaine,	73d Pa. Vols.,	Washington, D. C.
E. H. Fobes,	131st N. Y. Vols.	
D. D. Fox,	16th Ill. Cav.,	Aurora, Ill.
J. Fritz,	11th Tenn. Vols.	
S. A. Fay,	85th N. Y. Vets.,	Olean, N. Y.
C. W. Frost,	85th N. Y. Vets.,	Rochester, N. Y.
O. M. Fish,	2d Mass. Artillery,	Boston, Mass.
A. L. Fluke,	103d Pa. Vols.,	Kittaning, Pa.
M. C. Foot,	92d N. Y. Vols.	Cooperstown, N. Y.
J. D. Fox,	16th Ill. Cav.,	Aurora, Ill.
J. O. Goodrich,	85th N. Y. Vets.,	Scottsville, N. Y.
S. A. Geasland,	11th Tenn. Cav.	Kingston, Tenn.
A. Gude,	51st Ind. Vols.,	Bruseville, Ind.
H. Gamble,	73d Ind. Vols.	
Jno. A. Garces,	1st Md. Cav.	
Thos. G. Ro(t d,	1st Md. Cav.	
C. M. Cross,	100th O. Vols.	
G. W. Grant,	88th Pa. Vols.,	Reading, Pa.
A. Goodwin,	82d O. Vols.	
O. Grierson,†	45th N. Y. Vols.	

† Shot and mortally wounded by a sentinel on the stockade at Macon, Ga., June 11th, 1864. See account of murder in the chapter on Macon.

F. C. Gay,	11th Pa. Vols.,	Donegal, Pa.
C. F. Gutland,	134th N. Y. Vols.	
E. G. Gorgus,	90th Pa. Vols.	
J. A. Gilmore,	79th N. Y. Vols.	
S. P. Gamble,	63d Pa. Vols.,	Pittsburg, Pa.
E. L. Garrett,	4th Mo. Cav.	
F. M. Gilleland,	15th Ky. Vols.	
Geo. H. Gamble,	8th Ill. Cav.	
D. Garbet,	77th Pa. Vols.,	Hyde Park, Pa.
T. Gross,	21st Ill. Vols.,	Bement, Ill.
H. Gerhardt,	24th Ill. Vols.	
R. H. Gray,	15th U. S. Infty,	Cleveland, O.
J. M. Goff,	10th Wis. Vols.	
W. G. Galloway,	15th U. S. Infty.	

Name	Regiment	Location
J. H. Gagerly,	19th U. S. Infty.	
R. C. Gates,	18th U. S. Infty.	
C. W. Green,	44th Ind. Vols.	
J. B. Gore,	15th Ill. Vols.	
J. A. Green,	13th Pa. Cav.	
W. W. Glazier,	2d N. Y. Cav.,	Fowler, N. Y.
E. Gordon,	81st Ind. Vols.	
A. L. Gater,	10th Wis. Vols.,	Hustisford, Wis.
M. Gray,	13th N. Y. Vols.,	Naugatuck, Conn.
W. G. Griffin,	112th Ill. Vols.,	Cambridge, Ill.
C. E. Greble,	8th Mich. Cav.,	Battle Creek, Mich
Geo. Good,	84th Pa. Vols.	
M. E. Green,	5th Md. Cav.	
J. B. Holmes,	6th O. Vols.	
Jno. Hood,	80th Ill. Vols.	
R. J. Harmer,	80th Ill. Vols.	
W. H. Harvey,	51st Ind. Vols.	
G. D. Hand,	51st Ind. Vols.,	Shelbyville, Ind.
D. H. Harns,	3d O. Vols.	
Jno. Haideman,	129th Ill. Vols.	
S. H. Horton,	101st Pa. Vols.	
W. E. Hodge,	5th Md. Vols.,	Baltimore, Md.
W. Hawkins,	5th Md. Vols.	
D. W. Hakes,	18th Conn. Vols.	
J. D. Higgins,	18th Conn. Vols.	
W. Heffner,	67th Pa. Vols.,	Pottsville, Pa.
F. A. Hubbell,	Pa. Vols.,	Honesdale, Pa.
J. C. Hagenbach,	67th Pa. Vols.,	Philadelphia, Pa.
J. Hersh,	87th Pa. Vols.	
J. Hall,	87th Pa. Vols.	
P. Horney,	110th O. Vols.	
T. J. Higginson,		
J. G. Hallenburg,	1st O. Vols.,	Louisville, Ky.
A. Hauf,	5th N. Y. Vols.	
H. H. Hinds,	57th Pa. Vols.,	Montrose, Pa
Thos. Huggins,	2d N. J. Cav.	
Eug. Kepp,	82d Ill. Vols.	
C. P. Heffley,	142d Pa. Vols.,	Berlin, Pa.
J. M. Henry,	154th N. Y. Vols.,	Olean, N. Y.
G. Halpin,	116th Pa. Vols.,	Philadelphia, Pa.
E. H. Harkness,	6th Pa. Cav.	
J. D. Hatfield,	53d Ill. Vols.	
A. W. Hayes,	34th O. Vols.	
J. F. Hammond,		
H. Hubbard,	12th N. Y. Vols.	
W. S. Hatcher,	30th O. Vols.	
Jno. J. Hine,	100th O. Vols.	
M. B. Helms,	1st Va. Cav.,	Rosby's Rock, W. Va.
C. B. Hall,	1st Va. Cav.	
Eli Holden,	1st Va. Cav.	Barre, Vt.
B. Howe,	21st Ill. Vols.	
P. W. Houlchen,	16th U. S. Infantry.	
C. D. Henry,	4th O. Cav.,	Tiffin City, O.
J. Hanon,	115th Ill. Vols.	
C. E. Harrison,	89th O. Vols.,	Higginsport, O.
Geo. Harris,	70th Ind. Vols.	

W. B. Hamilton,	22d Mich. Vols.,	Romeo, Mich.
S. S. Holbruck,	15th U. S. Infty.	
L. D. Henkley,	10th Wis. Vols.,	Wanfrau, Wis.
E. H. Higly,	1st Vt. Cav.,	Castleton, Vt.
W. M. Hudson,	92d O. Vols.	
H. Horway,	78th Ill. Vols.	
C. T. Hall,	13th Mich. Vols.;	Battle Creek, Mich.
G. C. Houston,	2d N. Y. Cav.,	Concord, N. H.
P. A. Hagen,	7th Md. Vols.	
J. R. Hutchinson,	2d Va. Cav.,	Pittsburg, Pa.
G. W. Hale,	101st O. Vols.,	Upper Sandusky, O.
R. Huey,	2d E. Tenn. Vols.	
W. P. Hodge,	2d E. Tenn. Vols.	
E. Harbour,	2d E. Tenn. Vols.	
B. F. Harrington,	18th Pa. Cav.,	Waynesburg, Pa.
Jas. Heslit,	3d Pa. Cav.,	Baltimore, Md.
Jno. Hoffman,	5th Iowa Vols.	
W. Hayes,	5th Iowa Vols.	
J. M. Holloway,	6th Ind. Vols.	
C. M. Hart,	45th Pa. Vols.,	
D. W. Hicks,	9th O. Cav.	
H. R. Hubbard,	119th Ill. Vols.	
J. B. Helm,	101st Pa. Vols.,	Shellsburg, Pa.
S. W. Hawkins,	7th Tenn. Cav.,	Huntingdon, Tenn.
T. J. Hastings,	15th Mass. Vols.,	Worcester, Mass.
L. C. Herrick,	1st N. Y. Cav.,	Syracuse, N. Y.
S. Harris,	5th Mich. Cav.	
T. H. Heppard,	101st Pa. Vols.,	Philadelphia, Pa.
W. Hamilton,	2d Mass. Art'y,	West Amesbury, Mass
G. L. Hastings,	24th N. Y. Batt'y,	Oswego, N. Y.
C. G. Hampton,	15th N. Y. Cav.,	Brockport, N. Y.
H. P. Hoppin,	2d Mass. Art'y,	Cambridge, Mass.
W. C. Holman,	9th Vt. Vols.,	West Braintree, Vt.
J. B. Hill,	17th Mass. Vols.,	Averill, Mass.
A. W. Hunter,	2d U. S. Art'y,	New Hudson, Mich.
C. C. Huntley,	16th Ill. Cav.,	Huntley, Ill.
C. L. Irwin,	78th Ill. Vols.	
W. H. Irwin,	103d Pa. Vols.,	Alleghany City, Pa.
H. H. James.	6th Ind. Cav.,	Montezuma, Ind.
G. Johnson,	16th Conn. Vols.,	Hartford, Conn.
J. P. Jones,	55th O. Vols.,	Norwalk, O.
C. W. Jones,	16th Pa. Cav.,	Duncannon, Pa.
P. O. Jones,	2d N. Y. Cav.,	Brooklyn, N. Y.
J. A. Jones,	21st Ill. Vols.,	Olney, Ill.
J. H. Jenkins,	21st Wis. Vols.,	Oskosh, Wis.
R. W. Jackson,	21st Wis. Vols.,	" "
T. W. Jackson,	10th N. Y. Cav.,	Wolcott, N. Y.
H. P. Jordan,	9th Me. Vols.	
H. Jones,	5th U. S. Cav.,	Washington, D. C.
R. B. Jones,	2d E. Tenn. Vols.	
H. H. James,	6th Ind. Cav.,	Montezuma, Ind.
John King,	5th Ill. Cav.	Geneva, Ill.
M. D. King,	3d O. Vols.,	Barnesville, O.
A. J. Kuhn,	5th Md. Vols.	
H. V. Knight,	20th Mich. Vols.,	Battle Creek, Mich.
J. S. Kephart,	5th Md. Cav.,	Franklin, Ind.

Name	Regiment	Location
Jas. Kerin,	6th U. S. Cav.,	Washington, D. C.
J. B. King,	10th N. Y. Cav.	
G. Keyes,	18th Conn. Vols.	
J. N. Kibbe,	18th Conn. Vols.	
A. Kresge,	67th Pa. Vols.	
R. A. Knowles,	116th O. Vols.	
H. Kendler,	45th N. Y. Vols.	
M. Kupp,	167th Pa. Vols.	
Jas. Kane,	13th Pa. Cav.	
R. C. Knaggs,	A. D. C.,	Ann Arbor, Mich.
J. Kunkel,	45th N. Y. Vols.	
J. W. Kennedy,	134th N. Y. Vols.	
J. C. Kellogg,	6th Mich. Vols.	
D. O. Kelly,	100th O. Vols.,	Kelly's Island, O.
J. D. Kautz,	1st Ky. Cav.,	Dent, O.
T. A. Krocks,	77th Pa. Vols.	
T. D. Kimball,	88th Ind. Vols.,	
Wm. Keruger,	2d Mo. Vols.,	St. Louis, Mo.
E. E. Knoble,	21st Ky. Vols.	
E. M. Knowles,	42d Ind. Vols.,	
J. Kenniston,	100th Ill. Vols.,	Joliet, Ill.
S. Koach,	100th Ill. Vols.	
C. E. Keith,	19th Ill. Vols.,	Chicago, Ill.
Theo. Kendall,	15th U. S. Infty,	Brooklyn, N. Y.
H. B. Kelly,	6th Ky. Cav.	
D. F. Kittrell,	3d E. Tenn. Vols.	
F. H. Knapp,	9th O. Cav.	
W. M. Kirby,	3d N. Y. Art'y.	
T. King,	101st Pa. Vols.,	Bradford, Pa.
W. H. H. Keister,	103d Pa. Vols.,	Hillsville, Pa.
J. B. Kirk,	101st Pa. Vols.,	" "
G. W. Kirkpatrick,	15th Iowa Vols.,	Smyrna, Iowa.
W. S. Lyon,	23d O. Vols.,	Leeville, O.
T. Lennig,	6th Pa. Cav.,	Philadelphia, Pa.
F. A. Leyton,	18th Ind. Vols.	
Sam. Leith,	132d N. Y. Vols.	
A. W. Loomis,	18th Conn. Vols.,	Tolland, Conn.
A. H. Lindsay,	18th Conn. Vols.,	Greenville, Conn.
L. Lapton,	116th O. Vols.	
W. H. Locke,	18th Conn. Vols.,	Willimantic, Conn.
J. Leydecker,	45th N. Y. Vols.	
L. Lindemeyer,	45th N. Y. Vols..	New York City.
H. G. Lombard,	4th Mich. Vols.	
W. L. Laws,	18th Pa. Vols.	
A. T. Lamson,	104th N. Y. Vols.,	Genesee, N. Y.
A. W. Locklin,	94th N. Y. Vols.,	Great Bend, N. Y.
G. R. Lodge,	53d Ill. Vols.,	Ottawa, Ill.
T. S. C. Lloyd,	6th Ind. Cav.,	Terre Haute, Ind.
C. H. Livingston,	1st Va. Cav.,	Union Town, Pa.
J. L. Leslie,	18th Pa. Cav.,	Titusville, Pa.
D. R. Locke	8th Ky. Cav.	
J. Ludlow,	5th U. S. Art'y,	
A. Leonard,	71st N. Y. Vols.	
M. J. Lintz,	8th Tenn. Vols.,	
J. H. Longnecker,	101st Pa. Vols.,	Woodbury, Pa.
W. C. Lyon.	23d O. Vols..	Leeville, O.

W. B. Madera,	6th W. Va. Vols.,	Morgantown, Va.
H. A. D. Merritt,	5th N. Y. Cav.,	Hoboken, N. J.
O. McCall,	103d Pa. Vols.,	Rimersburg, Pa.
J. M. Myers	101st Pa. Vols	
C. McHenry,	85th N. Y. Vet.,	East Bloomfield, N.Y.
W. G. Miller,	16th Conn. Vols.	
J. McKinstry,	16th Ill. Cav.,	Matoon, Ill.
W. R. Moore,	2d Md. Cav.,	Wilmington, Del.
N. J. McCafferty,	4th U. S. Art'y,	Pittsburg, Pa.
T. W. McClure,	6th U. S. Art'y,	Wabash, Ind.
C. W. Morse,	16th Conn. Vols.,	New Hartford, Conn.
Jno. McAdams,	10th Va. Vols.	
L. Markbreit,	A. D. C.	
J. McKinley,	28th O. Vols.	
T. Milward,	31st O. Vols.	
W. H. McDill,	80th Ill. Vols.	
W. S. Marshall,	51st Ind. Vols.	
J. H. Murdock,	3d O. Vols.	
C. A. Maxwell,	3d O. Vols.,	Springfield, O.
H. S. Murdock,	73d Ind. Vols.,	Logansport, Ind.
J. D. Munday,	73d Ind. Vols.,	LaPorte, Ind.
J. S. Mettee,	5th Md. Vols.	
Jno. McCumas,	5th Md. Vols.	
W. J. Morris,	5th Md. Vols.,	Baltimore, Md.
T. F. McGinnes,	18th Conn. Vols.	
F. McKeag,	18th Conn. Vols.,	Norwich, Conn.
H. Morningstar,	87th Pa. Vols.,	Hanover, Pa.
J. S. Manning,	100th O. Vols.	
Thos. Mosby,	12th Pa. Cav.	
W. J. McConnel,	4th Iowa Vols.,	Wintersett, Iowa.
D. McCully,	75th O. Vols.	
O. Missehl,	68th N. Y. Vols.	
H. H. Mosely,	25th O. Vols.,	Summerfield, O.
Thos. Myers.	107th Pa. Vols.,	Chambersburg, Pa.
C. Murray,	15th Mo. Vols.,	St. Louis, Mo.
B. N. Mann,	17th Mass. Vols.	
J. A. Mitchell,	82d O. Vols.	
A. McDade,	154th N. Y. Vols.,	Westfield, N. Y.
J. A. Mendenhall,	75th O. Vols.,	Ringgold, O.
J. R. Meil,	82d Ill. Vols.,	Deerfield, O.
V. Mylieus,	68th N. Y. Vols.	
F. Moran,	73d N. Y. Vols.,	New York City.
J. Mooney,	107th Pa. Vols.,	Dushone, Pa.
F. Murphy,	97th N. Y. Vols.,	Salisbury Centre, N.Y.
G. H. Morisey,	12th Iowa, Q. M.	
H. E. Mosher,	12th N. Y. Cav.	
S. F. C. Merwin,	18th Conn. Vols.,	Norwich, Conn.
Thos. Maver,	100th O. Vols.	
T. H. McKee,	21st Ill. Vols.	
J. W. Messick,	42d Ind. Vols.,	Evansville, Ind.
D. F. McKay,	18th Pa. Vols.,	Meadesville, Pa.
A. M. Murray,	U. S. Artillery.	
R. G. McKay,	1st Mich. Vols.,	Beloit, Mich.
Wm. McElroy,	3d Ill. Vols.	
N. S. McKee,	21st Ill. Vols.	
J. Mitchell.	79th Ill. Vols.	

Name	Unit	Location
J. McGowan,	29th Ind. Vols.	
M. Mahon,	16th U. S. Infty.	
J. T. Mackey,	16th U. S. Infty,	Ballas City, Ill.
C. H. Morgan,	21st Wis. Vols.	
A. S. Mathews,	22d Mich. Vols.,	Pontiac, Mich.
J. S. Mahony,	15th U. S. Infty,	Prairie Depot, O.
S. McNeal,	51st O. Vols.,	Spring Mountain, O.
L. C. Mead,	22d Mich. Vols.	
A. U. McLane,	2d O. Vols.	
M. V. B. Morrison,	32d O. Vols.,	Chillicothe, O.
A. H. McKinson,	10th Wis. Vols.,	Pine Hill, Wis.
W. H. Mead,	6th Ky. Cav.	
A. Morse,	78th Ill. Vols.,	Macomb, Ill.
A. Morris,	4th Ky. Cav.	
H. Morey,	10th N. Y. Cav.	
G. W. Morse,	9th Md. Vols.,	Lovington, Tenn.
H. F. Meyer,	9th Ind. Vols.	
R. A. Moon,	6th Mich. Cav.,	Big Rapids, Mich.
M. M. Moore,	6th Mich. Cav.	
Jno. Millis,	66th Ind. Vols.,	Paoli, Ind.
J. McDonald,	2d E. Tenn. Vols.	
J. McColgen,	7th O. Cav.,	Georgetown, O.
D. T. Moore,	2d E. Tenn. Vols.,	Clinton, Tenn.
J. H. Mason,	21st O. Vols.	
J. McBeth,	45th O. Vols.,	Zanesfield, O.
R. H. Montgomery,	5th U. S. Cav.	
F. Moore,	73d Pa. Vols.	
J. McGovern,	73d Pa. Vols.	
A. McNiece,	73d Pa. Vols.	
G. Maw,	80th O. Vols.	
J. T. Morgan,	17th Mich. Vols.,	Ysilanti, Mich.
C. Miller,	14th Ill. Cav.	Chicago, Ill.
W. J. Nowlan,	14th N. Y. Vols.	
A. N. Norris,	107th Pa. Vols.	
Wm. Nelson,	13th U. S. Infantry.	
J. C. Norcross,	2d Mass. Cav.,	Farmington, Me.
J. F. Newbrandt,	4th Mo. Cav.,	Cincinnati, O.
Wm. Nyce,	2d N. Y. Cav.,	Hainesville, N. J.
B. H. Niemeger,	11th Ky. Cav.	
O. P. Norris,	11th O. Vols.	
Jas. O. Connor,	59th O. Vols.	
O. C. Ong,	2d Va. Cav.,	Meigsville, O.
W. O'Conner,	13th Pa. Cav.,	Philadelphia, Pa.
J. G. Oats,	3d O. Vols.,	Greenwich, O.
G. W. Pitts.,	85th N. Y. Vets.,	Short Tract, N. Y.
L. S. Peake,	85th N. Y. Vets.,	Hinsdale, N. Y.
E. C. Pierson,	85th N. Y. Vets.,	Waterloo, N. Y.
W. Phares,	46th W. Va. Vols.	Seneca, W. Va.
F. Phillips,	5th Pa. Cav.,	Philadelphia, Pa.
E. W. Pelton,	2d Md. Cav.,	Cumberland, Md.
E. W. Parcey,	80th Ill. Vols.	
S. B. Piper,	3d O. Vols.,	Barnesville, O.
G. A. Potter,	2d Ky. Vols.,	Cincinnati, O.
J. B. Pumphrey,	123d O. Vols.,	Marseilles, O.
W. G. Purnell,	6th Md. Vols.	
C. G. A. Peterson,	1st R. I. Cav.,	Providence, R. I.

Name	Unit	Location
E. B. Parker,	1st Vt. Artillery,	Providence, R. I.
Henry S. Platt,	11th Mich. Vols.	
E. C. Parker,	94th N. Y. Vols.	
H. C. Potter,	18th Pa. Cav.,	Philadelphia, Pa.
T. Paulding,	6th U. S. Cav.	
J. F. Poole,	1st Va. Cav.,	Martinsburg, W. Va
J. L. Powers,	107th N. Y. Vols.	Hamilton. N. Y.
D. B. Pettijohn,	2d U. S. Infty,	Fort Snelling, Minn.
G. H. Potts,	75th O. Vols.	
C. P. Potts,	151st Pa. Vols.,	Pottsville, Pa.
E. D. Potter,	6th Mich. Vols.,	Jeddo, Me.
E. L. Palmer,	57th N. Y. Vols.,	Montville, Conn.
J. S. Paul,	122d O. Vols.	
Z. R. Prather,	116th Ill. Vols.	
G. Pentzel,	11th N. Y. Vols.	
Jas. P. Perley,	13th Mich. Vols.,	New York City.
H. Perlen,	2d O. Vols.	
J. B. Patterson,	21st O. Cav.	
M. N. Paxton,	140th Pa. Vols.	
E. W. Pelton,	2d Md. Vols.,	Cumberland, Md.
C. Powell,	42d O. Vols.	
L. D. Phelps,	8th Pa. Cav.,	Colchester, Conn.
C. M. Prutzman,	7th Wis. Vols.,	Plainfield, Wis.
A. E. Patelin,	10th Wis. Vols.	
M. B. Pulliam,	11th Ky. Cav.	
R. H. Pond,	12th U. S. Infantry.	
Wm. P. Pierce,	11th Ky. Cav.	
L. B. Pettrie,	126th O. Vols.	
Wm. Randall,	80th Ill. Vols.	
Jno. Ritchie,	3d O. Vols.	
J. C. Roney,	3d O. Vols.,	Newark, O.
Wm. Reynolds,	73d Ind. Vols.	
A. C. Roach,	51st Ind. Vols.,	Indianapolis, Ind.
E. Reynolds,	73d Ind. Vols.	
E. Reed,	3d O. Vols.	
J. M. Rothrock,	5th Md. Vols.	
J. P. Rockwell,	18th Conn. Vols	
J. Ruff,	67th Pa. Vols.,	Philadelphia, Pa.
J. F. Robinson,	67th Pa. Vols.,	Scott, Pa.
W. F. Randolph,	5th U. S. Artillery.	
John Ryan,	60th Pa. Vols.	
W. E. Rockwell,	13th N. Y. Vols.,	Esperance, N. Y.
J. H. Russell,	12th Mass. Vols.,	Boston, Mass.
J. O. Rockwell,	97th N. Y. Vols.,	Booneville, N. Y.
J. A. Richardson,	2d N. Y. Cav.,	Stoneham, Mass.
N. A. Robbins,	4th Me. Vols.,	Union, Me.
H. E. Rulon,	114th Pa. Vols.	
H. Richardson,	19th Ind. Vols.	
J. Remie,	11th Mass. Vols.	
Geo. King,	100th O. Vols.	
D. P. Rennie,	93d O. Vols.	
T. J. Ray,	49th O. Vols.	
W. L. Retilley,	51st O. Vols.,	Roscoe, O.
G. W. Robertson,	22d Mich. Vols.,	Mount Cheneus, Mi
J. M. Rader,	8th Tenn. Vols.	
S. H. Reynolds,	42d O. Vols.	

E. W. Rubbs,	1st E. Tenn. Vols.	
G. F. Robinson,	80th O. Vols.	
J. L. Robinson,	7th Tenn. Cav.,	Huntington, Pa.
J. A. Reid,	2d N. C. Vols.,	Whitestown, Pa.
I. Risedon,	11th Tenn. Vols.,	Huntsville, Tenn.
G. Roberts,	7th N. H. Vols.,	Dover, N. H.
G. Ross,	7th Vt. Vols.,	Vergennes, Vt.
J. R. Roger,	157th Pa. Vols.,	Lancaster City, Pa.
E. E. Strong,	16th Conn. Vols.,	North Manchester,
R. B. Sinclair,	2d Mass. Heavy Artillery,	Worcester, Mass.
D. M. Spence,	113th Pa. Vols.,	Pittsburg, Pa.
J. W. Stoke,	103d Pa. Vols.,	Orrville, Pa.
G. A. Sharp,	19th Pa. Cav.,	Philadelphia, Pa.
A. A. Scudder,	35th Pa. Vols.	
H. C. Scoville,	92d Ill. Vols.,	Rockford, Ill.
L. S. Smith,	14th N. Y. Vols.,	Littleton, N. H.
D. J. Shepherd,	5th Ky. Cav.	
H. Silver,	16th Ill. Cav.,	St. Louis, Mo.
G. Scuttermore,	80th Ill. Vols.	
Th. Segaros,	80th Ill. Vols.,	Chester, Ill.
D. B. Stevenson,	3d O. Vols.	
E. E. Sharp,	51st Ind. Vols.,	Hokoma, Ind.
E. J. Spaulding,	2d U. S. Cav.,	Galesburg, Mich.
A. Stole,	6th U. S. Infantry.	
D. M. V. Stuart,	10th Mo. Vols.	
M. H. Smith,	123d O. Vols.,	Monroeville, O.
T. H. Stewart,	5th Md. Vols.,	Philadelphia, Pa.
John Socks,	5th Md. Vols.	
Jno. Sweadner,	5th Md. Vols.,	Liberty, Md.
J. F. Schuyler,	123d O. Vols.,	Attica, O.
C. H. Sowro,	123d O. Vols.	
E. L. Schroeder,	5th Md. Vols.,	York, Pa.
G. W. Simpson,	67th Pa. Vols.,	Mauch Chunk, Pa.
A. G. Scranton,	18th Conn. Vols.	
J. Smith,	67th Pa. Vols.,	Latrobe, Pa.
C. P. Stroman,	87th Pa. Vols.,	York, Pa.
A. M. Stark,	110th O. Vols.	
H. L. Sibley,	116th O. Vols.,	Racine, O.
S. Stearns,	4th Me. Vols.	
G. L. Synder,	104th N. Y. Vols.	
A. W. Sprague,	24th Mich. Vols.	
Geo. Schuele,	45th N. Y. Vols.	
H. B. Seeley,	86th N. Y. Vols.,	S. Troupsburg, N. Y.
W. S. Stevens,*	104th N. Y. Vols.	
E. Schrouders,	74th Pa. Vols.	
G. C. Stevens,	154th N. Y. Vols.,	Machias, N. Y.
D. C. Sears,	96th N. Y. Vols.	
H. Schroeder,	82d Ill. Vols.	
J. B. Samson,	12th Mass. Vols.,	W.Bridgewater, Mass
Jno. Sullivan,	7th R. I. Vols.	
M. R. Small,	6th Md. Vols.	
E. Shepard,	6th O. Cav.	Newburg, O.
J. M. Steele,	1st W. Va. Vols.,	Wellsville, O.
C. B. Smith,	4th N. Y. Cav.,	New York City.
Jno. Sterling,	3d Ind. Vols.	
F. Spencer,	17th O. Vols.,	Wilmington, O.

Name	Regiment	Location
A. W. Songer,	21st Ill. Vols.,	Xenia, O.
Wm. Stewart,	16th U. S. Infantry.	
W. H. Smythe,	16th U. S. Infantry.	
J. D. Simpson,	10th Ind. Vols.	
F. Schweinfurth,	24th Ill. Vols.,	Chicago, Ill.
A. C. Spafford,*	21st O. Vols.	
E. G. Spalding,	22d Mich. Vols.,	Port Huron, Mich.
E. S. Scott,	89th O. Vols.	
A. C. Shaeffer,	2d N. Y. Cav.,	Newton, N. J.
H. C. Smith,	2d Del. Vols.	
Jno. Spindler,	73d Ill. Vols.	
G. L. Sollers,	9th Md. Vols.	
L. L. Stone,	Regtl. Q. M.	Mt. Indus Falls, Vt
R. F. Scott,	11th Ky. Cav.,	Kirksville, Ky.
J. C. Shaw,	7th O. Cav.	
G. W. Sutherland,	126th O. Vols.,	Smithfield, O.
T. B. Strong,	11th Ky. Cav.,	Louisville, Ky.
Chas Trommel,	3d O. Vols.	
H. H. Tillotson,	73d Ind. Vols.,	Calumet, Ind.
A. V. Thomas,	73d Ind. Vols.	
D. Turner,	118th Ill. Vols.,	Warsaw, Ill.
Ira Tyler,	118th Ill. Vols.	
M. Tiffany,	18th Conn. Vols.	
H. O. Thayer,	67th Pa. Vols.	
A. A. Taylor,	122d O. Vols.,	Cambridge, O.
R. Tyler,	6th Md. Vols.	
R. Thompson,	67th Pa. Vols.,	Stoddardsville, Pa.
L. Thompson,	2d U. S. Cav.	
M. Tower,	13th Mass. Vols.	
E. A. Tuthill,	104th N. Y. Vols.,	Nunda, N. Y.
J. R. Titus,	3d U. S. Cav.	
H. Temple,	2d N. Y. Cav.,	Brooklyn, N. Y.
E. M. B. Timoney,	15th U. S. Infantry.	
G. W. Thomas,	10th Wis. Vols.	
H. C. Taylor,	21st Wis. Vols.	
A. J. Teter,	2d O. Vols.,	Steubenville, O.
R. F. Thorn,	5th Ky. Cav.,	Gardner, Kansas.
S. H. Tresouthick,	18th Pa. Cav.	
J. Turner,	Regtl. Q. M.	
H. Taylor,	65th Ind. Vols.	
J. E. Terwilliger,	85th N. Y. Vols.,	Almond, N. Y.
W. M. True,	16th Ill. Cav.,	Chicago, Ill.
A. J. W. Ulem,	3d O. Vols.,	Wooster, O.
J. R. Uptigrove,	73d Ind. Vols.	
M. Undutch,	9th Md. Vols.	
F. Vinay,	85th N. Y. Vols.	New York City.
G. A. Vanness,	73d Ind. Vols.,	Nogansport, Ind.
Geo. Veltford,	54th N. Y. Vols.,	New York City.
R. N. Vannetter,	1st Mich. Cav.	
D. Vansbury,	4th Md. Battalion,	
D. L. Wright,	51st Ind. Vols.,	Indianapolis, Ind.
A. H. Wonder,	51st Ind. Vols.	
Wm. Willis,	51st Ind. Vols.	
J. D. Whiting,	3d O. Vols.,	New York City.
A. R. Wolbach,	3d O. Vols.,	Wooster, O.
J. C. Woodrow.	73d Ind. Vols.	

C. P. Williams,	73d Ind. Vols.	
J. B. Williamson,	14th W. Va. Vols.	Middlebourne, W. V
Jos. F. Warwick,	101st Pa. Vols.,	Beaver, Pa.
J. C. Welch,	85th N. Y. Vols.,	Angelica, N. Y.
J. J. Wallace,	7th Tenn. Cav.,	Dowagiac, Mich.
R. P. Wallace,	120th O. Vols.,	Loudonville, O.
Thos. Worthen,	118th Ill. Vols.,	Warsaw, Ill.
L. Weiser,	1st Md. Cav.	
Wm. A. Williams,	123d O. Vols.	
J. W. Worth,	5th Md. Vols.,	Baltimore, Md.
J. B. Wilson,	5th Md. Vols.	
J. E. Woodard,	18th Conn. Vols.	
P. A. White,	83d Pa. Vols.	
E. J. Weeks,	67th Pa. Vols.,	Phœnixville, Pa.
T. J. Weakley,	110th O. Vols.,	New Carlisle, O.
W. H. Welsh,	78th Pa. Vols.,	York, Pa.
A. Wallber,	26th Wis. Vols.	
A. H. White,	27th Pa. Vols.	
D. Whiston.	13th Mass. Vols.	
T. Wuschow,	54th. N. Y. Vols.	
M. C. Wadsworth,	16th Me. Vols.,	Pittston, Me.
J. N. Whitney,	2d R. I. Cav.,	Raymond, Me.
M. T. Williams,	15th Ky. Vols.	
M. Wilson,	14th Pa. Cav.	
J. Woods,	82d Ind. Vols.	
C. N. Winner,	1st O. Vols.	
W. L. Watson,	21st Wis. Vols.,	Waupaca, Wis.
Wm. Willotts,	22d Mich. Vols.,	Birmingham, Mich.
J. Weatherbee,	41st O. Vols.,	Port Washington, O.
J. M. Wasson,	40th O. Vols.	
Jas. Wells,	8th Mich. Cav.	
H. Wilson,	18th Pa. Vols.,	Houston, Pa.
J. R. Weaver,	18th Pa. Vols.,	Latrobe, Pa.
W. H. H. Wilcox,	10th N. Y. Vols.,	New York City.
A. B. White,	4th Pa. Cav.,	Alleghany City, Pa.
C. F. Weston,	21st Wis. Vols.	
W. F. Wheeler,	9th Md. Vols.	
N. L. Wood, Jr.,	9th Md. Vols.	
E. Willhart,	2d E. Tenn.	
J. W. Wiltshire,	45th O. Vols.,	Cincinnati, O.
J. W. Wright,	10th Iowa Vols.,	Desmoines, Iowa.
J. B. Williamson,	14th W. Va. Vols.,	Middlebourne, W. V
E. D. York,	2d N. C. U. Vols.,	Friendship, N. Y.
C. H. Yates,	96th Ill. Vols.	
J. D. Zeigler,	114th Ill. Vols.	

ADDITIONAL LIST OF PRISONERS.*

---

* This list does not include those officers who were specially exchanged while at Charleston.

[The following is an additional list of officers captured during the spring, summer, autumn, and winter of 1864, after the removal of the old prisoners from Richmond on the 7th of May. They were imprisoned at Macon, Savannah, Charleston, Columbia, Charlotte, Raleigh, and Goldsboro':]

COLONELS.

Names.	Regiment, or Command.	Residence.
J. H. Ashworth,	1st Ga. U. S. Vols.	
T. H. Butler,	5th Ind. Cav.,	Clifty, Ind.
S. J. Crooks,	22d N. Y. Cav.,	New York City.
J. Frazier,	140th Pa. Vols.	
Pennock Huey,	8th Pa. Cav.,	Westchester, Pa.
F. C. Miller,	147th N. Y. Vols.,	Oswego, N. Y.
W. Shedd,	13th Ill. Vols.,	Aledo, Ill.
Daniel White,	31st Me. Vols.,	Bangor, Me.

LIEUTENANT COLONELS.

M. P. Buffum,	4th R. I. Vols.,	Providence, R. I.
J. B. Conyngham,	52d Pa. Vols.	
C. W. Clancy,	52d O. Vols.,	Smithfield, O.
M. A. Leeds,	153d O. Vols.,	Bantam, O.
C. C. Watson,	6th Ind. Cav.,	Greencastle, Ind.
D. B. McCreary,	145th Pa. Vols.,	Erie, Pa.
O. Moulton,	25th Mass. Vols.	
Benj. B. Morgan,	75th O. Vols.,	Franklin, O.
H. R. Stoughton,	2d U. S. S. S.	
A. H. Sanders,	16th Iowa Vols.,	Davenport, Iowa.
T. J. Thorp,	1st N. Y. Drag.,	Almond, N. Y.
G. Von Helmrick,	4th Mo. Cav.,	St. Louis, Mo.
G. Wallace,	47th O. Vols.,	Morning Sun, O.

MAJORS.

J. H. Dewees,	13th Pa. Cav.,	Philadelphia, Pa.
M. Dunn,	19th Mass. Vols.	
W. N. Denny,	51st Ind. Vols.,	Vincennes, Ind.
D. English,	11th Ky. Cav.,	Owening, Ky.
C. K. Flemming,	11th Vt. Vols.,	Bellows Falls, Vt.
G. B. Fox,	75th O. Vols.,	Cincinnati, O.
W. H. Forbes,	2d Mass. Cav.	
J. H. Filler,	55th Pa. Vols.,	Bedford, Pa.
T. J. Hasley,	11th N. Y. Vols.,	Dover, N. J.
W. P. Hall,	6th N. Y. Cav.,	Brooklyn, L. I.
R. Harkness,	10th Wis. Vols.,	Elkhorn, Wis.
J. H. Isett,	8th Ind. Cav.,	Wappello, Iowa.
W. M. Kendall,	73d Ind. Vols.,	Plymouth, Ind.

C. M. Lynch,	145th Pa. Vols.,	Erie, Pa.
P. M. Lernan,	22d N. Y. Cav.,	Memphis, N. Y.
C. P. Mattock,	17th Me. Vols.	
P. Nelson,	66th N. Y. Vols.,	Westchester, N. Y.
J. E. Pratt,	4th Vt. Vols.,	Bennington, Vt.
W. L. Parsons,	2d Wis. Vols.	
H. L. Pasco,	16th Conn. Vols.,	Hartford, Conn.
D. Quigg,	14th Ill. Cav.,	Bloomington, Ill.
W. H. Reynolds,	14th N. Y. Artillery,	Utica, N. Y.
J. Steele,	2d Pa. Cav.,	Pittsburg, Pa.
L. B. Speece,	7th P. V. R. Corps,	Wilkesbarre, Pa.
T. A. Smith,	7th Tenn. Cav.,	Lexington, Tenn.
M. H. Soper,	5th Ind. Cav.,	Sheldon, Ill.
D. Thomas,	135th O. Vols.,	Newark, O.
D. Vickers,	4th N. J. Vols.,	Philadelphia, Pa.
G. G. Wanger,	24th N. Y. Cav.,	Rochester, N. Y.
J. W. Young,	76th N. Y. Vols.,	Cherry Valley, N. Y.

CAPTAINS.

J. B. Alters,	75th O. Vols.,	Spring Dale, O.
W. N. Algbaugh,	51st Pa. Vols.,	Morristown, Pa.
H. B. Andrews,	17th Mich. Vols.	
John Aigan,	5th R. I. Artillery,	Pawtucket, R. I.
M. Auer,	15th N. Y. Cav.,	Syracuse, N. Y.
C. B. Amory,	A. A. Gen.,	Jamaica Plain, Mass.
James Belger,	1st R. I. Artillery.	
C. H. Burdick,	1st Tenn. Cav.,	Nashville, Tenn.
G. Bradley,	2d N. J. Vols.	
C. W. Boutin,	4th Vt. Vols.,	Chester, Vt.
C. A. Bowen,	18th Conn. Vols.	
B. Bennett,	22d N. Y. Cav.,	Hammondsport, N. Y.
N. Bostwick,	20th O. Vols.	
J. F. Benson,	120th Ill. Vols.,	Vienna, Ill.
B. C. Beebe,	13th Ind. Vols.,	Seneca Falls, N. Y.
A. N. Benson,	1st D. C. Cav.	
E. A. Burpee,	19th Me. Vols.,	Rockland, Me.
J. W. Bryant,	5th N. Y. Cav.,	Washington, D. C.
H. Biebel,	6th Conn. Vols.,	Bridgeport, Conn.
J. A. Barrett,	7th Pa. R. C.,	Philadelphia, Pa.
G. A. Bayard,	148th Pa. Vols.	
Geo. A. Blanchard,	85th Ill. Vols.,	Havanna, Ill.
S. Bremen,	3d Mich. Vols.,	Georgetown, Mich.
A. T. Bliss,	10th N. Y. Cav.,	Peterboro', N. Y.
H. D. Baker,	120th Ill. Vols.,	Golconda, Ill.
W. F. Bennett.	39th Iowa Vols.,	Osceola, Iowa.
J. H. Brown,	17th Iowa Vols.,	Desmoines, Iowa.
S. D. Barnum,	23d U. S. C. T.,	North Rome, Pa.
W. F. Baker,	87th Pa. Vols.,	Gettysburg, Pa.
H. H. Burbank,	32d Me. Vols.,	Limerick, Me.
O. E. Bartlett,	31st Me. Vols.,	Showhegan, Me.
J. T. Chalfant,	11th Pa. Vols.,	Pittsburg, Pa.
C. H. Call,	29th Ill. Vols.,	Inkster, Mich.
J. D. Clyde,	76th N. Y. Vols.,	Cherry Valley, N. Y.
C. R. Chauncey,	34th Mass. Vols.,	Westfield, Mass.
A. F. Cole,	59th N. Y. Vols.,	Lowville, N. Y.

J. P. Carr,	93d Ind. Vols.,	Austin, Ind.
H. P. Cooke,	A. A. Gen.,	Deckartown, N. J.
T. B. Camp,	52d Pa. Vols.,	Camptown, Pa.
L. S. Clark,	62d N. Y. Vols.,	Saratoga, Sp's, N. Y.
H. C. Chapin,	4th Vt. Vols.	Elmira, N. Y.
F. S. Case,	2d O. Cav.,	Wellington, O.
T. Coglin,	14th N. Y. Heavy Aty,	Rochester, N. Y.
J. W. Colville,	5th Mich. Vols.,	East Saginaw, Mich.
L. M. Carperts,	18th Wis. Vols.	
E. N. Carpenter,	6th Pa. Cav.,	Germantown, Pa.
M. W. Clark,	11th Iowa Cav.,	Columbus City, Iowa.
E. S. Daniels,	35th U. S. C. T.,	Old Cambridge, Mass.
C. C. Dodge,	20th Mich. Vols.,	Marshall, Mich.
O. J. Downing,	2d N. Y. Cav.,	Long Island, N. Y.
J. G. Derrickson,	66th N. Y. Vols.,	New York City.
J. B. Dennis,	7th Conn. Vols.	
T. F. Davenport,	75th O. Vols.	
C. Z. Dirlan,	12th O. Vols.,	Clyde, O.
W. Dusbrow,	40th N. Y. Vols.,	New York City.
A. Duzenburgh,	35th N. Y. Vols.	
E. B. Doane,	8th O. Cav.,	Salem, Iowa.
W. H. Davis,	4th Md. Vols.,	Baltimore, Md.
G. B. Donohey,	7th Pa. Res.	
L. B. Davis,	93d Ind. Vols.,	Patriot, Ind.
E. C. Dicey,	1st Mich. S. S.,	Detroit, Mich.
J. Dibeler,	45th Pa. Vols.,	Bainbridge, Pa.
S. S. Elder,	1st U. S. Art.	
B. W. Evans,	4th O. Cav.,	Kirkersville, O.
M. Eagan,	15th W. Va. Vols.	
N. C. Evans,	184th Pa. Vols.,	Rainsburg, Pa.
W. V. Farr,	106th Pa. Vols.	
E. W. Ford,	9th Minn. Vols.,	Austin, Minn
J. W. Funk,	39th N. Y. Vols.,	New York City.
W. M. Fisk,	73d N. Y. Vols.,	
J. L. Francis,	135th O. Vols.	
D. Flamsburg,	4th Ind. Battalion.	
J. Fiedler,	Eng. R. C. U. S. A.	
J. P. Fall,	32d Me. Vols.,	South Berwick Me.
W. W. Fay,	56th Mass. Vols.	
J. B. Gillespie,	120th Ill. Vols.,	Vienna, Ill.
E. C. Gilbert,	152d N. Y. Vols.,	Butternuts, N. Y.
A. W. H. Gill,	14th N. Y. Vols.,	Brooklyn, N. Y.
E. Grant,	1st Vt. Cav.	
E. H. Green,	107th Pa. Vols.,	Maytown, Pa.
A. Grant,	19th Wis. Vols.	
A. L. Goodrich,	8th N. Y. Cav.,	Churchville, N. Y.
J. L. Galloway,	A. A. G.	Pensacola, Fla.
J. L. Green,	A. A. G. U. S. A.,	Monroe, Mich.
C. Gutjahr,	16th Ill. Vols.	
P. Grayhaur,	54th Pa. Vols.,	Johnstown, Pa.
H. B. Huff,	184th Pa. Vols.,	Altoona, Pa.
W. R. Hitt,	13th Ill. Cav.,	Urbana, O.
W. Harris,	24th Mo. Cav.,	Mount Vernon, Mo.
C. A. Hobbie,	17th Conn. Vols.,	Stamford, Conn.
T. A. Heer,	28th O. Vols.,	Tell City, Ind.
G. D. Hart.	5th Pa. Cav.	

Name	Regiment	Location
H. B. Hoyt,	140th N. Y. Inf'y,	Rochester, N. Y.
D. J. Hume,	19th Mass. Vols.,	Boston, Mass.
R. C. Hutchinson,	8th Mich. Vols.	
C. W. Hastings,	12th Mass. Vols.	
E. Hayes,	95th N. Y. Vols.,	Sing Sing, N. Y.
M. C. Hobart,	7th Wis. Vols.,	Fall River, Wis.
J. A. Hayden,	11th P. R. V. C.,	Union Town, Pa.
W. L. Hodge,	120th Ill. Vols.,	Golconda, Ill.
H. A. Haines,	184th Pa. Vols.	
J. B. Heltermus,	18th Ky. Vols.	
S. Hymer,	115th Ill. Vols.,	Rushville, Ill.
P. Heinrod,	105th O. Vols.,	Waterford, Pa.
F. W. Heck,	2d Md. Vols.,	Baltimore, Md.
V. H. Hill,	2d Md. Vols.,	Manchester, N. H.
A. J. Holmes,	37th Wis. Vols.	
L. Ingledew,	7th Mich. Vols.,	Janesville, Wis.
B. A. Jobe,	11th Pa. R. V. C.,	Salem Cross R'ds, Pa.
D. Jones,	14th N. Y. Artillery,	Utica, N. Y.
S. C. Jones,	7th N. Y. Artillery.	
S. C. Judson,	106th N. Y. Vols.,	Ogdensburg, N. Y.
H. Jenkins,	40th Mass. Vols.	
C. G. Jackson,	84th Pa. Vols.,	Berwick, Pa.
J. D. Johnson.	10th N. J. Vols.,	Hamisports, N. J.
J. G. Kessler,	2d Ind. Cav.	
G. E. King,	103d Ill. Vols.,	Middleport, Ill,
P. D. Kenyon,	15th Ill. Battalion,	Mt. Carroll, Ind.
F. Kenfield,	17th Vt. Vols.,	Morristown, Vt.
W. S. Logan,	7th Mich. Vols.,	Richland, Mich.
J. S. Little,	143d Pa. Vols.,	Nicholson, Pa.
C. W. Lyttle,	145th Pa. Vols.,	
G. Law,	6th W. Va. Cav.,	Ellenboro', W. Va.
E. C. Latimer,	27th U. S. C. T.,	Canton, O.
W. W. McCarty,	18th O. Vols.,	McConnellsville, O.
J. W. Morton,	4th Mass. Cav.	
J. W. McHugh,	69th Pa. Vols.,	Philadelphia, Pa.
W. M. McFadden,	50th N. Y. Vols.	
H. McCray,	115th Pa. Vols.	
J. May,	15th Mass. Artillery.	
N. H. Moors,	7th N. Y. Artillery,	Albany, N. Y.
S. F. Murray,	2d U. S. S. S.,	Candia, N. H.
L. Maish,	87th Pa. Vols.	
A. C. Mattison,	12th N. J. Vols.	
J. Metzger,	55th Pa. Vols.	
LeRoy Moore,	72d O. Vols.,	Fremont, O.
S. M. Morgan,	A. A. Gen.,	Lindy, N. Y.
H. P. Merrill,	4th Ky. Vols.	
M. McGraylls,	93d Ind. Vols.	
H. J. McDonald,	11th Conn.,	Kingston, N. J.
M. Melkhhorn,	135th O. Vols.,	Ada, O.
J. A. Manley,	64th N. Y. Vols.	
A. G. Mudgett,	11th Me. Vols.,	Newburg, Me.
R. J. McWitt,	1st Pa. Cav.,	Milroy, Pa.
—— McIntyre,	15th Wis. Vols.	
L. Moore,	72d O. Vols.,	Fremont, O.
R. J. Millard,	2d Pa. Artillery,	Towersville, Pa.

Name	Unit	Location
J. H. Nutting,	27th Mass. Vols.	
L. Nolan,	2d Del. Vols.	
C. H. Nichols,	6th Conn. Vols.	
E. E. Norton,	24th Mich. Vols.	Detroit, Mich.
W. H. Nash,	1st U. S. S. S.,	New York City.
E. Newsome,	81st Ill. Vols.,	Carbondale, Ill.
A. Nuhfer,	72d O. Vols.,	Woodville, O.
C. Newlin,	7th Pa. Cav.	
J. Norris,	2d Pa. Artillery,	Washington, D. C.
C. S. Noyse,	31st Me. Vols.,	Mt. Desert, Me.
H. W. Ogan,	14th O. Vols.	
H. V. Pemberton,	14th N. Y. Artillery,	New York City.
J. Parker,	1st N. J. Vols.,	Trenton, N. J.
J. P. Powell,	146th N. Y. Vols.,	Clinton, N. Y.
L. B. Paine,	121st N. Y. Vols.,	Garratsville, N. Y.
J. T. Piggott, Jr.,	8th Pa. Cav.,	Philadelphia, Pa.
W. B. Plase,	87th U. S. Infty.,	Dayton, O.
D. H. Powers,	6th Mich. Cav.	
A. C. Paul,	A. A. Gen.,	Newport, Ky.
G. Pettit,	120th N. Y. Vols.,	Lexington, N. Y.
D. B. Pendleton,	5th Mich. Cav.,	Detroit, Mich.
D. M. Porter,	120th Ill. Vols.	
S. C. Pierce,	3d N. Y. Cav.,	Rochester, N. Y.
B. B. Porter,	10th N. Y. Artillery,	Taylor, N. Y.
J. A. Paine,	2d Ind. Cav.	Bridgetown, Ind.
T. Ping,	17th Iowa Vols.,	Ashland, Iowa.
J. Rourke,	1st Ill. Artillery,	Milwaukee, Mich.
H. Ritter,	52d N. Y. Vols.,	Philadelphia, Pa.
W. J. Reynolds,	75th O. Vols.	
A. C. Rosencranz,	4th Ind. Cav.,	Evansville, Ind.
—— Reed,	107th N. Y. Vols.	
R. C. Richards,	45th Pa. Vols.,	Ontario, N. Y.
W. J. Reynolds,	4th R. I. Vols.,	Wickford, R. I.
Geo. W. Reir,	107th N. Y. Vols.	
C. Robinson,	81st U. S. C. T.	
J. Snyder,	14th N. Y. Vols.,	Heuvelton, N. Y.
G. F. C. Smart,	145th Pa. Vols.,	West Greenville, Pa.
H. J. Smith,	53d Pa. Vols.,	Huntingdon, Pa.
D. Schooley,	2d Pa. Artillery,	Pittston, Pa.
H. W. Strang,	30th Ill. Vols.,	Collins Station, Ill.
J. H. Smith,	16th Iowa Vols.,	Lyons, Iowa.
A. S. Skilton,	57th O. Vols.	
W. Shuttz,	37th O. Vols.,	Toledo, O.
A. B. Smith,	48th Ill. Vols.	
R. R. Swift,	27th Mass. Vols.,	Springfield, Mass.
S. A. Spencer,	82d Ind. Vols.	
J. R. Stevens,	40th N. Y. Vols.,	Brooklyn, N. Y.
E. J. Swan,	76th N. Y. Vols.,	Cherry Valley, N. Y.
E. Schofield,	11th Pa. V. R. C.	Brookville, Pa.
C. B. Sutcher,	16th Ill. Vols.	
E. Shurtz,	8th Iowa Cav.	
M. L. Stansbury	95th O. Vols.	
J. G. Snodgrass,	110th O. Vols.,	New Madison, O.
H. R. Sargent,	32d Me. Vols.,	Portland, Me.
S. U. Sherman,	4th R. I. Vols.,	Providence, R. I.
R. T. Stewart,	138th Pa. Vols.,	Morristown, Pa.

D. W. Scott,	23d U. S. C. T.,	Pottsville, Pa.
L. D. C. Tyler,	100th Pa. Vols.,	Philadelphia, Pa.
S. C. Timbson,	95th N. Y. Vols.,	New York City,
H. Tilbrand,	4th N. H. Vols.	
J. H. Turner,	16th Iowa Vols.,	Muscatine, Iowa.
H. G. Tibbles,	12th O. Vols.,	Dayton, O.
J. Thomson,	4th O. Cav.	
C. L. Unthank,	11th Ky. Cav.	
H. A. Uffar,	A. A. Gen.	
J. W. Underwood,	57th O. Vols.	
A. Von Keiser,	30th N. Y. Battery.	
Z. Vaughn,	1st Me. Cav.,	Freeman, Me.
A. Von Haack,	68th N. Y. Vols.	
J. H. West,	11th Ky. Vols.	
E. T. Wyman,	———— ————,	Augusta, Me.
W. Washburn,	35th Mass. Vols.,	Boston, Mass.
A. R. Willis,	8th Me. Vols.,	Biddeford, Me.
U. S. Westbrook,	135th O. Vols.,	Zanesville, O.
B. F. Wright,	146th N. Y. Vols.,	Utica, N. Y.
W. M. Wilson, Jr,	122d O. Vols.,	Zanesville, O.
H. B. Wakefield,	55th Ind. Vols.,	Azailia, Ind.
G. Webb,	2d Pa. Artillery,	Murcy, Pa.
J. Wilson,	57th O. Vols.	
R Williams,	12th O. Vols.,	Dayton, O.
M. Wiley,	1st Tenn. Vols.	
E. B. Whittaker,	72d Pa. Vols.	
R. J. Wright,	6th O. Vols.,	Springfield, O.
H. H. Walpole,	122d N. Y. Vols.,	Syracuse, N. Y.
M. W. Wall,	69th N. Y. Vols.	
D. G. Young,	81st Ill. Vols.,	De Soto, Ill.
F. K. Zarracher,	18th Pa. Cav.,	Philadelphia, Pa.

LIEUTENANTS.

J. G. B. Adams,	19th Mass. Vols.,	Groveland, Mass.
E. P. Alexander,	26th Mich. Vols.,	Detroit, Mich.
H. M. Anderson,	3d Me. Vols.	
J. F. Anderson,	2d Pa. Artillery,	Philadelphia, Pa.
A. L. Abbey,	8th Mich. Cav.,	Armada, Mich.
A. O. Abbott,	1st N. Y. Dragoons,	Almond, N. Y.
A. S. Appleget,	2d N. J. Cav.,	Hightstown, Pa.
Robert Allen,	2d N. J. Dragoons.	
G. A. Austin,	14th Ill. Bat.,	Woodstock, Ill.
G. C. Alden,	112th Ill. Vols.,	Annawan, Ill.
W. C. Adams,	2d Ky. Cav.,	Star Furnace, Ky.
E. T. Afflec,	170th Nat. G.,	Bridgeport, O.
E. A. Abbott,	2d O. Vet. Vols.,	Olmsted Falls, O.

Count S. Braiday,	2d N. J. Cav.,	Vienna, Austria.
A. Bulow,	3d N. J. Cav.	
J. H. Bryan,	184th Pa. Vols.,	Harrisburg, Pa.
C. W. Baldwin,	2d N. J. Vols.,	New York City.
H. E. Barker,	22d N. Y. Cav.	
C. H. Bigley,	82d N. Y. Vols.	
M. Burns,	13th N. Y. Cav.	
C. A. Brown,	1st N. Y. Artillery.	
W. R. Bosford,	1st N. Y. Vols.	
J. L. Barton,	49th Pa. Vols.	
W. Buchanan,	76th N. Y. Vols.,	Cohoes, N. Y.
W. Blane,	43d N. Y. Vols.,	Albany, N. Y.
J. H. Briston,	1st Conn. Cav.	
H. H. Bixby,	9th Me. Vols.,	Norridgewock, Me.
D. W. Burkholder,	7th Pa. Vols.,	Shippensburg, Pa.
S. Brum,	81st Ill. Vols.	
W. H. Brady,	2d Del. Vols.,	Wilmington, Del.
J. Breon,	148th Pa. Vols.,	Potters Mills, Pa.
G. M. Burnett,	4th Ind. Cav.,	Terre Haute, Ind.
W. J. Boyd,	5th Mich. Cav.	
S. W. Burrows,	1st N. Y. Vet. Cav.	
M. Blickenhoff,	42d N. Y. Vols.,	New York City.
H. Buckley,	4th N. H. Vols.	
A. T. Barnes,	Ill. Vet. Vols.	
J. L. Beasley,	81st Ill. Vols.,	Fredonia, Ill.
A. Barringer,	44th N. Y. Vols.,	Nassau, N. Y.
E. P. Bishop,	4th Tenn. Cav.	
C. T. Bowen,	4th R. I. Vols.,	Wickford, R. I.
Wm. Bateman.	9th Mich. Cav.,	Ypsilanti, Mich.
Wm. Baird,	23d U. S. C. T.,	North Rome, Pa.
J. N. Biller,	2d Pa. Artillery,	Martinsburg, W. Va.
F. S. Bowley,	30th U. S. C. T.,	Worcester, Mass.
C. Boettger,	2d Md. Vols.,	Baltimore, Md.
W. A. Barnard,	20th Mich. Vols.,	Lansing, Mich.
Wm. Blasse,	43d N. Y. Vols.,	Albany, N. Y.
C. O. Brown,	31st Me. Vols.,	Moro, Me.
R. K. Beecham,	23d U. S. C. T.,	Sun Prairie, Me
A. M. Brisco,	Cole's Md. Cav.,	Baltimore, Md.
H. M. Bearce,	32d Me. Vols.,	West Minot. Me.
A. J. Braidy,	54th Pa. Vols.	
C. A. Bell,	A. D. C.	
R. Burton,	9th N. Y. Artillery.	
H. E. Beebee,	22d N. Y. Cav.	
V. L. Coffin,	31st Me. Vols.,	Harrington, Me.
L. A. Campbell,	152d N. Y. Vols.,	Cherry Valley, N. Y
C. W. Carr,	4th Vt. Vols.	

J. Cunningham,	7th Pa. R. C.,	Leesport, Pa.
C. Coslett,	115th Pa. Vols.,	Philadelphia, Pa.
R. Cooper,	7th N. J. Vols.,	Jersey City, N. J.
C. H. Crawford,	188th Pa. Vols.,	Philadelphia, Pa.
S. O. Cromack,	77th N. Y. Vols.,	Bennington, Vt.
H. Correll,	2d Vt. Vols.,	New Haven, Vt.
C. H. Cutter,	95th N. Y. Vols.,	Boston, Mass.
G. W. Creacy,	35th Mass. Vols.,	Newburyport, Mass.
R. H. Chute,	59th Mass. Vols.,	Chelsea, Mass.
H. M. Cross,	59th Mass. Vols.,	Newburyport, Mass.
H. A. Chapin,	95th N. Y. Vols.	
W. Chahill,	76th N. Y. Vols.,	Solon, N. Y.
J. L. Casler,	76th N. Y. Vols.,	Otsego, N. Y.
H. Chisman,	7th Ind. Vols.,	Cincinnati, O.
H. Cribben,	140th N. Y. Vols.,	Rochester, N. Y.
G. M. Curtis,	140th N. Y. Vols.,	Rochester, N. Y.
J. S. Caldwell,	16th Ill. Cav.,	Chicago, Ill.
S. Crossley,	118th Pa. Vols.,	Philadelphia, Pa.
L. B. Carlisle,	145th Pa. Vols.,	Suthersburg, Pa.
J. P. Codington,	8th Iowa Cav.,	Dubuque, Ia.
W. H. Curtis,	19th Mass. Vols.,	Randolph, Mass.
J. W. Clark,	59th N. Y. Vols.,	Butler, O.
J. H. Clark,	1st Mass. Artillery,	Boston, Mass.
D. L. Case, Jr.,	102d N. Y. Vols.,	Lansing, Mich.
J. D. Cope,	116th Pa. Vols.,	Uniontown, Pa.
J. W. Core,	6th W. Va. Cav.	
W. J. Colter,	15th Mass. Vols.,	Clinton, Mass.
J. Casey,	45th N. Y. Vols.,	Tuckahoe, N. Y.
W. H. Carter,	5th Pa. R. C.,	Elimsport, Pa.
J. L. Chittendon,	5th Ind. Cav.,	Knoxville, Tenn.
W. H. Canney,	60th N. Y. Vols.,	New York City.
W. F. Campbell,	51st Pa. Vols.,	Slifer, Pa.
J. F. Cameron,	5th Pa. Cav.,	Philadelphia, Pa.
M. Clegg,	5th Ind. Cav.	
H. R. Chase,	1st Vt. Heavy Artillery	Guilford Centre, Vt.
W. H. Conover,	22d N. Y. Cav.,	Norwich, N. Y.
B. F. Califf,		Salem, Mass
D. B. Chubbuck,	19th Mass. Vols.	
M. Cunningham,	42d N. Y. Vols.,	Norwich, Conn.
A. M. Charters,	17th Iowa Vols.,	Leavenworth, K'ns's,
W. A. Copeland,	10th Mich. Vols.	
T. Clemmens,	13th Ill. Vols.	
W. C. Cook,	9th Mich. Cav.,	Tecumseh, Mich.
C. P. Cramer,	21st N. Y. Cav.,	West Troy, N. Y.
Geo. Corum,	2d Ky. Cav.,	Greenupsburg, Pa.
M. B. Case,	23d U. S. C. T.,	Ottawona, Minn.

D. J. Cline,	75th O. V. M. I.,	Logan Hocking, O.
C. G. Conn,	1st M. S. S.	
M. Cunningham,	1st Vt. Heavy Artillery.	
H. L. Clark,	2d Mass. Artillery,	Rochester, N. Y.
C. D. Copeland,	58th Pa. Vols.,	Fall River, Mass.
C. P. Cashell,	12th Pa. Cav.	
J. R. Channell,	1st Ill. Artillery,	Ottawa, Ill.
W. S. Damrell,	13th Mass. Vols.,	Boston, Mass.
W. G. Davis,	27th Mass. Vols.	
S. V. Dean,	145th Pa. Vols.,	West Springfield, Pa.
J. S. Drennan,	1st Vt. Artillery,	Morrisville, Vt.
J. Dunn,	64th N. Y. Vols.,	New York City.
A. J. Dunning,	7th N. Y. Artillery.	
J. Donovan,	2d N. J. Vols.,	Elizabeth, N. J.
E. B. Dyer,	1st Conn. Cav.,	Derby, Conn.
W. C. Dorris,	11th Ill. Vols.	
H. G. Dodge,	2d Pa. Cav.,	Philadelphia, Pa.
C. Downs,	33d N. J. Vols.,	Patterson, N. J.
J. Duren,	5th N. H. Vols.,	Keene, N. H.
W. H. Dorfee,	5th R. I. Vols.,	Newport, R. I.
G. Durboyne,	66th N. Y.	
W. H. Diffenbach,	7th Pa. R. C.,	Huntingdon, Pa.
R. DeLay,	4th Iowa Cav.,	Centerville, Iowa.
O. W. Demmick,	11th N. H. Vols.,	Strafford, Vt.
L. Dick,	72d O. Vols.,	Fremont, O.
E. Dickerson,	44th Wis. Vols.	
D. Driscoll,	24th Mo. Vols.,	Cannonsburg, Mich.
H. G. Dorr,	4th Mass. Cav.,	Boston, Mass.
J. M. Drake,	9th N. J. Vols.,	Trenton, N. J.
H. A. Downing,	31st U. S. C. T.,	Poughkeepsie, N. Y.
J. W. Davidson,	95th O. Vols.,	Big Plains, O.
G. H. Drew,	9th N. H. Vols.,	Milford, N. H.
Chas. Everett,	70th O. Vols.,	Cleveland, O.
P. R. Eastman,	2d Pa. Cav.,	Mt. Clemens, Mich.
J. L. F. Elkin,	1st N. J. Vols.,	New Brunswick, N.
J. W. Eyestone,	13th Ind. Vols.,	Washington, Ia.
T. E. Evans,	52d Pa. Vols.,	Hyde Park, Pa.
T. K. Eckings,*	3d N. J. Vols.	
John Eagan,	1st U. S. Artillery.	
John Elder,	8th Ind. Vols.	
J. Fairbanks,	72d O. Vols.,	Rollersville, O.
G. E. Finney,	19th Ind. Vols.,	Elizabeth, Ind.
J. M. Ferris,	3d Mich. Vols.	
E. M. Faye,	42d N. Y. Vols.,	New York City.
J. Furgeson,	1st N. J. Vols.,	Philadelphia, Pa.
D. Flannery,	4th N. J. Vols.,	Trenton, N. J.

H. M. Fowler,	15th N. J. Vols.,	Newark, N. J.
G. W. Fluger,	11th Pa. R. C.,	Butler, Pa.
C. A. Fagan,	11th Pa. R. C.,	Ebensburg, Pa.
H. French,	3d Vt. Vols.,	Hartford, Vt.
L. W. Fisher,	4th Vt. Vols.,	Danville, Vt.
S. Fatzer,	108th N. Y. Vols.,	Rochester, N. Y.
E. Fontaine,	7th Pa. R. C.,	Washington, D. C.
D. Forney,	30th O. Vols.,	Coshocton, O.
S. Fisher,	93d Ind. Vols.	
D. S. Finney,	14th Ill. Vols.,	Beardstown, Ill.
D. Fitzpatrick,	146th N. Y. Vols.,	Brooklyn, N. Y.
L. D. C. Fales,	——— ———.	
H. C. Foster,	23d Ind. Vols.,	Jeffersonville, Ind.
John Foley,	59th Mass. Vols.,	Boston, Mass.
Louis Faas,	14th N. Y. Artillery,	Attica, N. Y.
R. J. Frost,	9th Mich. Cav.,	Albion, Mich.
G. J. George,	40th Ill. Vols.	
T. M. Gunn,	21st Ky. Vols.,	Shelbyville, Ky.
J. Gottshell,	55th Pa. Vols.	
J. M. Goodown,	12th Ind. Vols.,	Fort Wayne, Ind.
H. D. Grant,	117th N. Y. Vols.	
J. A. Goodwin,	1st Mass. Cav.,	Medford, Mass.
C. M. Granger,	88th N. Y. Vols.	
C. O. Gordon,	1st Me. Cav.,	Phillips, Me.
J. W. Goss,	1st Mass. Artillery,	Ipswich, Mass.
H. M. Gordon,	143d Pa. Vols.,	Shickshinny, Pa.
J. Gallagher,	4th O. Vets.,	Brookfield, Vt.
E. A. Green,	81st Ill. Vols.	
T. Griffin,	55th U. S. C. T.,	Pulaski, Ill.
M. L. Godley,	17th Iowa Vols.,	Ashland, Iowa.
Philip Grey,	72d Pa. Vols.	
A. M. Hall,	9th Minn. Vols.	
E. R. Hart,	1st Vt. Artillery,	Danvers, Mass.
J. F. Hodge,	55th Pa. Vols.	
R. F. Hall,	75th O. Vols.,	Cincinnati, O.
J. T. Haight,	8th Iowa Cav.,	Tipton, Iowa.
G. W. Hill,	7th Mich. Cav.,	Detroit, Mich.
E. J. Hazel,	6th Pa. Cav.,	Baltimore, Md.
R. Herbert,	50th Pa. Vols.,	Lebanon, Pa.
S. H. Horton,	101st Pa. Vols.	
W. B. Hurd,	17th Mich. Cav.,	Jackson, Mich.
E. Holder,	1st Vt. Cav.,	Barre, Vt.
S. P. Hedges,	112th N. Y. Vols.,	Jamestown, N. Y.
H. C. Hinds,	102d N. Y. Vols.,	Richfield Sp'gs, N. Y
J. Hopper,	2d N. Y. Cav.,	Scranton, Pa.
C. O. Hunt,	5th Me. Battery.	

W. R. Holland,	5th Md. Cav.	
G. N. Hull,	13th O. Vols.	
D. W. Hazelton,	22d N. Y. Cav.,	Peterboro', N. Y.
C. P. Holaham,	19th Pa. Cav.,	Philadelphia, Pa.
G. L. Hastings,	24th N. Y. Battery,	Albany, N. Y.
H. N. Hamilton,	59th N. Y. Vols.,	Belleville, O.
E. S. Huntington,	11th U. S. Infantry.	
W. H. Hoyt,	16th Iowa Vols.,	Camanche, Iowa.
R. M. Hughes,	14th Ill. Cav.,	Vandalia, Ill.
J. Hewitt,	105th Pa. Vols.	
J. Heston,	4th N. J. Vols.,	Sing Sing, N. Y.
J. Heffelfinger,	7th Pa. V. R. C.,	Mechanicsburg, Pa.
J. L. Harvey,	2d Pa. Artillery,	Philadelphia, Pa.
H. V. Hadley,	7th Ind. Vols.,	Indianapolis, Ind.
M. V. B. Hallett,	2d Pa. Cav.,	Osceola, Pa.
A. J. Henry,	120th Ill. Vols.	
V. G. Hoalladay,	2d Ind. Cav.,	Wintersett, Ind.
D. Havens,	85th Ill. Vols.,	Manito, Ill.
C. A. Hays,	11th Pa. Vols.,	Eagle, Pa.
J. L. Hastings,	7th Pa. V. R. C.,	Salona, Pa.
J. W. Harris,	2d Ind. Cav.,	Terre Haute, Ind.
P. Herzberg,	66th N. Y. Vols.,	New York City.
E. H. Higley,	1st Vt. Cav.,	Castleton, Vt.
W. H. Hendryks,	11th Mich. Battery.	
J. Huston,	95th O. Vols.,	Clayhick, O.
R. Henderson,	1st Mass. Art.,	Lawrence, Mass.
A. N. Hackett,	101st O. Vols.,	Masillon, O.
S. P. Hand,	43d U. S. C. T.,	Binghamton, N. Y.
T. B. Hurst,	7th Pa. V. R. C.,	Dillsburg, Pa.
Geo. Hopf,	2d Md. Vols.,	Baltimore, Md.
O. M. Hill,	1st Mo. Artillery.	
J. B. Hogue,	4th Pa. Cav.	
L. E. Haywood,	58th Mass. Vols.	
A. B. Isham,	7th Mich. Cav.,	Detroit, Mich.
H. A. Johnson,	3d Me. Vols.	
C. K. Johnson,	1st Me. Cav.,	Carmel, Me.
G. W. Jenkins,	9th W. Va. Vols.,	Portland, O.
J. C. Justus,	2d Pa. V. R. C.,	Philadelphia, Pa.
J. W. Johnson,	1st Mass. Artillery,	Methuen, Mass.
Alfred Jones,	50th Pa. Vets.,	Reading, Pa.
J. Jacks,	15th W. Va. Vols.	
P. Krohn,	5th N. Y. Cav.,	Oswego, N. Y.
E. Kendrick,	10th N. J. Vols.,	New York City.
S. C. Kerr,	125th O. Vols.,	Salineville, O.
H. T. Kendall,	50th Pa. Vols.,	Reading, Pa.
A. Kelly,	126th O. Vols.,	Barnesville, O.

Name	Regiment	Location
J. Keen,	7th Pa. V. R. C.,	Bart, Pa.
J. D. Kennuly,	8th O. Cav.,	Piqua, O.
J. P. Kempton,	75th O. Vols.	
J. H. Kidd,	1st Md. Artillery,	Port Deposit, Md.
R. H. Kendrick,	25th Wis. Vols.,	Potosi, Wis.
G. C. Kenyon,	17th Ill. Vols.	
G. C. Kidder,	113th Pa. Vols.,	Danton, Ill.
G. Knox,	100th Pa. Vols.,	Philadelphia, Pa.
J. M. Kelly,	4th Tenn. Vols.,	Athens, Tenn.
F. H. Kempton,	58th Mass. Artillery.	
J. R. Kelly,	1st Pa. Cav.,	Patterson, Pa.
J. C. Knox,	4th Ind. Cav.,	Ladoga, Ind.
Abe King,	12th O. Vols.,	Xenia, O.
J. Keheart	13th O. Vols.,	Russell Station, O
J. Kellow,	2d Pa. Artillery,	Honesdale, Pa.
G. L. Kibby,	4th R. L Vols.,	Providence, R. L
C. E. Lewis,	1st N. Y. Drag.,	Nunda, N. Y.
J. B. Laycock,	7th Pa. V. R. C.	
H. H. Lyman,	147th N. Y. Vols.,	Pulaski, N. Y.
J. Lyman,	27th Mass. Vols.,	East Hampton, Mass
W. H. Larrabee,	7th Me. Vols.,	Portland, Me.
A. Lee,	152d N. Y. Vols.,	Utica, N. Y.
J. L. Lynn,	145th Pa. Vols.,	West Greenville, Pa.
E. De C. Loud,	2d Pa. Artillery,	Philadelphia, Pa.
M. S. Ludwig,	53d Pa. Vols.,	Philadelphia, Pa.
D. W. Lewry,	2d Pa. Artillery.	
J. O. Laird,	35th U. S. Infantry.	
M. Laird,	16th Iowa Vols.,	Desmoines, Iowa.
J. C. Luther,	1st Pa. V. R. C.,	Ridgeway, Pa.
M. W. Lemon,	14th N. Y. Artillery,	Canton, N. Y.
L. M. Lane,	9th Minn. Vols.	
T. D. Lamson,	3d Ind. Cav.,	Venny, Ind.
A. Limbard,	McLaughlin's Squ.,	Delphee, O.
G. K. Lawrence,	2d N. Y. Mounted Rifles,	Buffalo, N. Y.
C. H. Long,	59th Mass. Vols.	
J. Monaghan,	62d Pa. Vols.,	New York City.
J. C. McIntosh,	145th Pa. Vols.,	Erie, Pa.
F. W. Mather,	7th N. Y. Artillery,	Albany, N. Y.
P. B. Mockrie,	7th N. Y. Artillery,	Albany, N. Y.
E. T. McCutcheon,	64th N. Y. Vols.,	Gowanda, N. Y.
E. J. McWain,	1st N. Y. Artillery,	Rochester, Vt.
J. McKage,	184th Pa. Vols.,	Hollidaysburg, Pa.
S. F. Muffley,	184th Pa. Vols.,	Howard, Pa.
H. F. Mangus,	53d Pa. Vols.,	Winfield, Pa.
J. McLaughlin,	53d Pa. Vols.,	James Creek, Pa.

W. A. McGinnes,	19th Mass. Vols.,	Boston, Mass.
A. D. Mathews,	1st Vt. Artillery,	Brownington, Vt.
A. Morse,	1st Vt. Artillery,	Fayetteville, Vt.
J. H. Morris,	4th Ky. Vols.	
J. McGeehan,	146th N. Y. Vols.,	Brooklyn, N. Y.
H. W. Mitchell,	14th N. Y. Vols.	
H. G. Mitchell,	32d Me. Vols.,	Portland, Me.
J. C. McCain,	9th Minn. Vols.,	Logansport, Ind.
T. McGuire,	7th Ill. Vols.,	St. Charles, Ill.
J. W. Miller,	14th Ill. Cav.,	Lincoln, Ill.
H. Miller,	17th Mich. Vols.,	Detroit, Mich.
J. Murphy,	60th N. Y. Vols.,	Newark, N. J.
J. Mallison,	94th N. Y. Vols.,	Brandon, Wis.
J. A. Mullegan,	4th Mass. Cav.,	Biddeford, Me.
W. F. Mathews,	1st Md. Vols.,	Martinsburg, W. Va.
N. J. Menier,	93d Ind. Vols.,	Leopold, Ind.
P. W. McManus,	27th Mass. Vols.,	Davenport, Iowa.
E. McMahon,	72d O. Vols.	
G. C. Morton,	4th Pa. Cav.	
E. Mather,	1st Vt. Cav.,	Fair Haven, Vt.
C. McDonald,	2d Ill. Artillery,	Tamaroa, Ill.
G. W. Mayer,	37th Ind. Vols.,	Lawrenceburg, Ind.
J. McCormick,	21st N. Y. Cav.,	Troy, N. Y.
A. J. Marshland,	2d Pa. Artillery,	Nicetown, Pa.
W. H. Mix,	19th U. S. C. T.,	Warsaw, N. Y.
T. J. Munger,	37th Wis. Vols.,	Madison, Wis.
A. McNure,	73d Pa. Vols.,	Philadelphia, Pa.
J. D. Marshall,	57th Ohio Vols.,	Wapakourutta, O.
—— McLane,	9th Minn. Vols.	
W. McNettervill,	12th U. S. Infantry.	
C. Niedenhoffen,	9th Minn. Vols.,	Winona, Minn.
A. Nelson,	66th N. Y. Vols.,	Westchester, N. Y.
J. B. Needham,	4th Vt. Vols.,	Shrewsbury, Vt.
H. L. Noggle,	2d U. S. Infantry,	Janesville, Wis.
J. Norwood,	76th N. Y. Vols.,	Slaterville, N. Y.
O. H. Nealy,	11th U. S. Infantry,	Boston, Mass.
W. Neher,	7th Pa. R. V. C.,	Philadelphia, Pa.
A. Neal,	5th Ind. Cav.	
D. M. Niswander,	2d Pa. Artillery,	Welch Run, Pa.
H. J. Nyman,	19th Mich. Vols.	
W. R. Nulland,	5th Ind. Cav.,	Lafayette, Ind.
R. V. Outcolt,	135th O. Vols.	
J. O'Harre,	7th N. Y. Artillery,	Cohoes, N. Y.
F. Osborne,	19th Mass. Vols.,	Byfield, Mass.
D. Oliphant,	35th N. J. Vols.	
E. O'Shea,	13th Pa. Cav.,	Philadelphia, Pa.

P. O'Connell,	55th Pa. Vols.,	Johnstown, Pa.
J. Ogden,	1st Wis. Cav.,	Winona, Minn.
G. C. Olden,	112th Ill. Vols.	
A. C. Pichenpaugh,	6th W. Va. Vols.,	Morgantown, W. Va.
H. Picquet,	32d Ill. Vols.,	Olney, Ill.
J. T. Parker,	13th Iowa Vols.,	Sigourney, Iowa.
G. M. Parker,	45th Ill. Vols.,	Carmi, Ill.
J. S. Purveance,	130th Ind. Vols.,	Huntington, Ind.
E. B. Parker,	1st Vt. Artillery.	
A. Phinney,	90th Ill. Vols.,	Rockford, Ill.
W. M. Provins,	84th Ill. Vols.,	Vermont, Ill.
T. Purcell,	16th Iowa Vols.,	Muscatine, Iowa.
W. H. Powell,	2d Ill. Artillery.	
D. H. Piffard,	14th N. Y. Vols.,	New York City.
C. A. Price,	5th Mich. Vols.,	Maple Rapids, Mich.
W. H. Partridge,	67th N. Y. Vols.,	Brooklyn, N. Y.
H. H. Pierce,	7th Conn. Vols.,	Unionville, Conn.
G. W. Pitt,	85th N. Y. Vets.,	Short Tract, N. Y.
D. S. Peake,	85th N. Y. Vets.,	Hinsdale, N. Y.
E. C. Pierson,	85th N. Y. Vets.,	Waterloo, N. Y.
M. P. Pierson,	190th N. Y. Vols.,	LeRoy, N. Y.
A. P. Pierson,	9th Mich. Cav.,	
D. Pentzell,	4th N. Y. Cav.	
J. C. Petrey,	95th Ohio Vols.,	London, O.
A. L. Preston,	8th Mich. Cav.,	Mt. Clemmuns, Mich.
G. Peters,	9th N. J. Vols.,	Elizabeth, N. J.
J. H. Pitt,	118th N. Y. Vols.,	Canton, N. Y.
James Post,	149th Pa. Vols.,	Shickshinny, Pa.
W. D. Peck,	——— ———,	Syracuse, N. Y.
G. W. Patterson,	135th Ohio Vols.,	Alexandria, O.
J. C. Price,	75th Ohio Vols.	
Z. Perrin,	72d Ohio Vols.,	Clyde, O.
S. H. Platt,	34th Mass. Vols.,	Pittsfield, Mass.
L. G. Porter,	81st Ill. Vols.,	Tamaroa, Ill.
J. H. Palmer,	12th Ohio Vols.,	Ripley, O.
W. A. Pope,	18th Wis. Vols.	
D. B. Pyne,	3d Mo. Vols.,	Alden, Iowa.
Worthington Pierce,	17th Vt. Vols.,	Woodstock, Vt.
W. B. Phillips,	2d Pa. Artillery,	Hyde Park, Pa.
C. O. Poindexter,	31st Me. Vols.,	Bridgeton, Me.
Chas. A. Price,	3d Mich. Vols.,	Maple Rapids, Mich.
M. Rees,	72d Ohio Vols.,	Rollersville, O.
W. B. Rose,	73d Ill. Vols.	
J. M. Ruger,	57th Pa. Vols.	
L. S. Richards,	1st Vt. Artillery,	West Concord, Vt.
G. Rieneckar,	5th Pa. Cav.	

O. Kahn,	184th Pa. Vols.,	Duncannon, Pa.
G. A. Rowley,	2d U. S. Infantry.	
B. E. Robinson,	95th Ohio Vols.,	Reynoldsburg, O.
W. E. Roach,	49th N. Y. Vols.,	Rochester, N. Y.
H. W. Raymond,	8th N. Y. Artillery,	Elba, N. Y.
J. C. Rose,	120th Ill. Vols.,	Vienna, Ill.
E. R. Roberts,	7th Ill. Vols.	
J. H. Reed,	120th Ill. Vols.	
J. M. Richards,	1st W. Va. Vols.,	Wheeling, W. Va.
H. Rothe,	15th N. Y. Artillery,	Alexandria, Va.
E. K. Ramsey,	1st N. J. Vols.,	Phœnixville, Pa.
L. H. Riley,	7th Pa. V. R. C.	
C. H. Ross,	13th Ind. Vols.,	Zanesville, O.
A. Ring,	12th Ohio Vols.	
T. W. Rathbone,	153d Ohio Vols.	
C. L. Rugg,	6th Ind. Cav.,	Newport, Ky.
J. S. Rice,	13th Ind. Vols.,	Washington, Iowa.
J. Reode,	57th Mass. Vols.,	Milford, Mass.
A. J. Raynor,	19th U. S. C. T.,	Ontario, N. Y.
L. Rainer,	2d N. J. Cav.,	Freehold, N. J.
J. S. Robeson,	7th Tenn. Cav.,	Huntington, Tenn.
W. L. Riley,	21st N. Y. Cav.,	Brighton, N. Y.
W. H. Randall,	1st Mich. S. S.,	Ypsilanti, Mich.
W. B. Sturgeon,	107th Pa. Vols.,	Shippensburg, Pa.
M. H. Stover,	184th Pa. Vols.	
A. A. Sweetland,	2d Pa. Cav.	
E. B. Smith,	1st Vt. Artillery,	Newport, Vt.
C. Schurr,	7th N. Y. Artillery.	
W. H. Shofer,	5th Pa. Cav.	
M. G. Sargeant,	1st Vt. Artillery,	Newport, Vt.
C. H. Stallman,	87th Pa. Artillery,	York, Pa.
S. S. Smythe,	1st Ill. Artillery,	Elkhorn, Ill.
Geo. Scott,	10th Ind. Vols.,	Lebanon, Ind.
E. Swift,	74th Ill. Vols.,	Pecatomica, Ill.
J. L. Skinner,	27th Mass. Vols.,	Amherst, Mass.
F. Stevens,	190th Pa. Vols.	
C. Stuart,	24th N. Y. Vols.	
M. Shanan,	14th N. Y. Vols.	
M. S. Smith,	16th Me. Vols.,	East Livermore, Me.
E. Snowwhite,	7th Pa. R. V. C.,	Palmyra, Pa.
W. H. S. Sweet,	146th N. Y. Vols.,	Utica, N. Y.
J. R. Sitler,	2d Pa. Cav.,	Harmonsburg, Pa.
A. L. Shannon,	3d Ind. Cav.,	Hannover, Ind.
A. M. Smith,	1st Tenn. Cav.	
J. C. Smith,	24th Ind. Bat.	
J. B. Smith,	5th W. Va. Cav.	

J. P. Smith,	49th Pa. Vols.,	Spring Mills, Pa.
P. Smith,	4th Tenn. Cav.,	Morristown, Pa.
J. Smith,	5th Pa. Cav.	
S. B. Smith,	20th U. S. C. T.,	Woodbury, N. J.
W. Sandon,	1st Wis. Cav.,	Ontario, Wis.
J. G. Stevens,	52d Pa. Vols.	
Frank Stevens,	15th Pa. R. C. Vols.,	Meadow Gap, Pa.
C. T. Swope,	4th Ky. Vols.	
A. S. Stewart,	4th Ky. Vols.	
R. R. Stewart,	2d —— Cav.,	New York City.
E. P. Strickland,	114th Ill. Vols.	
J. W. Stanton,	5th Ind. Cav.,	Carmel, Ind.
W. H. St. John,	5th Ind. Cav.,	Greensburg, Ind.
F. E. Scripture,	Regtl. Q. M.	
A. B. Simmons,	5th Ind. Cav.,	Union City, Ind.
H. P. Starr,	22d N. Y. Cav.,	Rochester, N. Y.
B. Spring,	75th Ohio Vols.	
A. C. Stover,	95th Ohio Vols.,	Urbanna, O.
C. P. Stone,	1st Vt. Cav.,	Brattleboro', Vt.
J. Stebbins,	77th N. Y. Vols.	
C. S. Schwartz,	2d N. J. Cav.,	Philadelphia, Pa.
J. Sailor,	13th Pa. Cav.,	Newport, Pa.
H. C. Smyser,	2d Md. Vols.,	Ashland Furnace, Pa.
M. W. Striblings,	61st Ohio Vols.,	Circleville, O.
J. O. Slout,	McLaughlin's Sq. O. Cav.,	Wooster, O.
M. N. Shepstrong,	60th Ohio Vols.	
J. P. Sheehan,	31st Me. Vols.,	Dennysville, Me.
J. F. Shull,	28th U. S. C. T.,	Bloomington, Ind.
B. F. Stauber,	20th Pa. Cav.,	Lewiston, Pa.
H. Schulter,	43d N. Y. Vols.,	Albany, N. Y.
L. D. Seely,	45th Pa. Vols.,	Knoxville, Pa.
T. D. Scofield,	27th Mich. Vols.	
C. B. Sanders,	35th U. S. C. T.	
P. A. Simondson,	23d U. S. C. T.	
N. W. Shaefer,	24th Ind. Cav.	
H. S. Tainter,	82d N. Y. Vols.	
D. Tanner,	118th Ill. Vols.	
H. V. Tompkins,	50th N. Y. Vols.	
B. W. Trout,	106th Pa. Vols.,	Canton, Pa.
J. S. Tompson,	10th Vt. Vols.	
L. E. Tyler,	1st Conn. Cav.,	Preston City, Conn.
A. Timm,	16th Iowa Vols.,	Davenport, Ind.
O. Todd,	18th Wis. Vols.,	Adrian, Mich.
A. W. Tiffany,	9th Minn. Vols.,	Carver, Minn.
J. Taylor,	2d Pa. R. C. Vols.	
D. W. Tower,	17th Iowa Vols.,	Farmington, Iowa.

F. Tomeon,	17th Iowa Vols.	
E. C. Taw,	67th N. Y. Vol.	
A. F. Tipton,	8th Iowa Cav.,	Elkader, Iowa.
David Turner,	118th Ill. Vols.,	Warsaw, Ill.
C. Tobel,	15th N. Y. Artillery,	New York City.
J. P. F. Toby,	31st Me. Vols.,	Machiasport, Me.
S. H. Tinker,	93d Ind. Vols.,	Allensville, Ind.
D. D. Von Valack,	12th U. S. Infantry.	
D. Van Doren,	72d Ohio Vols.,	Fremont, O.
C. Van Rensalaer,	148th N. Y. Vols.,	Seneca Falls, N. Y.
W. C. Van Alin,	45th Pa. Vols.,	Fleming, Pa.
A. Von Bulow,	3d N. J. Cav.,	New York City.
O. W. West,	1st N. Y. Dragoons,	Dansville, N. Y.
J. B. Warner,	8th Mich. Cav.,	Marshall, Mich.
Geo. Williams,	8th Mich. Cav.	
J. Winters,	72d Ohio Vols..	Townsend, O.
J. Warner,	33d N. J. Vols.,	Newark, N. J.
J. F. Wheeler,	149th N. Y. Vols.,	Salina, N. Y.
F. Watdmann,	16th Iowa Vols.,	Davenport, Iowa.
J. Walker,	8th Tenn. Vols.,	Bull's Gap, Tenn.
T. A. Weesner,	14th Ill. Vols.,	Greenfield, Ili.
D. J. West,	6th Conn. Vols.,	Bridgeport, Conn.
G. H. Wing,	14th N. Y. Artillery,	Glens Falls, N. Y.
C. W. Wilcox,	9th N. H. Vols.	
J. C. Watsen,	126th Ohio Vols.,	New Salem, O.
F. M. Woodruff,	76th N. Y. Vols.,	Oswego, N. Y.
Geo. Weddle,	145th Ohio Vols.,	Perrysburg, O.
C. W. Woodrow,	19th Iowa Vols.,	Mt. Pleasant, Iowa.
H. H. Willis,	40th N. Y. Vols.,	Aurora, Ill.
J. Winship,	89th Ill. Vols.,	Chicago, Ill.
R. Wilson,	113th Ill. Vols.,	Chicago, Ill.
E. S. Wilson,	1st Mass. Cav.,	Havana, Cuba.
R. P. Wilson,	5th U. S. Cav.,	Philadelphia, Pa.
B. F. Whitten,	9th Me. Vols.	
J. W. Warren,	1st. Wis. Cav.,	Beaver Dam, Wis.
D H. Warren,	Ass't Surgeon 8th Iowa Cav.,	Glencoe, O.
W. Williams,	8th Mich. Cav.	
T. H. Ward,	59th U. S. C. T.,	Westerville, O.
J. Wheaton,	59th U. S. C. T.	
B. W. Whittemore,	5th N. Y. Cav.	
H. A. Wentworth,	14th N. Y. Artillery,	Randolph, N. Y.
W. H. Wilker,	4th Ohio Vols.,	Arcadia, O.
J. H. York,	63d Ind. Vols.	
A. Young,*	4th Pa. Cav.,	Newark, N. J.
W. J. Young,	111th Ill. Vols.,	Xenia, Ill.

T. P. Young,	4th Ky. Vols.	
Aaron Zeigler,	7th Pa. R. C. Vols.,	Myerstown, Pa.
A. Zimni,	15th Iowa Vols.	
C. Zobel,	15th N. Y. Art.	

ALSO FROM LEONAUR
AVAILABLE IN SOFTCOVER OR HARDCOVER WITH DUST JACKET

THE LIFE OF THE REAL BRIGADIER GERARD VOLUME 1—THE YOUNG HUSSAR 1782-1807 by *Jean-Baptiste De Marbot*—A French Cavalryman Of the Napoleonic Wars at Marengo, Austerlitz, Jena, Eylau & Friedland.

THE LIFE OF THE REAL BRIGADIER GERARD VOLUME 2—IMPERIAL AIDE-DE-CAMP 1807-1811 by *Jean-Baptiste De Marbot*—A French Cavalryman of the Napoleonic Wars at Saragossa, Landshut, Eckmuhl, Ratisbon, Aspern-Essling, Wagram, Busaco & Torres Vedras.

THE LIFE OF THE REAL BRIGADIER GERARD VOLUME 3—COLONEL OF CHASSEURS 1811-1815 by *Jean-Baptiste De Marbot*—A French Cavalryman in the retreat from Moscow, Lutzen, Bautzen, Katzbach, Leipzig, Hanau & Waterloo.

THE INDIAN WAR OF 1864 by *Eugene Ware*—The Experiences of a Young Officer of the 7th Iowa Cavalry on the Western Frontier During the Civil War.

THE MARCH OF DESTINY by *Charles E. Young & V. Devinny*—Dangers of the Trail in 1865 by Charles E. Young & The Story of a Pioneer by V. Devinny, two Accounts of Early Emigrants to Colorado.

CROSSING THE PLAINS by *William Audley Maxwell*—A First Hand Narrative of the Early Pioneer Trail to California in 1857.

CHIEF OF SCOUTS by *William F. Drannan*—A Pilot to Emigrant and Government Trains, Across the Plains of the Western Frontier.

THIRTY-ONE YEARS ON THE PLAINS AND IN THE MOUNTAINS by *William F. Drannan*—William Drannan was born to be a pioneer, hunter, trapper and wagon train guide during the momentous days of the Great American West.

THE INDIAN WARS VOLUNTEER by *William Thompson*—Recollections of the Conflict Against the Snakes, Shoshone, Bannocks, Modocs and Other Native Tribes of the American North West.

THE 4TH TENNESSEE CAVALRY by *George B. Guild*—The Services of Smith's Regiment of Confederate Cavalry by One of its Officers.

COLONEL WORTHINGTON'S SHILOH by *T. Worthington*—The Tennessee Campaign, 1862, by an Officer of the Ohio Volunteers.

FOUR YEARS IN THE SADDLE by *W. L. Curry*—The History of the First Regiment Ohio Volunteer Cavalry in the American Civil War.

AVAILABLE ONLINE AT **www.leonaur.com**
AND FROM ALL GOOD BOOK STORES

ALSO FROM LEONAUR
AVAILABLE IN SOFTCOVER OR HARDCOVER WITH DUST JACKET

LIFE IN THE ARMY OF NORTHERN VIRGINIA by Carlton McCarthy—The Observations of a Confederate Artilleryman of Cutshaw's Battalion During the American Civil War 1861-1865.

HISTORY OF THE CAVALRY OF THE ARMY OF THE POTOMAC by Charles D. Rhodes—Including Pope's Army of Virginia and the Cavalry Operations in West Virginia During the American Civil War.

CAMP-FIRE AND COTTON-FIELD by Thomas W. Knox—A New York Herald Correspondent's View of the American Civil War.

SERGEANT STILLWELL by Leander Stillwell—The Experiences of a Union Army Soldier of the 61st Illinois Infantry During the American Civil War.

STONEWALL'S CANNONEER by Edward A. Moore—Experiences with the Rockbridge Artillery, Confederate Army of Northern Virginia, During the American Civil War.

THE SIXTH CORPS by George Stevens—The Army of the Potomac, Union Army, During the American Civil War.

THE RAILROAD RAIDERS by William Pittenger—An Ohio Volunteers Recollections of the Andrews Raid to Disrupt the Confederate Railroad in Georgia During the American Civil War.

CITIZEN SOLDIER by John Beatty—An Account of the American Civil War by a Union Infantry Officer of Ohio Volunteers Who Became a Brigadier General.

COX: PERSONAL RECOLLECTIONS OF THE CIVIL WAR--VOLUME 1 by Jacob Dolson Cox—West Virginia, Kanawha Valley, Gauley Bridge, Cotton Mountain, South Mountain, Antietam, the Morgan Raid & the East Tennessee Campaign.

COX: PERSONAL RECOLLECTIONS OF THE CIVIL WAR--VOLUME 2 by Jacob Dolson Cox—Siege of Knoxville, East Tennessee, Atlanta Campaign, the Nashville Campaign & the North Carolina Campaign.

KERSHAW'S BRIGADE VOLUME 1 by D. Augustus Dickert—Manassas, Seven Pines, Sharpsburg (Antietam), Fredricksburg, Chancellorsville, Gettysburg, Chickamauga, Chattanooga, Fort Sanders & Bean Station.

KERSHAW'S BRIGADE VOLUME 2 by D. Augustus Dickert—At the wilderness, Cold Harbour, Petersburg, The Shenandoah Valley and Cedar Creek..

AVAILABLE ONLINE AT **www.leonaur.com**
AND FROM ALL GOOD BOOK STORES

www.ingramcontent.com/pod-product-compliance
Lightning Source LLC
Chambersburg PA
CBHW020938230426
43666CB00005B/78